THE BIBLE
I NEVER KNEW

A CLOSER LOOK AT
CHRISTIANITY'S MAIN THEMES

PETER J. BYLSMA

BYBLIO
PRESS
Inspire, Inform,
and Transform

Byblio Press
11410 NE 124th St., #260
Kirkland, WA 98034 USA
www.bybliopress.com
info@bybliopress.com

Ordering Information: This book may be ordered by contacting the publisher at the address or email above. Special discounts are available on quantity purchases by corporations, associations, and others. For details, contact the publisher at any of the above addresses.

College professors and secondary school teachers may order free examination copies of this book by contacting Byblio Press at the address or email noted above.

The views expressed in this work are solely those of the author and do not necessarily reflect the views of the publisher, and the publisher hereby disclaims any responsibility for them.

Cover © created by Peter J. Bylsma
Maps created by David C. Hoerlein
Printed in the United States of America
ISBN: 978-1-964060-03-3 (sc)
ISBN: 978-1-964060-02-6 (hc)
ISBN: 978-1-964060-04-0 (e)

Library of Congress Control Number: 2024908162

CONTENTS

PREFACE

As I was leaving one career and waiting for the COVID pandemic to subside in 2020, I thought about what I should do next. During my various careers, I had developed a set of skills that helped me study complicated topics and communicate the main issues to busy readers in easy-to-understand ways. I had been a Christian for more than 50 years but still didn't feel like I knew the Bible very well. So I decided to summarize the Bible, and *The Short Bible: A Chronological Summary of the Old and New Testaments* was published in 2021.

This book is a logical extension of that book. It goes into depth on many important topics that aren't clearly explained in the Bible. This book also provides contextual information that helps us better understand the stories that were written for people at a different time in another place. Key facts that weren't included in the Bible are also included. Unlike *The Short Bible*, which was written for both Christians and non-Christians, this book is meant for Christians who want to develop a more informed and mature faith. Writing this book opened my eyes to misunderstandings I have had about some of the Bible's teaching, and what I learned has changed the way I live.

I acknowledge all those who influenced my faith journey, especially my parents, Bud and Patti Bylsma, who served in Young Life and other ministries around the world for more than 60 years. I also am indebted to Belinda Kelly, Marian Raikes, Nashira Reisch, and Mike Sullivan for providing useful comments when reviewing a draft of this book. In honor of all those who helped me on my faith journey, 90% of the royalties I receive from this book, my other books, and any related products will be given to the Bylsma Foundation to support groups that help those in need, promote justice in the world, seek and spread the truth, help others understand the stories of the Bible, and encourage those who need good news.

Peter J. Bylsma,
February 2024

CHAPTER 1

INTRODUCTION

In 1995, Philip Yancey wrote *The Jesus I Never Knew* (Zondervan) because people didn't understand who Jesus really was. When the COVID pandemic and political events in the United States unfolded prior to a controversial election in 2020, some Christians engaged in political discussions but seemed unfamiliar with the Bible they said they followed. I wondered if anything like Yancey's book had been written about the entire Bible, and I found nothing like it.[1]

I realized most people don't know much about the Bible, so I decided to use my writing and analytical skills during the pandemic to summarize the Bible. I had been a Christian for more than 50 years, but the Bible, with its many themes, was still a bit of a mystery to me. Reading it was like working on a puzzle without a picture on the box, and I hadn't put all the pieces together.

I published *The Short Bible: A Chronological Summary of the Old and New Testaments* (WestBow Press) in 2021 and used simple language to make the Bible easier to understand. While writing it, I learned a great deal about both the context and the content of the Bible, and I gained deeper insights into the main themes that run through all its books. When I finished, I was able to connect the pieces of the puzzle and see the big picture. But to keep the book short and readable, I only included a few sentences about the main themes that run from Genesis through Revelation.

I then decided to write this book to bring clarity to the Bible's essential messages, expand on what I learned, and provide information on related topics. Scripture verses are included so readers can find the

---

[1] John Calvin was a French lawyer and later an influential theologian and pastor who explained key messages of the Bible in *The Institutes* (or *Instruction*) *of Christian Religion*, first published in Latin in 1536 (translated into English in 1845). The unabridged version has 80 chapters and is more than 1,000 pages long.

relevant text.[2] (The Bible books and their abbreviations are found in Appendix F.)

While much has been written on each topic, this book summarizes the main ideas in short chapters. It aims to help Christians gain a better understanding of the Bible so they can develop a more mature faith and apply it to their lives. With a better grasp of the Bible's key ideas, Christians can focus on its key messages and not be overwhelmed by less important details. Greater insights help us be better messengers from God in a world that knows little or nothing about the Bible.

IGNORANCE OF THE BIBLE IS WIDESPREAD

The Holy Bible is the most read book in history and a source of knowledge and comfort for millions. But it's also misunderstood in many ways. Most people haven't read the Bible or heard its stories, and those who have read all or parts of it often don't understand its overall themes. There are many reasons why this is the case.

Most People Haven't Read the Bible

Most people don't know anything about the Bible because they have their own religions and haven't explored other viewpoints. There may be restrictions on having the Bible printed in their country, or they may use a language that doesn't have a Bible translation. In some areas, there are no Christians to introduce or explain the basic Christian messages in terms they can understand, and some people haven't learned to read. (The Bible is now available in audio format, so they can hear it at their own pace if they have the right technology and if it has been translated into their language.)

Others aren't interested in reading the Bible because they don't feel the need to believe in any God. In affluent areas of modern societies, most people have their needs met and live comfortable lifestyles because they have a decent income and the government provides what they need. When life is good, who needs God? When the Israelites in the Old Testament were at peace with their neighbors and their

---

[2] The quotes are not taken from any translation. The text has been reworded and sometimes shortened to make it easier to read and understand while also ensuring the text stays true to its original meaning.

basic needs were met, they ignored God. Some countries in Europe have created a church tax to maintain the old cathedrals in their cities because church attendance is so low that the congregation can't pay for the needed maintenance. Governments support the cathedrals because as tourist attractions, they help the economy. The percentage of people in affluent countries in northern Europe who say they are religious ranges from 22% to 39%.[3] In general, as the education and income of a person increases, the level of religious commitment declines.[4]

Some people have never read the Bible because of the negative reputation Christians have among non-Christians. Historically, the Bible has been used to manipulate or oppress others. The Crusades spoiled the name of Christianity in some parts of the world, and scandals among church leaders have soiled the church's image. In addition, many who say they are Christians don't follow the teachings of Jesus. Some people have had bad experiences with Christians who want to convert them, so they don't want to have anything to do with Christianity. The "hypocrisy of religious people" is now a major reason people in the USA doubt religion, according to a 2022 study of teenagers and adults conducted by the Barna Group, a leading research company that focuses on faith-based issues.

Finally, many people aren't interested in reading the Bible because they don't believe God exists. Atheists and agnostics believe religion is based on superstitions and that miracles didn't happen or were just a coincidence. To them, the Bible contains teachings that are old-fashioned and outdated in a science-based world that emphasizes objective truth and empirical reasoning. The miracles in the Bible reinforce their view that Christians believe in some kind of "magic" that defies scientific laws.

---

[3] This region includes Denmark, Estonia, Finland, Germany, Latvia, Norway, and Sweden. The percentage of people in the USA and Canada who said they were religious in 2017 was 56% and 37% respectively. The percentage of "nones" in the USA, those who have no religious affiliation, increased from 16% in 2007 to 29% in 2021. (Sources: WIN/Gallup International Association Survey, 2017; Pew Research Center, 2021)

[4] Students of statistics know this correlation doesn't mean education and money *cause* religious commitment to decline. Many factors influence one's commitment, and many who are wealthy and highly educated take their faith seriously.

Most People Don't Understand the Bible

Those who have read the entire Bible faced a daunting task. As a collection of 66 "books," it's very long and very complex, and it's not organized in chronological order like a normal book. Its many themes are scattered throughout the books, and it contains many details that aren't important to modern readers. The Bible was also written at a different time in a different geography for people in a culture that is very different from the western world. As a result, what was written is unclear to many of us, and important details were not written down because people who lived at that time already knew them. In addition, the text can be very wordy and unclear — extensive editing was not possible and the text contains some strange metaphors and analogies. All these factors make the Bible hard to understand.

Many who try to read the Bible don't get very far — they become confused and/or bored. Those who continue make slow progress. If the Bible was printed like a normal book, it would be 2,000 pages long. The initial stories are interesting but readers can quickly get bogged down in detailed descriptions of things that aren't interesting or important to us today. There is also duplication and repetition in some of the speeches and stories. Many people make a resolution to read the entire Bible but don't complete the task.

Time constraints also limit our ability to study the Bible. Most adults stay busy managing their jobs and families, dealing with unexpected crises, and staying informed about a rapidly changing world. Thus, few people have time to read a long, challenging, and somewhat disorganized book.

Instead, Christians usually focus on reading certain parts of the Bible, usually in the New Testament, and the parts being emphasized by their church leaders or fellowship group. Some spend a few minutes in devotions reading or listening to short sections of scripture along with brief explanations of the text. For many, the only knowledge they have about the Bible comes from a few stories they learned as a child or what is read or explained in a church service, which typically is just a few minutes each week.

Focus On What's Important

When we are busy and get new information every day about a world that rapidly unfolds around us, we need to make good use of our limited time. In 1970, futurist Alvin Toffler predicted a time when the rate of change was so fast that we would enter a state of *Future Shock*. The advances the world has experienced since then have fulfilled his prediction, and life for many seems to be spinning out of control. Computers and smartphones inundate us with uncensored news. Some of it is useful and well-packaged, but the internet, social media, and one-sided news sources can inundate us with false and manipulative messages that hide the truth. Scientific advances provide a greater understanding of nature, our bodies, and the universe that allow us to improve our world, but the news can also make us anxious and depressed.

When we face information overload, we need to use "critical thinking" skills (the ability to evaluate information and apply knowledge to solve problems). But we also need to exercise "critical ignoring" skills so we can focus on what's important. Schools don't teach either of these skills, so we need to learn to focus on the main points and the right things rather than being distracted by unimportant details. We need to separate the wheat from the chaff as we analyze information, prioritize our time, and make good choices about what to focus on and what to ignore. In 1890, William James said, "The art of being wise is the art of knowing what to overlook."[5] It was true then and it's even more true now. When we are swamped with too much information, what is true and important is hard to grasp, which makes it hard to understand the big picture.

The best way to learn something is to start by understanding a topic's main ideas. A headline and topic sentence of a paragraph provide this framework for learning, and what follows them are the details. When too many details are presented without first having the general framework of a topic, what we read is confusing and we can miss the key ideas. Because of how the Bible was written and organized, we are

---

[5] William James, *The Principles of Psychology* (1890), New York: Henry Holt and Company, chapter 22. James was an American philosopher and psychologist who also wrote *The Varieties of Religious Experience* (1902).

often unaware of the Bible's main ideas and themes. It takes effort and careful analysis to identify the Bible's fundamental truths.

The Importance of Being a Learner

The importance of deep and ongoing study can't be stressed enough. Most professions require some form of continuous learning for people to develop in their field, and those who are serious about maturing in their faith need to study the scriptures in more advanced ways. Christians are called to be salt and light in the world, and we are to make "disciples," which means "learners" (*mathētēs* in Greek, *discipulus* in Latin). "Sanctification" is the gradual process of being transformed by the Holy Spirit to become more like Jesus in every way, including in our desires, thoughts, and actions. The Holy Spirit, through our Bible study, personal reflection, and continuous learning, helps us to become more like Christ (Rom 12:2, Phil 2:12–13, 2Pet 3:14–18). We are to strive for perfection and excellence (Lev 11:44, 19:2, 20:26; Matt 5:48; Phil 4:8; 1Pet 1:15–16). When we realize we fall short of high expectations, we are motivated to learn and improve.

Learning requires a desire to be better informed and an open and discerning mind. Being open to the possibility that we lack understanding or may hold an incorrect belief is a key first step to learning. We also need to care about having the right beliefs. A good thinker not only acknowledges one's ignorance, but is also eager to learn, curious about the world, and committed to having a correct understanding. John Dewey, an American psychologist and education expert, said, "All learning begins when our comfortable ideas turn out to be inadequate."

Having a learner mindset and intellectual humility are important because we often overestimate our knowledge of a topic. Having some knowledge can be dangerous; humility involves recognizing our limitations and biases and being teachable. Non-learners often become confident, rigid, and complacent with what they know and aren't open to new information. I'm reminded of when I taught a class called The Life of Christ to middle-school students at a Christian school. The children of Christian professionals didn't think they needed to study the gospels because they "already knew" the stories. But they lacked a deep understanding of the gospel's complexity and themes, and they often failed the first exam. Many Christians think they know the Bible, but I've found that some who serve in Christian "careers" (pastors, missionaries, parachurch staff) are unaware of some key Biblical principles. H.L. Mencken once wrote, "For every complex problem, there's a solution that is simple, neat, and wrong." Not knowing what we don't know, and having confidence in what we believe, can also lead to pride, just as it did among the Pharisees.

A Literary Analogy

Here is an analogy to show how continuous learning improves our understanding and focuses our efforts. Young children learn letters, then words, and string them together to speak sentences that make sense. When we start school, we learn to read and write simple stories, and gradually our abilities advance so we can read and write about specific subjects. Some people don't go far in school, so their reading and writing levels are limited, which limits their learning and ability to express themselves. Those who continue their education learn about different types of literature and ways of writing, and by the time a student reaches age 15, they "know how to read and write." But there is still much more to learn. There are many different kinds of writing, and it takes time and effort to produce clear messages about complicated topics that others can easily understand. Good writing involves subtle nuances and strategies that differ based on the audiences. Good readers know what to focus on and what to ignore. Professional writers and readers analyze the works of others closely and can teach and comment intelligently about them. A select few earn Nobel and Pulitzer prizes.

Many start their faith journey like eager children. They have simple knowledge and drink spiritual milk. As they learn more about the Bible and God's unique call on their lives, they consume solid food and develop more complex diets. Greater insights makes it easier for them to see the Bible's patterns and important themes and to understand the details in their context. Mature Christians lead lives that are in sync with God's principles, and they make doing the right things a priority. Those with a good grasp of the truth can easily spot counterfeit beliefs and actions and can justify what they believe and how they act.

Becoming a Mature Christian

It takes discipline to become a mature Christian. In the parable of the sower and soils, a farmer spreads seeds on four types of ground, which represent the hearts of people. Some seeds fall on a path and are quickly eaten by birds. Seeds that develop roots in two types of soils produce no crop — one refers to those who fall away when things get hard because they aren't yet mature in their faith, and the other refers to those who are choked by life's worries, riches, and pleasures. It's only the last soil where the seeds are continually nurtured and develop deep roots and produce a bountiful harvest. This parable is included in three books of the Bible (Matthew 13, Mark 4, Luke 8). Developing deep roots and maturity requires study, time, and tending. Staying focused on the important things and the big picture keeps us from being distracted by tiny, less important details. (Don't major in minor things.)

This book is intended to help Christians develop deeper roots of a more mature faith. The Bible is a cohesive story of God's love for all of creation and how we should live in the world. I encourage readers to keep an open mind while reading — we often resist different ideas and perspectives when we first hear them. The Pharisees knew the scriptures well but didn't understand the simple truths that God wanted them to know and do. They focused on the details of correct religious practices but missed the point of their beliefs. We need to keep learning and deepening our knowledge and understanding in order to carry out God's challenging call on our lives. This book aims to help in this effort.

ORGANIZATION AND USE OF THIS BOOK

This book has four sections. Part One has seven chapters that cover basic information about the Bible and God. Part Two has eight chapters that discuss the main themes found in the Bible. Part Three has three longer chapters on specific topics of interest for today's readers. The book ends with an epilogue and appendixes that provide brief but useful summaries and reference materials.

The issues in this book can be studied in more depth, either individually or in groups, by looking at the scripture verses provided. Sometimes a topic is mentioned in one chapter but is covered in more depth in other chapters, so be sure to look at all the references when studying a topic. In addition, because these chapters are summaries of issues that can be explored in much greater detail elsewhere, you may want to investigate what has been written by others. On controversial topics where more than one view exists, closely examine all the views, including the context of the verses, before coming to your own conclusions about what to believe and how they apply to your life.

The Bible has much to say about other topics that aren't covered in this book. Various study bibles have lists of scriptures and explanations about other topics. But everybody should start by understanding the basics, the broad fundamentals of the faith, that are found in this book.

PART ONE

BASIC INFORMATION ABOUT THE BIBLE

CHAPTER 2

BIBLE HISTORY AND STRUCTURE

This chapter provides basic facts about the Bible, including its basic content and structure, how its "books" were created and selected, when the Bible was translated into other languages, and information about the authors and the length of the books.

BASIC FACTS ABOUT THE BIBLE

The Holy Bible is a collection of 66 ancient documents written by many authors over a 1,600-year period. The *Bible* means "the authoritative set of little books," and its content is called *scripture*, which means "something written."[6]

This small library has two parts, the Old Testament and the New Testament. A period of 400 years separates the events described in the two parts.

- The Old Testament has 39 books and spans about 1,100 years of history of the Israelites (400 years of history aren't included). It also provides accounts of world events that go back to when the universe was created as well as stories about the earliest humans who lived on earth.
- The New Testament has 27 books that were all written during a 50-year period in the first century (AD 45–95) to describe the main events and teachings related to Jesus and his initial followers in Canaan (now called Palestine) and the eastern Mediterranean Sea region.

---

[6] The Jewish Bible has additional books and no New Testament, and the Catholic and Orthodox Bibles have additional books. This book does not provide information about these other books.

How the Books Were Created

The authors of the documents usually described events and ideas to a writing secretary who was sometimes given latitude to put the author's ideas into their own words. The words were initially recorded on papyrus, and more durable materials (e.g., sheepskin) were used later. The original documents were copied by others so more people could read them. As demand for the documents increased, many copies were made, and sometimes those producing the copies made minor errors and clarifications along the way, which were then copied by others. Some authors reviewed the original books and corrected misunderstandings that had been recorded earlier. Thus, there are slightly different accounts of some events.

The letters of Paul and others were written on sheets of papyrus that were close in size to the sheets of paper we use now. Most of the time, only one sheet was used for a letter. When longer letters were written, they were connected to each other at the edges and then rolled up to form a scroll. Sometimes professional scribes wrote the letters while the author dictated them. Long letters probably required multiple scribes, and the authors may have done some editing along the way.

None of the original documents have been recovered. However, a copy of every Old Testament book except Esther was discovered in 1947 by Bedouin shepherds in a set of caves in the mountains around Qumran, near the Dead Sea. The scrolls had been created by the Essenes who lived apart from others in society about 2,000 years ago. As the Roman army advanced toward their settlements, they hid their scrolls in the remote caves and camouflaged their entrance to keep their documents safe from any invader. The scrolls were well preserved in the cool dry caves, and a recent analysis of the scrolls revealed that their contents were almost identical to the Bible books we use now.

How the Bible Was Compiled

For several hundred years after Jesus lived on earth, many documents were written about him and the actions and teachings of his followers. Some people wrote using false names in order to create an air of legitimacy for their documents.

Church leaders in the region met periodically to discuss the documents and issues related to Christian doctrine and church supervision. A group of Christian leaders met in Carthage (a major port city in Tunisia) in AD 397 to review the documents that were circulating about the life of Jesus and what various Christian leaders had written about Christianity. The leaders at the Council of Carthage wanted to decide on a final set of documents that would be considered divinely inspired and authoritative.

Historical documents about these meetings reveal the leaders used several criteria to determine which documents were true, authoritative, and divinely inspired.

1. *Was the document written by a prophet of God?* If so, then it was the word of God.
2. *Was the document confirmed by acts of God?* Miracles are acts of God, and true prophets often performed miracles. Miracles confirmed the authority of the author as speaking for God.
3. *Did its message tell the truth about God?* The church leaders used the policy, "If in doubt, throw it out." This policy was an extra step to ensure the validity of the documents that were included in the final set of documents.
4. *Did the content come with the power of God?* The early church leaders believed the word of God had the power to transform and build a person. If a document didn't have this quality, it was not included.
5. *Was it accepted by the people of God?* When a document was received, collected, read, and used by the people of God, it was regarded to be authoritative and inspired.

The leaders at the Council of Carthage had disagreements about which documents should be in the final set of documents that were considered authoritative and inspired. There were 14 books that had an unknown author or had a doubtful origin, and they were not included in the final set. (They are known as the *Apocrypha* and are included in the Catholic Bible.) For example, the Gospels of Thomas and Judas were not included in part because they promote a gnostic form of theology that was incompatible with the perspectives of two New Testament authors, Paul and Peter.[7] After much discussion, a final set of documents was created, and the set was known as the *canon* (a Greek word that means "rule" or "measuring stick," as if the overall criterion was, "does it meet the highest standard"?).

The 39 Old Testament books were also included in the canon because they were viewed as the original set of authoritative and inspired documents. While there were some debates about the Old Testament canon, by AD 250 nearly everybody agreed on the authority of the Hebrew scriptures. These ancient documents provided an important context for the Christian message and were often quoted by Jesus and other Christian leaders. Jews called these books the *Tanakh*, an acronym of the Hebrew initials of each of the three divisions: the Torah ("Teaching," the five books of Moses), Nevi'im ("Prophets"), and Ketuvim ("Writings"). The books were not put in chronological order. Instead, they appear in the Bible in four general categories: five Books of the Law (also called the Pentateuch), 12 Historical Books, five Poetical Books, and 17 Prophetic Books (five "major" prophets followed by 12 "minor" prophets).

Once the Council selected the documents to be included in the final New Testament canon, they were organized in their present order. Like the books of the Old Testament, the New Testament books were not arranged chronologically. Instead, the books were put in a logical narrative order: 1) the four gospels tell the life of Jesus and his teachings; 2) one book describes the acts of the apostles and disciples of Jesus who spread the Christian faith; 3) 21 letters to churches and Christian leaders explain the meaning and implications of the faith; and 4) one book describes future events. Paul's letters to members of local churches were the first to be written. Mark was probably the first gospel written (it's the shortest), but Matthew's account of the life of Jesus is the first in the New Testament because it begins with a direct connection to the Old Testament and shows that Jesus was a direct descendent of many Israelite leaders. This provided evidence to the Jews that Jesus was the Messiah.

---

[7] Gnostics believed that gaining knowledge is required for salvation. The term comes from the Greek word *gnostikos*, meaning "one who knows." Gnostics also believed all matter is evil and only the spirit is good.

BIBLE TRANSLATIONS AND VERSIONS

The Old Testament books were almost entirely written in Classical Hebrew (Aramaic was used for 268 verses in three books, 1.2% of the total). Over time, the books were translated into Greek in a set known as the *Septuagint,* which was widely used by Greek-speaking Jews. The New Testament books were all written in "common" Greek, the dominant language used in the eastern part of the Roman Empire. Once the entire canon was finalized, all the books were translated into Latin.

The first translation of the Bible into English occurred in the late 1300s by people supervised by John Wycliffe. It was a literal translation from Latin and was hard to understand. Another translation was written by a different author a few years later that was easier to read. The two translations were called the Wycliffe Bible and it was banned by the Catholic Church in England in 1409 because Wycliffe had led a movement that criticized some of the teachings of the church.

The first English Bible that appeared in print was written by William Tyndale in 1526. The idea of a Bible in English was scandalous at that time because the church in England was still governed from Rome and all the church services were conducted in Latin. But most people in Europe couldn't understand Latin, and Tyndale believed that all people should be able to read or hear the Bible in a language they could understand. Some Bibles existed in local languages in parts of Europe, and the translation of the Bible into other languages was a political act of defiance against the Catholic Church during a time when the Reformation movement was growing. Martin Luther translated the Bible into German in 1534. Tyndale's Bible was banned and he was convicted of heresy and executed in 1536.

Various versions of the Bible have been written over the centuries.[8] The earliest English version was commissioned in 1604 and published in 1611 by religious scholars working for King James of England. The translation from the original Hebrew, Greek, and Aramaic (not Latin) was done by 47 leading biblical scholars who worked in six groups.

---

[8] A *version* is a special kind of translation. It involves many experts working together to ensure the translation is accurate and understandable.

The creation of this version prompted work on translations into many other languages. The earliest translations didn't reflect insights learned from later discoveries about the meanings of the original Greek and Hebrew words. Archeological findings and analyses of the original words during the past 150 years have also added further insights into the meaning of the books and what the Bible says and means. Many more versions of the Bible have emerged based on these insights, and there are now 60 different free English translations available on the internet.

Paraphrased Translations

Several paraphrased versions of the Bible have been written to make the text more easily understood by those living in modern times and in different cultures. Here are the most noteworthy paraphrases.

- The *New Testament in Modern English* was written by J.B. Phillips, an Anglican clergyman. He translated only the New Testament by referring to the original Greek text. His translation was published in 1958 using British spellings, and some editions don't include verse numbers.
- The *Good News Bible* is a translation of the Bible by the American Bible Society. The New Testament was originally published in 1966 using the name *Good News for Modern Man*. The complete Bible was finished in 1976. It uses simplified language that children can read. This paraphrase is also known as the *Good News Translation* and is used in many countries and by many denominations.
- *The Living Bible* was created in English by Kenneth Taylor in 1971 and has been translated into many languages. He wrote it so his children would understand the biblical text when his family conducted their devotions. An updated version (*New Living Translation*) was published in 1996 based on the recommendations of a team of experts who understood the original Hebrew and Greek texts.
- *The Message: The Bible in Contemporary Language* was written by Eugene Peterson, an American Presbyterian pastor and author. This translation uses American idioms and slang to convey a more modern understanding of the original text. Experts in the Old and

New Testaments reviewed it to ensure it stayed true to the meaning of the original text. This translation of the entire Bible was finished in 2002.

LENGTH AND AUTHORS OF THE BIBLE BOOKS

The length of the Bible is underestimated because of how it's prepared for today's readers. When printed on very thin paper using small print and narrow margins, the entire Bible resembles a normal book. But reading the entire Bible is like reading 8–10 normal books, and much of it is much more difficult to read and understand than a modern book. The Bible has about 800,000 words in English, not including the section titles and notes that are usually added for clarification purposes. (The number of words in the Bible differs depending on the translation used and the language in which it is translated.)

Some sections of the Bible contain many details, but some of the details aren't important for most modern readers. For example, the detailed descriptions of Noah's ark and the Temple, the names of all the families in the census found in Numbers, and the cleaning rules found in Leviticus are not helpful to today's readers. Some books are quite long, while others are only a few paragraphs. Jeremiah is the longest book, and John's second and third letters are the shortest. The graphs at the end of this chapter shows the variation in the length of the books in the order they appear in the Bible.

Centuries after the books were written, they were divided into chapters and verses so readers could find specific texts more easily. Unlike modern books, chapters are rarely more than one page long, and sometimes these divisions don't occur in logical places. The chapter divisions used today were developed by the Archbishop of Canterbury around 1227 AD. The Wycliffe Bible was the first Bible to use this chapter pattern. There are nearly 1,200 chapters in the entire Bible (78% are in the Old Testament).

A Jewish rabbi Nathan divided the Hebrew Old Testament into verses in 1448 AD. In 1555, Robert Stephanus numbered the New Testament verses we use today. There are more than 31,100 verses in the Bible (74% are in the Old Testament).

Bible Authors

Of the 28 known primary authors, 20 wrote Old Testament books and 8 wrote New Testament books. All but one of the known authors were Jewish (Luke was a Gentile and wrote two books). Some books had more than one author. We don't know who wrote 12 books, and scholars still debate who the authors were.

All the known authors were men, and they sometimes identified themselves as the author. In a patriarchal culture, women were not respected and men didn't read what women wrote. Hence, women didn't identify themselves as an author and may not have been given credit if they helped write a document. It's therefore possible that a woman wrote parts or all of some books. A close analysis of the book of Job reveals it may have been written by a woman.[9]

The authors had their own styles, which reflected various literature genres (see chapter 4). Eight authors wrote more than one book. The table below shows the author of each book and the number of chapters and verses that appear in each of the 66 books.

---

[9] People assume a man wrote Job, but it was likely a well-educated woman promoting women's rights. Many clues justify this idea. First, no author is named, which is consistent with what a woman author would do (men didn't read what women wrote). Second, the book was written before Moses wrote Genesis and the location of the events and the characters in the story are not part of Israel's history, so there is no connection between Job and the Israelite traditions. Third, the ending provides several clues to support the idea of a female author. The three daughters were given the same share of the inheritance as the seven sons (this was never done at that time). The daughters were also the only children named (usually only sons were named) and were said to be the most beautiful women in all the land. Finally, women were (and still are) much more acquainted with undeserved grief than men, so a female would be more motivated than a man to write such a story.

Books	Author	Chapters	Verses
Genesis	Moses	50	1,533
Exodus	Moses	40	1,213
Leviticus	Moses	27	859
Numbers	Moses	36	1,289
Deuteronomy	Moses	34	959
Joshua	*Unknown*	24	658
Judges	*Unknown*	21	618
Ruth	*Unknown*	4	85
1 Samuel	*Unknown*	31	810
2 Samuel	*Unknown*	24	695
1 Kings	*Unknown*	22	816
2 Kings	*Unknown*	25	719
1 Chronicles	Ezra	29	942
2 Chronicles	Ezra	36	822
Ezra	Ezra	10	280
Nehemiah	Nehemiah	13	406
Esther	*Unknown*	10	167
Job	*Unknown*	42	1,070
Psalms	David*	150	2,461
Proverbs	Solomon*	31	915
Ecclesiastes	Solomon*	12	222
Song of Solomon	*Unknown*	8	117
Isaiah	Isaiah	66	1,292
Jeremiah	Jeremiah	52	1,364
Lamentations	Jeremiah	5	154
Ezekiel	Ezekiel	48	1,273
Daniel	Daniel	12	357
Hosea	Hosea	14	197
Joel	Joel	3	73
Amos	Amos	9	146
Obadiah	Obadiah	1	21
Jonah	*Unknown*	4	48
Micah	Micah	7	105
Nahum	Nahum	3	47
Habakkuk	Habakkuk	3	56
Zephaniah	Zephaniah	3	53
Haggai	Haggai	2	38
Zechariah	Zechariah	14	211
Malachi	Malachi	4	55

Books	Author	Chapters	Verses
Matthew	Matthew	28	1,071
Mark	Mark	16	678
Luke	Luke	24	1,151
John	John	21	879
Acts	Luke	28	1,007
Romans	Paul	16	433
1 Corinthians	Paul	16	437
2 Corinthians	Paul	13	257
Galatians	Paul	6	149
Ephesians	Paul	6	155
Philippians	Paul	4	104
Colossians	Paul	4	95
1 Thessalonians	Paul	5	89
2 Thessalonians	Paul	3	47
1 Timothy	Paul	6	113
2 Timothy	Paul	4	83
Titus	Paul	3	46
Philemon	Paul	1	25
Hebrews	*Unknown*	13	303
James	James	5	108
1 Peter	Peter	5	105
2 Peter	Peter	3	61
1 John	John	5	105
2 John	John	1	13
3 John	John	1	14
Jude	Jude	1	25
Revelation	John	22	404
Totals for 66 books		***1,189***	***31,103***

*Primary author

Words in the Old Testament

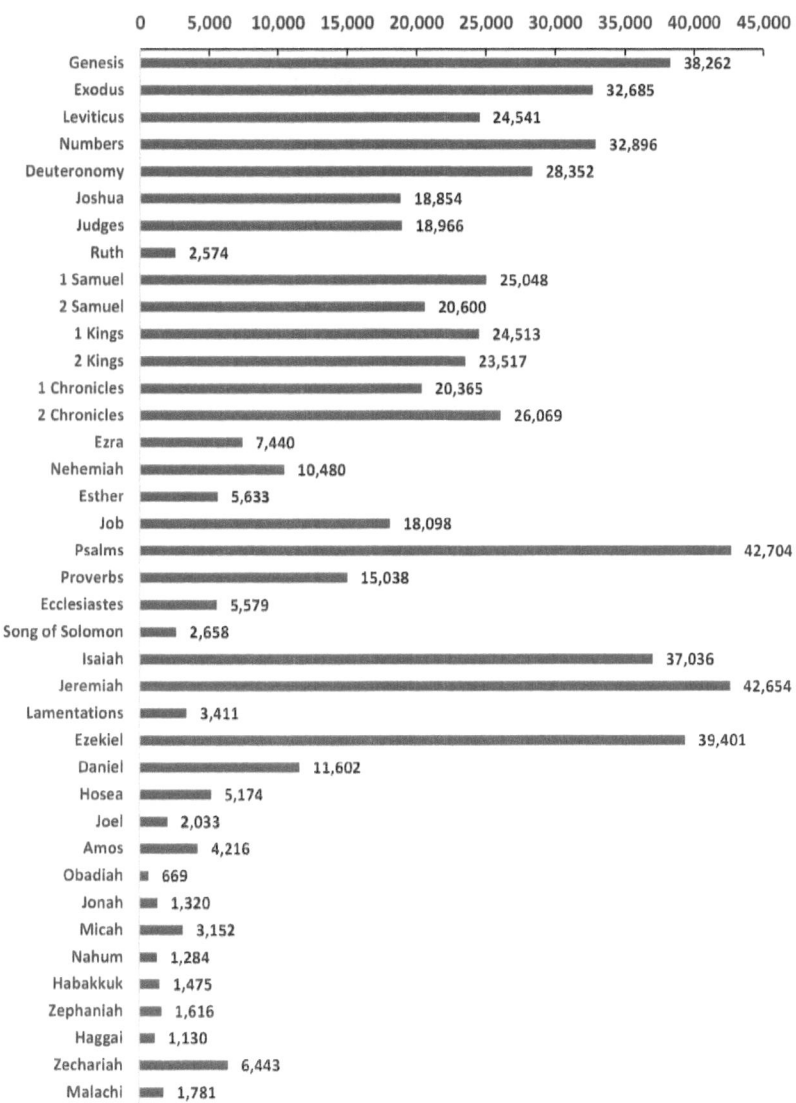

Book	Words
Genesis	38,262
Exodus	32,685
Leviticus	24,541
Numbers	32,896
Deuteronomy	28,352
Joshua	18,854
Judges	18,966
Ruth	2,574
1 Samuel	25,048
2 Samuel	20,600
1 Kings	24,513
2 Kings	23,517
1 Chronicles	20,365
2 Chronicles	26,069
Ezra	7,440
Nehemiah	10,480
Esther	5,633
Job	18,098
Psalms	42,704
Proverbs	15,038
Ecclesiastes	5,579
Song of Solomon	2,658
Isaiah	37,036
Jeremiah	42,654
Lamentations	3,411
Ezekiel	39,401
Daniel	11,602
Hosea	5,174
Joel	2,033
Amos	4,216
Obadiah	669
Jonah	1,320
Micah	3,152
Nahum	1,284
Habakkuk	1,475
Zephaniah	1,616
Haggai	1,130
Zechariah	6,443
Malachi	1,781

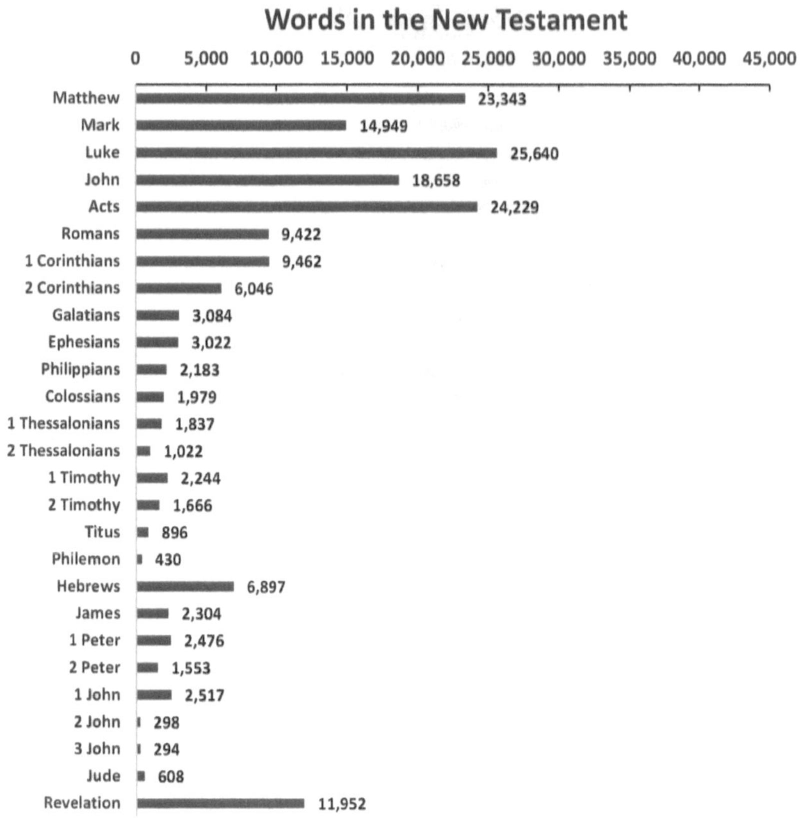

Words in the New Testament

	0	5,000	10,000	15,000	20,000	25,000	30,000	35,000	40,000	45,000

Matthew 23,343
Mark 14,949
Luke 25,640
John 18,658
Acts 24,229
Romans 9,422
1 Corinthians 9,462
2 Corinthians 6,046
Galatians 3,084
Ephesians 3,022
Philippians 2,183
Colossians 1,979
1 Thessalonians 1,837
2 Thessalonians 1,022
1 Timothy 2,244
2 Timothy 1,666
Titus 896
Philemon 430
Hebrews 6,897
James 2,304
1 Peter 2,476
2 Peter 1,553
1 John 2,517
2 John 298
3 John 294
Jude 608
Revelation 11,952

Note: Although the precise number given for each book implies great precision in the count, the length of each book is an estimate. Many different estimates have been made, and an analysis of the actual number of words in six books in the New International Version found that there were more words in the books than what others estimate. A mathematical formula based on these six books was applied to the other 60 books to estimate the number of words in each book and the total number of words in the Bible.

CHAPTER 3

IMPORTANT MISSING DETAILS

Even though the Bible is extremely long and complicated and has tremendous value, there are still many details missing that modern readers need to know to understand the overall story and messages. This chapter discusses some important details that are missing from the Bible.

REASONS DETAILS ARE MISSING

There are many reasons why important details aren't included in the Bible. Here are the main reasons.

- The authors of the books had specific audiences and purposes in mind when they wrote their documents. This narrowed the scope of what they wrote.
- The authors didn't think people would be reading their writings more than 2,000 years later. Although a few books were written for historical purposes and were expected to be relevant for many years, the idea that a collection of documents by multiple writers over many centuries would be combined into a single collection and referred to collectively didn't occur to most of the authors. They didn't think about what readers hundreds and thousands of years in the future would need to know about their situation.
- The authors assumed their audiences understood the local culture and customs, social and economic conditions, geographical features and locations, and major historical events that affected their society. In their mind, they didn't need to include details that were obvious to their readers.
- While many documents existed that described events and characters in the ancient world, the Council of Carthage was very careful when selecting the books they considered inspired and authoritative. This limited the information we have about what happened at that time. As a result, we need to find other sources

of information to understand their context and their world. If we limit our understanding of the ancient world to just the scriptures in the canon and a few courses we take in world history, we risk being ignorant about the local context, which can lead to a misunderstanding about what was written.

- Most people who lived at that time were not educated and could not read. As a result, the stories and teachings were often given in oral form rather than being written down. There was less need for written forms of communication at that time, and there is a limit to what people can remember.

- Those who lived after Jesus went to heaven thought he would soon return to earth. They didn't feel an urgency to record everything they had seen and heard when they interacted with Jesus. It would be about 20 years after his death and resurrection before accounts about his life started to be compiled. Many amazing things happened when Jesus was alive, but as John wrote in the last verse of his account, "Jesus did many other things as well. If they were all recorded, the whole world wouldn't have enough room for all the books that would be written" (John 21:25).

- Too many things happened over the course of 2,000 years to have them all recorded in the scriptures. We will never know everything about the stories and characters in the Bible. Many details were not written down, and while many stories have been passed down through the centuries about what happened to Mary and Joseph, the disciples, and early apostles, the scriptures are silent on most of the details.

- Finally, the urban and rural cultures at that time were vastly different from the world we live in today. While there are some similarities between the ancient and modern worlds and basic human nature has not changed, we now deal with many complex issues that were not a concern to people who lived thousands of years ago. For example, we now deal with climate change, weapons of mass destruction, an integrated international economy, complex political systems and global alliances, scientific discoveries that expand what we know about the world, and technological advances that accelerate the pace of change. Thus, the Biblical writers have little or nothing to say about some issues we confront today. This means we must search the scriptures for general principles that apply to our situation and the issues we debate today.

KEY EVENTS OCCURRING BETWEEN THE OLD AND NEW TESTAMENTS

Those who have been a Christian for many years acquired much knowledge about the context of the New Testament. This awareness is gained through Bible study, listening to sermons, and attending classes about the contents of the books. However, people who read the Bible for the first time are confused when they move from the Old Testament to Matthew. Many new ideas and groups of people are introduced in the New Testament without explanation, and significant historical events that took place that affected the region and culture aren't described.

Malachi's prophecies were written in 420 BC and are the last record of the prophets in the Old Testament. Many Jews lived outside of Palestine at the time, mainly in Babylonia and Egypt, and their communities became quite large. To maintain their faith, their communities set up places of worship (synagogues) that were led by a religious scholar (rabbi) who read and explained the books (Tanakh) written about God's covenant with the Israelites.

During the 400 years that followed Malachi's prophecies, many notable events took place in that part of the world, and major political changes continued to influence the Jews. This period is sometimes called "the silent years," but many important events took place that a new reader needs to understand.

- Over a 10-year period (336–326 BC) the Greeks, led by Alexander the Great, conquered Asia Minor and then the Egyptians, Assyrians, Babylonians, and Persians to create an empire reaching all the way to India. The Greeks brought new ways of thinking about the world through their religious and political philosophies. They also influenced the architecture and arts throughout the empire, and the Greek language became widely spoken and written (Hebrew and Aramaic were also used by the Jews). Jewish communities enjoyed relative peace during Alexander's reign.
- When Alexander died in 323 BC, he was replaced by two of his generals, who created their own dynasties. The followers of one

general banned Judaism in Palestine, and a few devout Jews started a rebellion against the rulers who required Jews to make pagan sacrifices. This Maccabean revolt spread throughout Palestine, and after 25 years of fighting, the Greeks were expelled in 142 BC, and respectable religious activities returned to Palestine. (Hanukkah celebrates the victory over these Greek oppressors.)

- The Romans conquered Palestine and took control of Jerusalem in 63 BC. They had no tolerance for rebellion and ruthlessly executed many priests and Jewish leaders. In 37 BC Herod the Great got Rome to declare him the king of the Jews and started constructing many buildings, including a larger Temple in Jerusalem. When he died in 4 BC, Rome put other leaders in his place.

The People and Land of Palestine

During this 400-year period, Greek (Hellenistic) ways of thinking became attractive to many of the Jews, and differences emerged among the Jews about how they should interact with the Hellenistic world while preserving their faith.

- The *Pharisees* were a small but influential group who focused on strict obedience to God's commands. They also wanted to be separate from the world rather than "mingle" with nonbelievers. They stressed maintaining personal piety and held a legalistic view of right and wrong. Independence from foreign influence was especially important to the Pharisees, and they followed additional rules (the Talmud) that were made to ensure Jews didn't come close to breaking any of God's essential commands. They thought this would please God and would create conditions that would lead to the coming of the Messiah (*Christ* in Greek). They were proud of their faith and expressed their religious beliefs to others in very visible ways.

- The *Sadducees* were another small influential group, but they focused on morality and rejected the idea of supernatural powers. They were more accepting of foreign influences, especially the ideas of the Greeks and the principles of ethical philosophy. The Sadducees were typically wealthy and well-educated, and they didn't accept the additional rules followed by the Pharisees.

- The *Essenes* focused on self-control and withdrawing from the world. This small group of mystics retreated to remote parts of the region, mainly into the desert west of the Salt (Dead) Sea.
- *Zealots* wanted to use physical force to ensure no foreign power controlled the lives of God's people. They were willing to die for their cause.

There were other subgroups of people within Palestine who were distinct. Some were labeled based on where they lived, such as the impure Samaritans and Galileans who were viewed with contempt because they had often intermarried with non-Jews or were not Jewish at all. (Galilee was the northern part of Palestine, Samaria was the central part, and Judea was the southern part that was previously known as Judah.) Galileans were also known for being rebellious against foreign authority.

Some groups were distinct based on their profession, such as the scribes, who wrote important documents (often religious in nature) and were experts in the Law, and members of the Sanhedrin, a large and diverse group of leaders who watched over the religious life of the Jews and had the power to punish Jews.

Some were known for their allegiance. Herodians were Jews who followed Roman traditions and beliefs, while Hellenists were Jews who followed Greek traditions and beliefs. Nazarites still existed (they took a vow to dedicate themselves to God, usually for a limited amount of time); they promised to not consume any form of a grape, not touch a dead person, and not shave their head (a sign to others that they had taken the vow).

Because of the immigration of non-Jews into Palestine and the emigration of Jews out of Palestine, most of the people living in Palestine 2,000 years ago were not Jews, and most Jews lived elsewhere. Of the estimated four million Jews in the Roman Empire, only about 700,000 lived in Palestine. There were more Jews living in Alexandria, Egypt, than in Jerusalem and more living in Syria than in Palestine.

Although the Romans established a good infrastructure of roads throughout the empire mainly using slave labor from peoples they conquered, the transportation system in Palestine was not well developed. People usually walked from place to place or traveled by donkey or mule. Some inns existed along the roads, but they were generally dirty, so affluent travelers relied on their network of friends and family for lodging when they traveled.

Some of the Israelite prophets wrote about a Servant-King who would come and bring the nation back to glory. The Jews wondered when God would send the person and why it was taking so long. Events in the region were certainly ripe to have the Jews think that somebody would deliver them from the grip of powerful nations. Roman oppression reminded them of when their ancestors were oppressed in Egypt and when they were conquered by the Assyrians and Babylonians. It had been 400 years since they last heard from a prophet about somebody who would suddenly appear. They were watching closely for the coming Messiah, the Anointed One who would come and save them as Rome crushed Jewish rebel leaders and executed them slowly by nailing them alive to crosses that dotted the region.

GEOGRAPHICAL DETAILS

The Middle East is a large area and received its name when the British Empire existed. London was the "center of that world" and the Middle East was not as far away from it as the Far East (eastern Asia). The region is now sometimes called southwest Asia, which is more accurate geographically and doesn't recognize any location of the world as being a reference point of where east and west begin. Parts of northern Africa are sometimes considered to be part of the Middle East.

People who lived in the region during Biblical times were familiar with the geography of the Fertile Crescent. When Abram moved from Ur around 2000 BC by first going to Haran and then to Canaan, people knew where these cities were located.[10] But most modern readers don't know that Ur was located on the Euphrates River in present-day Iraq (part of Mesopotamia) about 150 miles from the Persian Gulf, and Haran is still a city in southern Turkey. When Moses wrote Genesis 600 years after Abram's move, the Jews understood the extended family had traveled hundreds of miles to Canaan, first going northeast through modern-day Iraq, Syria, and Turkey in order to bypass inhospitable

---

[10] The ancient dates mentioned in this book are estimates. There is little agreement about when many of the key ancient events took place. Rarely are exact dates important to know.

areas. While some parts of the family stayed in cities along the way, the rest of the clan, including Abram's nephew Lot, headed south toward Canaan. But when Abram got to Canaan, conditions were not suitable for his extended family, so they all traveled to Egypt before returning to Canaan.

The trip took several years to complete and covered more than 1,000 miles. One can imagine the nature of the family conversations that occurred during the long trip. This was a permanent migration — they weren't going back. Knowing these details gives us a greater appreciation for the steadfast faith Abram and Sarai had in God.

Many cities and areas are mentioned in the scriptures, and some of them no longer exist. Those who don't live in the region or haven't visited it don't understand how far it is between these locations or the living conditions. Nazareth was located near the Sea of Galilee, about a 90-mile walk north of Jerusalem using routes west and east of the central highlands. The most direct route went through Samaria and would have saved several days of walking (many Jews avoided traveling this route because they didn't like the Samaritans.

Before the expansion of the Israelite kingdom during the time of David and Solomon, the region of Canaan was about 10,000 square miles (26,000 square kilometers), which is slightly larger than the state of Vermont (half the size of Costa Rica).

Canaan's Typography and Vegetation

The typography of the region is not fully understood by those who haven't been to Palestine. Jerusalem is near the top and in the middle of a range of tall hills, with an elevation of 2,500 feet (760 meters). The range is about 75 miles long (120 kilometers) and runs north-south through the middle of the area known as the Hill Country. The hills have an average elevation of 2,000 feet (610 meters) and several valleys cut across the hills from east to west. The hills south of Jerusalem are more rugged and more difficult to cultivate compared to the hills north of Jerusalem.

The Dead Sea, about 15 miles east of Jerusalem, is the lowest surface on earth (elevation of −1412 feet, or −430 meters), and both the Sea of Galilee and the Jordan River are also well below sea level. The

Mediterranean Sea (at sea level) is located to the west, about 50 miles away. A coastal region along the sea has no natural port for ships on the coast, so the Israelites had no navy and didn't use ships to trade with others. A fertile valley in the north provides an ideal place to raise animals and grow crops, and several tall mountains in the north generate snow and rain that provide water for several rivers. The very large Negev Desert in the south ends at the Gulf of Aqaba, which extends south to the Red Sea. (The maps in the last appendix provide a visual representation of the region.)

The variation in the land within relatively short distances and the large changes in elevation made travel difficult. The roads and paths could be steep, and a trip to Jerusalem is uphill for most people. When the Bible said somebody went "up" or "down" to a location, they were often referring to walking uphill or downhill, not going north or south.

The vegetation within this small region is quite diverse because of the variation in the level of rainfall in the region. The land east of Jerusalem is rocky with limited vegetation because of its lack of rainfall. The gentle western slope down from Jerusalem toward the coast gets more rain and is better for growing crops and raising animals. The region has rainy and dry seasons, and it can be very hot, so water is a precious resource. Although there are hundreds of plants mentioned in the bible, the main crops grown in the area were wheat, barley, grapes, olives, figs, and date palms. The main animals raised on the land were cattle, sheep, and goats that all provided food, milk, and clothing; horses, donkeys, and camels provided transportation for people and goods.

When Moses sent scouts to report on conditions in Canaan, the region was described as "flowing with milk and honey." Compared to the wilderness, the region was lush. Besides the presence of cattle and goats that provided milk, the reference to honey probably related to both the presence of pollinating bees that generated honey and palm trees that produce dates, which are still used to make honey. The terms "milk and honey" symbolize ample food from both animals and plants.

Canaan's Strategic Location Had Its Dangers and Benefits

Understanding the overall geographic location of Canaan is also important. The relatively tiny region occupies a narrow strip of land squeezed between the Mediterranean Sea on the west and desert-like conditions less than 100 miles to the east. The region was a crossroad for the main trade routes connecting Africa, Asia, and Europe.

As a result of its strategic location, the region was constantly traversed by outsiders and frequently invaded and controlled by larger empires that wanted to expand their territory (Egyptians, Assyrians, Babylonians, Greeks, Romans). Those who lived in Canaan built cities with large walls to protect them from various invaders, and the cities and those living near them formed alliances with each other to fight against common opponents. The Israelites were also surrounded by less powerful nations that they sometimes battled: the Ammonites, Amorites, Edomites, Hittites, Moabites, and Philistines. It was in this narrow stretch of land that God called the Israelites to be an example to the world, and the world came to them!

Cultural Details

Those living during biblical times shared a lifestyle and traditions that are very different from those who live in western cultures today. Those who currently live in Palestine, Arab countries, and less-developed countries would feel much more comfortable traveling back in time to be in that culture than modern westerners who feel culture shock when they visit these places.

Most families cooked their food outside when the weather allowed it; cooking took place inside during the cold winter weather. Women often used dried dung, sticks, dried grass, or thorny shrubs as fuel for their fire. Charcoal was also used to build and sustain fires. Olive oil was used in cooking and for lamps to provide light. The Bible characters knew nothing about candles.

Three classes of people lived in those days. First, nomads (Bedouins) were shepherds who lived in tents. Abraham, Isaac, and Jacob lived most of their lives in tents, as did the Israelites who survived 40 years in the wilderness. Many Israelites who lived in Canaan when it was first occupied continued living in tents. Those who visit Palestine today still see communities of nomads — their lifestyle has changed little since biblical times.

Second, poor farmers usually lived in villages in a one-room house. These homes took the place of tents and usually had a dirt floor, sometimes with pieces of stone. The walls were made of stone or bricks made from dried mud. In some cases, dried dung became part of the walls. Everybody slept together in one room on some type of cushion-mattress. Third, city dwellers usually had homes with more than one room, and they often had a nice courtyard within the bland external walls.

The Context of the Prodigal Son Story

The close living quarters of all three groups meant that everybody knew everybody and everything that was happening. Normal conversations were easily overheard by others, and every family scandal would be gossiped about — there were few family secrets.

Knowing this context provides new insights into the radical nature of God's love described in the story of the Prodigal Son (Luke 15:11–32).

- The father would have been shamed and embarrassed in the community when his younger son asked for his share of the inheritance. The son's act was scandalous, and the father would have had to sell half his estate to give the son his half share. One can imagine the content and extent of the gossip in such a close community.
- The son was disgraced when he wasted his money and spent time with pigs. Jews didn't touch pigs.
- The story says that when the son was still far away, the father saw him approaching and recognized his walk. This means the father spent every day watching for his son to return. People in the community would have thought the father was overly obsessed with being reunited with his spoiled son and probably was wasting his time watching for him instead of getting back to his own business. The waiting time was probably many months and perhaps years.
- The father disgraced himself by running toward his son and embracing him in an excessive manner. In that culture, older men didn't run, for it would expose their legs, which was not socially acceptable. The physical expression of the father's joy would also have been seen as excessive.

- The grand celebration upon the son's return would have been seen as unwise and disproportionate. Everybody would have known what initially happened and would have seen what the son looked like when he returned, frail and disheveled. People would have expected the father to first get an apology and would have put the son to work to repay what he had received. The son didn't deserve anything good.

- The reaction of the older brother was predictable when he became angry and refused to join in the celebration. He was disgusted because his loyalty wasn't honored and his brother was an embarrassment.

The story followed the parable of a lost sheep and coin and is part of Jesus's teaching about extreme joy at finding the lost. The term *prodigal* means spending resources freely and recklessly or being wastefully extravagant. Most people apply the term to the son, but in the context of Jesus's other teachings about God's concern for those who are lost and God's generosity, a better title for the story is "the prodigal father" because of the extravagant love the father had for his lost son.

* * * * * *

Many of the customs in Palestine have changed little since ancient times. The Bible is an "eastern" book, and those living in developed countries must work hard to understand the context of the Bible's stories in order to gain insight into what was written. Often the most important points were understood by people at that time and were therefore not written.[11]

Of course, some issues we confront in modern times were not mentioned anywhere in the Bible. The authors didn't know what would happen many centuries in the future. In addition, the Bible intentionally contains little or nothing about many disciplines (e.g., the natural and social sciences, technology) and the ethical issues related to them. While the Bible doesn't contain all the details we might want, it still provides an abundance of stories, teachings, and principles that can help guide our individual lives and tell us how we should live together on earth.

---

[11] For more details about the customs and culture during Biblical times, see *Manners and Customs for Bible Lands*, Northwestern Theological Seminary.

CHAPTER 4

THE BIBLE AS LITERATURE

GENERAL CONTENT

The books of the Bible reflect many types and elements of literature because it had multiple authors. Readers move from one genre to another, from gut-wrenching tragedies to edge-of-your-seat epics, examples of scandalous and courageous leadership, sound moral teachings, and emotion-laden poetry. The variety of the Bible's content is partly responsible for its worldwide appeal.

The first authors described how the world began and wrote narratives about various heroes, historical accounts, legal presentations and speeches, and biographies. Some authors wrote poetry, recorded genealogies and census information, provided wisdom literature and proverbs, and wrote short stories, parables, and letters of inspiration and exhortation. They used symbolism and sometimes wrote highly symbolic predictions about the future.

Most of the writings occurred when farming was the main occupation, so there are many references and metaphors using common items at that time (sheep, goats, soil, seeds, water, wheat, fish, vineyards, the desert, the wilderness). For example, Psalm 1:3–4 describes godly and wicked men using similes.

> He is like a tree planted by streams of water,
>> which yields its fruit in its season; his leaf does not wither.
> But the wicked are like chaff the wind blows away.

The overall tone of the Bible is somber and serious. The Bible has little humor — one rarely laughs when reading through the entire set of books. While one of the Bible's main themes relates to love, there is little romance. There are many touching encounters between people, and some of the sexual encounters are perverse in nature. There are many sad parts, but there are also many heroes and victories. Most of the Bible is non-fiction; some fictional stories were written to convey important messages.

All the complexities of life appear in the writings: life and death, good and evil, guilt and forgiveness, justice and judgment, grace and mercy, love and hate, reason and emotions, individualism and community life, sibling rivalry, reflections of the past and visions of the future, patience and expediency, discipline and impulsiveness, power and servanthood, selfishness and sacrifice, health and sickness, trust and deception, sequential logic and paradox, idealism and realism. The stories often have rich symbolism, and dialogue is mixed in with narration. The range and depth of the stories in the Bible and the different styles of writing are reasons why the entire set is essential reading for any educated person and why the Bible is considered the greatest "book" in all of history.

Elements of the Plot

The collection of the writings in its entirety has a beginning that moves progressively to a conclusion. No one document tells the entire story, but together they build on many common themes. Despite their diversity, the documents all contribute to a plot that centers on the nature of God and the invisible conflict between the spiritual forces of good and evil in the world.

Although there are many authors who write over hundreds of years, the overall plot of the Bible includes a number of unifying themes that run from the beginning to the end.

- The world has two planes of reality — one that is physical and can be seen and measured, and another that is invisible, supernatural, and spiritual, which cannot be measured empirically.
- Invisible forces have unusual "supernatural" powers. Some forces have good and loving motives, but others have evil motives that destroy what is good.
- There is only one true and supreme being (God) who simultaneously has three relational "persons." Some people believe there are many gods, but these gods don't have the characteristics or power of the true God. The three "persons" of God are collectively known as the

Trinity. (The term "persons" is used because God has a personality, emotions, and an intellect and makes rational decisions.)

- A special kind of love, one that sacrifices for others and expects nothing in return, is the most important quality in the world. This theme is described in more depth in chapter 9.

In modern literature, a plot unfolds gradually, often over hundreds of pages with much character development and detailed descriptions of the context and minor characters. The few key points of the story are sometimes implied along the way or near the end of the book. Sometimes the points are made clearly, but they are often implied. The primary purpose of much of today's fiction is for entertainment.

The Bible is different from modern literature in several ways. Most of its stories are relatively short, they lack detailed descriptions of the setting and characters, and its teachings are usually clear and explicit. It's more like nonfiction that informs, teaches, and exhorts.

The Bible has many tragedies and heroes, many disappointments and victories, and they are sometimes described in several forms of literary plots. A *romance* describes an ideal picture of human experience. A story that moves from romance to disaster is a *tragedy*, and a story that moves in the opposite direction is a *comedy*. A comedy's plot often unfolds as a hero's character develops as they overcome obstacles and ultimately achieve a successful outcome. The rest of this chapter describes the various forms of literature found in the Bible.

THE STORY OF ORIGINS

The first three chapters of Genesis provide a special kind of history and a logical beginning of the book. The story is similar to the creation stories about pagan gods, but Genesis is different in important ways. In contrast with the typical description that many gods were created out of the chaos of the world, Genesis asserts that God existed before the world began and created it in an orderly fashion. Most people at that time believed there were many gods, but Genesis describes one God who created the entire world, and the human race as special among all of creation. There is no battle among the gods for power and control of the world; God is in control and there is harmony between God's "persons."

The world is described as being good, not full of fear and chaos. Life began as a perfect paradise, and it stayed that way as long as humans obeyed God's instructions. But the story describes how turning away from God has negative consequences. Paradise was lost, but the acts of a loving and creative God saved the finest but flawed creation from danger and death. It foreshadows key stories in the Bible about how God saves flawed people and that paradise would eventually return.

Humans, both males and females, were created in the "image of God" and take on certain characteristics of God. Humans can distinguish between right and wrong, have self-consciousness and an awareness of our surroundings, can have meaningful relationships with God and others, and are able to love others in sacrificial ways. These qualities give people unique insights into the nature of God. In contrast with the descriptions of the pagan gods who were worshipped and feared and demanded sacrifices to be appeased, the true God of the universe wants a loving relationship with humans. God created and loved the world, and humans are to love God, take care of the world, and love one another.

The origin story is meant to lay out the general concepts of the universe; it doesn't provide specific details in a historical narrative about how the world began. The time and place covered in these chapters are not stated, and attempts to use the genealogies to determine when the world began don't seem reasonable in light of what we now know about ancient civilizations and the universe. The "days" of creation described in Genesis 1 are symbolic of an orderly process that took place over an unknown amount of time. The Garden of Eden symbolizes paradise where God is present and there is no evil. Evil is introduced into the world, and Adam, Eve, and their children symbolize the sinful tendencies of humans. Genesis 1–4 is best seen as an introduction to several main themes that will unfold in more detail all the way through to the last book, Revelation.

The story of Noah and the flood also lacks details to place it in history. Many civilizations have stories about a great flood, and the dimensions given for Noah's ark would make it similar in size to a modern cargo ship. Nevertheless, the account is best seen as another symbolic story that describes the natural tendency for humans to resort to corruption, wickedness, selfishness, and violence when dealing with others. Warnings of judgment went unheeded, foreshadowing events to come centuries later. The account also foreshadows God's pattern of saving a small percentage of people from harm (a "remnant") that allowed humans to continue to relate to God. The rainbow was a constant reminder to people that God would forgive and not destroy the world.

Finally, the nine verses in Genesis 11 provide a brief account about the construction of the Tower of Babel, which symbolized human pride in their achievements. The dispersed workforce due to language differences is a reminder that God can humble human efforts that lead to pride. Language differences continue to lead to many humbling experiences!

Moses wrote Genesis around 1400 BC during his time when he led the Israelites in the wilderness. The stories about creation and everything up until he wrote Genesis had been passed on through generations of oral storytelling. These stories include the events about 500 years earlier about Abraham's call by God to move to Canaan.

HEROIC NARRATIVE

A *heroic* narrative is a specific type of narrative that describes the events in the life of heroes and the conflicts they encounter. The story of Abram/Abraham is the first to appear in great detail, although the short story about Noah could also fall in this category. Abraham's heroism is spiritual in nature — he has faith in God and is obedient to God's will.

God is always another character in the Bible's heroic narratives. God gives Abram and his wife a new name — they are changed people. The stories about Abraham, Isaac, and Jacob all reveal their flawed character, but God continues to stand with them and honors their agreement, which shows the loving and forgiving nature of God. Flawed people can accomplish great things if they obey God. The story of Joseph being sold to traders but ending up saving his entire family reveals that God can use evil and undeserved suffering for good. Joseph overcomes many hardships, and his faith and good decisions pay off and enable him to build the nation of Israel.

The story of David is a classic heroic narrative that spans several books. He is the most complex of all the Old Testament characters and has many talents and roles. As a political leader, he is most like a conventional hero who appears in ancient literature. He grew up from a humble position, became famous by killing a formidable enemy (Goliath), was victorious in many battles, and became the greatest king of Israel. While he exhibited many good character traits, he also had flaws that caused him to suffer. Throughout his tragedies and triumphs, his spiritual journey was constantly present and evolving.

The heroic story of Daniel's life unfolds in several settings. Like the story of Joseph, he is portrayed in idealistic terms and is a model of virtue and integrity when confronted with difficult circumstances. As a person with a strong faith while he served in secular positions of power, he doesn't compromise his core values, even though he faced negative consequences. He is a religious hero whose life is centered in God. There were other Old Testament stories that fall into this category of literature, including the stories of Joshua and Gideon.

Three women are described in heroic narratives: Ruth, Deborah, and Esther. The romantic story of Ruth, a foreign migrant who becomes part of Jewish society, describes a brave and gentle woman of integrity. After first experiencing several tragedies, she eventually becomes the wife and mother in the royal line of David. Deborah is a prophet and honest judge who leads the Israelites in their successful battle against the very strong Canaanite army based in Hazor, along with a reluctant Barak. The victory led to 40 years of peace. Esther is a young orphan who wins a beauty contest and becomes the queen of Persia and risks her life when she tells the king about a decree that threatens the lives of all the Jews in the empire. The story is nationalistic in nature rather than spiritual.

The Epic of Exodus

An *epic* is a long story with many different episodes and is a specific type of heroic narrative. The unified plot centers on the character of Moses, a political leader, and the people of God, the Israelites. It records historical events over 40 years and a journey from Egypt on the way to the Promised Land. There is no story in the Bible like it, and it takes four books to tell the entire story (Exodus, Leviticus, Numbers, Deuteronomy).

Unlike the traditional epic that magnifies human heroes, the epic of Exodus centers on the nature and power of God. In fact, this epic flips the traditional epic structure on its head — people often fail to have faith and act wisely. God's power and love are what sustains the Israelites during the journey, not human actions and decisions. If it wasn't for a few key leaders who acted with conviction and wisdom with a faith in God, the journey would have turned into a disaster many times. Even the main character, Moses, was a flawed man and felt inadequate to do what God wanted him to do. As a reluctant leader, others helped and advised him as he led the Israelites out of Egypt while the stubborn people constantly complained. God is the true hero in the story.

With God at the center of the entire story, the epic has a highly moral and religious theme. Many rules for correct living take up vast amounts of the story. There are constant reminders about how to live and warnings about how not to live. The story ends with reminders from Moses that God had been faithful to the Israelites, and their victories were not something they accomplished on their own: God was solely responsible for bringing the entire nation out of Egypt to the doorstep of the Promised Land.

SATIRE

The Bible sometimes reflects *satire*, which makes a point by highlighting the moral shortcomings of a person or group of people. Sometimes it causes laughter by the reader, but a satire can also be bitter and angry.

The prophet Amos was a simple farmer who used satire in a blistering attack from God to the Israelites. The region was experiencing easy living during a time of prosperity, but wealth was not distributed evenly and many social injustices existed within the culture. He first condemned injustice in other nations, saying that divine judgment would be their punishment. But he then condemned the wickedness of the Israelites who were proud about how religious they were, and he condemned the social evils, injustice, immorality, and profanity that existed in society. He wrote that if foreign nations deserved punishment, so did Israel. In fact, it was even worse because the Israelites were God's chosen people and should know better!

Jesus used satire when he told parables that attacked materialism, the love of money, a lack of compassion, and the emphasis on looking good to others. The hypocritical Pharisees were often the object of these messages in his series of "woe" statements, and he often used dramatic metaphors to emphasize his points (e.g., calling Pharisees "whitewashed tombs").

The unknown author of Jonah wrote the 2-page satire to make many universal messages. Jonah is afraid to do what God calls him to do (preach about the future destruction of Nineveh, Israel's main enemy) and travels 2,000 miles in the opposite direction. After suffering during the trip, he goes to preach his message. But ironically, he pouts about his situation and lacks the qualities of compassion, forgiveness, and universal love shown by his God for his enemy.

BIBLICAL TRAGEDY

A *tragedy* is a narrative that moves from prosperity to catastrophe, a fall in fortune from a high to a low place, usually because of some weakness in character. It can be an individual, or a group, or even a great nation. The responsibility for the fall is a logical consequence of action or inaction, not by chance. The tragic hero is often both an agent and victim of the failure. The fall of the Roman Empire was a tragedy. (This doesn't mean a tragedy is "tragic" — good things can come from a tragedy.)

The life of Samson is a tragedy. His great strength made him a famous hero, but his ignorance and unwise decisions led to his early death. The life of Saul, Israel's first king, also follows the tragedy pattern. Although he had the physical attributes of a leader, his insecurities and bad decisions led to his downfall. The life of King Solomon is a third example of a Biblical tragedy. As the favorite son of King David, he became the richest and wisest man on earth. But after he built the Temple, he allowed his many wives to corrupt the correct religious practices, and his success and prosperity tainted his judgment. The nation fell apart soon after his death. Both Saul and Solomon started with great promise, but decisions and personality weaknesses soiled their reputations.

POETRY

Poetry is the most precise and condensed form of writing and is used in many parts of the Old Testament. Some books were entirely poetry, and Psalms is a collection of 150 lyric poems that contain the strong thoughts and feelings of an individual. Most of the psalms were written by David and many reflected the thoughts and emotions he had while certain events took place among the Israelites. The writings interpret life and events using vivid images and symbols and employ many figures of speech, especially metaphors and similes. Rather than reflecting rhyme, the psalms contain a repetition of ideas using parallel structure.

Most psalms relate in some way to the concepts of good and evil. The authors have a clear preference for pursuing good and benefiting from God's goodness while rejecting evil ways that lead to negative consequences. About half of the psalms deal with prayers during times of trouble, and some simply praise God. A few reflect a patriotic nationalism based on a shared cultural experience. Some were meant to be sung or accompanied by music.

Various Old Testament authors used poetry to convey their messages to the Israelites. Isaiah used poetry extensively as he wrote to multiple audiences, and he quoted God's words in poetry (e.g., 2Ki 19). Lamentations, probably written by Jeremiah, is a book of poetry that describes what happened during Babylon's destruction of Judah and the people's incredible sense of loss following the fall of Jerusalem, the destruction of the Temple, and their exile to Babylon. The Song of Solomon was written in poetry, and most of the book of Job was written in an ancient poem format. Songs are written as poetry (e.g., David's praise in 2Sam 22), sometimes characters within a story use poetry, and some prayers appear in poetry form (e.g., Hannah's prayer in 1Sam 2).

WISDOM LITERATURE

Wisdom literature is a general category for a host of different types of writings. Its characteristics include having a wise narrator who declares truth and insights to others about human experiences. The author often makes short, concise statements or stories about what is true in a proverb. These statements often deal with the right and wrong way to do things. In general, the proverbs tell people to follow these truths to avoid evil and be rewarded; those who don't follow the advice are warned that they will suffer negative consequences.

Sometimes these statements are strung together to make an extended short story on a common theme. Parallel ideas are sometimes strung together, as are comparisons between something that is good and something that is bad. Moral and spiritual truths in a world that has both good and evil forces are often the subject of biblical wisdom literature.

The book of Proverbs contains the best examples of wisdom literature, and most of it was written by King Solomon. Positive and negative statements are often coupled to provide a contrast between good and evil. Sometimes these are just one sentence long. For example, Proverb 3:35 states, "The wise inherit honor but fools inherit dishonor." In other cases, there are clusters of proverbs that discuss the same idea. Many of the sayings and short stories deal with money, justice, and sexual morality (many verses talk about avoiding the temptations of sex-related sins and making money the wrong way). The book has many reminders to its readers that they must constantly pursue wisdom and avoid doing evil things.

The book of Ecclesiastes was also written primarily by Solomon, and he asserts that he is an experienced wise man. He wants to share his observations in order to teach others about the world. His writing style involves making short statements and telling stories that summarize basic truths based on what he has learned as he pursued the good life.

THE GOSPELS AND EPISTLES AS LITERATURE

The four *gospels* (Matthew, Mark, Luke, John) that begin the New Testament stand alone as a unique kind of literature — there is nothing like them in secular literature. The gospels combine historical facts with a few biographical details, contain both dialogue and narration, include satire and wisdom literature, and the parables of Jesus are allegories.

The gospels have a single purpose: to tell the story of one man, Jesus. Unlike the Old Testament heroic narratives that have a logical hero and a single plot, the gospels include many stories that don't tie closely together, and they have numerous themes. And Jesus is no ordinary hero — he is a suffering servant rather than a mighty victor. Instead of beating his opponents, he is executed as a criminal. And the overall story cannot be considered a tragedy in part because of what Jesus's death means for the world, and because the resurrection suddenly changes the scenario from death to eternal life.

The teachings of Jesus are saturated with metaphors and symbols, and he created fictional stories to make his points. Leland Ryken, professor emeritus of English at Wheaton College (IL), says, "He drew upon one area of human experience to shed light on another... Sending the disciples to minister in a hostile world was similar to sending 'sheep in the midst of wolves'" (Matt 10:16).[12]

An *epistle* is a type of literature that is written in the form of a letter. Since they mainly contain teachings about Jesus and the implications of being a disciple, they can be considered an extension of the gospels. Some are general while others are quite personal. Some are well crafted while others are somewhat random, as if they were written via a stream of thought.

Paul wrote 13 letters that are included in the New Testament (he wrote other letters that were never found). Nine of his letters were sent to churches and were well-designed and general in nature. For example, his longest letter was sent to the house churches in Rome, which had both Jewish and Gentile believers. He didn't know most of the people who would hear his message, so his writing is more formal. His letter explained the general principles and implications of the faith as if his epistle was a legal case. Paul also wrote four much shorter and more personal letters to individual Christian leaders he knew (Timothy, Titus, Philemon).

Four other Christian leaders wrote general letters to believers: the apostles Peter and John and the two half-brothers of Jesus, James and Judas (calling himself Jude). These letters were meant to encourage and guide Christians during difficult times and to point out false teachings about the faith that were circulating at the time.

---

[12] Leland Ryken, *The Literature of the Bible* (1974), Grand Rapids: Zondervan Publishing House, p. 291.

Another letter, Hebrews, was written by an unknown author to Jews in general to convince them that Jesus was superior to all the heroes of the Old Testament. The letter is impersonal and structured like a sermon or essay, and it aimed to keep Jewish believers from reverting back to Judaism.

OTHER FORMS OF LITERATURE

A few other forms of literature appear in the Bible and are worth mentioning. In some cases, a book has a mixture of several types of literature, and there may not be agreement about what type of literature a book or story represents. For example, the well-designed book of Job is unique because it has elements of a tragedy, comedy, drama, satire, wisdom literature, and poetry.

Romance and Pastoral Literature

Song of Solomon is a *romance* describing an ideal picture of a loving human relationship, although some consider the book to be an allegory of God's love for the nation of Israel and now for the church. The story of Ruth and her marriage to Boaz could be considered romance literature. *Pastoral* literature, which uses rural settings and characters (especially shepherds), often has a theme of love and depicts the good life or an ideal setting. Jesus was described as the "good shepherd" who loved and cared for his sheep.

Encomium

An *encomium* is a form of literature that praises a general character type or an abstract quality. Psalm 1 is an encomium that praises a godly person. Psalm 15, shown below, uses general terms to exalt the character of a godly person.

> Lord, who may live in your sacred tent?
> Who may live on your holy mountain?
> The one whose walk is blameless,
>   who does what is right,
>   who speaks the truth from their heart;
> Whose tongue says no slander,
>   who does no wrong to a neighbor, and

> who does not cast a slur on others;
> Who despises vile people and honors those fearing the Lord;
> Who keeps their promise even when it hurts, and
>   does not change their mind;
> Who lends money to the poor without interest,
>   who does not accept a bribe against the innocent.
> Whoever does these things will never be shaken.

Proverbs 31 contains an encomium that praises the qualities of the good wife. Isaiah 52 and 53 describe the Messiah in a paradoxical encomium that ties a suffering servant to one who is high and exalted. John 1:1–18 praises Jesus and his essential role on earth as the human form of God. 1 Corinthians 13 praises the abstract quality of love, and Hebrews 11–12:2 describes the faith of others with exhortations for believers to follow their example.

Parables

The *parables* in the Bible are allegories, a form of literature in which details have conceptual meanings. While we are most familiar with the parables of Jesus, they also appear in nine Old Testament books (most are in Jeremiah, Ezekiel, and Zechariah). They are easy to understand because they are usually short and describe situations that are familiar to the audience.

Jesus probably made up his parables on the spot to use a short story to make a point. He used them to teach unconventional truths about topics that were misunderstood by his listeners. Most of his parables didn't need any explanation because his point was obvious, but sometimes he explained the details to his listeners who were confused about its meanings (e.g., the parable of the sower and soils).

The use of fictional stories is an effective way to teach eternal truths. Parables are vivid and interesting stories to think about, and short stories are easy to remember. Sometimes, spontaneously making up a story is the best way to make a point, and fiction can be used to simplify and emphasize important facts that are true.

Apocalyptic Literature

John's "revelation" (*apocalypsis* in Greek, meaning "unveiling") was written in the form of apocalyptic literature that was popular at that time. It used highly symbolic language in the form of visions, numerology, and archetypes and often lacked important details. This makes the content hard to understand, and there are many ways to interpret its content.

This mysterious type of literature was used earlier by the Old Testament prophets, especially by Isaiah, Jeremiah, Daniel, and Ezekiel, and by some New Testament authors. John's book refers to many other apocalyptic books that were circulating at the time that his audience would have known about but are not included in the Bible.

Since Christians were being persecuted at that time for not obeying any Roman laws that violated the principles of their faith, John could not communicate with members of the church in a transparent way in his letter, now called Revelation. Those receiving his letter would be in danger if the letter was found by the Romans, so John used terms that had double meanings or would only be understood by believers. He talked about the evils of Babylon, but he was really talking about the evils of the Roman empire. He used the number seven to symbolize completeness (e.g., seven cities and hills, seven seals, seven stars, seven trumpets). This approach is similar to how an athletic team or members of an underground community use secret signs and language to communicate with each other — his words were in code and were not to be taken literally. As a prisoner in exile, he had time to write a carefully crafted letter to circulate among churches in seven cities connected by major roads in Asia Minor.

The overall conflict is the spiritual struggle between the forces of good and evil. The book is disjointed and hard to follow, and its meanings are the subject of much debate. Nevertheless, the final climax, the defeat of evil and the description of a new heaven and earth, makes Revelation a fitting end to the entire collection of books in the Bible. Like the end of a movie after a long titanic struggle, we finally know which side wins. In the midst of much ongoing carnage that seems like it will never end, this is a comforting thought that brings hope during our trials on earth.

* * * * * * *

The variety of the types of literature used in the Bible, along with its range of characters, interesting stories, complex plot details, and compelling truths about society and the human condition, has made it a timeless classic. Every educated person should read and understand the Bible, even if they don't believe in God, because it is the basis for understanding historical trends and engaging our discourse about local and world problems and their possible solutions.

CHAPTER 5

UNDERSTANDING THE BIBLE

Given the variation in literature forms and figures of speech used in the Bible, the different authors and their audiences, and the different geographic and cultural context of the books, it can be a challenge to have an accurate understanding of certain passages. The authors and speakers used different literary devices to convey essential meanings: allegories and parables, metaphors and similes, irony and satire, and hyperbole (exaggerations). The authors used these devices to convey their messages, and their audiences knew they were meant to make a point rather than to be taken literally or report historical facts. While the biblical writings convey timeless truths, not everything that was written is literally true. Readers need to know when to take any particular message or story literally or figuratively.

GENERAL CONCEPTS FOR INTERPRETING THE BIBLE

Interpreting the Bible often requires careful study. The field of study related to the interpretation of the Bible is called *hermeneutics*, and the term *exegesis* refers to the interpretation of a specific Biblical text. The process of interpreting scripture starts by trying to understand what the author meant to say, not what the text means to a reader now, which would impose our belief system on the Biblical text.

To understand what a Bible passage means (in contrast to what is *says*), we need to know five things:
- The literary form the passage was written in;
- The cultural and historical context of the passage;
- Who the author was writing to and for what purpose(s);
- The meaning of the words that were written; and
- What other scripture passages say about the topic.

In many cases, what was written or said was not meant to be taken literally — they may have been metaphors or hyperbole. When we read that "God is our fortress," we know this is a metaphor — God doesn't look like a castle structure; being in the "shadow of God's wings" doesn't mean God has the wings of a bird. The "hand of God" is an anthropomorphic term, a literary method to give a human characteristic to something that is invisible in order to convey a commonly understood concept. Jesus said we should cut off our hand or pluck out our eye if they offend us, but he didn't mean for people to actually do it — it was hyperbole.

Some people misunderstood the Christian movement because they took terms literally. Nicodemus was confused when Jesus said he had to be "born again" and pointed out the difficulty of re-entering his mother's womb. Some people said Christians were cannibals who "ate the body of Christ" and "drank his blood" (many people stopped following Jesus when he used this metaphor). Some thought Christians were incestuous because they married their "brothers and sisters." Some said Christians were atheists because their God was invisible and didn't believe in the Roman gods that could be seen. We know Jesus used symbolism when he said, "Destroy this temple and I will rebuild it in three days" (John 2:19).

When it comes to interpreting a story, the author may tell the audience its meaning. At other times, the author just tells a story without describing its significance, usually because the audience understood the point being made. So we need to understand the context to understand the meaning of some stories.

We must also understand the meaning of the words used, which might not be translated accurately into other languages. For example, the English word *love* has many meanings: we love certain foods, parents love their children, friends love each other, and people "make love." Knowing the difference between the three Greek words for love — *eros, philia,* and *agape* — is key to understanding the "love" chapter of the Bible, 1 Corinthians 13.[13]

"Fear" is another word with different meanings. For example, Proverbs 9:10 has been translated, "The fear of the Lord is the beginning

---

[13] Paul used the Greek term *agape* as the word for love in this chapter, which involves action and sacrifice for others. The term love in this chapter doesn't mean an emotional feeling, mutual friendship (*philia*), or physical love (*eros*).

of wisdom," but other translations use the terms respect, reverence, and awe. These are better terms in this context because we are told "fear not" or "don't be afraid" more than 140 times in the Bible. In ancient Near Eastern literature, the terms "fear" and "love" were associated with covenant loyalty — fearing God is to have an allegiance (love) for God and the instructions, values, convictions, and behaviors of God. So we shouldn't be afraid of God. This example shows us that in-depth study may be important to understand the meaning of a verse.

Finally, some verses use metaphors that were understood at the time but are unfamiliar to today's readers. For example, Isaiah and Malachi refer to a person who will "prepare the way of the Lord, make his paths (crooked places) straight and the rough places smooth," verses that later applied to John the Baptist, God's messenger crying in the wilderness (Isa 40:3–4, Mal 3:1, Matt 3:3, Mark 1:2–3, Luke 3:4). But the verses make more sense when we know their underlying meaning. In ancient times, before a king went on a journey, he sent workers ahead to ensure the route was as direct and straight as possible and any ruts or bumps in the road were made flattened, which made the king's trip faster and more comfortable. John preceded the king and prepared the way, which implied the king was heading their way.

LITERAL INTERPRETATIONS MAY NOT APPLY OR BE UNDERSTOOD

Some passages are meant to be taken literally but they may be cultural and no longer apply, or we don't understand the context and therefore miss the point. Since the local context influenced what was written, specific instructions provided to people in one place at a particular time may not relate to those living in other areas or times — the guidance may be cultural instructions rather than universal truths for all to always follow.

For example, in 1 Corinthians 11, Paul said women believers should cover their heads, and he made comments about the length of a person's hair. These instructions were valid because they related to the local customs of Corinth at the time. However, they have been interpreted by some to be mandates to be followed at all times. Leviticus 19:28 says a person should not get a tattoo, but the context of the verse relates to people who cut themselves as part of a pagan ritual related to the dead. Paul commanded Christians to "greet one another with a holy kiss" (Rom 16:16, 1Cor 16:20, 2Cor 13:12, 1Th 5:26, 1Pet 5:14), but this was the traditional greeting in the Mediterranean world at that time. While this is what the verses *say*, it's not what they *mean*, which was to express warmth and friendliness to others, not literally pressing one's lips together in a romantic way.

There were many instructions given in the Old Testament that Christians no longer follow because circumstances have changed. For example, the Israelites were forbidden to eat pork, but Jesus said that it's not what a person consumes that defies them (Matt 15:11), and pork was part of what Peter saw in a vision as acceptable food before he visited Cornelius (Acts 10). The correct interpretation of the instructions in the Bible are those that are consistent with the main themes running through all the books of the Bible, and the direct teachings of the New Testament take priority over those in the Old Testament (Jesus often clarified what the Law meant).

Some verses were meant to be taken literally at the time but are widely misunderstood now because we live in a different environment. For example, Proverbs 25:21–22 was quoted by Paul in his letter to Christians in Rome: "If your enemy is hungry, feed them; if they are thirsty, give them water to drink. This will heap burning coals on their heads, and the Lord will reward you" (Rom 12:20). These verses should be taken literally within the context of the culture, and the meaning applies universally, not just to those who lived in Israel and Rome.

At the time, somebody who was running out of material to keep their fire going would ask many neighbors for a small amount of wood or a few coals. Eventually this would provide enough material to keep their fire going through the night. Paul says that by providing a large amount of wood or charcoal (heaping burning coals) to a neighbor, it relieves the neighbor from having to get these items from many others — it's a sign of extreme generosity. Moreover, people often carried things on their heads, so in this context, the heaping coals were put on the person's head to carry home. Paul quoted Proverbs in the context to tell Christians to do their best to be at peace with everybody and to let God provide vengeance to their enemies — God loves those who are generous. Yet some pastors used this passage to imply that serving one's enemy is a way to harm them and get revenge in a subtle way.

But the phrase, taken literally at that time, doesn't mean that at all — serving an enemy is *not* a way to hurt them by burning their head.

Several verses say that what was written shouldn't have anything added or removed, but these verses apply only to what was written in that particular document, not to all of scripture. The idea is first mentioned in Deuteronomy 4:2 and is repeated later (Deut 12:32, Prov 30:6). But many other books of the Bible were written later, including all the books of the New Testament. Revelation 22:18–19, written in John's prophecies about the end of time, also contains the idea. The verses relate only to his letter — John wrote them when others were writing their own prophecies about the persecutions of the Christians. If these verses were taken literally, no other book would be included in the Bible after Deuteronomy. Since the books of the Bible were not approved as being authoritative until centuries later, authors didn't know their writings would become part of a highly respected Bible. Moreover, if these verses applied to all scriptures, anybody who writes about the Bible and explains its meanings would be guilty of violating these admonitions. Nobody argues that books with Bible stories that are simplified for children should never be written.

Verses that are meant to be taken literally can also have deeper meanings. The idea of "heaping burning coals on your enemy's head" illustrates the psychological value of showing extreme generosity to others. While the next verse says God will reward the generosity of the giver, there are other benefits from the generosity. The gesture increases the chances of a more peaceful relationship between two parties. This happens when innocent civilians find themselves in the middle of a battle and are confronted by fighters from the opposing side. It also happens when two parties are at odds with each other — the first one to make a generous gesture can start the reconciliation process. Finally, the gesture communicates that the generous person values people more than money or material possession, which is a kingdom value.

Some Biblical accounts describe situations that were normal at the time, but this doesn't mean they are justified. Slavery, for example, is mentioned hundreds of times in ways that seem to justify it as an acceptable social practice or ordained by God. Christians justified slavery for centuries, but over time we developed a better understanding of the context and the underlying principles of scripture, and we now see slavery as an unacceptable practice. Polygamy was a normal part of Jewish society and no verse condemns it, but this doesn't make it the correct marriage model. Passages about women were written in a patriarchal culture, and simple interpretations of isolated versions, along with traditional views toward women and previous assumptions about what the texts mean, must be examined in light of what we know now about women's capabilities. We need to allow new facts and insights from the Holy Spirit inform our understanding of what the scriptures mean and not just strictly follow what they say.

Individual vs Authoritative Actions

Some literal interpretations can appear to contradict each other. For example, in Genesis 9:6, God says a person who kills another person should be put to death. Later, the sixth commandment (Exod 20:13) says "Do not murder" but God commanded the Israelites to kill all the inhabitants of Canaan when occupying the land.

The apparent contradictions that sometimes occur in scriptures are usually explained by having a correct interpretation of the verses. There is no contradiction in these examples because the command not to kill is directed to individuals, and governing authorities carry out the death sentence to administer justice and keep peace in the community. All civil authority works on behalf of God's authority (see chapter 17), so God uses humans to punish evil. A soldier in the military is a tool of the government and may kill an enemy, but the soldier must not kill somebody when he is not in that role.

This raises the issue of how a loving God can punish those who do evil or issue a command to kill all the Canaanites, including women and children. These orders were meant to remove evil from society before the Israelites moved into the region. There are several points to keep in mind when grappling with this apparent contradiction.

First, a loving God hates evil but allows it to continue until the time comes when all evil will be destroyed. Second, allowing evil to continue unchecked would be irresponsible and would destroy those who are good. In fact, Revelation says that God will intervene to destroy evil permanently. In the meantime, God is the administrator of justice. Romans 12:19 says, "Don't take revenge, leave that to God's righteous anger. The scriptures say, 'I will take revenge, I will repay,' says the Lord." (Chapter 17 provides a lengthy discussion about this topic.)

Third, the cleansing of Canaan was a one-time situation meant to create a clean environment for the Israelites and remove those who followed evil practices. This is like what a family would do before moving into a new but filthy house — everything that is not clean must be eliminated. Who would move into a house full of poisonous vermin and dangerous substances without doing a deep and thorough cleaning first? Without it, whatever survived will regenerate and cause havoc to the inhabitants again. (This is exactly what happened: Canaan was only partially cleaned and the Canaanites who remained in the area undermined the Israelite beliefs and culture.) This cleansing was similar to the destruction of all humans during the time of Noah.

In sum, God hates evil so much that at some point, all evil will be eliminated. Nevertheless, God's loving nature and sacrifice to cover people's sins continues to give humans the opportunity to turn from evil, be reconciled with God, and be a force for good in the world. Civil authorities are responsible for providing a safe and just society, and when a government doesn't carry out this duty, they may need to be removed.

INSPIRATION, AUTHORITY, AND IMPORTANCE

The Bible claims to be the "inspired" word of God (*theopneustos* in Greek, meaning "God-breathed") and "is useful to teach us what is true and help us realize what we have done wrong" (2Tim 3:16). Both Paul and Peter said the teachings in scriptures didn't come from human understanding — the writers were moved by the Spirit and spoke for God (1Cor 2:12–13, 2Pet 1:20–21). So God is the true author of the Bible and used humans as scribes, and this makes it authoritative and true when it was first written.

No scripture verse exists that says no mistakes or errors were made in the documents that were compiled in the Bible. The various authors assumed that what they wrote had no mistakes (grammatical or factual), so they didn't need to mention this idea. Since God is the true author of the Bible and God doesn't make mistakes (Heb 6:18), we infer that everything that was written had no errors, a concept known as "inerrancy." Those who affirm this concept usually say that any error or inconsistency that occurs in the Bible can be attributed to human authors who made errors at some point, perhaps because they lacked a complete understanding of a situation, or when the documents were copied and then distributed by others (the Bible we use today is based on copies, not the original documents).

Some church groups say that people who have a true faith must believe the Bible we read today is totally accurate, including its accounts related to history, science, and a man's role in the church and family.[14] This has been the church's traditional position. Nearly 400 years ago, Galileo was arrested and ordered to deny his belief that the sun, not the earth, was the center of the universe. Many churches say women have limited roles and that wives must submit to their husbands. Many Christians now question this way of viewing scripture.

Being inspired, authoritative, and true doesn't mean every part of the Bible has equal importance. In some cases, what was written had temporary historical value (e.g., census figures, genealogies, detailed description of the dimensions of buildings and other structures). Moreover, the names of some people and places are not important to most people today. Although the scriptures were inspired, there are many parts that are not inspiring, and the writing is often difficult to understand.

Reading and understanding such a long book is a daunting task, especially because it's not organized chronologically and omits details a modern reader needs to know to understand what was written. People are often unfocused while studying the Bible and often rely on certain sections more than others. This is like studying individual trees in parts of a forest without understanding the contours of the forest itself. For the modern reader who has limited time, the initial challenge is to understand the main ideas. Once these are understood, much of the rest of the Bible's content makes sense and can be seen in its proper perspective as it provides additional details or supporting evidence as well as more explanations or duplications of the various ideas and themes. Appendix A provides a brief chronology of the events and

---

[14] Chapters 8, 18, and 19 discuss these issues.

characters in the Bible, Appendix B briefly summarizes each book, and Appendix C provides a "nutshell" version of the Bible. These appendixes provide the "big picture" so the Bible can be more easily understood.

CHAPTER 6

THE NATURE OF GOD

During ancient times, people believed there were many gods, which were impersonal, aloof, and unknowable. The God of the Bible is the opposite — personal, near, and knowable. The one God of the Bible has three different "beings" who are collectively known as the Trinity: God the Father, God the Son (Jesus), and God the Holy Spirit .

Unseen spiritual entities also exist, including angels who are agents of God and demons that use their powers in evil ways. For example, Exodus describes how Pharoah's magicians used their powers in their confrontations with Moses. Demons know who Jesus is and Satan, the most powerful angel and the prince of darkness, wants to be powerful like God. However, God is above these spiritual forces and used power to serve, protect, help, and punish others. Satan is controlled by God's power and will be defeated forever in a final battle described in mysterious language in Revelation (see chapter 16).

This chapter describes the names and attributes of God and details about the three forms of God.

THE NAMES OF GOD

The Hebrew term *God* (*Elohim* in Hebrew) is a plural noun for a powerful being that has multiple dimensions. The Hebrew name God gave Moses was YHWH (pronounced Yahweh, Hebrew doesn't have vowels), but eventually it was not spoken because it was considered too holy to say — the term *Jehovah* was used instead. The term *Lord* (*Adonai* in Hebrew) is another word for God that is often used in the Bible. Thus, the words Elohim, Jehovah, and Adonai are all used when referring to God.

The terms used for God were typically masculine (*he, his, him*) or *Father*. However, God is not a masculine deity and has no gender. Both males and females were made in God's image. The Holy Spirit is commonly referred to as a gender-neutral "Spirit." The scriptures sometimes assign no gender to God — the God who appeared to Moses in the burning bush in Exodus 3 had no gender and Elijah experienced God as a gentle whisper.

The term *Father* has been used because God was the father of Jesus and the original creator, similar to how the founder of a country is sometimes referred to as a "founding father" and because in most societies, the father is the main provider. Jesus taught the disciples to address their prayer to the Father.

Even though the Bible was written in a patriarchal society, it contains verses and words that refers to God in feminine terms or with attributes of femininity. In many languages, nouns have a feminine or masculine gender, but English doesn't have gendered nouns. The word for God's Spirit in Hebrew is the feminine noun *ruach*, and the Greek term for "wisdom" or the Spirit is *sophia*, a feminine word. Several verses in the Old Testament refer to God in feminine ways (Deut 32:18; Num 11:12; Isa 42:14, 49:15, 66:13; Hos 11:3–4, 13:8). In Exodus 33, Moses talked to God and used a term similar to *shekinah*, considered to be a feminine form of God's divine presence. In the New Testament, God is described as a hen that gathers her chicks under her wings (Matt 23:37, Luke 13:34) and as a mother looking for a lost coin (Luke 15:8–10).

It's not wrong to refer to God with male pronouns, but it can limit our understanding of God and have negative social and theological consequences if we refer to God with only male pronouns. It exalts males at the expense of others, and it can limit our theological imagination — using many pronouns for God emphasizes that God is a mystery beyond our human labels.

Given that God has multiple forms and is neither male nor female, perhaps "they" is the best term when referring to God. But since there are many words for God, there is no one correct word, so individual believers should use what they want to use and should not be judged for doing so. Ultimately, using many titles, pronouns, and images when referring to God recognizes the multidimensional nature of God. All of them are applicable in some way, and God is far more than all of them.

The Bible refers to God and Jesus using many other names. For many centuries, people were identified by their family, so people knew

Jesus as the son of Joseph and Mary. In the Old Testament, the coming Messiah referred to Jesus with many names, and during and after his ministry, people referred to Jesus using other names. Here are many of the names used to refer to God, Jesus, and the Messiah.

Advocate	Jehovah Jireh (Provider)	Righteousness
Almighty One	Judge	Risen Lord
Alpha and Omega	King of Kings	Rock
Ancient of Days	Lamb of God, Lamb	Root of David
Banner	Light of the World	Savior
Branch	Lion of Judah	Shepherd
Bread of Life	Master	Son of Man, the Son
Bridegroom	Messiah/Christ	Teacher, Rabbi
Comforter	Mighty God	The Door
El Shaddai *	Most High	The Life
Everlasting Father	Overcomer	The Truth
God, Lord	Prince of Peace, Prince	The Way
Good Shepherd	Master	The Word
Great High Priest	Redeemer	True Vine
Head of the Church	Refuge	Wonderful Counselor
Healer	Resurrection and the Life	

*God Almighty

KEY ATTRIBUTES OF GOD

God is all powerful (*omnipotent*) and controls everything in the universe. There are more than 50 verses in the Bible that mention God's universal power, including creating the entire universe (for example, Gen 1:1–26; Psa 33:6, 135:6; Isa 44:24; Job 42:1–2; Jer 32:27; Matt 19:26; Luke 1:37).

God is totally good and loving (*omnibenevolent*). In Psalm 86:15, the Lord is described as "a compassionate and gracious God, slow to anger, abounding in love and faithfulness." This means God cannot do certain things — being holy and perfectly good, God cannot do anything evil. God cannot perform any immoral act — destroying evil is a loving act.

God is always present everywhere (*omnipresent*). This means God was, is, and will be "with us" in every situation; God has not left us alone and is never absent. The biblical name for Jesus is *Immanuel*, "God with us" (Isa 7:14, Matt 1:23). God is eternal, with no beginning and no end. Jesus said, "I am the Alpha and the Omega, the first and the last, the beginning and the end" (Rev 22:13).

God knows everything (*omniscient*), including the past and future. God is aware of all things; John wrote, "God knows everything" (1Joh :30). King David wrote about God's omniscience and omnipresence in Psalm 139. Here are a few verses from the poem.

> Lord, You have searched me and known me.
> You know when I sit down and when I get up;
> You understand my thoughts from far away. (vs 1–2)
> Where can I go from Your Spirit?
> Or where can I flee from Your presence?
> If I ascend to heaven, You are there;
> If I make my bed in the deepest depths,
> Behold, You are there. (vs 7–8)
> You created my innermost parts;
> You wove me in my mother's womb.
> I am awesomely and wonderfully made. (vs 13–14)

These characteristics of God never change and remain the same forever (*immutable*). Verses in both the Old and New Testament confirm this fact (Num 23:19; Isa 40:8; Mal 3:6; Psa 102:27, 110:4; Jam 1:17; Heb 13:8). However, God's methods can be unpredict-able, flexible, and can change depending on the situation. People come to understand God after seeing miracles or by using logic. God's creativity and complexity are revealed in how divine acts unfold in our lives and how God communicates with us.

God appears to be influenced when hearing people's sincere requests ("prayers"), when circumstances change, or out of the goodness of God's character. The Old Testament has many verses about God deciding not to bring planned calamity (Exod 32:14; 2Sam 24:16; Jona 3:4–4:2; Amos 7:1–6; Jer 26:3,13, 42:10). In some cases, God's promise to bring destruction was "conditional" and was not carried out because people repented. In the New Testament, James 5:16 and 1 John 5:14 talk about prayers being a way to have God intervene in human affairs. Jesus changed his mind several times when he was asked for help (Matt 15:21–28, John 2:1–11), and he told the parable of the persistent widow who was given justice (Luke 18:1–7). Jesus told his disciples they needed much faith and prayer when dealing with evil spirits (Matt 17:15–20, Mark 9:17–29).

God's character has many positive dimensions, including being creative, loving, faithful, trustworthy, compassionate, kind, merciful, good, moral, pure, holy, patient, forgiving, just, and wise. God wants us to be loyal and is jealous when we stray away intentionally. God is concerned for us when we are lost and seeks to bring us back into the flock of believers. God protects us from evil and guides us on the right path when we are in danger. God is in complete control, so we have nothing to worry about and nothing to fear, for "perfect love casts out fear" (Josh 1:9, 1Joh 4:18). The phrase "don't be afraid" (or its equivalent) appears more than 100 times in the Old Testament and more than 40 times in the New Testament.

THE TRINITY

This section looks at the three "persons" of the Trinity: God the Father, God the Son (Jesus), and God the Holy Spirit. Being one, the three have the same characteristics, but they have different functions. While the term "Trinity" doesn't appear in the Bible, the concept of God having three dimensions was discussed and debated for several centuries. The idea of the Trinity eventually became an accepted Christian doctrine by the end of the 4th century. Several stories include the simultaneous appearance of all three persons of God, such as during the baptism of Jesus by John the Baptist.

God the Father

As noted above, God the Father has different names, including Jehovah, Elohim, and Adonai. Sometimes the simple term "God" is used when referring to God the Father. It was the Father who appeared to Moses in the burning bush, and Isaiah refers to God as the Father (Isa 63:16–17, 64:8–9), which implies a connection between God and the Israelites — God is the Father of the Israelites, who are the children of God. Jesus used the Aramaic word "Abba" meaning "Father" (Mark 14:36) and Paul used it as well (Rom 8:15, Gal 4:6). Jesus prayed to the Father on several occasions, including when he was facing arrest and later when he was on the cross. The Lord's Prayer starts with "our Father."

God the Father was literally the father of Jesus. This was a miracle because Mary was a virgin, so Jesus refers to the invisible God as his Father. The Father is also a perfect example for all good earthly fathers, who should always listen, live correctly, be just and fair, and most importantly, show the many attributes of love, for God is love (1Joh 4:8).

The term "father" only occurred twice in the Old Testament (Isa 63, 64), but the term is implied when Israelites were described as the children or sons of God. So the Jews were surprised when Jesus talked about God as his father. He first mentioned this when he was 12 years old and was left behind by his parents in Jerusalem during the Passover Feast. When they found him in the Temple debating the religious leaders, he said, "Didn't you know I had to be in my Father's house?" But they didn't understand what this meant (Luke 2:49–50). He later defended healing a sick man on the Sabbath, saying it was proper for him to do it: "My Father is always working, and I am working" (John 5:17). The religious leaders then wanted to kill him because he broke the Sabbath and called God his Father, which made himself equal with God.

God the Son — Jesus, the Messiah (Christ)

The Old Testament scriptures predicted a coming Messiah who would be born from a young virgin and be God with us (Isa 7:14, Matt 1:20–23). He would save the Israelites by making a new covenant, removing their sins, and being a king forever (Jer 31:31–34, Isa 9:1–7). The events and teachings in the New Testament confirmed that Jesus was a human form of God and the Messiah (*Christ* in Greek). He fulfilled all the prophecies of the Messiah, including being preceded by a prophet (John the Baptist) and his death and resurrection.

Although Jesus was born as a child in Bethlehem, he already existed before the beginning of creation. John begins his gospel with the following statement about Jesus:

> In the beginning was the Word, and the Word was with God, and the Word was God. Jesus was with God in the beginning, and through him everything was made; without him, nothing was made. The Word became flesh and lived among us. (John 1:1–3,14)

When Jesus argued with the Pharisees, he referred to himself as being God and said God was his father.

> Everything was given to me by my Father. Nobody knows the Father except the Son and those the Son chooses. If you know me, you know God. If you know me, you will know the truth, and it will set you free. "Before Abraham was born, I am!"
> (John 8:18,19,32,42,58)

After hearing these words, the Pharisees were so angry that they looked for stones to kill him, but Jesus slipped away to safety. Jesus also told his disciples that he was a form of God, and those who know him know God: "If you know me, you will know the Father" (John 14:7, Matt 11:27).

Paul wrote to those in the early church about who Jesus was. In Colossians 1:10–22, he describes the role of Jesus in a nutshell and the implications for those who follow him.

> Jesus is the visible image of the invisible God, the firstborn of all creation: he created everything, both in the heavens and on earth, visible and invisible, and all earthly powers — everything was created through and for him. He existed before anything existed, and he holds everything together. He is also the head of the church. He is the beginning and will be first in everything. It was the Father's desire that all of God's characteristics be shown in him and that he would reconcile all things to himself, whether things on earth or in heaven, having made peace through the blood of the cross. Even though you were alienated, had a hostile attitude, and did evil things in the past, Jesus has reconciled you to God through his death in order to present you to God holy, blameless, and beyond reproach.
>
> Walk in a way that pleases the Lord in every way, bearing fruit in every good work and increasing your knowledge of God, strengthened with all of God's power, showing your perseverance and patience, and giving thanks with joy to the Father who has included us in the inheritance of the saints. God rescued us from the powers of darkness and transferred us to the kingdom of Jesus, who redeemed us and has forgiven our sins.

In Philippians 2:6–11, Paul describes what Jesus did and what happened as a result.

Although Jesus was God, he didn't consider being equal to God as something he should use to his advantage. Instead, he came to earth as a human and became a humble servant. He obeyed his Father to the point of being humiliated and killed on a cross! As a result, God exalted him to the highest possible place in heaven and gave him the highest possible name. It's in the name of Jesus that every knee will bow in heaven, on earth, and under the earth, and every tongue will acknowledge that Jesus Christ is the Lord of all, to the glory of God the Father.

There are many instances when we are told to pray to the father "in the name of Jesus." Since there is one God, praying to the Father is the same as praying to Jesus and the Spirit. There is no one way to pray, nor is there a communication "chain of command." Mentioning the name of Jesus is a way to recognize the authority of Jesus. While mentioning the name of Jesus has become a tradition, invoking the name of Jesus is especially important when dealing with evil spirits, which are especially fearful of the name of Jesus and must obey him.

Holy Spirit

The third being in the Trinity is the "holy spirit" (sometimes called the "holy ghost" or *paraclete*, meaning helper, advocate, intercessor, and comforter[15]). The word "paraclete" is used several times in the New Testament. Jesus said, "I will ask the Father, and he will give you another *helper*, to be with you forever; the helper is the Spirit of truth... you know the Spirit because it remains with you and will be in you" (John 14:16–17). John later writes, "I write these things so you will not sin. But if anyone sins, we have an *advocate* with the Father, Jesus Christ the righteous one" (1Joh 2:1). Paul writes in Romans 8:26–27, "The Spirit helps us in our weakness. We don't know what we should pray for, but the Spirit intercedes for us because we may not have the words to express our deepest emotions. God knows our heart and the mind of the Spirit, and the Spirit intercedes for God's people according to God's will." Some versions of the Bible translate paraclete as *comforter.*

As one dimension of God, the Spirit has always existed and has all the same attributes of God. However, an outpouring of the Spirit

---

[15] The Greek word *paraklētos* means "someone called to come alongside someone else."

occurred 50 days after Jesus died. He had gone to heaven and those following Jesus waited in Jerusalem for the time when they would receive God's spirit that Jesus promised to send them. As they waited in a large house, a sound like a violent wind filled the house and something resembling tongues of fire touched each one of them. They were all filled with the Spirit and began speaking other languages. They went into Jerusalem where Jews from Asia, Africa, and Europe had gathered for the festival of Shavuot. The men started speaking about Jesus in the other languages, and the Jews were amazed to hear Galileans speaking their language. (Those who didn't know the other languages made fun of the disciples who spoke as if they were drunk.) This arrival of the Spirit on the 50th day is known as Pentecost.

The ability to speak another language without being trained is one of the "gifts" of the Spirit. All Christians are given one or more special gifts from the Spirt, and Paul explains these different gifts and roles in his letters to believers in several churches (see Rom 12, 1Cor 12–14, Eph 4).[16] The gifts and roles are meant to build, equip, and strengthen the church — they are like the many parts of a body that must work together. Some are more obvious than others, but all are important in some way. We don't earn the gifts given by God, although they can be developed, and the gifts often exhibit themselves in our daily lives and vocations as well as within the church.

The lists of spiritual gifts found in scripture overlap while having some variations. This suggests that none of the lists are intended to be comprehensive. Instead, they show the diversity of ways God equips Christians to serve the body of Christ, which means others are possible (e.g., intelligence, memory, business sense, linguistic, oratory, literary, analytical, logic, rhetoric, music, visual arts, athletic, strength). Here are the gifts in Paul's lists.

- *Prophecy*: declaring a message from God with confidence, often to build up, encourage, and console others, but also to confront evil or predict a future event.
- *Wisdom*: having insight to make good decisions based on the situation.

---

[16] Peter also mentions a few gifts (1Pet 4:10–11).

- *Knowledge*: having a comprehensive understanding of an issue or situation.
- *Faith*: having strong trust in God and an ability to inspire others to trust God in any situation.
- *Teaching*: able to help others understand a topic or issue using different methods.
- *Leadership*: providing vision, overseeing, shepherding, training, feeding, coaching, and motivating people in the church.
- *Administration*: able to keep things organized, effective, and efficient.
- *Healing*: able to use God's power to cure a person who is ill, wounded, or suffering.
- *Miracles*: able to display signs and miracles that show God's power and truth.
- *Discerning Spirits*: able to recognize if something is from God or is righteous.
- *Tongues*: able to communicate in an unfamiliar foreign language; also the Spirit's language for individual use.
- *Interpreting Tongues*: able to interpret the speech and writings of a different language for others to understand.
- *Service/Mercy/Helps*: having an unusual desire and capacity to serve and help others.
- *Giving/Contributing*: releasing material resources in generous ways to further the work of the church.
- *Exhortation*: motivating others to action and purpose.
- *Encouragement*: identifying with and coming alongside others to provide comfort and emotional support.

Those who have the Spirit and follow Jesus are gradually transformed into people who are more like Christ. They develop the "fruits" of the Spirit as they grow in "spiritual" maturity. Paul lists these fruits as strong evidence that God's spirit is alive in a person: "The fruit of the Spirit is love, joy, peace, patience, kindness, goodness, faithfulness, gentleness, and self-control" (Gal 5:22–23). He gave a similar list to guide Titus when appointing leaders for the local churches and included being hospitable and disciplined.

The Spirit guides our life and conscience. Following the Spirit is essential to living a Christian life. Paul writes in Romans 8:5–6, "Those living with a sinful mindset desire earthly things, but those living with a holy mindset focus on what the Spirit desires. Focusing our mind on earthly things leads to death, but a Spirit-led mind gives life and peace."

WHY JESUS CAME TO EARTH

God first made a promise to Abraham and the Israelites to bless them so they could be a blessing to others. They were to show the world what a relationship with God and a just society looked like. But the Israelites were often unfaithful to God, disobeying the commands they received, and not providing love and justice to others. They were to make sacrifices to show their sorrow and remorse for their sins. But due to their continued disobedience, God removed the blessings that were given to the Israelites. Only a remnant stayed faithful and hopeful as they waited for the day when a king (Messiah) would come and save them.

So God came to earth in human form (Jesus, the "incarnation") for three main reasons. First, he came because people need concrete examples and constant reminders of a model human being. As the visible form of an invisible God, he was a living demonstration of God's character and he modeled how God's people should live on earth. He had the right values and told us what we should do and believe. He left behind indelible memories and permanent changes among those he encountered, which motivated them to tell others about him.

Second, Jesus came to clarify aspects of the initial covenant and to teach about the good news of God's love for the human race. Some of the rules that were initially given provided a framework for worship and justice (e.g., an eye for an eye), but individuals are to live differently (e.g., love your enemies). When he taught, he would sometimes say, "you have heard it said…, but I say to you…." Life was not to be lived according to rigid rules, but according to the rule of love. When the Pharisees scolded the disciples for picking grain on the Sabbath, which was forbidden, Jesus said, "The Sabbath was made for mankind; we weren't made for the Sabbath" (Mark 2:27). He also taught that God's kingdom had come. He provided insights and guidance about God's unconditional love, blessings, forgiveness, how we should live in the world, and our purpose for living. He brought light into darkness, saves the lost, and gives us an abundant life (John 12:46, Luke 19:10, John 10:10).

Lastly, Jesus came to be the final sacrifice for all people and erase the natural consequences of sin, being separated from God. His death became the last and perfect sacrifice that saves *all* people from their sins, not just the Jews, and allows all people to come to God blameless and clean. His death and resurrection conquered sin, death, and Satan, and the Gentiles are welcomed (adopted) into God's family. Therefore, we no longer need to make sacrifices to show our sorrow for our sins or worry about our salvation. Jesus paid the price for our sin and reconciled us to God. There is nothing we must do, other than follow Jesus, to be saved from permanent death. We don't earn our way to heaven. Being spiritually free enables Christians to live without fear and like Christ. Believers are God's representatives (ambassadors) of God's kingdom to those who live in earthly kingdoms.

Having Jesus come to earth wasn't God's "plan B" after the initial effort to have the Israelites be a model society on earth didn't work. Rather, God had to show everybody that it's impossible for people to have a close relationship with an invisible supreme being by following rules, making sacrifices, and having a high priest intervene on their behalf. It was always God's plan to send Jesus to earth to model service, sacrificial love, generosity, and forgiveness, and to demonstrate that God accepts all people. The old covenant foreshadowed the new covenant and then became obsolete (Heb 8). Through the unleashed Spirit, everybody can have a close interactive relationship with a living God and be saved from damnation. This is certainly good news! When we are loved and forgiven just as we are, we gain emotional and spiritual freedom that enables us to love and serve others in the same way Jesus did when he was on earth. He fulfilled the prophesies about the Messiah made in the Old Testament, and his profound teachings and example has endured centuries after his 3-year ministry among the Israelites and a few Gentiles who lived in the region.

* * * * * * *

A complex God uses many different strategies and tactics to exhibit power and authority and to meet the overall goals of showing the world how we are to live. The intrinsic nature of God's character and qualities doesn't change, but God can influence people in unpredictable ways. Many characters in the Bible speak for God, and some of them acted and spoke in unusual and bizarre ways. Different types of miracles occur, punishment comes in different forms, and God still influences individuals and society in unexpected ways. The next chapter looks at the different ways God communicates with people.

CHAPTER 7

COMMUNICATING WITH GOD

One of the unique things about the human species is that we have the ability to understand and interact with God. We were made in God's image, and part of that "image" includes having meaningful relationships with other thinking and feeling creatures. It might be said that God would be lonely if the universe had no humans in it — being made in God's image, we are the only ones who can relate to God.

Relationships require different forms of communication. This chapter describes various ways God and people communicate with each other and some of the dynamics of this process.

How God Communicates With Humans

God communicates with humans in many ways. Although the events discussed in the Bible took place centuries ago, there is ample evidence that God still communicates with people in all kinds of ways.

1. The awesome beauty of the universe and its predictable cycles and "laws of nature" have inspired humans to see the planet and the universe as an orderly and beautiful creation that is not randomly designed. This way of communicating by God is called "natural revelation."

2. As noted in the previous chapter, God communicates using a "Spirit" who influences the human mind and emotions and provides direction to humans about their choices. When humans take time to listen and seek direction, the Spirit can communicate through insights and an inaudible "voice" in the mind. This process is called "prayer."

3. Sometimes God communicates with people directly through dreams, visions, and messages from angels or "holy strangers."

4. Humans can be inspired by the Spirit to speak the words of God to others in extraordinary and convincing ways. This is accomplished through "prophecy."

5. On rare occasions, God disrupts the normal laws of nature to intervene directly in human activities, sometimes causing rare natural events to occur at strategic times. These events are called "miracles" and are described in more detail in the next chapter.
6. Some people speak for God and provide godly advice and may rebuke others by using their "spiritual gifts."
7. The Bible itself is available to study so we can learn about God's ways long after the events occurred.
8. Finally, God took on a human form in the person of Jesus who lived on earth. Jesus gives us the most concrete example of how we are to live and love one another.

Of all the ways God communicates with people, what is written in the Bible is the ultimate authority. What is revealed through all the other methods must be measured and interpreted in light of what the Bible teaches. When there is a conflict in a message, what the Bible says takes priority. This is why it's so important to study the Bible and understand what it teaches. It's also why controversies involve different interpretations about what the Bible says and means.

PRAYER

Prayer is an invisible interaction with God that is initiated by a person. The Greek term "*proseuche*" is the most common term that is translated as "prayer" in the Bible and appears more than 125 times in the New Testament. The terms for "pray" or "prayer" occur more than 300 times in the Bible (and many more times in some translations). In the Old Testament, a prayer was sometimes made in the form of a vow to God. For example, Hannah told God that if she had a son, she would dedicate him to the Lord (1Sam 1:8–11). When she gave birth to a son, she named him Samuel (meaning "God has heard").

Jesus taught about how to speak to God. Those who pray shouldn't use flowery language to impress those who are watching and listening, and they shouldn't say prayers by saying the same things over and over again. Instead, people should pray in private and be honest, telling God about their deepest thoughts and feelings. Although God knows what we need, even before we ask for it (Matt 6:5–8, Rom 8:27), praying shows God both our willingness to engage in a relationship and our dependence on God.

Jesus provided a sample prayer that contained certain basic elements (the "Lord's Prayer" is found in Matthew 6:9–13 and Luke 11:2–4). These elements included (1) a recognition that God is holy, (2) a desire for the kingdom of God to influence this world so it becomes more like heaven, (3) a desire to have God's will be done on earth, (4) asking for the basic necessities we need to survive, (5) asking for forgiveness for our sins and for help to forgive others, and (6) seeking protection and deliverance from evil forces in the world. Thus, prayers can focus on *praise*, *thanksgiving*, and *requests*.

Jesus said God loves it when people pray and wants everybody to depend on God to have their needs met.

> Everyone who asks will receive, those who seek will find, and those who knock will have the door opened. Which of you, if your children ask for bread, will give them a stone? Or if they ask for a fish, will you give them a snake? If those who are evil know how to give good gifts to their children, how much more will your God in heaven give good gifts to those who ask! (Matt 7:7–11, also Luke 11:9–13)

Jesus didn't have a specific time or place when he prayed; it seemed to be happening all the time. His awareness of God was constant and continual, and listening to God through silence was part of the process. He often retreated to quiet and private places to eliminate distractions and be alone when interacting with God.

Scripture tells us to pray at any time and that God hears our prayers. We should pray when we are sad, afraid, facing temptation, and in need of something, including guidance or protection. We pray when seeking forgiveness from our sins, and Paul says to "pray continually" (1Th 5:17); the psalmists say to pray in the morning, noon, and night (Psa 5:3, 55:57).

What and Who We Should Pray For

In addition to what Jesus taught in his example prayer, scripture singles out specific people and topics we should pray for. We are to pray for:
- Christians (Jam 5:16; Rom 1:9; Eph 1:18, 6:18; 2Th 1:11–12);
- Physical and spiritual healing (Psa 6:2, 34:18; Jam 5:13–16; 3Joh 1:2);

- Those in spiritual leadership positions (Eph 6:19–20, Col 4:3);
- Political leaders (1Tim 2:1–3);
- More people to preach the gospel (Matt 9:36–38);
- Our enemies and those persecuting us (Matt 5:44; Acts 7:59–60);
- Everybody (1Tim 2:1); and
- Ourselves, especially that we persevere and don't give in to evil and temptations (Gen 24:12; Matt 14:30; Luke 21:35–36, 23:42; Matt 26:41; John 17:15; Phil 4:6).

Although many people pray for others to become Christians, there is no scriptural basis for this. This doesn't mean we shouldn't do it — we are told to pray for whatever we want, and Paul tells Timothy to pray for everybody. However, these are general instructions, and there is nothing specific about praying for a person's conversion. The closest a verse comes to this idea is when Jesus says to pray for more people to spread the good news (Matt 9:36–38). Paul mentions this in Romans 10:14–15: "How will people believe in (Jesus) if they have not heard? And how will they hear without a preacher?"

What We Should Know About Prayer

The scriptures offer some conflicting views about prayer. Jesus said we can ask for anything and we will get it (Mark 11:24; Matt 7:7, 18:19). But elsewhere, he and others added new statements about prayer. The use of general language and hyperbole explains the differences among some of the verses.

Here are some general principles about prayer.

- God hears our prayers when they are made honestly in the right spirit. God says that when we humble ourselves and pray, seeking God and turning from our wicked ways, God hears us and forgives us (2Chr 7:14). Other verses make the same point (Jer 29:12; Job 22:27; Prov 15:8,29; Psa 145:18; Matt 6:5–6; Luke 18:9–14; Jam 4:3)
- We should always be ready to pray. Paul told the Christians in Thessalonica that they should "always rejoice and never stop praying, giving thanks in every situation" (1Th 5:16–18). Paul told the Philippians, "Don't worry about anything. In every situation,

present your requests to God in your prayers with thanksgiving" (Phil 4:6).

- We should pray with confidence. We are to approach God confidently because "if we ask anything according to his will, God hears us (1Joh 5:14). James says we should ask in faith without wavering (Jam 1:6).

- We should pray that God's will is done on earth and in our lives, which is a key concept in the Lord's Prayer. Jesus prayed this way in the Garden of Gethsemane when he wanted to avoid being killed, but it was God's will that he become the ultimate sacrifice for the world.

- We don't automatically get what we pray for. God isn't a "genie in a bottle" who grants us our every wish. Our prayers may not align with God's will, and we should assume that if we don't get what we pray for, our prayer may be answered later (and sometimes much later, so patience is needed). Our prayers may also be answered in ways we don't expect or with a "no" (for some reason, God doesn't want to give us what we asked for). When our requests are not granted, we may later understand why when we examine our past and see how God guided our steps in a different direction.

- In some cases, we need to pray with persistence and not give up when our prayers aren't answered (Luke 11:5–13, 18:1–7; Matt 15:21–28). Jesus tells a parable of an evil judge who gives a widow justice because of her persistence, saying God will do the same for us (Luke 18:1–8). Some people in the Bible waited many years before having their prayers answered. Many barren women prayed for years to have a child before their prayers were answered. God told Simeon that he wouldn't die until he saw the Messiah. He was very old when he saw Jesus at the Temple soon after Jesus was born. He held Jesus in his arms and said, "Lord, you can take me now in peace" (Luke 2:29).

Paul's life provides examples of some of these prayer principles. He had a "thorn in the side" and persistently prayed to have the problem taken away, but God didn't remove it. We don't know the nature of his affliction, but whatever it was, Paul came to understand that God didn't remove it in order to keep him humble — he was good enough just as he was, and God's power was shown in his weakness.

ANGELS, AGENTS OF GOD

Another way God communicates with people is through angels, spiritual beings created by God before the physical world existed. The term "angel" comes from the Greek word *aggelos*, meaning "messenger" or "envoy," and is used more than 400 times in the Bible. The number of angels that exist is unknown but appears to be so vast that they are uncountable.

Only three angels are given names in the Bible. Satan (also called the devil, Lucifer, and Beelzebul) is the leading angel that rebelled and was expelled from heaven. Many other angels chose to follow the devil and were expelled as well — they are called "demons." Satan is still active and can deceive people because he can be disguised as an "angel of light" (2Cor 11:14). The two other named angels are good. Gabriel tells Zechariah that his elderly wife, Elizabeth, will have a baby (Luke 1:19) and is also mentioned in Daniel 8 and 9. Michael, the highest-ranked angel (archangel), closed the mouths of lions to save Daniel and will lead God's army in the final battle against evil (Dan 11:13; Rev 12:7; he's also mentioned in Jude 1:9).

Angels serve God in several ways. They give messages to God's people, praise and worship God, provide protection for God's people, and carry out God's judgment. The unnamed "angel of the Lord" serves as God's messenger and appears many times in both the Old and New Testaments. Angels also took care of Jesus after his last temptation in the wilderness.

Angels can appear in different forms. They can be invisible, like the angel that stopped Balaam's donkey (Num 22:22–35). They can be visible in the air, like the angels that sang to the shepherds when Jesus was born. They can appear on earth, sometimes in human form. Hebrews 13:2 says, "Don't neglect to show hospitality to strangers, for some have unknowingly entertained angels." Two angels warned Lot about the coming destruction of Sodom, and they looked like handsome men. Some angels have a fantastic appearance. For example, the angel that rolled back the stone in front of the tomb of Jesus sat on the stone and its "appearance was like lightning and its clothes were white like snow" (Matt 28:3). Angels are distinctly different from God's spirit, which is also invisible.

Angels provided protection for various people in the Bible, sometimes in amazing ways. An angel guided the Israelites as they traveled through the wilderness after leaving Egypt. Daniel said an angel closed the mouths of lions when he was thrown into the den after he defied a royal decree. The psalmist wrote about these "guardian angels" in Psalm 91:9–12.

> If you dwell in the Most High, the Lord who is my refuge,
> Then no harm or disaster will come to you.
> For God will command his angels to guard you in all your ways.

Angels often caused fear in those who saw them. They sometimes arrive suddenly, startling those who see them, so they often start by saying, "Don't be afraid."

People still experience angels or the protection of angels. I and members of my family can describe times when unusual strangers or invisible forces helped us or protected us from danger. On three occasions, I should have died or been severely injured in a car crash, but I and all those with me survived without a scratch. My father once drove a bus full of teenagers going to a Christian camp off a narrow mountain road to avoid oncoming traffic. The bus went down a steep slope and its wheels crossed over a large ditch, yet it remained upright. The tow-truck driver couldn't believe the bus didn't roll over many times — it had defied the laws of physics. Those serving on the mission field tell unusual stories about how angels protect them from evil forces as they spread the gospel in inhospitable areas where evil spirits are strong. God protects us, so we shouldn't be afraid.[17] The action of angels is a type of "miracle," which is discussed in the next chapter.

---

[17] Those working in areas where the gospel has not been introduced may encounter spirits that are benevolent ("white magic") and spirits that are selfish and have evil motives ("black magic"). Pharaoh's magicians who opposed Moses displayed "magical" powers, and several accounts in the New Testament refer to magicians. Many accounts in the New Testament refer to demons and those who have a demon, and demons knew that Jesus was the Messiah. The use of magical powers was condemned by God because the power didn't come from God. When Christians who communicate the gospel in a new culture encounter magicians, they may work with those practicing white magic and let them see

CHAPTER 8

SCIENCE, TRUTH, AND MIRACLES

God has communicated with humans through the natural world that was designed with incredible detail and consistent laws of nature. God gave humans superior brains compared to all the other living organisms so we can understand and appreciate the creation. God also interacts with the world through various types of miracles.

Some people don't believe in miracles because they believe everything can be explained in some natural and scientific way. They say that either the miracle never happened, it had a scientific explanation, or it was just a coincidence. Some who believe in the merits of science also believe that only what can be objectively measured using scientific methods is true. These people tend to be either agnostics or atheists. This chapter looks closer at both science and miracles and this point of view.

SCIENCE AND TRUTH

Science is a general field of study of different parts of the world. Its goal is to understand the truth about our universe and our interactions with nature and each other in order improve the quality of life on earth. Science has three general areas.

- The *natural* sciences focus on the physical world (e.g., physics, chemistry, life sciences, earth sciences) and are sometimes called the "hard" sciences because they assume there are a number of fixed or "hard" rules operating in the universe.
- The *social* sciences study human behavior and interactions (e.g., anthropology, education, history, politics, psychology, sociology) and are sometimes called the "soft" sciences because their general principles are not fixed — they vary based on the context. As a

---

that the source of their power comes from God. This aids in the evangelism process and builds on what the local culture already knows about God.

result, the "soft" sciences are much harder to study than the "hard" sciences. Statistical analysis and probability are often part of the study of social sciences.

- The *formal* sciences involve systems to create and explore knowledge (e.g., mathematics, statistics, computer science, information technology).

Each of these three general fields has multiple subfields which sometimes overlap. For example, meteorology (the study of weather) is one of the earth sciences among the natural sciences, and paleontology combines biology and geology.

The Scientific Process

The term "science" is also used to define a process of learning and discovery in order to understand the truth about a topic. The process often involves making educated guesses (hypotheses) based on theories about a specific issue, then making systematic observations and accurate measurements related to the issue; this can include experiments or statistical models that control important variables. Analyses of the results lead to further steps to study the issue in a more informed way, and the process continues.

Although the term "scientist" was first used in the early 1800s, many people consider Aristotle to be the first scientist. Living in Greece in the third century BC, he pioneered techniques of observation and inquiry that are still used today. Galileo, the Italian astronomer and physicist, was the first to use the scientific process. Building on the ideas of Copernicus, he questioned conventional wisdom and used scientific methods in the early 1600s to discover the earth was not the center of the universe. He was arrested by the Inquisition in 1633 and ordered to deny his beliefs, but his methods of study revolutionized Europe and sowed the seeds for the Enlightenment in the 18th century. (In 1992, Pope John Paul II said the church had wronged Galileo.)

The scientific process and the tools and techniques associated with it are now used in many fields of research. The goal of research is to collect evidence that leads us to a better understanding of a specific topic, which can lead to making more accurate predictions, better decisions, and better products for the world to use.

Historically, the church has been suspicious of science and its methods because they sometimes appear to undermine religious faith. For example, the Scopes "monkey trial" in 1925 pitted science and the teaching of evolution against literal interpretations of creation described in the Bible. A Tennessee state law prohibited the teaching of evolution, and the trial was broadcasted nationally by radio. A highly critical journalist ridiculed Biblical teachings during the trial, which caused some Christians to oppose science and the press because they were seen as anti-Christian forces. A "fortress" or "circle the wagons" mentality developed among some Christian groups who felt the faith was being attacked, and they thought true believers needed to be protected from sinful and unorthodox influences in the world. These groups viewed science, the press, and intellectuals as secular forces that opposed the faith.[18]

In actuality, science is simply a way to seek and find knowledge — it's politically neutral. The knowledge gained by science has been used for evil and selfish purposes, but it has also increased our understanding of the world and improved our standard of living, which have brought about change. But change can be hard, and compelling evidence is often not enough to change our behavior. Moreover, biased studies and research that support a particular point of view are dangerous despite their disguise as authoritative truth. This is why the work of science and the methods used should always be transparent so others can check and replicate the findings in order to verify the truthfulness of the claims.

---

[18] Two years after the trail, Bertrand Russell, a British philosopher, wrote an essay, *Why I Am Not a Christian* (1927, reprinted by Touchstone in 1967) that further distanced religion from science. He wrote, "Fear is the basis of (religion) — fear of the mysterious, fear of defeat, fear of death. Fear is the parent of cruelty, so it's no wonder cruelty and religion have gone hand-in-hand. We can now begin to understand and master things with the help of science, which has forced its way against the Christian religion. Science can help us to get over this craven fear in which mankind has lived for so many generations. Science can teach us to no longer look for imaginary supports, to not invent allies in the sky, but rather to look to our own efforts to make this world a fit place to live in" (edited for brevity).

The Pursuit of Truth

Science tries to discover truth. The field of study that deals with knowledge is called *epistemology*: how to discern truth and what it means to "know" something. Having knowledge means we understand something, its relative importance, and how it can be used (or abused) in daily life. Our beliefs are developed through the influence of family, friends, social circles, media, political leaders, and our experiences with each of these.

Knowing the truth leads to emotional, psychological, and spiritual freedom. Jesus spoke these words to those who followed him: "If you continue in my word, then you are truly my disciples; you will know the truth, and the truth will set you free" (John 8:31–32). He was telling them that knowing him sets us free from sin, fear, condemnation, and worry, which gives us confidence and the freedom to do good in the world.

Lies and half-truths are the enemy of the truth, and evil forces use many types of deceptions to distort the truth. Those who lie take advantage of people's trust, gullibility, simplistic thinking, fears, beliefs in common myths, and trust in those who think like them. They tell us to use our intuition (not our brain) to reach conclusions about what is true and that truth is what is inside us. But our emotions are easily manipulated, our intuitions reflect deep prejudices, and we like to blame others for our problems. Jesus called the devil the father of lies and the evil one (John 8:44, Matt 13:19). Satan tempted a vulnerable Jesus in the wilderness by quoting the scriptures out of context, but Jesus knew the truth and countered the temptations with better quotes of his own. False and misleading information erodes trust and contributes to divisions within society. It also makes it harder to have conversations with friends, family, and neighbors when people don't share the same facts.

Constant exposure to the same perspective has a lasting impact on our ability to interpret events and messages. Being isolated from other points of view makes it easy for those with evil and biased motives to influence us by using disinformation (lies with no factual basis) and misinformation (knowingly or unknowingly telling lies or partial truths that distort or ignore the truth, such as using facts or statistics to make a point but leaving out details that would lead to a different conclusion).

Falsehoods and lies that are repeated many times become "truth" to the speaker/author and their listeners/readers because of the psychological influence repetitive messages have on our mind. Repetition deepens the neural pathways in our brain, just as walking the same dirt path over and over makes it wider and harder. Deep neural pathways are difficult to change and eliminate. This process of repetition has been termed "brainwashing" and is used worldwide in overt and subtle ways. When lies become our truth, we unwittingly spread falsehoods to others with sincerity.

It takes a tremendous amount of time, effort, and self-reflection to leave a path that has become deeply entrenched in our mind. Being constantly surrounded by incomplete, incorrect, or biased information makes it hard for us to be open to new ideas, even when they are correct. This is what had happened to the Jewish leaders who interacted with Jesus. He used the following analogy of wineskins.

> Nobody uses a piece of a new garment to patch an old one. If they do, they will have torn the new garment, and the patch from the new will not match the old one. And nobody pours new wine into old wineskins. Otherwise, the new wine will burst the skins; the wine will run out, and the wineskins will be ruined. No, new wine must be poured into new wineskins. Nobody who first drinks old wine wants the new wine: they say, "The old is better." (Luke 5:36–39)

Jesus was saying that new ideas are often incompatible with our traditional ways of thinking and acting, so we resist changing our mind and behavior. Embracing new ideas means giving up old ideas and established new habits, which can be a painful process that includes a sense of loss and failure. It's easier to be comfortable with our usual customs and practices than to entertain the validity of new ideas that challenge our habits and beliefs and may require us to change. The Jewish religious leaders were convinced they had figured out how they should live and what they should believe. However, their limited and inflexible perspectives conflicted with the teachings of Jesus, so they rejected him.

One way to identify a lie is to focus intently on what is true. The Christians in ancient Rome were surrounded by a pagan society, and Paul told them not to conform to that culture. Instead, they were to "be transformed by the renewing of their minds" (Rom 12:2). Having a strong grasp of the truth makes it easier to identify lies, false arguments, and misinformation. My father once told me that those in charge of identifying counterfeit coins mainly listened to the sound of legitimate coins bouncing on a table. That way, a fake coin stood out because it made a slightly different sound. (I'm not sure if this was actually done, but it's a good illustration. When we hear both lies and truths, it's hard to know what is true.)

Retaining our holiness in an evil world requires a consistent focus on God's word and being in the fellowship of others who speak the truth. Science has found that a changed focus helps us overcome depression, trauma, loneliness, heartbreak, and a sense of loss. Observing nature's beauty or acts of kindness and listening to music brings peace and reduces inflammation. God brings us "beauty from ashes" and blesses those who "meditate on God's words day and night" (Isa 61:3, Psa 1:1–2). Paul understood the importance of maintaining the right focus when he wrote, "Whatever is true, noble, right, pure, lovely, and admirable, anything that is excellent or praiseworthy, think about those things" (Phil 6:8).

The sciences have also shown us that understanding life and the universe is a challenge. When we first learn things as a child, the concepts are put into simple concepts and language, and what we first learn is easy to understand and remember. But as we grow older, we realize things aren't so simple. Paul says, "When I was a child, I talked like a child, thought like a child, and reasoned like a child. When I grew up, I put my childhood ways behind me" (1Cor 13:11). We should therefore resist the tendency to have simple answers to complex issues.

Instead, we should take time to understand the truth about our world. We need media literacy and should confirm "facts" from multiple sources. We need flexible minds that absorb new information and perspectives when warranted. Accurate information is crucial for making informed decisions. Jesus tells us to be "wise as serpents and pure as doves" (Matt 10:16). Jesus used this simile to convey the need for believers to make good use of their mind while being harmless, to be wide-eyed critical thinkers who discern the truth while retaining our innocence. (Jesus wasn't referring to the evil serpent in the Garden of Eden.) When we pursue knowledge, we shouldn't be afraid of what we find because, as St. Augustine and many others have said, "all truth is God's truth."

To learn the truth, we need to avoid biased information that (1) masquerades as news but has undisclosed sources, (2) mixes facts with opinions, (3) doesn't rely on objective facts, (4) intentionally excludes important facts, and (5) focuses on stories designed to incite strong emotions (e.g., fear and anger). Transparency and critical thinking are helpful remedies to combat lies.

Today's scientists acknowledge there are still many things about the world we don't know, and we don't know enough about all of nature's laws to say any event violates them. Our "laws of nature" are simple summaries of what we know now and are subject to change. New discoveries occur that make us rethink our theories, and the more we know, the more we realize we still have much to learn. As our circle of knowledge grows, so does our circle of awe and awareness of our own ignorance and the complexity of life. Cosmologists base their theories of the universe on the existence of "dark matter" (a gravitational anomaly), but more than 100 years after Fritz Zwicky, a Swiss astronomer, discovered this anomaly in 1933, we still don't know what it is. Nevertheless, we know it exists because we can see and predict its influence and use its mathematical properties to study the universe.

Humility is the natural response to understanding how little we know. Pride, arrogance, hubris, conceit, and cockiness are characteristics of those who lack insight into their own ignorance (or they are trying to mask it). Atheists hold a position that implicitly believes they have all knowledge, which means they know what exists and what does not exist. Such a position is intellectually untenable — no human knows everything, but their assertion that God doesn't exist provides them comfort while being blind to their ignorance — they don't know what they don't know.

Science and Religion

Some see science and religion as opposite ends of a "truth" spectrum and contradicting each other, but this is based on a misunderstanding of both. Some Christians believe everything in the Bible is to be taken literally, which would make it at odds with what we have learned by studying the world. But they are mistaken — as noted in chapters 4 and 5, the Bible is full of different types of literary devices, and the context of what was written must be taken into account. Not everything is to be taken literally — something can be true without being factual. Some stories in the Bible were told to make a point rather than report actual facts or events; the stories and lessons weren't written to describe scientific truths.

Instead, science and religion complement and inform each other. Science reveals the majesty of God's creation that has natural laws throughout the universe. Everywhere we look, the laws of physics are the same. Albert Einstein wrote, "The most incomprehensible thing about the world is that it is comprehensible." In other words, the fact that such a vast universe is comprehensible is a miracle. The natural world is exceedingly complex, but it's also somewhat predictable, so it can be studied, understood, and changed. The world makes sense and reflects a knowable God. In addition, the earth appears to have been uniquely created over time specifically so humans can thrive, which makes it different from anything else in the universe (this is known as the "anthropic principle"). Our advanced technologies that explore the universe have not yet found any evidence of any other form of life outside the earth, let alone "intelligent" life.

Our investigation of the universe and its properties reveals it is billions of years old, and through natural processes, it has taken almost all that time for conditions on earth to be ready for productive human activity. The idea that the world would only be a few thousand years old but was made to look billions of years old would mean God created the universe as a giant hoax. Time is part of God's creation, and God uses time to create change.[19] Genesis 1 says God created the world over time, which was to "bring forth" life using natural processes.

But we still don't know how life started on earth, how it led to complex organisms, and when and how humans, made in the image of God, came into being. A belief in a divine creation doesn't rule out

---

[19] On earth, a "day" is 24 hours because that's how long it takes for our planet to rotate one time. But other planets take more time, so the term "day" is relative. We should not insist on interpreting the word "day" as a literal 24-hour period — this would define time in the entire universe in terms of our own ideas of hours and days. The days of creation are commonly interpreted as meaning a long period of time.

the validity of ideas and theories about how life changed on earth over time. Pierre Teilhard de Chardin, a paleontologist and Jesuit priest, noted that evolution is a process in which simple things become more complex. It's humbling to realize a powerful God made an amazing universe that is constantly changing.

Finally, in an age where our scientific knowledge helps us create all types of inventions and technologies, religion should raise moral and ethical questions about their use. This applies to different types of weapons used in war and medical questions related to the beginning, middle, and end of life (e.g., cloning, genetic engineering, fertility, organ and tissue donations and transplants, life support, and assisted suicide). Since technology can be used for both good and evil purposes, decisions about if and when certain procedures should be conducted require collaboration with theologians and scientists sitting at the same table. We should have neither uncritical devotion to our past beliefs nor uncritical enthusiasm for new ideas and ways. Our pursuit of knowledge and progress must be guided by a moral compass in order to avoid creating destructive forces.

MIRACLES

A miracle is a rare event, usually initiated by a supernatural power, which has a specific purpose and doesn't reflect the normal laws of nature in the physical universe. Most miracles are initiated by God, although angels and humans can be used to carry out some form of divine intervention. Sometimes the terms "signs" and "wonders" are used to describe miracles. Evil powers can also perform certain types of miracles.

While atheists and agnostics may not believe that miracles can occur and that a supernatural world doesn't exist, our personal experiences that defy explanation provide evidence that something else is going on in the world besides what we can see or measure. Many scientists and medical personnel know the "laws of science" sometimes don't occur in the usual ways. In sum, we know miracles can occur because they *do* occur.

Many miracles are mentioned in the Bible. In some cases, a miracle has a natural explanation but occurred at a rare or strategic time. Other miracles defy nature's laws or simply demonstrate unusual intervention by God in the life of people. Answers to prayers are not usually thought of as miracles because they happen all the time, but these interventions by God in our lives could be considered miracles because they cannot be explained with scientific reasoning. This part of the chapter discusses the types of miracles that occurred in the Bible and some general principles and concludes with examples to provide evidence that miracles still occur today.

Miracles Show God's Power

The first natural miracle in the Bible occurred when God appeared to Moses in a burning bush (Exodus 3). Moses then used a wooden staff in various ways and a "changing hand" that could turn to leprosy to show God's power to Pharaoh and his magicians (Exodus 4 and 7). Moses used the staff to change water into blood and brought plagues on the Egyptians to force Pharaoh to release the Israelites from slavery. God's power was then shown when all the first-born children and cattle died, except for those of the Israelites who put blood outside their door; God's wrath passed over these homes.

God's power was shown many times after the Israelites left Egypt. Moses used the staff to separate part of the Red Sea so the Israelites could escape the Egyptian army, and to get water out of rock. God provided two unusual forms of food (manna and "meat" from dying birds) to sustain the people while they traveled in the wilderness. Pillars of smoke and fire led the way. An earthquake swallowed up defiant Israelites, and the Jordan River stopped flowing to let the Israelites enter Canaan. In some cases, the same natural event has occurred at other times, but the miracle was in the timing — the sea has parted and the river has stopped on very rare occasions, but these events also occurred just when the Israelites needed them to happen. The Israelites knew they were signs that God was protecting them and in control of their future.

Other unusual natural events took place in the Old Testament at strategic times. For example, when an unusual thunderstorm flooded the Kishon River, the forces of Deborah and Barak slaughtered the soldiers of the vastly superior army of Hazor (Judges 4). Elijah started a drought during the reign of King Ahab, and it ended after he called down lightning to burn his sacrifice in his confrontation with the prophets of Baal (1Ki 17–18). Elisha, Elijah's successor, performed many miracles, some of which involved natural events. For example, when the Syrian army surrounded the city of Samara and its people were so hungry that they started killing their children for food, Elisha heard about this and told the people they would have real food the next day. That night, God caused thunder to sound like a charging army, which scared away the Syrian army. The next day, four homeless people with leprosy walked into the enemy camp and only found the food and animals the Syrian army had left behind (2Ki 6–7). When a large gang of cocky young men made fun of Elisha because he was holy and bald, he cursed them in the name of the Lord and two bears then ran in from the forest and mauled 42 of them (2Ki 2:23–24).

The first miracle Jesus performed was using his power to turn approximately 180 gallons of water into high-quality wine. He was reluctant to use his power and authority in this way at the wedding in Cana, but he agreed to help the groom's family when the party was running out of wine (John 2). The Sea of Galilee was the scene of two miracles that showed God's power: Jesus both walked on the water and calmed the waves during a storm (Matt 8,14; Mark 4,6; Luke 8; John 6).

Jesus also expelled evil spirits from people who acted in violent ways — the spirits knew who he was and that he had superior powers to theirs. Jesus also used his power to raise several people from the dead. One woman was healed simply by touching his clothes as he walked past her. Jesus stopped everybody and asked who touched him because he felt power leave him (Mark 5:25–34). Jesus knew where the fish were swimming when he gave advice to fishermen, and he somehow was able to produce an abundance of food after speaking to large crowds. John ends his book by saying Jesus did so many amazing things that the world wouldn't have room for all the books that could be written about them.

Miracles of Physical Healing

God cared about people's health and bodies, and God's power to heal was demonstrated several times in the Bible. In the Old Testament, both

Elijah and Elisha raised boys from the dead, and Elisha had Naaman, a Syrian military leader, wash in the Jordan River to heal his leprosy (2Ki 5). A dead man even came back to life when touching Elisha's dead body in his tomb (2Ki 13:21). An unnamed prophet healed the withered hand of the evil King Jeroboam, who became the king of Israel after Solomon died (1Ki 13). After Isaiah told a very sick King Hezekiah that he was going to die, God told Isaiah to return and tell the king that God heard the king's earnest prayer to stay alive and would heal him. The king lived another 15 years (2Ki 20:1–6).

Jesus miraculously healed many people, a practice he started soon after starting his public ministry: Matthew 4:23–24 says Jesus began teaching in the synagogues, proclaiming the good news about the kingdom, and healing every kind of disease and sickness among the people in Galilee. News about this reached Syria, and people from all over the region with many different types of ailments, afflictions, and disabilities were brought to him, and he healed them. He had great compassion for those who were ostracized or in pain.

As his ministry unfolded, Jesus healed those who were paralyzed or crippled, those who were blind or deaf or couldn't speak, and those with leprosy or epilepsy. He quickly healed the ear of the servant who tried to arrest him in the Garden of Gethsemane (Peter cut it off in an initial skirmish). Sometimes Jesus healed people on the Sabbath to make a point that helping others was more important than keeping strict rules about the Sabbath — the Pharisees followed strict rules to prove their holiness to God, but their legalism blinded them to the more important point of God's command to love others.

Finally, God intervened in miraculous ways to allow women to have children at unusual times during their lives. Being childless at that time was considered worse than being dead — the physical limitation was accompanied by social embarrassment, emotional shame, and depression. The list of women who were barren for many years who eventually had a son includes Sarai (Isaac), Rebekah (Esau, Jacob), Rachel (Joseph, Benjamin), the unnamed wife of Manoah (Samson), Hannah (Samuel), and Elizabeth (John). The conception of Jesus in Mary was clearly a miracle.

Miracles Among the Apostles

The book of Acts records a number of miracles. Jesus had told his disciples that they would do "greater things" (more in number) than he had done when they were done in his name (John 14:12–14). Acts 2:43 and 5:12 both say the apostles performed many miracles, and Acts records some of them. For example, Peter healed the disabled man who begged at the Temple entrance: God's power and the man's faith healed him, and Peter was jailed because of it (Acts 3–4). In Acts 5, a married couple died on the spot after Peter caught them lying. The sick and those with evil spirits were placed on the street so Peter's shadow would fall on them and they could be healed. After Peter was arrested again, God opened the jail doors to let him escape. Acts 9 records that Peter healed Aeneas and raised Dorcas from the dead, and God freed him from a Roman prison (Acts 12). The apostles Stephen and Philip also performed miracles (Act 6,8).

Paul performed miracles after his miraculous conversion on his trip to Damascus and after his blindness was healed through Ananias. Paul's many miracles are documented in Acts 12–28, and on several occasions, he miraculously escaped from jail like Peter had done earlier. Paul first used logical reasoning to convince the Jews in the synagogues that Jesus was the Messiah and to present the gospel in the major cities of Asia Minor and Greece, but his demonstrations of God's power to others provided confirming evidence that his words about God and Jesus were true.

People Given Special Powers

Some individuals were given unusual abilities to further God's purposes. Joseph was given the ability to interpret dreams, and while Samson was a seriously flawed individual, God gave him great strength that freed the Israelites from domination by the Philistines for 20 years. Samuel was a unique prophet that God used to reform the nation of Israel and select its first king. Elisha knew in advance what strategies the Syrian army had, and Daniel was given the ability to know and interpret dreams and understand strange messages. Some prophets, especially Isaiah, were given insight into the signs of the coming Messiah and events related to the end of the world.

In addition, many of the gifts of the spirit manifest themselves in miraculous ways. In fact, there are gifts of miracles and healing, and one could say that speaking in tongues is a miracle, for it's not possible for a person to speak another language without first learning it.

PRINCIPLES OF MIRACLES

We can conclude certain things from the miracles that occurred during Biblical times and throughout history. There are many examples of how people were healed because of their faith or how rare natural events occurred at strategic times. Jesus didn't perform many miracles in his hometown of Nazareth because the people had little faith. However, having faith is not a requirement for a miracle to occur. Moreover, having faith does *not* mean a miracle *will* occur. Like prayer, sometimes our desires and wishes are not answered when or how we want them to be — God is not a "genie" who grants our every wish.

Faith is Not Always Needed

Some miracles occur because God is good and wants people to be safe and healthy. This means it's not necessary for people to believe something miraculous will happen for a miracle to occur. For example, Jesus raised people from the dead because he had compassion on the families, not because they had faith that a miracle would happen. Those who had demons were saved even though they didn't have faith, and the fishermen doubted Jesus knew where fish would be caught. Jesus healed 10 lepers but only one was thankful.

Another example of a healing without faith occurred when the disciples saw a man who was blind from birth and asked Jesus if the blindness as a result of his parents' sins. Jesus said the man's parents hadn't done anything wrong. Rather, the man was blind so God's power could be shown. Jesus made mud from his spit, put it in the man's eyes, and told him to wash in the Pool of Siloam. The man did so and received his sight. It happened on the Sabbath, so there was a big investigation about who the man was and how he was healed. The man didn't know how it happened, and there is no evidence that the man thought he would be healed. After repeated questioning, he told the Pharisees, "All I know is that I was blind and now I can see" (John 9:25). Later, he met Jesus and believed in him.

Faith May Not Lead to a Miracle

Some people believe that a miracle will occur if we have enough faith. Jesus said on several occasions that if a person had enough belief, a supernatural miracle could occur. People use these verses to say that if a person wants a miracle to happen but it doesn't, the person doesn't have enough faith. However, these verses were a form of hyperbole to make a point and were not meant to be taken literally (Matt 17:20, 19:26; Mark 9:23). Do we really think a person's faith could move a mountain from one place to another?

While having a strong belief (faith) that a person will be healed may result in a healing, it sometimes doesn't happen. The best example in the Bible to support the view that faith isn't enough for a miracle to occur is Paul's prayer that his "thorn in the side" be removed. He prayed for this three times, but the "thorn" didn't go away. Paul never disclosed any facts about his affliction, but he said God's power was made perfect in weakness. Paul was good enough just as he was, and his limitations kept him humble — when he was weak, he was strong, and he was not afraid of hardships (2Cor 12:7–10).

The Apostles didn't think they should pray to heal everybody who was sick. Paul didn't pray to heal Timothy's illnesses; he simply advised him to add wine to his diet (1Tim 5:23). Also, a miracle may happen gradually and become obvious much later rather than instantly. The healing of our emotions and spirits may take time to become evident. We shouldn't expect God to automatically answer our prayers for a miracle, for God works in mysterious ways and does not owe us anything.

Miracles Happen to Unusual Characters

God causes miracles to occur in unusual ways and among unusual people. Some of the strangest healings took place among foreigners, which shows God's universal love of all people, even though they didn't appear to deserve it. When Jesus first preached in Nazareth, he impressed his friends in the synagogue but then mentioned two foreigners who were helped by God, a widow in Phoenicia who aided Elijah during a long famine and who miraculously had an endless supply of food, and Naaman, a Syrian military leader, who was healed of leprosy by Elisha. This infuriated the crowd and they wanted to kill him (Luke 4). In Numbers 22, we learn that a donkey was given the ability to see an angel and then speak to its rider, Balaam, when he was on his way to meet an evil Moabite king.

Several miracles among foreigners and outcasts are mentioned in the New Testament. A persistent Greek woman living in Phoenicia got Jesus to heal her daughter who had an evil spirit (Matt 15). Jesus changed his normal routine and took a boat to the region of the Gerasenes, east of the Sea of Galilee, to cast out demons living in two men. The men lived in caves, cut themselves, and terrorized the region. (The gospels give slightly different versions of the story: Matt 8:28–34, Mark 5:1–20, Luke 8:26–39.) The interaction between Jesus and the Samaritan woman at the well is a miracle of a changed spirit. She was changed when she met a respectful man who broke the social norms and told her he was the Messiah. The miracle of her transformation resulted in many Samaritans becoming followers of Jesus.

A Multidimensional Miracle: Peter and Cornelius

The long story in Acts 10 about Peter and Cornelius, the Roman centurion who lived in Caesarea, contains several miracles. An angel told Cornelius to have soldiers find and bring to him a man known as Peter, who was staying in Joppa (40 miles away) in the home of a man named Simon. While the soldiers were on their way, Peter was hungry and went into a trance and saw forbidden food coming down from heaven. This happened three times, and each time, Peter was told to eat it, but he said he wouldn't eat it because it was all unclean. But a voice in the trance told him, "Don't call anything impure that God says is clean" (Acts 10:15).

Just as Peter came out of his trance, the soldiers showed up at Simon's home and found Peter. After a 2-day journey, they all returned to Cornelius' home. Peter asked why he was asked to come, and Cornelius said an angel told him to find Peter and listen to him. Although righteous Jews weren't allowed to interact with Gentiles,

Peter realized that the messages in his trance were instructions for him to welcome Gentiles into the faith. The Gentiles heard Peter's message and were filled with the Holy Spirit.

This series of events demonstrated the inclusive nature of the gospel and laid the foundation for evangelism worldwide. Our creative God unites people from multiple locations in unusual ways to work together to further the kingdom — this has become a common pattern for miracles to unfold throughout history.

MIRACLES STILL OCCUR

Many people still experience miracles, and some have written books about their experiences. For example, in *Proof of Heaven: A Neurosurgeon's Journey into the Afterlife* (Simon & Schuster, 2012), Eben Alexander, an atheist doctor, documents his experience while being in a coma (he's no longer an atheist). *Bruchko* (first published as *For This Cross I'll Kill You*, Creation House, 1973) is a personal account by Bruce Olson that describes his experience after he moved into the Amazon forest when he was 19 years old. He describes various miracles that took place during his ministry with a stone-age tribe.

I and members of my family have also experienced God's direct intervention. My father, "Bud" Bylsma, experienced a number of them during his 65+ years of working in various Christian ministries around the world. Here is a summary of one miracle that I know happened, as described in his autobiography. (Details about this and other miracles in his life can be found in his life story, *Living HIStory: Doing God's Will On Earth*.)

> In November 1978, I was driving on a two-lane highway from Bend, Oregon to Eugene on a very cold but clear day. As I passed a truck at 70 mph, I found myself going sideways, sliding on "black ice." I spun off the road and hit a big tree sideways. I had an out-of-body experience as I twirled upward and thought, "I'm going to beat you home, Patti" (his wife). Then I don't remember anything else.
>
> The truck driver called the ambulance and I was found on the ground in the bushes. If the car had hit the tree at my door (one foot away), I would have been killed instantly. I had 15 broken bones, mostly in my back but also my hip and several ribs. The med-evac helicopter ride

to Portland was very painful, and I was in traction in the hospital for 10 days. After being discharged, I was in pain every time I took a step.

We attended a church in Portland and during communion six months later, the pastor invited people in the congregation to come forward if they wanted prayer. I walked slowly forward. When asked, what I wanted prayer for, I said, "I can't take a step or bend over without pain." The pastor put some oil on my wrist and prayed quietly while the congregation sang songs. I don't remember what he said, and when he said Amen, I limped back to my seat.

When I was home later that day, I dropped something and bent over to get it. When I stood back up, I realized I had bent over without any pain. I bent over several more times to see if I would be in pain, and all my pain was gone. I just started laughing, and the pain never returned.

There is no explanation for this healing other than God's love and compassion. Nothing happened between the prayer and the healing — no medication was taken, nothing special was eaten, and he didn't expect to be healed! He just did what God tells us to do. During a scientific investigation, all conditions are held constant while one variable is introduced to determine its effects. God's power is the only thing that changed to account for my father's healing, and he lived 43 more years without pain.

* * * * * * *

There is an overwhelming amount of documentary, physical, testimonial, circumstantial, and anecdotal evidence that miracles have occurred and that God exists and is still active in the world. I have spent decades as an analyst, researcher, and data scientist studying different topics, and I know that discovering truth doesn't depend on the certainty found in a narrow type of scientific inquiry. Many have experienced things that have no logical explanation and defied scientific principles. We don't need hard, scientific proof of God's existence in order to believe and obey — some things that count can't be counted. Miracles are like the stars — we see them all around us when looking under the right conditions. However, there is a vast gap between them, and we may never see them if our vision is impaired or don't have eyes that see.

PART TWO

MAIN THEMES

CHAPTER 9

LOVE, THE BIBLE'S MAIN THEME

The Bible is essentially a long and complex love story. The word *love* has many meanings and we use it in many ways. The Greeks had three words for love: *eros* (physical, passionate love), *philia* (friendship or reciprocal love), and *agape* (sacrificial love for others without expecting anything in return). The love described in the Bible takes on many forms, but its most common use is within the context of a relationship that serves and sacrifices for others.

The Bible makes this clear: *Love is the most important quality in the world.* Paul defined love using the term *agape* and stressed the importance of being a loving person when he compared it to spiritual gifts and the attributes of generosity, faith, and hope in his letter to the Corinthians.

> If I speak in other tongues but don't have love, I'm just making noise. If I have the gift of prophecy and can understand all mysteries and knowledge, or if I have so much faith that I can move a mountain, but I don't have love, I am nothing. If I give everything I have to the poor and sacrifice my body but don't love others, I gain nothing. (1Cor 13:1–3)

> Love is patient and kind. It doesn't envy or boast or dishonor others. It's not proud or self-seeking. It's not easily angered, and it keeps no record of wrongs. Love doesn't delight in evil but rejoices with the truth. It bears and believes all things; it's always hopeful and it endures all things. Love never fails. When I was a child, I talked and thought like a child. Now that I've matured, I've put away my childish and selfish ways. Prophecies, tongues, and knowledge will all pass away. All that remains are faith, hope, and love, and the greatest of these is love. (1Cor 13:4–11,13)

GOD IS LOVE AND LOVES THE WORLD

Love is one of God's enduring qualities (omnibenevolent), as noted in chapter 6. The mighty God first created an amazing universe, then our planet with all its physical and living attributes. Finally, God made the most important creation, humans, who were given some characteristics of God: creative, having a moral dimension that enables people to distinguish between right and wrong, capable of having meaningful relationships with others, and able to love others in sacrificial ways.

These qualities give people unique insights into the nature of God, and we are unique compared to animals and the pagan gods who were feared and didn't have a loving relationship with humans. "There is no fear in love. Perfect love drives out fear because fear is associated with punishment" (1Joh 4:18).

The apostle John, the disciple who was the closest to Jesus, wrote extensively about God's love.

> God loved the world so much that he sent the Son into the world so that whoever believes in him will not die but will live forever. The Son existed before the creation of the world, and God didn't send him into the world to condemn the world. He has come to this world to save it. (John 3:16–17)

> Friends, let us love one another, for love comes from God. Everyone who loves has been born of God and knows God. Those who do not love do not know God, because God is love. This is how God showed his love for us: He sent his Son into the world so we would live through him. This is love: not that we loved God, but that God loved us and sent his Son as a saving sacrifice for our sins. (1Joh 4:7–10)

Two Main Commands: Love God and Others

The scriptures say we are to love God and our neighbor. When asked about what is required to earn eternal life, Jesus mentioned some of the 10 commandments and added, "You shall love your neighbor as yourself" (Matt 19:19, Luke 10:25–27). When religious leaders asked Jesus which commandment was the most important, he said "Love the Lord your God with all your heart, with all your soul, with all your mind, and with all your strength. This is the first and greatest commandment. And the second is like it: 'You shall love your neighbor as yourself.' All the Law and the Prophets hang on these two commandments" (Mark 12:30–31, Matt 22:37–40) .

Love God

The first three commandments related to loving and respecting God (Exod 20:2–7), which are summarized here.

> I am to be your only God. Do not make an idol or anything looking like a god, and do not worship or serve them. Do not use or say my name carelessly — treat it with great respect. I will punish those misusing my name.

God is jealous of people's allegiance and doesn't want us to focus our attention and love on anything that controls or preoccupies us. Loving others who love us is a natural reaction — we appreciate expressions of love shown to us by others. 1 John 4:19 says, "We love because God first loved us." Not loving those who love us is a sign of rejection to those who first love us.

Hosea took a prostitute as his wife so he would understand how God feels when dealing with an unfaithful partner. Israel was like a prostitute who had not been faithful and had fallen in love with other gods. As a result, God "divorced" them because they committed adultery. God desires recognition as well as mercy for others, not sacrifices and burnt offerings. "Israel must return to God and maintain love and justice" (Hos 12:6).

One way we show God our love is through our worship, which involves giving God our highest praise and honor for what was (and will be) done for us and for God's character. Worship also includes sharing our sorrow when we disobey God's commands. (In the Old Testament, worship included sacrifices to show repentance. That tradition continues through the voluntary giving of tithes.) The Lord's prayer starts by recognizing God's holiness and acknowledges our sinfulness, for which we need forgiveness. Jesus said our worship is in vain if we go through the rituals and say the right words but don't have humble hearts and don't repent sincerely (Isa 29:13, Matt 15:7–9, Luke 18:9-14). Because God loved us and shows us mercy, Paul tells us to offer our bodies as living sacrifices, which is a form of worship (Rom 12:1). Worship can occur with others in a structured way or individually, wherever we may be. Many of the Psalms are written forms of worship, and Christians have said and sung them for centuries as part of corporate worship.

Love Your Neighbor

The command "love your neighbor as yourself" appears for the first time in Leviticus 19:18. More than 1,300 years later, the Jewish religious leaders who interacted with Jesus quoted this verse as one of the two greatest commands (loving God was the greatest command). Paul quoted this Leviticus verse when he said "love is the fulfillment of the law" (Rom 13:8–10), and he told the Galatians that the entire law is summed up in one command: "Love your neighbor as yourself" (Gal 5:14). Jesus and James said the same thing (Matt 7:12, Jam 2:8).

Jesus also provided insights into who our neighbors are. The clearest explanation is found in his story of the Good Samaritan. A religious expert asked him what must be done for a person to inherit eternal life. Jesus responded that people should do what was written in the Law. The expert quoted the Law: "Love the Lord your God with all your heart and with all your soul and with all your strength and with all your mind" and "Love your neighbor as yourself."

After Jesus agreed, the expert wanted to look wise and asked Jesus, "Who is my neighbor?" Jesus replied with this story.

> As a man walked down the dangerous road from Jerusalem to Jericho, robbers attacked him. They stripped him of his clothes, then beat him and went away, leaving him half dead. A priest was traveling on the road and passed on the other side when he saw the man. A Levite also saw the man and passed him on the other side of the road. But a Samaritan came along and saw the half-dead man and took pity on him. He mended his wounds with oil and wine. Then he put the man on his own donkey, brought him to the nearest inn, and took care of him. The next day he gave two days' wages to the innkeeper and said, "Look after him, and when I return, I will reimburse you for any extra expenses you may have for taking care of him." (Luke 10:25–34)

Jesus asked the expert which man was a neighbor to the man who was attacked. The expert replied, "The man who showed him mercy." Jesus told the expert, "Go and show mercy to those who need it"

(Luke 10:35–37). Jesus was saying that when we encounter people in need, we should help them in extravagant ways.

Love Other Christians

Jesus added a new idea to the "love your neighbor" theme when he singled out the need to love those who followed him. In fact, he said that loving other believers is the mark of a Christian. When Jesus gathered with his 12 disciples for the last time before his arrest, he washed their feet and then gave them this command: "A new command I give you: Love one another. As I have loved you, so you must love one another. Everybody will know you are my disciples if you love one another" (John 13:34–35). Later, John said much more on this topic.

> This is how we know who the children of God are and who the children of the devil are: Anyone who doesn't do what is right is not God's child, nor is anyone who doesn't love their brother and sister. For this is what you heard from the beginning: We should love one another. Anyone who hates a brother or sister is a murderer, and you know murderers don't have eternal life living in them. This is how we know what love is: Jesus Christ laid down his life for us. And we ought to lay down our lives for our brothers and sisters. If anyone has material possessions and sees a brother or sister in need but has no pity on them, how can God's love be in them? Dear children, don't love with words or speech but with actions and truth. And this is God's command: to believe in the name of his Son, Jesus Christ, and to love one another as he commanded us. Friends, since God loved us, we should love one another. If we love one another, God lives in us and his love is completed in us. (1Joh 3:10–11,15–18,23; 4:11–12)

> This is how love completes us so we will have confidence on the judgment day. Whoever claims to love God but hates a brother or sister is a liar. For those who don't love their brother and sister, who they have seen, cannot love God, whom they have not seen. Jesus gave us this command: Anyone who loves God must also love their brother and sister. (1Joh 4:17–21)

Paul also wrote about the importance of loving others, and especially Christians: "Don't become weary in doing good, for we will eventually reap a harvest if we don't give up. So when you have the opportunity, do good to all people, especially to those in the family of believers" (Gal 6:9–10). He also said, "May the Lord increase your love for each other and for everyone else" (1Th 3:12).

The ultimate expression of love is being willing to die for others. Jesus said, "This is my command: Love each other as I have loved you. Nobody has greater love than those who die for their friends" (John 15:12–13). This is what Jesus did for everybody, not just for his friends. Paul says, "God's love for us is shown in that while we were sinners, Christ died for us" (Rom 5:8).

So, others will know we are Christians by our loving actions for each other, not because of what we put on our cars, the clothes and jewelry we wear, or what we say we believe. Our outward appearance and theological positions don't demonstrate love for others.

Love Your Enemies

Jesus emphasized that loving others includes loving our enemies. During his Sermon on the Mount, he said, "You have heard it said, 'Love your neighbor and hate your enemy.' But I tell you, love your enemies and pray for those who persecute you, that you may be children of your God in heaven" (Matt 5:43–45). Luke's account puts it slightly different: "To those who are listening, I say love your enemies, do good to those who hate you, bless those who curse you, pray for those who mistreat you" (Luke 6:27–28).

Previously in his sermon, Jesus talked about how to react to persecution.

> Blessed are those who are persecuted because of righteousness, for theirs is the kingdom of heaven. Blessed are you when people insult and persecute you and say all kinds of false and evil things against you because of me. Rejoice and be glad, for your reward will be great in heaven, for they persecuted the prophets who came before you. (Matt 5:10–12)

The idea of having a different mindset about our enemies was not a new concept. The Bible says God uses those with evil motives to bring about good outcomes.

- Joseph was sold as a slave by his brothers to traders traveling to Egypt, but God used it for good. For many years, his brothers thought he was dead, so they were surprised to see him as a leader in Egypt during the great famine. He told them twice that God used their evil actions for good: "You meant to harm me, but God used it for good and sent me ahead of you to save you and the lives of many" (Gen 45:4–8, 50:15–20).

- As discussed in chapter 5, Paul repeated the verse from Proverbs 25:21–22 when he wrote to the Romans: "If your enemy is hungry, feed them; if they are thirsty, give them water to drink. This will heap burning coals on their heads, and the Lord will reward you" (Rom 12:20).

- A related verse says, "When people please the Lord, they make even their enemies to be at peace with them" (Prov 16:7).

- Job defended himself from accusations of being sinful by saying he had not rejoiced at the misfortune of his enemies nor had he used a curse to end his enemy's life. (Job 31:29–30)

- Peter writes, "Don't repay evil with evil or insults with insults. Instead, repay evil with blessing, for you were called in order to obtain a blessing" (1Pet 3:9).

We are to love our enemies and not take revenge against them. Instead, we are to leave retribution to God. Proverbs 20:22 says, "Don't say, 'I will repay evil,' but wait for the Lord who will deliver you." Paul quotes Proverbs when he writes, "Don't take revenge, leave that to God's righteous anger. The scriptures say, 'I will take revenge, I will repay,' says the Lord" (Rom 12:19). Instead of seeking revenge, Paul said, "Bless those who persecute you; bless and don't curse them... Don't be evil to those who are evil. Be careful to do what is right in the eyes of everyone. If possible, as much as it depends on you, live at peace with everyone" (Rom 12:14,17–18).

IMPLICATIONS: GENEROSITY AND FORGIVENESS

Loving others means serving and sacrificing our own way for them. Since "we know God makes everything work for the good for those who love God," and "God is for us, so who can be against us," and we are not to worry because God will provide for all our needs (Rom 8:28,31; Luke 12:22–34), we are freed from worrying about our own needs and we can express lavish love for others. This includes being generous and forgiving those who have offended us.

Generosity

One theme that occurs over and over throughout the Bible is God's generosity toward people and the need for people to be generous toward others. God was very generous to the Israelites, even though they often neglected to love God in return. The early Christians were known for their unusual generosity for others — it distinguished them from others.

The gospels contain many examples of generosity, including acts performed by Jesus and some of his main teachings and parables. His first miracle was providing an overwhelming amount of high-quality wine several days into a wedding in Cana (John 2). He defended the anointing of his head and feet with expensive oil (Matt 26, Mark 14, Luke 7, John 12). He instructed people to sell one's possessions and give to the poor (Luke 11:41, 12:33, 18:18–22). He praised the widow who gave a small offering because it was all she had (Luke 21). The parable of the workers in the vineyard praised the generous landowner (Matt 20), and the parable of the wedding banquet showed how God favored those who didn't deserve to be invited to a lavish dinner (Matt 22). He said to give to those who ask, even when they cannot reciprocate (Luke 6:27–36, 14:12–14). He told his disciples, "Freely you have received, so give freely" (Matt 10:8).

Jesus was also generous with his time and power: he went out of his way to help others and used his power to heal many types of people. The concept of being generous to others is mentioned so often in the Bible that the next two chapters provide more details about the topic.

Finally, the Bible says nothing about considering how our generosity will be handled and the potential results, either immediate or long-term. This doesn't mean we should blindly help others, perhaps enabling them to be dependent on others. It just means we are to act with love and generosity and leave the results to God. An attempt to save a person who is drowning is a loving act, even if the person is not saved. I have passed many people on the street who ask for money, but there are occasions when I sense the person has a real need and have been prompted by the Spirit to support them in some way. But too often people are not generous or loving because they think their help may not benefit others in the long run. Such rationalization is not Biblical.

Forgiveness

The Old and New Testaments say God forgives those who have sinned and that we are to follow God's example and forgive others (Num 14:19–20; Isa 1:18, 43:25, 55:7; Jer 31:34; Psa 32:5, 103:12; Dan 9:9; Mic 7:18–19; Matt 6:14–15, 26:28; Mark 11:25; Luke 6:37, 17:3–4; Acts 3:19; Eph 1:7, 4:32; Col 1:13–14, 3:13; Heb 10:17; 1Joh 1:9).

Jesus provides the greatest example of forgiveness: he forgives our sins. When he publicly forgave sins, others were offended because only the perfect God could do this (Isa 53:5, Luke 5:20–21). He later forgave those who plotted to have him killed (Luke 23:34). The sacrifice of Jesus paid the debt owed by all people one last time. Our debt was forgiven, so we are to forgive the debts of others: "Forgive our debts as we forgive those who are indebted to us" (Matt 6:12; Luke 11:4).

At one point, Peter asked Jesus how often people should forgive others. The Jewish tradition was to forgive somebody three times, and Peter suggested the right number might be up to seven times, more than double what was taught in the past. But Jesus said the right number was 77 times, and then told this parable.

> The kingdom of heaven is like a king who wanted to close the debt of his servants. A man who owed him 10,000 bags of gold came to him and couldn't pay it, so the king said his entire family would be sold to repay the debt. But the servant asked for patience and promised to pay it back. The King had mercy, cancelled the debt, and let him go.
>
> But the man then went to a fellow servant who owed him a small amount of silver and started choking him, demanding to be paid. The servant begged for patience but the man refused and had the servant thrown into prison until he could pay the debt. The other servants saw this and told the King what happened.
>
> The King called the man back and said he was a wicked servant. The King said, "I canceled all your debts because you begged me to. You should have had mercy on your fellow servant." The King then had him sent to jail to be tortured until he paid all he owed. Jesus then

111

said, "This is how my Father in heaven will treat each of you unless you forgive your brother or sister." (Matt 18:21–35)

This parable of the unmerciful servant illustrates the great kindness of God and how we are to forgive others as well. There was no way the servant could ever pay the king what was owed. Jesus concluded by saying God would not forgive those who don't forgive others. By saying people should forgive others 77 times, he was really saying that people should always forgive those who ask for it.

Our acts of love for our neighbors and enemies, including our generosity and forgiveness of them, have practical benefits. They increase the likelihood of peace between ourselves and others. Loving our enemies is also an act of self-preservation. When we love others, we are like Jesus, the Prince of Peace who loved the world. Forgiveness also has positive benefits for the forgiver. Research has shown that those who forgive others, including their enemies, have fewer health and psychological problems, which are more likely to occur when we harbor resentment and dwell on past wrongs.[20]

WHEN LOVE AND THE LAW COLLIDE

Jesus broke many widely-held beliefs and traditions when he was alive. He touched unclean lepers, visited places normal Jews never went, talked to foreigners and praised them for their faith, healed on the Sabbath, didn't condemn a woman caught in adultery, and had many friends who lived scandalous lives. This raises the question about when something may be right when it's normally considered to be wrong. When are exceptions permitted or even encouraged?

We received 10 general commands, including that we must not lie or steal and we must honor the Sabbath. But Rahab was justified when she lied to the guards of Jericho to protect the Israelite spies (Josh 2,6; Heb 11; Jam 2), and the midwives were justified when they told Pharaoh the Israelite women delivered children so fast that they could not kill them at birth (Exodus 1). King Solomon seems to justify a starving person who steals food (Prov 6:30), and honoring the

---

[20] Information about the benefits of forgiveness and related issues can be found at the International Forgiveness Institute (www.internationalforgiveness.com).

Sabbath is a vague command about having everybody rest one day in the week (Exod 20:8–11). The Jewish leaders created many rules about how this commandment should be followed, and Jesus criticized them for misinterpreting its meaning.

But the right action to take doesn't always depend on the situation. Anthropologists tell us that some acts are universally condemned in all cultures, such as being cruel to children, committing rape, killing a person to obtain their possessions, and betraying those who help you. One absolute Biblical principle encompasses these ethical teachings and should always be followed: *show love to others*. This principle is explicitly and implicitly found in hundreds of places in the Bible. Everything is summarized in the command "love your neighbor," and everybody wants to be treated with love. This is what makes Christianity so attractive from a moral, ethical, and philosophical point of view.

So when a situation calls for an act of love that would violate an earthly law, we are to act in love, knowing we are breaking the law for a higher purpose. However, there may still be earthly consequences for that action. For example, a person may break several traffic laws in order to rush a person to the hospital in an emergency, but the person may also be fined for the violations; we may stand up to protest against injustice, but it may mean being taken to jail.

Our love for others must take priority in all situations and is a form of obedience to God. When the apostles were arrested and ordered not to preach by the religious leaders, they said they had to "obey God rather than human leaders" (Acts 5:29). Rahab broke the command not to lie, but she was being faithful to a higher priority command to honor God.

The one exception to always loving others is when it conflicts with our love for God. As noted early in this chapter, our first priority is to love God. Abraham was going to kill Isaac because of his faith in God, and Jesus said, "If anyone comes to me and doesn't hate their father and mother, wife and children, brothers and sisters, and even their own life, they cannot be my disciple. And those who don't carry their cross and follow me cannot be my disciple" (Luke 14:26–27). This appears to violate the 5th commandment — honor and respect your parents. Nevertheless, there needs to be balance. For example, those called to Christian ministry must not abandon those they have committed to care for — we can serve God and others at the same time. Normally, there is no conflict between loving God and loving others.

Thus, the general rule when making decisions is to love others, and how that looks depends on each unique situation. Our actions should be guided by one question: what is the most loving thing to do? The "laws" of loving God and others should always take priority because lesser commands are subordinate to them. Those who strictly follow a law rely on the safety of legalist solutions that may lack flexibility, judgment, and love. This was the view of the Pharisees that Jesus condemned. When no good option is available in this evil world, we should do the least non-loving thing, a position called "doing the lesser of two evils."

Love's Hierarchy

The above discussion leads us to conclude that there is a hierarchy in terms of determining what the right course of action should be in situations when there is no clear-cut option to act in a loving way or to obey all the commandments. In these cases, one must decide what to do to maximize love and minimize evil. Saving many innocent lives is better than saving a few, and saving a few righteous lives is better than saving many lives of the wicked. For example, Noah and his relatives survived while all the wicked in the world perished, many wicked people died in Sodom while Lot and his small family were saved, and the Israelites were told to exterminate the Canaanites. Also, breaking one of the 10 commandments is justified in the name of love. For example, the Hebrew midwives lied to Pharaoh and saved baby boys rather than kill them, and Rahab lied to the Jericho guards. Both were judged to have done the right thing.

The Bible supports another love principle: actual life is to be given priority over potential life. In nature, a tree is more valuable than a seed, and a fully developed human has greater value than an embryo. Causing the death of an embryo by miscarriage was not considered a capital crime, but causing the death of a person was (Exod 21:22).[21]

---

[21] This is one of only two sections of the Bible directly related to abortion (Numbers 5:11–31 implies that abortion is justified when a husband is jealous of his wife's adultery). Jewish religious scholars throughout history have held different views about abortion. The fetus

Moreover, one person is more important than any animal or non-living thing (money, jewels, etc.).

Finally, there is a hierarchy in terms of our works and our sins. Some acts are better than others, with corresponding rewards. In the parable of the talents, the servants acted in ways that earned them different rewards, and we will all be judged based on what we have done (2Cor 5:10, Rev 20:12). Those who teach will be judged with greater strictness (Jam 3:1). Similarly, some sins are worse than others (Matt 11:22–24, John 19:11, 1Cor 11:30, 1Tim 1:15, 1Joh 5:16). Jesus said one sin, speaking against the Holy Spirit (attributing the Spirit's work to the devil), was so bad that it would not be forgiven (Matt 12:32, Mark 3:28–30, Luke 12:10). While all sins are sin, they are not equally serious.

A Loving God and Hell

An ethical question often posed is how a loving God could create hell and send anybody there. The Bible has several passages about hell, and it's not a pleasant place to be — it's where the wicked go after death to endure eternal punishment and experience a total separation from God (Matt 8:12, 25:41; Luke 16:23,26; 2Th 1:8–9; Rev 20:15). Hell (*Hades* in Greek) is an area of darkness or an eternal fire or a lake of burning sulfur where there is "weeping and gnashing teeth." (The Hebrew term *Sheol* is a grave or "place of the dead" and isn't the same as hell.)

Hell may seem to be a hypocritical place that is inconsistent with the nature of a loving God, but it is not. Perfect and absolute love never forces somebody to do something. If people don't want to be with God, then God will not force them into a situation where they are with God. So, there must be a place for people to go where God doesn't exist. Hell is that place. C.S. Lewis said there are two kinds of people in the world: one who says to God, "thy will be done," and one to whom

---

has been considered part of the mother's body and doesn't have independent rights of its own until it takes a breath after birth. The silence of the Bible about penalties related to abortion, which was not uncommon during the time in certain situations, and the detailed instructions about other sins, raises questions about how abortion should be viewed. Therefore, the principles of love apply to situations when abortion is being considered, and no single course of action is the most loving thing to do in every situation.

God says, "thy will be done."[22] In more contemporary terms, God tells the latter, "have it your way." Having them go to heaven would force them to be someplace they don't want to be, and a loving God will not force them to do that.

The Bible contains nothing about what happens to people who haven't heard about Jesus and God, nor is anything written about what happens to those who haven't met the usual requirements mentioned to be a Christian (e.g., a profession of faith, water baptism). What we do know is that a loving God is the judge. When the criminal who was being crucified next to Jesus asked Jesus to remember him, Jesus told him he would be going to paradise. The criminal probably hadn't been baptized, but he respected Jesus and wanted to be with him after they both died. Jesus's response showed the consistency of God's grace and generosity and gives us insight about what happens to people after they die. It would be inconsistent for God to send somebody to hell without first giving them a chance to know about God.

The Bible has one story in which somebody who went to hell interacts with somebody in heaven. Jesus told the story of a rich man who selfishly lived in extravagance while Lazarus lived in poverty and pain (Luke 16:19–31). The rich man asked Abraham to warn his family about the terrors of hell, but Abraham said the family had enough evidence of what God wanted people to do while they are still alive. The rich man was also told that travel between heaven and hell wasn't possible. This story implies that once a person dies, their future is fixed. However, God is the ultimate judge about our eternal future, so we really don't know what will happen to those who have never heard about God and Jesus.

---

[22] C.S. Lewis, *The Great Divorce* (1945), Great Britain: Geoffrey Bles.

CHAPTER 10

JUSTICE, MERCY, AND GRACE

A logical extension of the Bible's theme of love is showing love to others in the forms of justice, mercy, and grace. God shows all three, and we should do so as well. This chapter looks at these three concepts.

JUSTICE

God uses people to show the world how life and relationships should look on earth. God's people are to exhibit specific qualities that distinguish them from others — they are to love and provide justice to others, especially those who are disadvantaged in some way: foreigners and the sick, poor, abandoned, despondent, and disenfranchised.

The importance of providing justice to others is one of the main themes running through the entire Bible. Justice can be defined as being fair to others, giving people what they deserve, and not giving somebody more or less than what they should get. The idea is that when we do good, we are rewarded; when we do something wrong, we are punished. Moreover, the size of the consequences should relate to what was done — major rewards and punishment for major actions, minor rewards and punishment for minor actions (an eye for an eye, nothing more, nothing less). Finally, justice is meant to be applied fairly without regard to who is being judged. The rich and poor are to be judged in the same way, based on facts and without favoritism based on who they are (Exod 23:3,6; Lev 19:15; Isa 1:17; Amos 5:12; Zech 7:9–10). God initially favored the Israelites but eventually showed a sense of equity and fairness by wanting a relationship with all people in the world, regardless of their actions, beliefs, gender, tribe, race, age, or birthplace.

The words *justice* and *righteousness* are very similar in both Hebrew and Greek (*díkaios*). Note the similarity of the terms rightness and righteousness, justice, justified, and justification. Matthew 5:6 has been translated using terms, which reflects the idea the words can mean the same thing: "Blessed are those who hunger and thirst for righteousness (justice), for they will be satisfied." When scripture says God is righteous, it also means God is just. God wants us to be righteous, which includes providing justice.

Providing justice is both a personal and collective responsibility. We are members of social groups, communities, and nations, and our collective acts can either help or hurt others. This is why God has always held families, cities, nations, and empires responsible for their collective actions. When God gave instruction to people about justice, they were told to take responsibility for one another's well-being.

Justice in the Old Testament

God administered justice many times in the Old Testament, starting in Genesis. Adam and Eve were expelled from the Garden of Eden when they sinned, and the flood killed nearly all people because of their wickedness. Sodom was destroyed because the people were wicked, and their lack of righteousness was cited as the reasons for their destruction. (Genesis 18 focuses on the people's lack of righteousness, and Genesis 19 talks about Sodom's sexual immorality.)

When Moses gave the laws for people to follow while they were in the wilderness, many of the laws related to justice. Leviticus has many rules related to justice within the community. People were commanded to "love your neighbor as yourself" and the rich and poor were both to be judged in the same way. Foreigners were to be accepted and loved just like everybody else, just as the Egyptians welcomed the Israelites during the famine. A field was not to be harvested to its edge, and the poor and foreigners were allowed to eat the food at the edge as well as anything that fell to the ground during the first harvest. During a sabbath year (the seventh year), land was not to be tilled, and the food coming from it was freely available to anybody who wanted it.

> Don't join a wicked person by being a false witness. When giving your testimony in a lawsuit, don't pervert justice and don't favor a poor person. If you meet your enemy's animal wandering away, you must return it to him. If you see a donkey belonging to your enemy lying helplessly under its load, you must help your enemy release the donkey. You must not take a bribe, for a bribe blinds the clear-sighted

and subverts justice. You must not oppress a foreigner, for you know what it's like to live in another land. Sow and harvest your land for six years, but in the seventh year, you must let it rest and lie fallow and let needy people eat from it. (Exod 23:1–5,8–10)

The Israelites were often punished by other nations during the period of the judges in part because they didn't provide justice in society. A consistent pattern emerged during these centuries. The Israelites honored God but soon got comfortable, conformed to the ways of the local culture, and gradually forgot to follow the ways of God. This led to oppression by others and the absence of God's blessings and protection. When things got very bad, the Israelites appealed to God for help, and different heroic leaders emerged to defeat the oppressors. The victories restored peace (*shalom* in Hebrew) and justice until the cycle of decline started again.

Israelite leaders were often guilty of injustice during the period of the judges and kings. Samuel was one of the few honest priests, but his two sons perverted justice when they became judges. Many prophets called attention to the injustice being done in the Northern and Southern Kingdoms.

- Amos wrote that moral corruption and complacency permeated Israel's culture, and that religious rituals are meaningless when injustice prevails.
- Hosea warned Israel that God wouldn't protect them because God desires mercy and recognition, not sacrifices and burnt offerings. "Israel must return to God, maintain love and justice, and always wait for God" (Hos 12:6).
- Isaiah emphasized the importance of justice many times. He first wrote that God condemns those in Judah and Jerusalem because they are corrupt and evil; their sacrifices and religious gatherings are meaningless because the people don't obey God. Through Isaiah, God said:

> Do you think I want all these sacrifices and offerings? I'm disgusted by the smell of your incense. When you raise your hands in prayer, I don't look at you; when you say many prayers to me, I'm not listening. Stop doing evil! There is blood on your hands and you need to wash

them, for you have not provided justice, defended the oppressed, or advocated for orphans and widows. (Isa 1:11,13,15–17)

You engage in religious rituals, fasting and praying, but you treat others with injustice. Do you expect me to listen to your prayers, be impressed, and bless you? Your rituals occur once a week. What I desire is for you to have a humble spirit and to offer encouragement and support to those with broken hearts. I'm pleased when I see my people loosening the chains of injustice, untying the cords of heavy yokes, feeding the hungry, providing shelter for the homeless, clothing the naked, and freeing the oppressed — these are signs of true religion. When I see these things happening, I will hear you and heal you, and light will rise in your darkness. But there will be no peace for the wicked. (Isa 58:3–10, 57:21)

When referring to the coming king, Isaiah said "Justice is the measuring stick, and righteousness is the plumb line" (Isa 28:17), and that the king would establish justice that extends to all nations, not just the Jews. (Jeremiah wrote something similar about Jesus.)

- Micah summarized God's demands: "provide justice, love mercy, and walk humbly with God" (Mic 6:8).
- Ezekiel said Sodom was destroyed because it didn't help the poor and needy (Eze 16:49).
- The prophets Nahum, and Habakkuk condemned nations because they didn't provide justice.
- Zechariah said the Messiah would replace wickedness with justice and peace, and told the Jews:

> Administer true justice. Show mercy and compassion to one another. Don't oppress the widow, the homeless, the foreigner, or the poor. Don't plot evil against each other. Those who came before you didn't listen, and they were scattered and became strangers in other nations. Therefore, speak the truth to each other, and make sound judgments in your courts. (Zech 7:9–14, 8:16)

Nearly all the prophets' warnings were directed to the Jews, God's people, but only a few Israelite leaders heeded these warnings. For example, when a prophet rebuked Jehoshaphat, he made reforms and installed impartial judges who emphasized justice rather than taking bribes. But most of the leaders were evil, didn't provide justice, and didn't listen to the prophets. As a result, the nation was conquered by foreign powers and the people were taken very far from Canaan. (Appendix D rates the kings who served during this time.)

Finally, Psalms and Proverbs have many references to justice and injustice.

Justice in the New Testament

The New Testament has fewer direct references to justice, although Jesus and his followers often provided justice in concrete ways to others (they showed mercy and grace more often). Jesus mainly modeled the importance of helping those who have been denied justice, who lived on the margins of society and were oppressed because of their lower social status. This includes caring for women and widows, foreigners, those who disrupted society, and those with various physical ailments (e.g., blindness, crippled, leprosy).

When Jesus started his ministry, he read from Isaiah, "The Spirit of the Lord is on me, because he has anointed me, to proclaim good news to the poor. He has sent me to proclaim freedom for the prisoners and recovery of sight for the blind, to set the oppressed free" (Luke 4:18). While his words are true in a spiritual sense, he displayed his concern for these people in concrete ways during his ministry.

Jesus later condemned the Pharisees and scribes for not providing justice and not treating people fairly, and he quoted Micah's verse to them about the need to provide justice. He inspired Zacchaeus, a despised tax collector, to repay those he cheated, and Jesus welcomed him into the Kingdom because of his change in heart that led to changes in his behavior. The parable of the sheep and goats emphasizes the importance of helping others as proof of a sincere faith.

Jesus also condemned income disparities. While his comments were not directed against all who are wealthy, he spoke against those who gained their wealth by trampling on others and who refuse to use it to help those who suffer. His story about the rich man who selfishly lived in extravagance while Lazarus lived in poverty and pain (Luke 16:19–31) taught people about proper justice — eventually the rich man went to hell while Lazarus went to paradise.

Paul's letter to the Romans notes that all people are guilty of the crime of not providing justice to others, which is part of our sinful nature. He tells those in Colossae to grant justice and fairness to their slaves, and the book of Hebrews mentions the faith of their ancestors who administered justice.

James makes many references to the Sermon on the Mount and the theme of justice. He warns against favoring the rich while mistreating the poor. He tells believers to demonstrate "works" along with their faith, specifically noting that they should care for the hungry and destitute. He ends the first chapter by talking about justice as "pure religion," visiting orphans and widows in distress.

Most people don't realize how much the New Testament stresses the importance of justice because the Greek term *dikaiosune* is usually translated as "righteousness." But the term can also be translated as "justice" or "fulfillment of the law," and justice or "rightness" may be a more accurate translation in some passages.

MERCY

People often don't understand the difference between mercy and grace because they are often mentioned together. For example, Moses was told that "the Lord, the merciful and gracious God, is slow to anger, full of love and faithfulness for thousands, and forgiving our sin, wickedness, and rebellion" (Exod 34:6–7). Psalm 86:15 says, "You, O Lord, are a God full of compassion, and gracious, patient, and abundant in mercy and truth." Psalm 145:8–9 says, "The Lord is gracious and full of compassion, slow to anger and great in mercy. The Lord is good to all and is merciful to all he has made." Psalm 112:4 says, "God is gracious, full of compassion, and righteous" (this one verse mentions grace, mercy, and justice).

However, mercy and grace are not the same. *Mercy* is defined as showing kindness and compassion for all things, especially human beings; when we receive mercy, we get kindness we don't deserve. On the other hand, *grace* is an undeserved favor, which is an extreme amount of mercy — we get *more* than we deserve. My father once told me a simple story to clarify the difference between justice, mercy, and grace. He said a guilty man appeared before a judge and is fined $1,000, which is *justice* — the man gets what he deserves. But a judge shows *mercy* when the man is pronounced guilty but the fine is cancelled — the man doesn't have to pay anything, his debt is forgiven. When the judge shows *grace*, the man is declared guilty and the judge *gives* the man $1,000.

The importance of showing mercy is mentioned many times in both the Old and New Testaments. God is merciful to us and shows mercy to those who disobey God's laws. Here are other examples related to God's mercy.

Through the Lord's mercies we are not consumed, because His compassion doesn't fail. They are new every morning; great is Your faithfulness. (Lam 3:22–23)

God doesn't stay angry forever because the Lord delights in mercy. God will have compassion on us and will address our sins. God will send all our sins to the bottom of the sea. (Mic 7:18–19)

Because of God's great love for us, our God, who is rich in mercy, made us alive with Christ, even though we were dead in our sins. (Eph 2:4–5)

When the kindness of God and our Savior's love for everybody appeared, we were saved, not because of the good deeds we have done, but according to God's mercy. (Tit 3:4–6)

I will be merciful and will not remember their sins. (Heb 8:12)

If we confess our sins to Jesus, he is faithful and just and will forgive our sins and purify us from all unrighteousness. (1Joh 1:19)

Grace, mercy, and peace come from God the Father and from Jesus Christ." (2Joh 1:3)

With God as our example, we are told to show mercy to others. This especially applies to how we treat the vulnerable and powerless in society, those who have the greatest need: widows, orphans, foreigners, the poor and disabled, and those in prison. Two long parables in Matthew, the parable about the unmerciful servant (chapter 18) and the parable of the sheep and goats (chapter 25), provide vivid examples of this requirement. Here are other examples in the Old and New Testaments.

> The Lord says: "Execute true justice, show mercy and compassion to others. Don't oppress the widow or fatherless, the alien or the poor." (Zech 7:8–9)

> God has shown you what is good. What does the Lord require of you? Provide justice, love mercy, and walk humbly with God. (Mic 6:8)

> Those who oppress the poor show contempt for their creator, but those who show mercy to the needy honor God. (Prov 14:31)

> Blessed are the merciful, for they shall obtain mercy. (Matt 5:7)

> Do to others whatever you want them to do to you, for this is the Law and the Prophets. (Matt 7:12, Luke 6:31; the verse is now known as the "Golden Rule")

> Woe to you, scribes and Pharisees, hypocrites! You tithe extravagantly but neglect the more important parts of the law: justice and mercy and faith. You should have done these in addition to giving your tithe. (Matt 23:23)

> Be merciful, just as your Father is merciful. (Luke 6:36)

> God comforts us in all our tribulation so we may be able to comfort those who are in any trouble in the same way God comforts us. (2Cor 1:4)

> Be kind to each other, tenderly forgiving one another, as God in Christ forgave you. (Eph 4:32)

> As people who God chose to be holy, show mercy, kindness, humility, patience, and gentleness. Forgive one another, just as Christ forgave you. (Col 3:12–13)

> You are judged without mercy when you show no mercy to others. Mercy is better than judgment. (Jam 2:13)

> You should all have a mindset of showing compassion for others. Love each other, be tender and courteous, and don't be evil when evil is done to you. Instead, bless others because you were called to this, that you may inherit a blessing. (1Pet 3:8–9)

Finally, showing mercy is a natural consequence of experiencing mercy yourself. One of the fruits of the Spirit is showing mercy (kindness, compassion) to others. In addition, we benefit when we show mercy. "Those who show mercy do good for their own soul, but those who are cruel trouble their own flesh. Those who despise their neighbor sin; but happy are they who show mercy to those in need." (Prov 11:17, 14:21)

GRACE

Grace is the ultimate sign of God's love for people. Grace can be defined as an undeserved gift or favor, and scripture says that it's God's goodness and extravagant unconditional love (grace) that saves us from our sins. We haven't done anything to deserve it, and there is nothing we can do to earn it.

Grace in the Old Testament

We tend to think of grace as a New Testament concept, but God showed grace in the Old Testament. While the noun "grace" is rare in the Old Testament, the adjective "gracious" is more common. The Hebrew term *khen*, which is typically translated as "grace," also means "favor." When Moses was on Mount Sinai chiseling the tablets with the 10 commandments, the Lord came to him and said, "the Lord, the merciful and gracious God, is slow to anger, full of love and faithfulness, always loving thousands, and forgiving our sin, wickedness, and rebellion" (Exod 34:6–7). God later wants Aaron, the high priest, to tell the Israelites this benediction: "May the Lord bless you and protect you; may the Lord smile on you and be gracious to you; may the Lord favor you and give you peace" (Num 6:23–26). Whenever the priest used this blessing, God promised to bless the people of Israel.

God often showed grace for the Israelites as a group and to individuals in the Old Testament. The people were rebellious, wicked, and sinful many times through the centuries, but God continued to bless them in order to maintain their relationship. In some cases, God provided justice, often slowly and after many warnings, but God showed mercy and grace much more often. God was even gracious to other nations — Jonah quotes Exodus 34:6–7 when he sees God has saved the hated Assyrians in Nineveh. God blessed and protected David even though he committed major crimes; several of the Psalms express the writer's desire and thanks for God's graciousness.

Grace in the New Testament

Several New Testament parables provide insights into God's grace. One of the best-known parables relates to the extravagant love of a father for his prodigal son, described in chapter 3. The son asked for his inheritance early and squandered it on wild living but is lavishly welcomed home later by a loving father. Those who added titles to the Bible stories applied the term to the son who lived in extravagance, but a better understanding of the story is to apply the term to the extravagant love the father had for his lost son. The "Prodigal Father" is really a story about giving grace, love for somebody who doesn't deserve it. A just father would have punished the son, and a merciful father would have accepted the son back into the family without requiring any payment and without a celebration. But a gracious father throws a feast!

Other parables relate to unexpected and extravagant rewards. In the parable of the workers in the vineyard, all the workers got the same amount, even though many of them didn't work very long (Matt 20). In the parable of the great banquet, the host ends up inviting many strangers, even those from far away, because the invited guests decided not to come (Luke 14). This story foreshadowed the greatest example of grace for all — what Jesus did to take away the sins of the entire world. Although he was totally innocent, he left the comforts of heaven and came to earth to show us the way to live and took on our sins when he was killed. He was the last sacrifice needed so all people can have an abundant life here on earth and live in heaven for eternity. He conquered death so we lose the spiritual chains of our sin, and that gift is available to everybody, an incredible undeserved gift!

This is why the scriptures say that we have been saved by the loving grace of Jesus when we have faith in him. Paul's letters to the Colossians and Ephesians stressed that people have done nothing to earn any special status with God. It's entirely God's grace, a free and undeserved gift that came to believers because of one's faith in Jesus. "You were previously dead in your sins, but now you are alive in Christ — your sins have been forgiven. It's by grace we have been saved because of our faith. It's God's free gift, not what we have done so we can boast about it" (Col 2:13, Eph 2:1,4,5,8,9).

Other passages in the New Testament talk about God's saving grace. At the Council at Jerusalem, Paul and Barnabas reported how the Gentiles were being converted, and some Jewish believers said the Gentiles had to be circumcised as required by the laws of Moses. But Peter said it was God's grace that saved people, not how they look. Later, Paul told the Galatians that grace didn't come to him because he was a devout Jew who obeyed the Jewish laws.

IMPLICATIONS FOR BELIEVERS

God is just, merciful, and gracious, and we are to be the same while we live in the world (John 13:34). Circumstances dictate when to apply each principle, just as God applies all three at different times. At a minimum, justice must prevail over injustice, so our laws should reflect fairness to all. In addition, mercy can be applied in many situations, and kindness that goes well beyond reason (grace) has its place in a world that seems to be falling apart.

We don't want justice from God for ourselves because if we got what we deserve, we would all be condemned to death. But we need to advocate for justice in society and call earthly authorities to provide justice. God's mercy and grace are given to individuals so we can live life abundantly. The English theologian and church leader John Stott once said, "The Gospel is good news of mercy to the undeserving. The symbol of the religion of Jesus is the cross, not the scales."

As I reflect on my own Christian upbringing in a devout Protestant family, our emphasis was on God's love, mercy, grace, and correct beliefs, but not on justice. I think there are several reasons why my parents didn't emphasize justice in my spiritual development. All relate to those who hold different perspectives.

1. Christians emphasize understanding the life of Jesus and the New Testament themes of love, grace, forgiveness, salvation, faith, and correct beliefs. In contrast, the Old Testament is very long and doesn't flow chronologically, which makes it hard to understand. As a result, most Christians don't know the Old Testament very

well. Since Jesus fulfilled the Messianic predictions and had new interpretations of the original Laws, the main Old Testament teachings, including justice, are rarely studied by many Protestants.

2. The Reformation was based on the realization that God's salvation was based on grace and faith, not doing good works, which meant the concepts related to justice and work in society associated with it are often ignored by Protestants. Catholics emphasize the importance of providing justice and caring for the poor — works and actions — and Protestants reacted by focusing on the importance of a person's faith and beliefs, not works (unless they were tools of evangelism that lead others to a Christian faith). This reaction is part of an anti-Catholic bias that has existed for more than 500 years.

3. A liberal theological movement in the early 1900s dismissed supernatural elements of the Bible and many traditional beliefs, including the existence of miracles and the resurrection. Liberal theologians emphasized the moral teachings of the Bible, which included providing justice and making changes in America's economic and political systems. Christians who held strong beliefs in the authority of scripture then associated providing justice as being part of a "liberal" theology. Showing justice, especially to the poor, was part of a movement known as the "social gospel."[23] Opposition to this agenda has grown stronger among a shrinking number of white Christians in the United States.

4. The issue of providing justice can be controversial and can cause divisions among people because it can become a political issue. In the interest of keeping the peace and not harming relationships, our family simply didn't discuss justice, which meant I was unaware of justice issues in the Bible.

Some of these reasons use "guilt by association" thinking about what correct beliefs and actions look like. Some Christians think little

---

[23] The "Social Gospel" was a religious reform movement in the United States in the late 19th and early 20th centuries that stressed the need for social reforms as well as personal salvation. Its leaders wanted to improve society through application of the Biblical principles of charity and justice. The Social Gospel was very popular among liberal Protestant leaders.

about providing justice if it's not part of a plan for evangelism. But those who take the Christian faith seriously should not ignore the Biblical teachings about justice just because of who supports this point of view. Serious Christians look at the entire Bible for direction about how to live in the world. Providing justice is not part of the Old Law — it's God's mandate. All the commandments are summed up in the verse, "Love your neighbor as yourself" (Lev 19:18; Matt 19:19, 22:36–39; Mark 12:28–33; Luke 10:27; Rom 13:9; Gal 5:14; Jam 2:8). True faith will always exhibit some form of works, and providing justice and being fair are signs of righteousness.

* * * * * * *

Providing justice, mercy, and grace to others, especially vulnerable and disenfranchised groups, is evidence of a God-like disposition. Acts of service, compassion, and sacrifice for others are considered "pure and undefiled religion" (Jam 1:27).

CHAPTER 11

MONEY, POSSESSIONS, AND PROSPERITY

Another logical extension of the Biblical theme of love is using what we own for the benefit of others, which is one way to provide justice, mercy, and grace. The Bible has hundreds of verses related to money, possessions, and prosperity that should be studied carefully to determine their themes. This chapter provides background information on these topics and summarizes the main ideas presented in scripture.

BACKGROUND

Money can be defined as something that has value and can be stored and exchanged for other things. It normally has a specific value that people can use to buy and sell things with one another. When compared to a barter system where the value of items is often difficult to establish, having a money-based economy makes it easier and more efficient to make exchanges. To do this, money needs to hold its value over time and be widely accepted. Many things have been used as money, including agricultural or natural products (e.g., barley, shells). Paper money was first used in China in the 7th century, so it didn't exist during Biblical times.

A person may not have much money but can own many possessions that have value and can be exchanged for money. In this way, it's better to look at the idea of "wealth" when considering the total value of what a person owns. Wealthy people can have many types of possessions that have great value (money, property, houses, vehicles, etc.), while poor people have relatively few possessions that have much monetary value.

The Bible refers to money and possessions in different ways. Terms like treasure, wealth, prosperity, talents, gifts, rewards, and possessions are used to describe a person's overall level of resources. These terms appear in many books of the Bible.

Several forms of money are mentioned in the Bible. Gold and silver were used as currencies during Biblical times and are mentioned many times. Different types of Jewish, Roman, and Greek coins are mentioned, and sometimes the same coin is given a different name in some translations. The named coins include the mite (the least valuable), penny, drachma, shekel, shilling, denarius (worth about four days wages), and mina (worth three months wages). Coins contained small amounts of silver or gold that determined their value. A "talent" was a large amount of gold, worth about 15 years of an average worker's wage.

EVERYTHING BELONGS TO GOD

As the creator of the universe, everything belongs to God. This concept runs against how we view money and possessions — we think of them as our own private property. But scripture is clear that what we think is ours really belongs to God.

> To the Lord your God belong the heavens, even the highest heavens, the earth and everything in it. (Deut 10:14)

> The earth is the Lord's, and everything in it, the world, and all who live in it. (Psa 24:1)

> The Lord God says, "Every beast in the forest is mine, the cattle on a thousand hills. I know every bird in the mountains, and everything that moves in the fields is mine. If I was hungry, I wouldn't need to tell you because the world, and everything in it, is mine." (Psa 50:10–12)

If everything we have, all our property and possessions, is not our own, the question becomes, "What are we to do with what belongs to God?"

We Are Stewards

People were created to populate the earth and take care of it. So, we are stewards (trustees) who are responsible for managing the affairs of the owner according to the owner's' instructions and values. Jesus made this point in his parables of the landowner and of the talents, which are summarized here.

- A landowner planted a vineyard, protected with a wall and tower, and hired workers to manage it while he was away. But the workers treated the vineyard as their own and beat or killed all the messengers who came to collect the harvest, including the landowner's only son, believing this would allow them to inherit what belonged to him. (Matt 21:33–39)

- A man was going on a journey and entrusted his possessions to his three servants. He gave gold to each based on their ability and were to use it wisely. One servant got five bags, one got two bags, and the third got one bag. The servants who received five and two bags of gold used the gold wisely and earned twice as much by the time the owner returned. But the servant who received one bag buried the gold to hide it. The two who used their gold wisely were praised and given more responsibility, but the servant who buried the owner's gold was severely punished. (Matt 25:14–30)

So, Christians are stewards who should use their resources wisely and for good purposes. This includes promoting peace and providing justice and mercy, especially to the disadvantaged and who are despised in society. God told Moses to tell the Israelites, "Although all the earth is mine, you will be for me a kingdom of priests and a holy nation" (Exod 19:5–6), and they were told to leave their land unused every seventh year and not to gather food at the edge of their land to allow the poor to gather food from it.

The Tithe

The tithe refers to giving 10% of one's annual income or production to support God's work in the world. The term comes from the Hebrew word "a tenth." We first learn that Abraham and Jacob offered a tithe to God (Gen 14, 28), and later, the Israelites were commanded to tithe from what they earned (Lev 27:30; Num 18:25–28; Deut 14:22–24; 2Chr 31:5–6). In Proverbs 3:9–10, we read, "Honor the Lord with your wealth and with the first fruits of all your crops; this will fill your barns and your vats will be full with new wine."

The Israelites largely neglected the tithe when they lived under evil kings in the Northern and Southern Kingdoms. When some of the Israelites returned to Jerusalem from exile, both Nehemiah and Malachi condemned them for neglecting to tithe — the Levites (priests) had to find other jobs to survive and religious activities were neglected.

In the New Testament, Jesus mentioned the tithe when he condemned the religious leaders for doing it but neglected providing justice and mercy, which were more important (Matt 23:23). He was indirectly confirming the importance of the title, although when he mentioned it during the Sermon on the Mount (Matt 5:23–24), he related it to offering sacrifices, which are no longer required because it was part of the old law — Christians have been released from obeying the old law (Rom 7:4,6; Eph 2:15). So, the tithe is not a requirement for Christians.

Although the tithe is not required, it not only helps others, but it helps us as an antidote to covetousness. The last Commandment says: "Do not covet." Jesus said, "Be on your guard against every form of greed" (Luke 12:15). Wanting things too much is dangerous to our souls, and Hebrews 13:5 says, "Let your character be free from the love of money; be content with what you have." Every time we give a tithe, we deal with our desire for what we might have bought for ourselves. To give is not to buy, and this is a challenge in a capitalist society.

Generosity

As discussed in the two previous chapters, generosity is a main theme in the Bible. God is generous and we are to be generous toward others. This giving is voluntarily and should be sensitive to inequalities. Paul explains these ideas in 2 Corinthians 8–9, which includes these verses:

> Remember: Those who give sparingly will reap sparingly, and those who give generously will reap generously. Each of you should give what you have decided to give, not reluctantly or under compulsion, for God loves a cheerful giver. (2Cor 9:6–7)

> We don't desire that others are relieved while you are hard-pressed, but that there might be equality. Right now, your plenty will supply what they need, and later, their plenty will supply what you need. The goal is equality, as it's written: "Those who gathered much didn't have too much, and those who gathered little didn't have too little." (2Cor 8:13–15, with a reference to Exod 16:18)

Christians in early church voluntarily shared their wealth with each other so nobody was in need. They devoted themselves to fellowship and "had everything in common and sold their property and possessions to help those in need" (Acts 2:44–45). The Greek word for fellowship is *koinonia*, which means "to have in common" or "to share." So, Christians are to be generous and willing to share. Paul tells Timothy: "Command those who are now rich not to be proud or put their hope in their riches, which are very uncertain, but to put their hope in God, who provides us with everything for our enjoyment. Command them to do good, to be rich in good deeds, and to be generous and willing to share" (1Tim 6:17–18). Paul also wrote, "Bear each other's burdens, and so fulfill the law of Christ" (Gal 6:2).

Some have been outspoken about the lack of generosity of believers. One study of the giving patterns among American Christians found that the median level of giving is less than 1% of their pre-tax income and 20% give nothing at all to the church, parachurches, or nonreligious charities. The study also found that poor Christians give more than middle-income Christians as a percentage of their income. Moreover, the study projected that if serious Christians in the United States (those who attend church at least a few times a month) gave 10% of their *after*-tax income, it would raise an extra $46 billion (in 2008, not adjusted for inflation), enough to eliminate world poverty.[24]

Prosperity Is a Mixed Blessing

Money is a tool used to facilitate transactions and can be used for good or evil purposes. In this sense, it can be considered neutral, neither a good nor bad thing, just like any other tool. It's the actions and attitudes associated with money — how it's acquired, used, and viewed — that are good, bad, or neutral (having no morality). Money can be a double-edged sword — it improves the efficiency and transparency of transactions, and it provides people more choices that enable them to have more control over their lives. But the improved efficiency also allows us to acquire more things much faster, which increases the likelihood of materialism. The internet and credit cards are other neutral tools that enable people to quickly buy more than they need.

---

[24] Christian Smith, Michael Emerson, and Patricia Snell, *Passing the Plate: Why American Christians Don't Give Away More Money* (2008), New York: Oxford University Press.

Wealth and Prosperity Are Good

The Bible often says that material blessings are good and we should enjoy them. We are also told that those who follow God will prosper — God rewards those who are obedient. In addition, gaining wealth is a logical consequence of hard work, and those who prosper can help others.

God created a physical world that was good. Gold, the most valuable metal, is first mentioned in the description of the Garden of Eden, along with other precious items (Genesis 2). Items made of gold were seen as honorable throughout the Bible. For example, the Ark of the Covenant and the Temple were decorated with gold, and some stories refer to objects made of gold in a positive manner. The wise men honored Jesus with gold, their most valuable gift, and the city and streets of heaven described in Revelation are made of gold (as well as many precious gems and pearls).

The Israelites were blessed with productive land and wealth because they were God's children (Deut 8:7–10,18). When Solomon asked God for wisdom, the Lord was pleased and gave him honor and wealth as well as wisdom. The material blessings of Job were rewards for his good behavior and faith in God. John rebuked the heresy of Gnosticism, which said that all matter is evil (the Gnostics said Jesus could not have been an actual person because good things are only spiritual). In Revelation, the Lamb is worthy to receive wealth (as well as many other things). Various jewels and gems are mentioned in the Bible in a positive way, and the book of Proverbs had many verses that view money, wealth, and wages in a positive way (except when they are gained using evil methods). However, the Bible never emphasizes the value of acquiring and accumulating wealth.

Prosperity also provides the means to help others. The blessings received by the Israelites were meant to be shared with others and those in need (Gen 12:2–3; Lev 19:9–10; Deut 15:10; Isa 58:10; Prov 14:31, 19:17, 22:9). The tithe supported those who worked for God and the religious infrastructure. Various women are mentioned as supporting the disciples financially, the wealth of Joseph of Arimathea allowed him to use his new grave to bury Jesus, and the wealthy church of Philippi supported Paul and his traveling companions.

John Wesley wrote a famous sermon entitled "The Use of Money" in 1760 that supports these notions. He said Christians should *earn* all they can, *save* all they can, and *give away* all they can. He wasn't against people having money and he didn't think money was evil, but he later noted that Christians were ignoring the third part of his sermon. He was pleading for Christian generosity and compassion for the poor and needy, and what mattered most was what people did with their money.

Oddly, what we do for others often happens to us as well — being generous results in blessings for the giver. Jesus said, "Don't judge others and you won't be judged. Don't condemn and you won't be condemned. Forgive and you will be forgiven. Give and it will be given to you" (Luke 6:37–38). Paul reiterates the same idea: "Remember, those who sow sparingly will also reap sparingly, and those who sow generously will also reap generously" (2Cor 9:6).

Money and Prosperity Can Be Bad

While wealth and prosperity can be good, the Bible also offers a second perspective on them. While money and prosperity may not be evil by themselves, the *love* of money is said to be the root of all evil and may cause some to lose their faith (1Tim 6:10). Money gives us control and power, both of which should be in God's hands, not ours. Having money allows us to get what we want, not just what we need. When we improve our standard of living and our possessions increase in quality and quantity, we gain prestige and popularity, become more comfortable, give ourselves credit for our progress, and are less likely to put our trust in God.

This occurred many times over several centuries among the Israelites during the period of the judges. After the Israelites honored God, they would be blessed and prosper, and eventually they didn't follow the ways of God, which led to calamity. Moses had warned the people about this. Here is a summary of what he told them before they entered Canaan.

> Be careful not to forget the Lord; keep God's commandments and Laws. If you forget, when you have eaten and are satisfied, when you have built good houses and lived in them, when your herds and your flocks multiply, and when your silver and gold and all that you

have multiplies, your heart will become proud and you will forget the Lord who brought you out of slavery in Egypt. God led you through the terrible wilderness that had scorpions and no water and brought water for you out of the rock and fed you manna, so you would be humble and tested and eventually do good. If you forget, you may say in your heart, 'My power and strength made me this wealth.' So remember that it's God who gave you the power to create wealth. (Deut 8:11–18)

Being wealthy can be dangerous and make it hard to be faithful and obedient to God's call for correct living. For example:

- God called Gideon to drive the Midianite army out of Canaan. When he was victorious, the people wanted to make him a king. He declined but asked for a gold earring from all those who took one from the enemy. Gideon received 43 pounds of gold and made an elaborate garment for himself with the gold, similar to what the high priest wore. He put it in his hometown, and "all the Israelites prostituted themselves by worshiping it there" (Judg 8:27).

- When exiled Jews living in Babylonia returned to Jerusalem, construction on a new Temple started. The prophet Haggai reminded the people that building the Temple was a higher priority than using their money to improve their houses that were already elaborate. Other prophets chastised the Israelites for not supporting the work of the priests and for not following the normal religious practices.

- In the New Testament, a rich young man came to Jesus and wanted to know how he could obtain eternal life. He had been faithful to the Law since his youth, and Jesus told him to sell all he had and give the money to the poor, then follow him. Jesus knew the man's faith was in his wealth. After the man left in sadness, Jesus told his disciples, "It's very hard for the rich to enter the kingdom of God. In fact, it's easier for a camel to go through the eye of a needle than for someone who is rich to enter the kingdom of God" (Matt 19:24, Mark 10:25, Luke 18:25).[25]

---

[25] The "eye of a needle" sometimes refers to a very small opening in a city's wall, which might be a small gate or door. This type of opening is easily guarded and allows people to enter a city late at night. If the opening is very small, a camel would need to be unloaded

- Jesus tells the story about a rich man and a poor man (Lazarus) who both die. The rich man goes to hell and sees Lazarus in heaven. The rich man is told he received his reward when he was alive, and he wants to warn his brothers so they can repent and avoid his fate. But he is told they were warned by Moses and the prophets. (Luke 16:19–31)
- In Revelation, John criticizes the church in Laodicea because it was complacent and self-sufficient. The prosperous city was a center of banking, but John said they were spiritually poor. He told them, "Because you are lukewarm, I'm about to spit you out of my mouth! You say, 'I'm rich, I have wealth and don't need anything.' But you don't realize you are wretched, pitiful, poor, blind, and naked. I rebuke and discipline those I love, so be sincere and repent" (Rev 3:16–17,19).

Jesus warned us about the dangers of accumulating possessions. He said, "Don't store up for yourselves treasures on earth, where moth and rust destroy them and where thieves break in and steal them. Instead, store up treasures in heaven, where moths, rust, and thieves can't do harm to them. For where your treasure is, that's where your heart will be" (Matt 6:19–21). Our treasure is anything we value and where we focus our attention. What we focus on dictates our actions, and when we focus on gaining wealth to acquire material things, we lose our focus on God, the one who provides for us.

When we have possessions and wealth, we rely on them for comfort and safety. In the parable of the sower and soils, one type of seed fell

---

and lying flat on a board, then dragged through on a plank, to get through the opening. It would be virtually impossible for a fully grown camel to do this. The message implies that a person cannot earn eternal life by being obedient or becoming poor — God's help is needed. One's possessions can be a stumbling block to following God, and we can't buy our way into heaven.

Some say the phrase is meant to be taken literally and no tiny opening existed. This view believes it's impossible for a rich person to be saved, and his disciples would have known about a gate with that name and not asked Jesus how it was possible. In the three gospel accounts, Jesus goes on to say, "All things are possible with God." However, Jesus initially said it was "very hard," not impossible. The reader must decide how best to understand this passage, but in either case, the point is that possessions can be a dangerous stumbling block to being an obedient Christian.

among thorns and the plant that emerged didn't mature because it was eventually choked by life's worries, riches, and pleasures.

We often worry when we lack wealth because we have come to rely on it. Jesus addressed this issue in his Sermon on the Mount. Here is a summary of that passage.

> You can't serve both God and money; nobody can serve two masters. So don't worry about your life, what you will eat or drink or about your body and what you will wear. Life is more than food and the body is more than clothes. Look at the birds — they don't sow or reap or store food in barns, but God feeds them. You are much more valuable than birds. You can't gain any time in your life by worrying about things — why worry about your clothes? See how the flowers of the field grow on their own — Solomon in all his splendor isn't dressed as well as these flowers! If God clothes the grass, which is eventually thrown into a fire, God will clothe you much more. So don't worry and say, "What will we eat and drink or wear?" Our God in heaven knows you need them. But seek first God's kingdom and righteousness, and all these other things will be given to you as well. Don't worry about tomorrow because each day has enough trouble of its own. (Matt 6:24–34)

Money can corrupt those with evil motives. Evil people often prosper by oppressing the poor and through injustice. Jesus became violent and angry when he cleansed the Temple of greedy merchants who set up businesses to make money and take advantage of vulnerable people who wanted to worship the correct way. We can take comfort that wealth gained by evil means will not last (Jam 2:6–7; Prov 10:2, 11:4, 13:11, 20:17, 22:16).

Poverty and Its Benefits

People can be poor for multiple reasons, including because they have (1) been oppressed or discriminated against by those who are wealthy or powerful, (2) experienced unfortunate things, (3) lacked opportunities, (4) not inherited certain benefits (e.g., money, possessions, land, intellect, a good name, a socially-acceptable physical appearance, being born in an affluent region), (5) lived a sinful life, (6) not worked hard, (7) not received needed support when experiencing a crisis, or (8) intentionally chosen to live with few possessions. Solomon wrote proverbs about how laziness causes people's poverty, and Micah said people are poor because they are oppressed by the powerful who want to maintain their lifestyles through their social, economic, and political privileges. In most cases, people are poor for reasons beyond their control.

The New Testament highlights the benefits of being poor. In contrast to the dangers of having and depending on wealth for survival and safety, the opposite is also true: those who are poor are more likely to rely on God. They are also more likely to share with others, as those in the early church did (most of them were poor). The poor are also less likely to focus on obtaining more possessions, and being unencumbered by possessions allows them to be more flexible and free to follow the Spirit. In addition, those who are poor are more likely to be content — riches provide only temporary pleasure in this life and never satisfy (Eccl 5:10). True happiness can't be gained without God; the Teacher in Ecclesiastes says many times that the pursuit of happiness is like "chasing after the wind."

Jesus himself grew up in a poor family and modeled simplicity. Although he was God and had great power, he came to earth in a humble manger and lived a simple life. His father was a simple carpenter who could only afford a cheap offering when Jesus was born. The family grew up in a disrespected region, and Jesus relied on others to support him during his ministry. He carried no money and had to get a coin from the mouth of a fish to show money to the religious leaders. He may have been homeless — he said, "Foxes have holes and birds have nests, but the Son of Man has nowhere to lay his head" (Matt 8:20). Jesus understood what it's like to be poor and could see the danger of having wealth. Those who are poor have more empathy for others who are poor and tend to be more generous than those with greater resources — they know what it's like to live day-to-day and rely on others. It's not surprising that the poor are among God's favored people (Deut 15:7–8; Isa 61:1; Zech 7:9–10; Luke 4:17–19, 6:20–21, 14:12–14; Matt 25:31–46; 1Cor 1:18–20; Jam 2:5).

Loans, Debt, and Investments

The Bible discusses other financial concepts related to wealth, money, and possessions that must be understood to grasp the meanings of some Biblical stories. A *loan* is given to somebody who "borrows" something and must repay it, with or without *interest* (a charge for "renting" money). Those who receive a loan have a *debt* to repay to those who gave them the loan. Loans are usually made with money, but any material possession can be loaned to another (e.g., a friend loans a car to a friend). *Investments* involve spending money on something with the expectation that the value of what was acquired will increase in value or contribute to greater wealth. Sometimes this can involve debt. For example, people who go to college often get a loan and assume they will be able to pay off the debt, plus make more money in the future, because they will earn a higher wage.

Three more terms apply to financial transactions. The *interest* rate of a loan can make the repayment easy or difficult, and when applied to an investment, it can make the *return* high or low (more or less money comes back to the investor). The *risk* of an investment refers to the degree of uncertainty that the return will be either a gain or loss — the higher the risk, the more likely there will be larger gains or losses.

Biblical Principles About Loans and Debt

The Old Testament describes acceptable loans that can be made to others and some general principles about obtaining a loan (going in debt). Specifically, the Bible allowed loans to be made to Israelites without any interest, but loans made to others could include interest (Exod 22:25, Deut 23:19–20). But despite this "law," some money-lenders charged interest when making loans to other Israelites.[26]

The Bible has other perspectives on making loans. Only one verse advises us not to make loans to others foolishly because a person may be unable to pay the debt (Prov 11:15). Several verses say a person could not recover a debt if it meant taking items that provided for a person's basic needs (Exod 22:25–27; Lev 25:35–37; Deut 24:6,10–13). In addition, the principle of forgiving loans and freeing slaves was established in the Old Testament to minimize wealth disparities, enhance justice, and promote generosity. Deuteronomy 15:1–11 describes how debts were

---

[26] *Usury* is the practice of making unethical or immoral loans with a very high interest rate that unfairly enrich the lender. Israelites who charged interest to other Israelites were practicing usury.

to be forgiven after seven years among the Israelites, which included freeing slaves. The Year of Jubilee, which came every 50 years, released people from their debts, released slaves, and returned property to the original owner (Lev 25:8–13). So the scriptures emphasize giving loans without interest with little regard to having the debt repaid, and wealth was to be redistributed periodically.

The New Testament stresses the importance of being generous, which included making loans to others, even if they are not able to pay off the debt. Jesus said, "Give to those who ask of you; don't turn away from those who want to borrow from you" (Matt 5:42). The book of Luke records several teachings by Jesus on this topic. However, these verses speak to individuals, not to businesses and their practices, which have their own set of principles.

> Give to those who ask you, and when somebody takes something from you, don't demand it back. If you lend to those who you expect to do the same to you, what credit is that to you? Even sinners lend to sinners in order to receive back the same amount. But love your enemies and do good; lend and expect nothing in return. For then your reward will be great and you will be sons of the Most High; God is kind to ungrateful and evil people. (Luke 6:30,34–35)

> A moneylender had two debtors: one owed 500 denarii and the other owed 50. When they were unable to repay, he canceled the debts of both. (Luke 7:41–42)

> When you prepare a meal, don't invite your friends or family or wealthy neighbors, for they will invite you to a meal in return, and you will get what you gave them. Instead, invite those who are poor and have disabilities. You will be blessed because they don't have the means to repay you, and you will be repaid at the resurrection of the righteous. (Luke 14:12–14)

The Bible has many warnings about being in debt. Borrowing from others creates a sense of "slavery" to the lender, and it should only be done when the debt can be repaid, for it's not right to be in debt and not pay what is owed (Deut 28:12; Prov 22:7,26–27; Eccl 5:5; Psa 37:21; Neh 5:3–5; Matt 6:24; Rom 13:7–8). It's also not right to go into debt to avoid work or get immediate gratification (Prov 6:1–11, 10:4, 14:23; Heb 13:5). So our mindset is to avoid debt when possible unless it generates more value in the future, and to be sure the debt can be repaid. This often means deferring gratification.

The Bible also discusses "spiritual" debt. In the Old Testament, sins separated the Israelites from God and put them in debt, so they made sacrifices to show their sorrow and regain God's approval. The sacrifice of Jesus paid the debt owed by all people one last time (Rom 6:23, Col 2:13–14). Our debt was forgiven, so we are to forgive the debts of others: "Forgive our debts as we forgive those who are indebted to us" (Matt 6:12; Luke 11:4). The parable of the servant who had his huge debt totally forgiven (Matt 18:21–35) illustrates the great kindness and generosity of God and how we are to forgive others.

Biblical Principles for Investments

The Bible includes stories and parables that indirectly relate to investments. We are given gifts and skills to build the church, and we are to make good decisions as God's stewards to make the world a better place. We are to plan our investments wisely, counting the cost and the benefits before we act (Prov 6:6–8, 13:11, 21:5).

The most famous story Jesus told that relates to being wise investors was the parable of the talents (a huge amount of gold) recorded in Matthew 25:14–30 (briefly mentioned earlier in this chapter). An owner gave three servants different amounts of gold to use while the owner was away. One servant got five bags, one got two bags, and the third got one bag. The servants who got five and two bags used them wisely and doubled the amount of gold. This is a very high return, which probably required a high-risk investment — they were not afraid to take risks to achieve great gains. However, the servant who received one bag hid the gold in a hole in the ground.

When the owner returned and asked for the gold, the servants who received five and two bags presented the owner with double the amount they were given. The owner told them, "Well done, good and faithful servants! You have been faithful with a few things — I will put you in charge of many things!" But the servant who buried his one bag made up excuses for doing nothing and retrieved the gold from the ground. The owner said to him, "You are wicked and lazy! Why didn't you put my money in the bank? I would have at least received the gold plus interest." The owner then had the servant thrown into the darkness where there is "weeping and gnashing of teeth." The owner also gave the one bag to the servant who had 10 bags — he had been very responsible with the large amount he received. Luke 19:11–26 records a similar story. Both stories emphasize being faithful with what we have, not the importance of making money.

On another occasion, Jesus told people that they should think carefully about the implications of following him. He used an investment analogy: "If you want to build a tower, won't you first estimate the cost to see if you have enough money to complete it? If you lay the foundation and can't finish it, everyone who sees it will ridicule you" (Luke 14:28–29).

The Bible gives no justification for accumulating wealth. In fact, practicing the principles of generosity, forgiving loans, freeing slaves, and returning property to the original owner means we should *not* accumulate wealth for ourselves. Instead, we are to store our treasures in Heaven (Matt 6:19–21, 1Tim 6:17–19).

We should also have flexible plans. When Jesus was asked about dividing an inheritance, he made fun of a hypothetical rich man who tears down barns to build new ones so he could store an abundant harvest and take life easy — "eat, drink, and be merry" — but the man died the next day. Being rich in this life isn't being rich in God's eyes (Luke 12:13–21). Proverbs 16:9 says, "People make plans in their hearts, but the Lord establishes their steps." James tells his readers:

> You say, 'today or tomorrow we will go to this or that city, spend a year there, carry on business, and make money.' But you don't know what will happen tomorrow. What is your life? You are a mist that appears for a short while and then vanishes. Instead, say, 'If it's the Lord's will, we will live and do this or that.' As it is, you boast with arrogant schemes, but such boasting is evil. (Jam 4:13–15)

Jesus told an unusual parable that praised a manager who mismanaged his owner's money and was about to be fired (Luke 16:1–9). The manager realized he had to do something quickly, so he contacted two men who had large debts with the owner and made large reductions in the amount that was owed (but he didn't collect what was owed). Later, the owner praised the manager for acting shrewdly. Jesus ended the story by saying people should use wealth to gain friends and that his followers need to be wise when operating in the world. The story also shows how generosity can benefit multiple people — those with the debt and those who forgive debtors (both the manager and the owner improved their reputation by reducing the debt).

Some of a Christian's investments need to have a long-term perspective that considers benefiting others, not just ourselves. God commanded Jeremiah to buy land in Anathoth, a town near Jerusalem where he was born.[27] At the time, the Babylonians controlled the town, so buying land appeared to be a foolish investment. But Jeremiah purchased the land in a very public way, even though he was confused about why God wanted him to do it. God told him that a time would come when Israel would regain control of the land (Jer 32). With our own future secured, we should be willing to help others in unusual ways. Practicing philanthropy is a sound way to invest in others.

Jesus tells us to be "wise as serpents and pure as doves" (Matt 10:16), to use our mind while remaining harmless. Being a Christian in a complicated world requires us to be wide-eyed critical thinkers who discern the truth. Having wealth is a big responsibility, and as stewards of God's resources, we should have no problem being generous — we are simply giving away what God owns. We are to be faithful with what we received, so we should make wise decisions about what God has given us and do what the owner asks us to do.

IMPLICATIONS

Wealth can be a sign of blessing, but it can also reveal a priority of living for ourselves and not being generous; we are to be ready to make loans and cancel debts. The world constantly and seductively emphasizes gaining possessions and wealth in order to be happy and accepted by others. Those with wealth need to be reminded often that we are stewards of God's resources, and to whom much is given, much is required. We must develop a mindset of generosity, as described in chapters 9 and 10, as an effective antidote to the culture's pressure and manipulation for us to acquire what we want, which usually exceeds

---

[27] The town was one of six "cities of refuge" run by the Levites that provided asylum and protection for anyone who unintentionally killed a person (manslaughter) until their case went to trial.

what we need. The Bible doesn't support any specific economic system, but the laws of Moses related to debt forgiveness and support for the poor helped prevent large wealth disparities within Israel's society. Any system that relies primarily on getting people to buy things they don't need also needs strong systems to support those in most need.

God specifically says we should support those who are disadvantaged in some way. Nothing in scripture says we should only give when it's a "good investment" or that we should consider why a person is poor. While we should be wise about using what God has given us, loving one's neighbor is evidence of one's sincere faith. This means helping those we encounter, as described in the story of the Good Samaritan (Luke 10:25–37).

Jesus said, "The poor will always be with you" (Mark 14:7), so there are many opportunities to be generous. While the poverty rate has slowly declined worldwide, as of 2022, nearly 20% of the people living in developing countries were living in multi-dimensional poverty.[28] Most of them live in Africa and south Asia, so they are largely invisible to those living in other regions. Given the wide range of reasons why people are poor, multiple strategies are required to support those in need. A proverb of unknown origin says, "Give people a fish and feed them for a day; teach them to fish and you feed them for a lifetime." There are times when we should do both, and we need to be ready, and have a disposition, to help those in need when we encounter them on our path.

We need to live within our means and be satisfied with what we have. When Paul was in prison, he wrote to the wealthy church in Philippi so they wouldn't worry about him, telling them, "I have learned the secret to be at peace in every situation. I can live simply and in prosperity. I can be content if I'm well fed or go hungry, having much and needing much. I can handle anything because Christ strengthens me" (Phil 4:11–13).

---

[28] *Global Multidimensional Poverty Index 2022: Unpacking Deprivation Bundles to Reduce Multidimensional Poverty*, United Nations Development Program (New York) and Oxford Poverty and Human Development Initiative (Oxford). The population of the 111 countries surveyed was 6.1 billion (76% of the world population), and 1.2 billion were living in multi-dimensional poverty, which is measured using various indicators related to health, education, and standard of living.

CHAPTER 12

LIFE IS NOT FAIR

Is life fair? Our idea of fairness comes from our understanding of justice, that people should get what they deserve. Some people talk about their belief in "karma," a Hindu term that means a person's actions will cause what happens to them in the future. In this sense, karma is another way of saying life will be fair — good things will happen when people do good things, and bad things will happen when people do bad things. It might be in this life, and it might be in the next life, but fairness will prevail.

The Bible stresses that justice is needed because much of our life on earth is *not* fair. We tend to think that we should be rewarded when we do something good, but often we are not. The reverse is also true: we think people should be punished when they do bad things, but often they are not. This should not come as a surprise. There are many examples in the Bible that show life isn't fair. In fact, more often than not, evil people reap rewards and bad things happen to those who are good. The idea of karma keeps people from fighting for justice. This chapter examines the concept of fairness and the many ways life is not fair.

JUSTICE: PEOPLE GET WHAT THEY DESERVE

Providing justice to others is a major theme of the Bible. Chapter 10 discusses this topic, and this section briefly summarizes the main ideas of that chapter.

Justice is another word for being fair to others, giving people what they deserve. Fairness is reflected when we are rewarded for doing something good and when we are punished for doing something wrong. Justice also relates to consequences that should be in proportion to what is done — major rewards and punishment for major actions, minor rewards and punishment for minor actions. An eye for an eye, nothing more, nothing less. Finally, justice is meant to be applied fairly without regard to who is being judged. Everybody should be judged in the same way.

God showed a combination of justice, mercy, and grace in the Old Testament. For example, justice was dispensed when Adam and Eve were kicked out of the Garden of Eden because they disobeyed. God also showed mercy and grace to those who didn't deserve them. The Israelites constantly complained, rebelled, and ignored God, but God continued to bless them. Life wasn't fair — the Israelites got far more than they deserved! Moses told them, "It's not because you are righteous or have integrity that you will take possession of Canaan. It's because of the wickedness of these nations. After all, God considers us a stubborn people" (Deut 9:5–6). But eventually, God gave them justice and they were punished.

In the New Testament, God showed a sense of equity and fairness by wanting a relationship with all people in the world, regardless of their actions, beliefs, gender, tribe, race, age, or birthplace. God's love for the entire human race reflects justice, mercy, and grace, but not always in that order.

EVIL PEOPLE PROSPER

It's human nature to be selfish, and those with power often use it to promote their own interests. This allows them to prosper and become even more powerful. Lord Acton, a British historian, said, "power tends to corrupt, and absolute power corrupts absolutely" (as power grows, so does immorality). Selfish people who have power gain more resources, which allows them to conquer others and take what doesn't belong to them. History is full of evil leaders who expand their empires and enrich themselves as they wage war on their weaker neighbors.

This doesn't only happen in empires and governments. Some businesses cheat, lie, cut corners, and exploit others to gain more profits (the love of money is the root of all evil). Criminals, both individuals and in groups, use violence and deception to exploit honest and vulnerable people to meet their own desires. In these cases, those acting in evil ways enjoy a better life at the expense of innocent people and often pass on the benefits gained from their evil deeds to their family and friends. These benefits and their related privileges are then passed from one generation to the next. It's not easy to watch evil people prosper — we want justice to prevail, but often it does not.

The Bible has stories about powerful people who took advantage of their position to help themselves. King David had Bathsheba's husband killed so he could marry her (if Nathan hadn't confronted him, he would have gotten away with it). Evil priests abused their power and lived a prosperous and easy life. Many prophets spoke truth to evil Israelite kings, but the kings ignored or killed them and continued enjoying the benefits and comforts of their powerful positions. Jeremiah complained to God about why the wicked were blessed and prospered while he, a Godly man, suffered (he was arrested, beaten, imprisoned, and received many death threats). The Jewish tax collectors and Roman soldiers used their positions to gain wealth for themselves during Jesus's time. As Job suffered, he wondered, "Why do the wicked continue to live and become very powerful? They watch as their descendants and their offspring live on without fear, and God's rod doesn't touch them" (Job 21:7–9).

Only one verse in the Bible says the wicked will not prosper (Eccl 8:13), but many verses say they do (Psa 37:7, 73:3; Job 12:6, 21:7–13; Lam 1:5; Dan 11:36; Mal 3:15; Jer 12:1). Although God's people were commanded to provide justice to others, especially those who are disadvantaged in some way and who lack the power to be treated fairly, it was the exception after they occupied Canaan, not the rule. When justice was provided, it was after long periods of injustice and it was often for a short amount of time.

In many cases, we are told that evil people will get justice only when they die and God punishes them. Jesus told this parable about the coexistence of the good and the bad until the end of time (Matt 13:24–30). A man's enemy sowed weed seeds into his wheat field, and when the wheat sprouted, the weeds also appeared. The man told his workers to allow both to grow together so the wheat would not be pulled up when the weeds were pulled. It's only when the harvesters come at the end of the season that the weeds are collected and burned. This parable doesn't provide much comfort to those who are forced to live alongside evil people and suffer.

Evil people have another advantage of an unjust system. Sometimes their punishment is weak and short-lived, and they may escape punishment entirely. Criminals take advantage of flawed or weak legal requirements and loopholes in the law, which may include high expectations to prove guilt, and they may get out of jail after a short visit, if they go at all. They are then free to continue their evil ways and exploit innocent people. Sometimes it takes a long time for justice to be served; justice delayed is justice denied. The evil in this world seems to be both widespread and enduring. It's been said that "crime doesn't pay," and in Hollywood movies, that's usually true — those who represent good causes usually win in the end. But in reality, crime often pays. Luckily, the wealth gained by evil means will not last (Jam 2:6–7; Prov 10:2, 11:4, 13:11, 20:17, 22:16).

GOOD PEOPLE SUFFER

If karma really exists, many good and innocent would not suffer. But as noted above, evil people prosper and sometimes it's at the expense of innocent and vulnerable people. Many verses say our rewards will come in heaven, not here on earth (Matt 5:10–12, 6:27; Luke 6:23,35; John 14:3; 1Cor 3:8,11–14, 9:18, 15:42–44; 2Cor 5:1–4; Gal 6:7–9; Phil 3:20; 2Tim 4:8; 1Pet 5:4; Rev 22:12). In the parable of the talents (Matt 25:14–30, Luke 19:15–19), the faithful servants get their rewards later, not immediately.

Two Old Testament books, Ecclesiastes and Job, discuss the unfairness of life and that good people suffer.

Ecclesiastes

The book of Ecclesiastes contains the reflections of a wise king, probably King Solomon later in his reign. In contrast to the black and white answers provided in Proverbs, wisdom is viewed with more realistic and nuanced eyes — there is neither blind optimism for doing right nor skeptical pessimism for doing wrong. Instead, life is seen with its complexities and frustrations.

Despite the false claim that "everything is meaningless" and that creating change to improve life is like "chasing the wind — nothing is new under the sun" (Eccl 1:2,9,14), the author extols the attributes of wisdom, even though life can be unfair.

Although a wicked person who commits a hundred crimes may live a long time, I know things will go better for those who respect and love God. Yet because the wicked don't respect God, things will not go well for them, and their days will not lengthen like their shadow. And here is something else that is meaningless: the righteous who get what the wicked deserve, and the wicked who get what the righteous deserve. (Eccl 8:12–14)

Everybody has the same destiny, both the righteous and the wicked, the good and the bad. Nobody knows when they will die; as fish and birds are suddenly caught in nets and traps, people are trapped by evil times. One sinner can destroy many who are good. (Eccl 9:2,12,18)

Because life holds many disappointments, the author concludes by encouraging people to enjoy life, work hard, and embrace life's surprises as opportunities given by God to learn and grow.

Story of Job

The book of Job is a long story (not part of the Israelite history) with conversations about faith and obedience, rewards and punishments, good and evil, and how good people should respond when bad things happen to them. Job is a very wealthy and righteous man who has nearly everything taken away from him because God allows Satan to torment him to see if he will remain faithful. Job stays faithful and doesn't blame God for his many problems: "The Lord gives and the Lord takes away. Blessed be the name of the Lord" (Job 1:21).

Job's friends tell him he must have sinned because God doesn't punish good people for no reason — they tell him he needs to repent and change his ways, and then everything will be good again. But Job disagrees, saying he hasn't done anything wrong.

Yet Job is perplexed by how his life changed so fast even though he did nothing wrong. He wonders how people can please a God who knows everything but can forgive those who deserve punishment. God's ways are beyond our understanding. His experience proves that suffering is not automatically linked to sinfulness, and he believes God will eventually say he is innocent. He doesn't know why certain things happen — life can be unfair and sometimes the wicked prosper. He gets irritated with his friends who falsely accuse him of doing something wrong, blaming the victim. He says even if he dies, he will live again; his faith brings him hope that God's love and judgment will result in a "not guilty" verdict for him in the afterlife. He says, "I know my redeemer lives and that in the end, God will still be standing. After my body is destroyed, I will still see God" (Job 19:25–26).

Job is humbled when God starts talking to him and he realizes how little he knows and understands. God becomes angry with his friends for incorrectly saying that suffering only occurs due to sin and that justice only occurs during one's lifetime. Easy answers don't apply in complex situations.

The story ends abruptly when God honors Job's humility and faithfulness and blesses him with more than he originally had — he goes on to live a long life and has many descendants. But the story has no closure about the deal between God and Satan; in the end, good prevails against evil because Job doesn't waver. The story also doesn't explain why the faithful suffer or why the wicked prosper, so readers are left to think about the answers for themselves.

INNOCENT PEOPLE SUFFER

Innocent people, including children and infants, have always suffered due to the sins of others. Sometimes it's related to the punishment of others. For example, all the Israelites had to live in the wilderness for 40 years because 10 men lacked faith. Later, the Israelites were punished because of their unfaithfulness, and innocent people were affected as well — most of the Jews were exiled or taken as prisoners to foreign lands. Today, innocent people die when greedy people commit criminal acts (e.g., online scams, taking shortcuts to create buildings that collapse and kill those inside, drug and human trafficking). People use weapons to rob or kill innocent people during a crime. Innocent people go to prison for crimes they didn't commit while the guilty remain free. Those in power make selfish decisions to protect their power and wealth, which robs innocent people of the support they need to live decent lives.

Innocent people suffer for other reasons. People are born with disabilities and may suffer their entire lifetime and may require constant care by compassionate adults who had other plans for their lives. People get killed or maimed in car and plane crashes. Millions are born and raised in countries that lack the resources needed to support the population, and poverty affects millions, which leads to high infant mortality and low life expectancy. Innocent people are affected by many types of natural disasters, and terrible diseases strike all kinds of people — nobody seems to be exempt. Jesus said, "God causes the sun to rise on the evil and the good and sends rain on the righteous and unrighteous" (Matt 4:45).

People experiencing these conditions ask, "Why is this happening to me?" and say, "This is unfair." Job asked these questions, and the answer is, in part, that life is unfair. Some lose their faith because they suffer for no good reason. Job's wife tells him to give up, her only spoken words in the story: "Are you still holding on to your faith? Curse God and die!" (Job 2:9).

The question about why innocent people suffer is hard to answer. We rarely know why things happen, and life can be unpredictable when good and evil forces coexist. God's ways are not our ways, God's timing is not our timing. Some say that when bad things happens, it's "God's will," but God doesn't want people to suffer. In a world that has both good and evil, everyone can suffer, and suffering has always been part of a Christian's life. Faithfulness to God and our response to our circumstances, especially during times of trial and when tempted by evil, matter the most. Job stayed faithful, even when he was not healed and his prayers were not answered, and eventually he was vindicated.

Suffering is not always a bad thing. Some people suffer as a consequence of their sin or reckless actions, and they may be held accountable by a justice system. Suffering may also occur be a result of one's voluntary service or sacrifice for others or obedience to God's call on their lives. Jesus suffered on the cross and prophets suffered or were killed for speaking out about wrongs and injustice. They knew their actions put themselves at risk, but doing and saying the right thing was more important, even if they suffered or died. History is full of examples of people who suffer for good causes. Suffering is not something to be avoided at all costs.

GOD CAN USE BAD THINGS FOR GOOD

Sometimes the crises of life and suffering can be used for good purposes. At an individual level, they test and deepen our character, build our stamina and grit, focus our priorities, and help us empathize with others who suffer. As dark shadows provide depth in beautiful paintings and diamonds are created under prolonged pressure and then carefully chiseled and polished by a master jeweler, so too are humans developed and shaped in difficult times. "Consider it pure joy when you face many kinds of trials. They test your faith and produce perseverance, which helps you mature" (Jam 1:2–4). Scar tissue is stronger and more resilient than regular skin, and we need to keep in mind the end result of our actions and sufferings. This gives new meaning to the phrase "the ends justify the means."

God can also use evil deeds to accomplish good things on a grand scale. The story of Joseph is perhaps the best example of how God sees the future and allows things to happen that look bad, but ultimately they are used for good. Joseph was Jacob's favorite son and his 10 older brothers hated him for it (they also hated him for telling Jacob all the bad things they did when they were not home). His brothers staged his death and made money by selling him to foreign traders traveling to Egypt. But through a series of unusual events and his God-given insights, he rose to power and Pharaoh put him in charge of managing all the food in the nation. When a famine affected the region, his brothers went to Egypt to get food, but they didn't know Joseph was there, and they didn't recognize him because they all thought he was dead. Eventually Joseph revealed his true identity, and they were afraid he would seek revenge for selling him as a slave. But Joseph told them:

> Don't be upset with yourselves; it was God who sent me here in order to preserve your life. We have had two years of famine but it will last five more years. God sent me here ahead of you to preserve our family and keep you alive. It wasn't you who sent me here, but God, who made me like a father to Pharaoh and lord of all his household and ruler over all the land of Egypt. (Gen 45:5–8)

Joseph provided food for the family and arranged for all of them to move to Egypt, where they were given the best land for their animals. After Jacob died, the brothers feared Joseph would seek revenge against them and told him they would be his slaves. But Joseph said again, "You wanted to harm me, but God intended to use what you did to save many lives" (Gen 50:20).

The New Testament also says God uses bad things for good purposes. John 9 records a conversation about why a man was born blind. Jesus said the man hadn't done anything wrong. Rather, it was so God's power could be shown. Jesus healed the man on the Sabbath, a scandalous act at the time. Many healings occurred that proved to people that God was real. Jesus was killed, but his sacrifice and resurrection ended up saving everybody. The persecution of the Christians made them flee Jerusalem, which forced them to go into Gentile areas, which spread the gospel. Paul summarized this concept when he wrote, "God causes all things to work together for good for those who love God" (Rom 8:28). For them, death is a comma, not a period, in a life that has no end.

WE GET FAR MORE THAN WE DESERVE

Chapter 10 had a lengthy discussion of grace, an undeserved gift or favor that expresses extravagant and unconditional love. God showed grace in both the Old and New Testaments and constantly gave people benefits and forgiveness they did not deserve. Our normal instinct is to focus on ourselves and seek our own interests; our selfish and sinful nature makes us guilty. But our imperfections are made clean and perfect through the sacrifice of Jesus's blood, and God's grace allows us to avoid justice — we can live forever in paradise rather than die. If we demand justice from God for ourselves, we would all be sentenced to death.

It's worth repeating here that New Testament parables show we get more than we deserve. The extravagant love of a father for his prodigal son ends up in a feast to celebrate the son's return. Workers in the vineyard get the same pay, even though some didn't work very long. Strangers are invited to a great banquet because the inviting guests decided not to come. We should be glad life isn't fair!

HEAVEN

Chapter 9 discussed hell, and this chapter ends with a short description of "heaven," the final reward for those who have faith and have followed Jesus. It's another example of people getting more than they deserve.

Several ancient religions talked about heaven having seven levels, but the Bible talks about only three types of heaven. The first is what we call the sky, the atmosphere around the earth. In the Old Testament, we read about the "birds of the heavens" and the "rain from heaven" (Gen 1:26, 8:2; Deut 11:17, 18:12). The Israelites received manna and meat from heaven (Exod 16:4,8; John 6:31), and Jesus will come back on the "clouds of heaven" (Matt 26:64).

The second type of heaven mentioned in the Bible is the physical universe we see when we look into the night sky — the stars and planets in the distance. God created the heavens and the earth, and the "waters under the heavens" gathered together (Gen 1:1,9). Abraham's descendants were to be like the "the stars of heaven" (Gen 22:17), and the Israelites were told not to "serve or worship other gods, or the sun or the moon or anything in the heavens" (Deut 17:3).

The third kind of heaven is what we normally think of when we talk about going to heaven — it's where Jesus and God are. While God is everywhere, the Old Testament says God is in heaven (Deut 26:15, 1Ki 8:30, 2Chr 7:14, Psa 103:19). The New Testament says we are to "give glory to God, who is in heaven" (Matt 5:16). Paul talks about a person (probably himself) who went to "the third heaven" and called it "paradise" (2Cor 12:2–3). Jesus told the thief who wanted to be remembered that he would be with him in paradise (Luke 23:43). This is where Jesus sits on a heavenly throne and where we want to go after we die. (The term "third heaven" appears only once in the Bible.)

John was given a vision in which he saw heaven, and he described it in great detail. Once all the evil in the world is destroyed, the "first heaven" will pass away and "the holy city of Jerusalem will come down from heaven and be restored on earth." A voice will come from the king on the throne:

> Look! God's dwelling place (heaven) is now among the people. God will dwell with them and they will be God's people. There will be no more tears in their eyes and no more death or crying or pain — the

old order of things has passed away and I have made everything new! It is done. To the thirsty I will give water without cost from the spring of the water of life. These victors will inherit all this. I will be their God, and they will be my children. (Rev 21:1–6)

This will be no ordinary city in its size or construction. The city will be massive — if taken literally, it's described to be the size of a large country (its area would make it the seventh largest country in the world). The city will be made of pure gold, its 12 gates will be made of pearls, and its walls will be more than 200 feet high. There is no Temple in the city because God and the Lamb are the Temple. There is no sun or moon because the glory of God provides the light; there is no darkness or night. Nothing impure ever enters the city. Those whose names are in the book of life will live as the bride of God forever. Just as in the book of Job, the pain and suffering of God's people are eventually rewarded — perseverance of the faithful results in a happy ending. The epic spiritual battles that have been waged will be over — there is total victory, and evil is annihilated forever. This vision of a glorious afterlife helped people endure great hardship and let them know that justice will eventually prevail.

So it appears heaven is a real place, not just a spiritual or symbolic state of mind. God can't be limited to any geographical place: King Solomon said while praying to the Lord, "Heaven and the heaven of heavens cannot contain You" (1Ki 8:27). Yet when Stephen was being killed, he knew he was going to a specific place and that he would be in the presence of the Lord; he was allowed to see it as he was being killed (Acts 7:55–56). We don't know where this heaven will be, but it appears to be a new place, not somewhere on this earth — there will be a new earth (Isa 65:17, 66:22; Luke 21:33; 2Pet 3:10–13; Rev 20:11, 21:1). In the meantime, Jesus said the Kingdom of God (the same thing as the Kingdom of Heaven) is already here on earth, although not in its complete form (Matt 6:10, 13:24–52; Mark 4:30–34; Luke 8:1, 18:29–30).

Levels of Heaven

Nothing in the Bible describes different levels of rewards within this "third" heaven, although some verses make an indirect reference to the idea that heaven might not be the same for everybody. While our salvation doesn't depend on our actions, there appears to be different rewards and crowns. God promises the "crown of life" to those who are faithful despite going through trials and tribulations (Jam 1:12; Rev 2:10). God promises a "crown of glory" to those who are faithful leaders of the church (1Pet 5:2–4), and Paul talks of the "crown" of righteousness, which the Lord will give to those who "longed for Jesus's appearing" (2Tim 4:8).

Other verses mention rewards. Jesus said, "Blessed are you when people insult you, persecute you and falsely say all kinds of evil against you because of me. Rejoice and be glad because your reward in heaven is great, for the prophets were persecuted the same way" (Matt 5:11–12). Jesus will "repay each person according to what he has done" when he returns (Matt 16:27). In the parable of the talents, Jesus differentiated among those who followed him: some received many talents while others received relatively few. He told those who used what was given to them wisely, "Well done, faithful servant. You have been faithful with the little you received, so I will put you in charge of much more" (Matt 25:14–29). We are expected to use what we have effectively, but we receive different things. So what we do in life matters to God: "Those who have been given much, much will be demanded" (Luke 12:48).

It seems fair that God would reward some people more than others based on what they did in their life. Will the thief who died next to Jesus get the same reward as Moses, Peter, Paul, and the many other pillars of the faith? Will every part of paradise be accessible to everybody who is there? We don't know the answers to these questions, but what we do know is that it's better to be there than in any alternative. We are glad that God gives us mercy and grace, but it's human nature for us to want our enemies to get justice, what they deserve — we want life to be fair to them, even when we get more than we deserve. We don't want life to be fair.

When Do We Go to Heaven?

Most people think we go to heaven when we die, but a careful reading of the Bible shows this isn't the case. In fact, no scripture says we will go to heaven when we die. Instead, everybody who dies enters an interim sleep-like state before moving later into a permanent status.

Many verses talk about death as if it's the beginning of a temporary sleep-like status (Job 3:11,13; 14:12; Psa 13:3; Dan 12:2; John 11:11,13; Acts 13:36; 1Cor 11:30; 15:18,20,51; 1Th 4:13,14; 5:10). Death, like sleep, is temporary. Peter said David was still in his tomb and had not gone to heaven (Acts 2:29,34). Paul said the dead will be raised when Jesus returns again, with "the dead in Christ" being the first to rise when God's trumpet sounds (1Th 4:15–16, 1Cor 15:51–52). If people rise from the grave, they haven't gone to heaven yet. Jesus is the only one who has gone to heaven, the first to be raised among those who are "asleep" (John 3:13, 1Cor 15:20).

So when we die, our souls wait until Jesus returns, when people will be raised on the "last day" (John 6:39–40) and then go to their final destination: "The hour is coming when all who are in the grave will hear His voice and come forth — those who have done good will be resurrected to life, and those who have done evil will be resurrected to condemnation" (John 5:28–29). The time will come suddenly, like the "twinkling of an eye" as if we are waking up instantly from a deep sleep (1Cor 15:52). Our natural body will be raised in a spiritual body, our mortal bodies become immortal. Death is conquered and has no sting (1Cor 15:42,44,54–55; Hos 13:14). According to Revelation 20:4, those who have been martyred for the faith will go to heaven first. But we don't know when this will happen (see chapter 16 for more details on this subject).

In the meantime, our souls exist after death without a physical body. We don't know what this is like, but people who have had a "near death experience" (NDE) give us some insights. It begins when a person's body stops working and they calmly rise out of their body without experiencing any pain. They float up and look down on themselves and others. They may travel through a long tunnel toward a bright light, and they may recall events in their life. Some sense love and peace on this journey. Those with NDEs return to their body and "reboot" instead of dying. Their experience is like a slow dream, and although the brain may not be working, the person still has self-awareness with a spirit or "soul" that continues after we die. Paul said he knew a man who had an out-of-body experience (2Cor 12:2–4). People from different religions and cultures around the world have had similar experiences.[29]

We don't know anything about this self-awareness for those who have not come back to life. We don't know how long we will have any awareness. It's possible we will have consciousness as we wait for Jesus to return: Matthew 27:52–53 says some dead saints came out of their tombs when Jesus died and after the resurrection, which indicates some consciousness may exist after we die. But there is no biblical support for the idea that people can look down on us from heaven after they die. Our souls continue to exist, with or without any self-awareness. Death might be like sleep when we can recall our dreams and often we remember nothing.

Yet the idea that people go to heaven after they die brings comfort to those who are still on earth. Our souls may exist and be active in some way, and the idea of speaking to those we love, who look down on us after they die, is a common one that brings solace in times of reflection. There is no need to correct a person's beliefs who may not have the right theological understanding of the afterlife if it helps them cope with their circumstances.

* * * * * * *

We need to accept that life isn't fair. When we do, we are less likely to become bitter when bad things happen to us and won't blame God for our problems. We will also be more likely to focus our efforts on making sure life is fair for others (justice) and providing mercy to those who suffer as a result of life's unfair nature. When life isn't fair, the prospect of living forever and being without pain when we die can comfort us and those left behind after we die.

---

[29] The serious study of NDEs began when Dr. Raymond Moody, a Christian psychiatrist, published *Life After Life* (1975, MBB Inc). Some of the cases in the book are accounts by people who had been declared dead. Out-of-body experiences (OBE) are similar to NDEs. People have had these experiences for thousands of years — according to Plato, Socrates had one.

CHAPTER 13

BEING SAVED (DELIVERED)

The Bible records a number of examples of how God makes promises to people and saves them. The first example was in the Garden of Eden when God forgave the sin of Adam and Eve and allowed them to live and multiply. God later saved Noah and his family from the great flood and promised never to destroy the human race again. Then in a series of agreements, God selected a family and their descendants to be a nation that sets an example for others to see how people should live on earth. In Genesis 17, God made a covenant with Abraham: his descendants would be very fruitful and rule the region as long as his descendants trusted and obeyed God. Abraham proved his faith in God when he was willing to obey the command to kill Isaac, his only son. God said, "Because you have not withheld your son, I will bless you and multiply your descendants to be like the stars in the sky and the sand on the seashore. Because you obeyed me, all nations of the earth will be blessed through your descendants" (Gen 22:16–18).

God continued to protect and bless this nation, the Israelites, even when they often ignored God's commands. But eventually, their continued disobedience and lack of interest in the relationship resulted in the Israelites losing their favored status, and God's protection was removed. Only a small percentage of Jews remained faithful to God, a remnant that continued the covenant between God and the nation of Israel.

Later, God saved all people from their sins, which allows everybody the opportunity to appear blameless before God. A new "nation" of God became a worldwide movement of people (the church) who are to be an example of God's love for others and share good news about the God who has saved everybody from their sins. This chapter looks at what the Bible says about the concept of "being saved."

THE MEANING OF THE TERM "SAVED"

The term "saved" is used in different ways in the Bible. In most cases, the term means "delivered" or "rescued" from some type of danger or crisis. The Israelites were saved from their enemies, from sickness, from slavery, and from death. The disciples were saved from drowning in a storm, and Christians can be saved from an empty and meaningless life. The Psalmists asked God to save them from evil, enemies, and physical dangers. For example, David appeals to God's love and mercy as he pleads for deliverance in Psalm 69:13–14:

> I pray to you, O Lord, at an acceptable time;
> In your great love, O God, answer me with your true salvation.
> Rescue me from the mire, don't let me sink;
> Deliver me from my enemies, and from deep waters.

In the New Testament, the words saved, salvation, and savior are nearly always used as synonyms of "deliverance." The term "saved" doesn't relate to receiving eternal life or going to heaven when we die, although these things happen when we are delivered from sin. Going to heaven involves several steps, including being delivered from sin, maturing in one's faith, and becoming a disciple. These steps involve many things: confession and repentance, believing and trusting Jesus (faith), and acting on these beliefs in accordance with what God wants us to do.

The word "saved" is used in connection to receiving salvation in several places in the New Testament.

- When Paul and Silas were imprisoned in Philippi, an earthquake shook the prison and freed them. But they didn't escape and they told the prison guard not to kill himself. The guard asked the two men, "What must I do to be saved?" They told him, "Believe in the Lord Jesus and you and your household will be saved" (Acts 16:30–31).

- Paul wrote to the Romans to say that faith brings salvation: "If you say that Jesus is Lord and believe in your heart that God raised him from the dead, you will be saved; your belief comes from the heart, which leads to holiness, and your mouth says what is in your heart, which leads to salvation" (Rom 10:9–10).

- Before Paul explained the importance of the death and resurrection of Jesus to the church in Corinth, he prefaced his comments this way: "This is the gospel I preached to you and you received, that enabled you to be saved" (1Cor 15:1–2).

- Paul explained the basic nature of the gospel to believers in Ephesus: "Our sinful human nature makes us deserve death, but because of God's great mercy and love for us, God made us alive with Christ. We were all dead in our sins, but God's grace has saved us... You have been saved by God's grace because of your faith" (Eph 2:3–5,8).

So "being saved" is something that happens because of God's grace and a person's faith and belief in God. (It's unclear how the faith of the prison guard also saved his family.) But as we will see later in this chapter, more is required than saying you believe something.

Christians sometimes use the questions "are you saved" or "have you been saved" or "have you asked Jesus into your heart" when they want to know about a person's spiritual status. These phrases are forms of Christian jargon and are confusing to those who don't know the meaning of the terms. It's better to ask different questions using terms people will understand. One of the main impediments to evangelism is the use of Christian terms that non-believers don't understand. Using terms people don't understand is not a good communication practice. (Chapter 14 provides more information about evangelism.)

How Are People Saved?

Both the Old and New Testaments say God is the one who saves people physically and emotionally from danger and from their invisible spiritual "disease" of sin. God chose Abraham and his descendants (the Israelites) to be part of an agreement: God would protect and save them from harm, and they would honor God and be a model for others to see how God interacts with humans. It was a *quid pro quo* — each party had a responsibility. God said, "*If* my people, those called by my name, humble themselves and pray, and seek me and turn away from their sinful practices, *then* I will hear them from heaven, and I will forgive their sin and heal their land" (2Chr 7:14).

But most of the time, the Israelites ignored their part of the agreement, even though they were often reminded about their duty to honor God, and even though God continued to love them despite their rebellious spirit and disobedience. But eventually, there were consequences for continued disobedience, and God's protection was removed — one party left the relationship, which ended in divorce. As a result, the nation of Israel was defeated and most of the Jews were taken prisoners to distant lands. A small number of Jews remained faithful and some of them returned to rebuild Jerusalem, which had been destroyed.

This cycle of events showed that people could not live up to what God required. The periodic sacrifices people made removed their sins temporarily, but sacrifices had to be made continually for people to be reconciled to God.

So the next step in the process was for God to become a human being, a living example to show us how God wanted us to live. Jesus, God in human form, came to earth to both show people the right way to live and to be the final and perfect sacrifice so other sacrifices are no longer needed. God also became accessible to all people, not just the Jews. In addition, the Holy Spirit helps people live the right way and is a direct link to and from God. In all these actions, God made salvation possible for all of humanity.

In order to be connected with God and enjoy the benefits of the relationship, people just need to decide whether or not they want to have that relationship. It's free — there's nothing we can do to earn it, and we certainly don't deserve it (that's the point about grace, it's God's gift to us). However, it does require a humble commitment to Jesus and a dedication to following his teachings.

This was the main point made by Jesus when he spoke to the Pharisee Nicodemus about the need to be "born again" (John 3:3). Nicodemus was confused because he took the statement literally, so Jesus clarified what he meant: a person needs to be born in the Spirit, that is, have a new beginning that puts God in control of our life.

Their conversation led to a concise statement by Jesus about why he came to earth. Starting with an Old Testament story (Num 4:9) that Nicodemus would understand, Jesus said:

Just as Moses lifted up the snake in the wilderness, so the Son of Man must be lifted up so that everyone who believes may have eternal life. For God loved the world so much that God sent the Son into the world so that whoever believes in him will not die but will live forever. God didn't send him into the world to condemn the world but to save it. Those who *believe* and *follow him* are not condemned; those who don't will stand condemned. (John 3:14–18, emphasis added)

Nicodemus was earnestly seeking the truth and was sincerely asking Jesus about what it takes to enter the kingdom of God, and he eventually became a believer (he later helped prepare Jesus's body for burial). Being born again requires repentance (*metanoia* in Greek, meaning "to turn around" or "a change in heart" or "re-formation"). If we are sincere about our new beliefs, it will be reflected in a changed lifestyle: "If anyone is in Christ, they become a new creature; the old ways are left behind and new things have taken over" (2Cor 5:17). Those who undergo a transformation will bear the fruits of the Spirit — a plant is known by the fruits it bears (Matt 7:15–20, Luke 3:8–9, Rom 7:4, Gal 5:22–23).

Zacchaeus is an example of a person who encountered Jesus and changed his life. He was a rich Jew and a hated tax collector who volunteered to give away much of his wealth and said he would return money he had gained from others through dishonest means. Jesus told him, "Today salvation has come to this Jewish house" (Luke 19:2–9).

CAN PEOPLE LOSE THEIR "DELIVERED" STATUS?

Historically, there are two views about whether a person can lose their salvation. One view says **no**, a person who decides to trust and follow Jesus can never lose their status of being saved from sin's curse. This view is called "eternal security" or "predestination" and was best explained by John Calvin, a French theologian who wrote a book about it during the Protestant reformation (*Concerning the Eternal Predestination of God*, 1552).

The other view is **yes**, those who decide to trust and follow Jesus can change their mind or drift away from following Jesus and lose the benefits of being delivered from sin's curse, which includes going to heaven. This view is called "free will" and was best explained by John

Wesley, an English priest and evangelist who led a revival movement within the Church of England starting in the 1730s. This perspective had its roots in the theology of a Dutch theologian, Jacobus Arminius, who reacted to Calvin's idea of predestination in the early 1600s.

Different denominations have developed based on these two perspectives. This section summarizes these two views, both of which depend on biblical teachings, and discusses a third perspective, which is also supported by scripture.

Eternal Security

Some people believe that if a person is a genuine Christian, they can never lose their salvation. Several verses support the idea that God chooses (predestined) people to be believers. How could they eventually lose their salvation if God predestined them to be part of God's family? The explanation about a person who rejects the faith after first accepting it is that the person either (1) was never a Christian in the first place (they were not chosen), or (2) has temporarily lost their faith and will eventually return to it, or (3) will not gain the benefits of the Christian life while on earth, but they will still go to heaven because God loves them. Some New Testament verses support this view (Matt 22:14; John 6:44, 10:28; 15:16,19; Acts 13:48; Rom 8:29; Eph 1:4–5,11; 1Joh 2:19). In these verses, there are no conditions attached, so eternal security is guaranteed. The concept is based on the idea that God knows what will happen in the future.

A logical objection to this perspective is that if a loving God could do that for one person, why isn't it done for everybody? And if God predetermined salvation for somebody, why would God punish them for rejecting the gospel — they had no choice about the matter! And just because no condition is clearly stated doesn't mean salvation is unconditional — God makes promises with and without mentioning conditions.

Free Will

Some say believers are responsible for the decisions they make, and as a result, may choose to stop following Jesus and even reject his instructions. If people are free to choose to follow Jesus, they can logically be free to reject that way of life. Many verses support this view (Eze 18:24; Luke 8:6,7,13; John 15; Acts 5:1–11; Rom 11:22; Heb 6:4–6, 10:26–29; 1Tim 1:18–20, Rev 3:5). People are excommunicated from the church because they don't follow the teachings of Christ or bear any fruits of the Spirit. In addition, several verses imply that it's possible for us to decide to walk away from God because of how difficult it can be to follow Jesus in this world (Heb 3:6,14, 4:14; Rom 11:22; Col 1:23; Acts 13:43, 14:22).

Events in the Old Testament support this view. The Israelites were God's chosen people, but they lost God's blessing and were punished for their lack of faith and disobedience. (It's unclear if God treats groups and individuals the same or differently.) Moses warned them many times about the consequences of not being faithful and gave the people this message from God:

> If you become corrupt and do evil in the eyes of the Lord, God will be angry, and you will quickly perish from the land. I give you this choice, life and happiness or death and adversity, a blessing and a curse. You will be cursed if you don't listen to my commandments and you turn away from me to follow other gods — you will perish. So choose life. (Deut 4:25–26, 30:15–19)

In this "free will" view of salvation, the Bible never portrays God as controlling the free will of individuals. So a person can decide to get a divorce from God. It would be inconsistent to suggest that someone can willingly follow Jesus but not willingly leave the relationship.

Some people believe that the ideas of both predestination and free will can coexist. The explanation for how they come to hold both views at the same time is very complicated.

A Third View: Faith Requires Action

There is also biblical support for the view that a person who *does have faith* may not go to heaven. This is not due to a conscious decision to reject Christ, but rather because of a lack of action that reflects true faith. Jesus told Nicodemus, "Those who *believe* and *follow* the Son are not condemned; those who don't will stand condemned" (John 3:18, emphasis added). Action must accompany beliefs.

Several other times Jesus implies that action is necessary to enter the kingdom of God. The greatest in the kingdom are those that *do* and teach the commandments (Matt 5:19). "Every tree that doesn't bear good fruit is cut down and thrown into the fire. Not everyone who says to Me, 'Lord, Lord,' will enter the kingdom of heaven; those who *do* the will of the Father in heaven will enter" (Matt 7:19–21). The family of God is made up of those who *do* God's will (Mark 3:35). After telling the story of the Good Samaritan, Jesus tells us to go and *do* likewise (Luke 10:37).

Three long passages also support this view. First, James 2:14–26 says that faith is not enough — correct action is a sign of true faith and obedience. A person's faith and actions work together, and James attacks those who see a difference between people who claim to have faith and those who do good deeds. "A person is considered righteous by what they do and not by faith alone. A person's faith is dead if it is not also accompanied by action" (Jam 2:17,26). The actions of Abraham and Rahab show the importance of actions, or "works."

The second passage is the parable of the sheep and goats, the only parable about who goes to heaven. Found in Matthew 25:31–46, Jesus distinguishes between those who acted and those who didn't act when they saw somebody with physical needs. The parable is like the story of the Good Samaritan — we are to love God and our neighbor as ourselves, and a good neighbor helps others. The goats in the parable represent faithful people who didn't act when seeing those in need. They are totally shocked to find out they were going to hell.

The third passage is the first very long parable told by Jesus in three gospels, the parable about seeds and soils related to the kingdom of heaven. He discussed what happened to four kinds of seeds scattered by a farmer among different types of soils, and then explained its meaning to his disciples (Matt 13, Mark 4, Luke 8). Here is a summary.

> Some seeds fell on the path where they were walked on and eaten by birds. Some fell on rocky ground, and when they sprouted, the plants withered because they lacked moisture. Other seeds fell among thorns, which grew up and choked the plants. Other seeds fell on good soil that grew up and produced a huge crop, a hundred times more than what was sown.

The seeds are the words of God. The seeds on the path are those who hear, but the devil takes away the word from their hearts, so that they don't believe anymore and are not saved. The seeds on the rocky ground are those who receive the word with joy, but they have no roots. They believe for a while, but when things get hard, they fall away. The seeds that fall among the thorns are those who hear, but as they live their lives, they are choked by life's worries, riches, and pleasures — they don't mature in their faith. But the seeds on good soil are those with good hearts, who hear the word, retain it, and produce a good crop because of their perseverance.

In this parable, the phrase, "they don't believe anymore and are not saved," applied to the first soil, supports the idea that a person may not go to heaven if they stop believing. The seeds in the second type of soil don't grow because there are no roots and the plants wither when life becomes too hard. Both types of soil relate to the "free will" perspective. The third soil, where seeds fall among the thorns, relates to this third view. This soil represents those who are preoccupied with worldly concerns and don't have a mature faith. One can infer that these people are not *doing* the will of God, even though they say they have faith. The inference of the parable is that the first three types of people won't enter the kingdom of heaven — it's only the last type of people, those who persevere during hard times and produce fruit, who enter the kingdom.

The parable of the builders also emphasizes the need for action.

Why do you call me, 'Lord, Lord,' but don't *do* what I say? All those who come to me and hear my words and *act* on them are like those who build a house with a foundation on a rock. When there was a flood, the river rose against their house but it was not shaken because it was well built. But those who hear and *do not act* accordingly are like those who build a house on the ground without a foundation. (Luke 6:46–49)

Lastly, Jesus told the religious leaders a story about a father who has two sons and tells them to work in his vineyard. The first son says he won't go but changes his mind and works. The second son says he will go and work but *doesn't* go. Jesus asked the leaders which son obeyed their father, and they correctly answer that it was the son who did what was asked. He then condemns them for not changing their ways (Matt 21:28–32).

Jewish Leaders Believed But Were Not Saved

The Jewish religious leaders fall into this third view. They were quite convinced that their correct beliefs and strict adherence to religious laws and their rules would justify them before God. However, the prophets and Jesus were very clear that their actions fell short of what God required.

Jesus quoted Isaiah's prediction that the Jewish leaders would be hypocrites when he wrote, "You honor me with your lips but your hearts are far from me. You worship me in vain, your teachings are just human rules" (Isa 29:13, Matt 15:7–9). John the Baptist scolded the leaders before Jesus started preaching, and Jesus warned the people about following false prophets.

> You brood of vipers! Produce fruit that reflects repentance. Don't say to yourselves, 'We have Abraham as our father.' God could raise children of Abraham from these stones! The ax is ready to cut the roots of the tree — every tree that doesn't produce good fruit will be cut down and thrown into the fire. (Luke 3:7–9)

> Watch out for false leaders who look like peaceful sheep, but inwardly they are like wolves. You will know them by their fruit. Do people pick grapes or figs from plants with thorns? Every good tree bears good fruit, but a bad tree bears bad fruit. Every tree that doesn't bear good fruit is cut down and thrown in the fire. So not everyone who calls me "Lord" will enter the kingdom of heaven, but only those who *do* the will of my God in heaven. Many will say to me on that day, "Lord, didn't we teach in your name and drive out demons and perform many miracles?" I'll tell them, "I never knew you. Get away from me, you evildoers!" (Matt 7:15–23)

Devout Jews didn't eat until they washed their hands in a certain way, and they observed many other traditions related to cleanliness. Some Pharisees and scribes saw some of the disciples eating food without washing their hands, and they asked Jesus why they didn't follow the tradition of the elders but ate their food with dirty hands. Jesus replied:

> You have let go of the commands of God and are holding on to human traditions. You've become good at putting aside God's commands in order to observe your own traditions! Eating with unclean hands doesn't defile anybody. Nothing outside a person defiles them. It's what comes out of a person's heart that defiles them. You Pharisees are hypocrites who clean the outside of the cup and dish, but inside you are full of greed and wickedness. A sign that you are clean inside is that you are generous to the poor. (Mark 7:8–9,14–15; Matt 15:20, 23:25; Luke 11:39,41)

Finally, the parable of the wedding feast provides another perspective about how the Jews had lost God's blessing. The parable talks about a king who invited many guests to a party, but none of them came — they were too busy doing other things. So the king invited many strangers to come, and they came (Matt 22:1–10; a similar story is found in Luke 14:16–24). The parable is about how the Jews were the chosen people but decided not to join the feast (follow Jesus), and they were destroyed because they were not worthy. Jesus said the kingdom of God would be taken from them and given to those who will produce fruit.

This third perspective is like the "free will" view in that some Christians may not be saved from sin's final curse. Those who say they have faith but have not acted with love for those in need may not have had faith after all, for if they had true faith, they would have followed God's commands. This is what Calvin would say if he found out these people were not going to heaven. Christians are known by their loving actions, not by having the right beliefs or a sound theology.

There seems to be more evidence in the scriptures that a person who says they have a faith may not really have faith or their faith can be neglected, misdirected, or not taken seriously. For all these reasons, it appears that Calvin's view of "eternal security" is based on a much narrower set of scriptures compared to other perspectives about whether a person can lose their salvation.

Ultimately, God decides whether a person is delivered from sin. A person's faith is expressed by their actions and their fruit. We don't really know if a person is a Christian, so we shouldn't dwell on whether or not they are. God knows and decides. It's tempting to spend time trying to solve theological questions like this, but it's mostly a distraction from more important things. What we should focus on is knowing and then following the commands of Jesus, which is often hard to do.

The Bible says it's not our job to earn or live right to earn our salvation. We will often fail and will always fall short of perfection, but we can have full confidence that God forgives us: "Our sins will be white as snow" (Isa 1:18, Psa 51:7). The blood of Jesus's sacrifice allows us to stand blameless before God when we act on his teachings.

CHAPTER 14

LIVING IN THE WORLD

As Christ's ambassadors and citizens of heaven, we represent God in the world with our words and actions. God created the world and loves it, but evil also exists in the world. Jesus said his disciples were not "of" this world and asked God to protect them while they were "in" it: "My prayer is not that you remove them from the world but that you protect them from the evil one. They are not of the world, even as I am not of it" (John 17:15–16). He was referring to human institutions and cultures in an earthly kingdom controlled by the devil, the prince of this world (John 12:31). Paul later said the same thing (Col 1:13, Eph 2:2). The challenge is how to live a Christian life when we are surrounded by evil influences.

LIVING IN AN EVIL WORLD

The existence of evil is first noted when a "serpent" entices Eve to eat from the tree of the knowledge of good and evil (Gen 2:17, 3:1–5,11–13). As a result, God put a curse on the serpent, Adam, and Eve (Gen 3:17–23). This serpent was the angel Satan (the devil, Lucifer, Beelzebul) who rebelled and was expelled from heaven (Luke 10:18).

Satan is described in different ways in the Bible. As an evil angel, he has no physical form, but he uses people to influence others to do what is wrong. He is intelligent and can be good looking, and he can deceive us because he poses as an "angel of light" but perverts the truth. Thus, he is like a wolf in sheep's clothing, the "father of lies" and the "evil one" (2Cor 11:14, John 8:44, Matt 13:19). He is arrogant but insecure because he knows his power is limited; he is controlled by God's power and will be defeated forever in a final battle described in Revelation (see chapter 16). He knows scripture but uses it out of context to manipulate others (Matt 4:1–10). He doesn't live in hell but is alive and the "god of this world;" as an active extrovert, he walks around like a roaring lion, looking for somebody to devour. He has power and uses miracles to show it, and he rules over the evil forces of darkness on earth and in the heavens. So, we are to put on all of God's armor to stand against him (2Cor 4:4, 1Pet 5:8, Exod 7:11, 2Th 2:9, Eph 6:11–17).

Satan would be classified as having an antisocial personality and is similar to narcissists and psychopaths. He is selfish and self-centered, cruel, sadistic, deceitful, corrupt, greedy, perverted, angry, impatient, manipulative, controlling, immoral, unforgiving, immature, socially cold and lacking compassion for others, unjust, profane, hostile, biased, foolish, vengeful, proud, power-hungry, conniving, insulting, dishonorable, untrustworthy, jealous, horrific, inhumane, lustful, vain, unloving, shrewd and subtle, filled with hate and loving death, sowing doubt about what is good and right, a creator of fear, and an opponent of truth. When his demise draws near, he will become more and more desperate, as described in Revelation. While some people may become *possessed* by one or more demons, many more are *influenced* by evil powers (sometimes unknowingly) and have these characteristics to some extent. The opposite of these characteristics describe a good God; just as we know Christians by their fruits, we know evil by its fruits.

Christians are often at odds with the evil world and are tempted to compromise and conform to the surrounding culture. Jesus said his disciples would be hated because they don't follow the ways of the world (John 15:18–19). A subtle strategy used by evil forces to compromise our message is to slowly influence Christians to conform to the values of the non-Christian world. The world's criteria for success include being wealthy, healthy, and living comfortably; happiness is pursued through sex and drugs; we strive for acceptance and love by making ourselves look good. Paul warned Christians about this and said we need to be different: "Don't conform to the ways of this world, but be transformed by the renewing of your mind" (Rom 12:2).[30]

Evil forces use other methods to undermine believers and their institutions. One evil strategy is to minimize and undermine the influence and messages of the church. This spiritual warfare tactic

---

[30] The religion practiced by the people in Canaan was clearly demonic, so they had to be killed before the Israelites could settle permanently in the region. Nevertheless, many Israelites adopted practices of the local culture after they settled in Canaan, despite being warned not to do so (*syncretism* is the practice of blending different religions or philosophies).

includes creating divisions and distractions, sowing doubts and discord, making small things important while more important things are ignored, and getting Christians bogged down in religious discussions instead of acting with love.

Evil forces don't just attack Christians and the church. They infiltrate many aspects of life and try to minimize and disrupt the forces of good in individuals, in human institutions, and in society's economic, social, and political systems. In both biblical times and now, oppression and injustice reflect evil influences. Paul said, "Our struggle is not against flesh and blood, but against the rulers, against the authorities, against the powers of darkness in this world and against the spiritual forces of evil" (Eph 6:12). Satan poses as "an angel of light" but perverts the truth and ultimately is revealed as a wolf in sheep's clothing.

Lifestyle Options

So how are we to live in an evil world? The answer is that individually and collectively, Christians are to model God's love, generosity, and forgiveness in this world. The church is to reflect a different value system and be the salt of the earth, preserving what is good and making everything more flavorful. Christians are to be lights that shine in darkness, areas of warm water in a cold pool. The church is God's "exhibit A" in the world's court about how people should live on earth — it is to promote love and peace in a chaotic, evil, and violent world.

But Christians can choose to live in this world in different ways. People have used three basic approaches to be models of the kingdom, and the models can be used at different times during our lives. First, some choose to completely separate themselves from the world and associate only with others who are like them. The *Essenes* were a small group of mystics that focused on self-control and withdrew from the world more than 2,000 years ago. They retreated to remote parts of Palestine, mainly into the desert west of the Dead Sea, where they copied the scriptures (the Dead Sea scrolls). John the Baptist lived in the wilderness until he emerged to announce the coming of the Messiah. Throughout history, highly religious people have retreated into the seclusion of monasteries, and others have settled into communes or small communities or lived by themselves in remote areas in order to avoid the world.

A second approach is living *in* the world but not really being part *of* the world. Those taking this approach have little interaction with others who don't share their beliefs. This was the view Jews had — they didn't mix with Gentiles. The Pharisees went even farther and separated themselves from Jews who were "sinners." Sometimes those who take this approach wear special clothes to distinguish themselves as being separate. Many Christians take this approach because we are not to "love the world or the things in it; God's love is not in those who love the world" (1Joh 2:15). The Psalms and Proverbs are full of verses warning us against keeping evil company, and some New Testament letters warn against being with evildoers (1Cor 15:33; 2Cor 6:14–17; 2Tim 3:5; Jam 1:27, 4:4). Those taking this approach have a circle of friends who live the same way, but they may not know their neighbors. It's easier to keep the faith when we live among those with whom we agree and share similar experiences and interests.

The unspoken strategy in this approach is that others will somehow be attracted to Christians who live this way. The flaw in this strategy is that if Christians don't know others who don't share their beliefs and values, others won't know the attractiveness of Christian perspectives. Christians taking this approach will also lack the relationships needed to connect with others. One cannot love your neighbor if you don't know them.

Those who decide to live this way may do so because they either 1) have little interest in sharing their faith with others, or 2) lack confidence in their ability to share their faith, or 3) don't want to be involved in the world, perhaps out of fear. Perhaps some live this way for all three reasons. Those taking this approach tend to focus on worshiping God and being thankful that Jesus died for them, but they neglect taking the next step and acting on why Jesus saved them. They joined the team but don't plan to play a game — they can be "so heavenly minded that they are of little earthly good."

Jesus had a perspective on this approach. He said in his Sermon on the Mount:

You have heard it said, "Love your neighbor and hate your enemy." But I say, love your enemies and pray for those who persecute you. If you just love those who love you, what reward will you get? The tax collectors are doing that! If you only greet your own people, are you doing any more than others do? The pagans do that! (Matt 5:43–47)

A third way to live in the world is to mix with all types of people, regardless of their background or lifestyle. Paul told those in Corinth, the port city with a nasty reputation: "I previously said not to associate with immoral people, but I didn't mean the immoral people of this world… for then you would have to leave the world" (1Cor 5:9–10). Jesus loved the world and interacted with all kinds of "sinners," giving him a bad reputation among the religious leaders. Jesus criticized the religious leaders because they were arrogant, hypocritical, judgmental, and followed rules but missed the point of their purpose in life. He told them to "take the log out of your own eye so you can see clearly and remove the speck of dust from another person's eye" and made a similar point when he compared a gnat to a camel ((Matt 7:1–5, Matt 23:24).

The advantage of this third approach is that we get to know "sinners" who can see our lives and values. Knowing non-believers puts us in a better position to know and love them. The danger is that we may gradually compromise our values and adopt the ideas and actions of those around us. This is why we need to stay in fellowship with others in the church, to spend time studying the scriptures in depth, and to be quietly reflective on a regular basis. These habits help us know and remember the Christ-like values we should embrace while we live in the world.

No matter how we decide to live in the world, the overriding principles that should guide a Christian's life relate to the main themes of the Bible: loving God and others, showing mercy and generosity to others, and promoting justice. When doing so, we become credible witnesses of Christ. Dietrich Bonhoeffer, a German pastor who was executed by the Nazis in 1945 because of his involvement in a plot to kill Hitler, said, "Your life as a Christian should make non-believers question their disbelief in God."

EVANGELISM AND DISCIPLESHIP

Since the world is full of evil, Jesus told his followers to tell others about him and help strengthen their faith. He said "make disciples of all the nations," teaching them to follow his commands, and being a witness in the world (Matt 28:19–20, Acts 1:8). Disciples are "learners" (*discipulus* in Latin) and *evangelism* is the process of sharing the gospel with others (*evangelium* in Latin, meaning "bringing good news").[31] The process of evangelism is being a witness with good news. My father, an evangelist, defined the process as "one beggar telling another beggar where to find bread." The term "witness" is a noun, not a verb — a person is a witness, somebody who testifies about the truth and what they experienced. One does not "witness" to others.

Elements of Effective Evangelism

The first step in the evangelism process is being an effective witness. Effective witnesses require good communication, which is about what is *heard*, not what is said. For a message to be heard, a message must come from a credible source.

The examples of Jesus and Paul, coupled with what we know from the fields of psychology and communications, reveal these six characteristics of effective evangelism.

1. A credible witness has *good character*. Ralph Waldo Emerson said, "Who you are speaks so loudly that I can't hear what you are saying." Our actions and attitudes speak louder than our words, so we need to have the attributes of honesty, integrity, genuineness, trustworthiness, concern, love, humility, and authenticity to be heard. Good character includes having "the fruit of the Spirit" (Gal 5:22–23). Without these characteristics and a good reputation, others won't listen to us. Being judgmental and self-righteous

---

[31] Evangelism is different from defending and promoting the faith (a discipline called *apologetics*). It's also different from *proselytizing* (*prosēlytos* in Greek, meaning "stranger" or "newcomer") that advocates for a particular position and tries to change a person's mind and have them believe what we want them to believe. When the term was first used in English in the 1600s, it related to recruiting religious converts. It tends to use a logical approach, but it can be aggressive and confrontational, which makes it less effective because it's less appreciated. Changing a person's mind rarely comes through confrontation, which makes people defensive.

destroys any possibility of having a decent conversation about our experiences; we must walk our talk.

2. Credible communicators have *competence*. They know what they are talking about, and they are honest about what they don't know. Their depth of expertise is revealed by their life experiences and in their ability to show unique insights and a nuanced understanding of different situations. Smart people who do excellent work are trusted and have credibility, and others want to be around them. People judge others based on their work and life, not their theology. If we want others to respect us, we must do good work.

3. Effective communicators *contextualize their message*. They adapt their message based on the situation because every encounter is different. They take time to know their audience so they can use the terms that will be understood and will stimulate curiosity based on what interests their listeners.

4. Contextualizing a message requires taking time to *develop relationships*. People share their thoughts and feelings with those they know and trust, and developing trust takes time. We won't listen to total strangers who start talking to us: they tend to have a hidden agenda. There first needs to be some kind of connection, and when people feel safe in the relationship, they are more likely to be honest and share their concerns and fears. People who genuinely care about others help others, connect on an emotional level, and show empathy. When we are interested in people's lives and their stories, we can reveal ours; in that context, we can share our own good news and are more likely to be heard. Our connections must be earnest and not just a means in a hidden agenda to present the gospel. It takes time to earn the right to be heard, and others can tell if we truly care for them and want to know them.

5. Effective communicators have a *clear message*. What they say is simple and logical, and the vocabulary is adapted to the audience; they don't use jargon that others won't understand. Providing clarity requires a good understanding of the subject matter and preparation to ensure the main ideas are presented clearly. Share from your own experience when it's a natural part of the conversation. Simply tell your story, don't push or preach, and don't give advice if it's not wanted.

6. Effective evangelists *go* to those who need to hear their message. They are action-oriented and don't wait for others to approach them. They leave the comforts of their situation and meet others where they gather. Building relationships is easier when a listener is comfortable and not defensive. Being with others where they gather also provides insights about their thoughts and ways, which allows a speaker to contextualize their message to the ideas and culture of the listener. Jesus told his followers to "*go* and make disciples of all nations" (Matt 28:19, Mark 16:15). God used the persecution of the Christians to force them out of Jerusalem into Gentile areas where they were witnesses in Judea, Samaria, and the rest of the world (Acts 1:8).

Jesus and the apostles used these elements when they shared the gospel. The story about Jesus and the Samaritan woman at the well had all these elements (the story lacks contextual details necessary for us to grasp their importance). Jesus took an unusual route, established rapport and interest, and the changed woman became an evangelist herself because of her encounter with him (John 4:4–42). Paul was a trained Pharisee who knew the scriptures well and spoke and wrote with authority, but after his dramatic conversion, he took time to develop his understanding about who Jesus was. He then crafted his messages for different audiences. He made dangerous trips to Gentile areas, spoke to Jews in the synagogue using terms and historical figures they knew, and his messages to Gentiles related to their situation. For example, when he went to Athens, he used Greek ideas and never mentioned the scriptures because his audience didn't know about them. Most of his letters were sent to those he knew, and his character and life story gave him credibility.[32]

Being an effective ambassador and model for the world isn't an easy task. Not only do human imperfections keep Christians from being perfect examples, but the strategies and tactics we use to tell others about Jesus and our faith can be ineffective and sometimes counterproductive. Asking a question or making a statement about a

---

[32] For another perspective on how to change the mind of others about an issue, see Howard Gardner's *Changing Minds: The Art and Science of Changing Our Own and Other People's Minds* (2006), Boston: Harvard Business School Press.

person's religious beliefs without first having some kind of relationship with them is unlikely to generate a meaningful dialogue. Repeating a generic message to total strangers is not an effective strategy and makes people think Christians are pushy and insensitive. Christians who don't exhibit the fruits of the Spirit soil God's reputation and are not good models for others to follow. We identify Christians by their love for others, not their correct theology or number of converts.

There is no biblical basis for trying to convince a person to believe in God if they resist our message. When Jesus sent out pairs of disciples to explain the gospel to non-believers, they were told to leave when people didn't welcome them, shaking the dust from their sandals (Matt 10:4, Luke 9:5, Mark 6:11, Acts 13:51). We are to tell others the good news, but we aren't responsible for bringing people to God. When we push a message on others who indicate they aren't interested in what we have to say, we violate the principles of effective evangelism. This approach also shows we are hypocrites and not loving and respecting others, which further deepens the skepticism of non-believers; we misrepresent who Jesus is and are not good ambassadors. Since beliefs are usually built on our experiences and emotions rather than logic and reason, it's better to move on to more fertile ground than spend time trying to convince somebody who resists our message. God says, "I stand at your door and knock. If you hear my voice and open the door, I will come in and eat with you" (Rev 3:20). We simply invite others to know God, but how they respond is their choice — we aren't to force ourselves on others.

The best way to attract people to the Christian faith is for Christians to exhibit love and the fruits of the spirit that are so different and attractive that others want to know more about us. When others are interested in who we are, the opportunity opens for a deeper conversation about the Christian life. We should be prepared for that discussion — Peter said, "Always be ready to give an answer to those who ask you why you are hopeful, speaking with gentleness and respect" (1Pet 3:15).

We aren't responsible for changing a person's head and heart — that's God's job. Our job is to live a Godly life and be credible messengers who can clearly explain the good news about Jesus. The parable of the farmer who sowed seeds among the different soils describes four possible results. Some will reject what we do, and two of the three types of seeds that take root will produce no crop, either because their faith doesn't mature or because life's worries, riches, and pleasures distract them. Only 25% of the listeners produce lasting fruit. This parable is included in three books of the Bible (Matt 13, Mark 4, Luke 8) .

The evangelism and discipleship process can involve many steps. Using the analogy of the parable of the soils, the hard ground of a person's spirit may first need to be broken up and then tilled to make it more receptive ground. More work is needed to plant seeds again, remove obstacles in the ground, and to provide nourishment for the seeds and soil. Immature plants require constant attention until they grow up. This is why my evangelist father said "a Christian is somebody who turns out to be one."

The lengthy process means we may not see any results from our efforts. It also means we shouldn't take credit for any person's conversion. Paul told the new believers in Corinth that he and Apollos were just servants who helped them to believe in Jesus — there was nothing special about either of them: "The Lord assigned each of us a task. I planted the seed, Apollos watered it, but God makes it grow. It doesn't matter who plants or waters" (1Cor 3:5–7). It may take years, even decades, for hard soil to become receptive and ready to receive the good news of the Gospel they hear from others. The life of a known Christian can a testimony of an unusual, sacrificial life. By the time a person decides to follow Jesus, a large portion of the preparatory work has been done, and a conversion is just the start of a marathon. It takes time to produce good fruit, so all the efforts of those who soften the ground, sow seeds, nurture the soil, and care for a new plant are not in vain.

We never know what kind of soil we are working with when we interact with others. God can use anybody to be a witness to others, even when they don't use the elements of effective evangelism. The simplicity of an authentic experience, spoken to those we know, can be used to share our spiritual insights with others. Jesus told the Gerasene man who was freed from his many demons to tell others about what happened to him. The Samaritan woman at the well went back to town and told everybody about Jesus, and many Samaritans came to believe he was the Messiah when they talked to him themselves. Jesus and an angel told women who went to the empty tomb to "go and tell" others that he was alive (Matt 28:5–10, Mark 16:1–10, Luke 24:10, John 20:17). The beggar who was blind from birth was healed by Jesus. After the Pharisees interrogated him and didn't believe he had ever been blind, he ended the conversation by telling them, "all I know is that I was once blind but now I see" (John 9:25). The experience of a person's changed life is powerful evidence of the existence of a good God.

The Challenges of Discipleship and Change

While salvation comes free, following Jesus has its costs. Jesus tells us to enter the "narrow gate" and using that path brings many difficulties (Matt 7:13–14, Luke 13:23). Many are invited, but the path is difficult, so relatively few truly choose to follow Jesus. Although Jesus had spoken to thousands of people, in the end there were only 120 people who still followed him, and this was *after* his resurrection and he went to heaven!

Many who conduct evangelism efforts down-play the cost of following Jesus. Being a Christian is much more than making an initial decision. We are to make disciples, not converts, and true disciples make a life-long commitment to live a very different lifestyle within their culture (see chapter 15). We make decisions every day to follow the ways of Jesus, and often this isn't easy.

When we infer that everything will be fine once a person becomes a Christian, we aren't being honest. This sets them up for either disillusionment or a half-hearted commitment that makes little difference in the world. When people know that being a Christian comes with a high personal cost, that they may fall away from the faith when things get hard or that life's worries and riches may distract them from being fully committed, they are more likely to persevere and produce abundant fruit.

Jesus wanted those who listened to him to think carefully about what it meant to follow him, for it was not going to be easy. He said, "If someone comes to me but loves their family or their own life more, they can't be my disciple. Whoever doesn't carry their cross and follow me can't be my disciple" (Luke 14:26–27). Then he made several analogies.

Suppose you want to build a tower. Won't you first sit down and estimate the cost to see if you have enough money to complete it? For if you lay the foundation and can't finish it, everyone who sees it will ridicule you. Or suppose a king is thinking about going to war. Won't he first consider whether his 10,000 men can defeat the 20,000 men of another king? If not, he will send a delegation and offer terms of peace. In the same way, those who don't give up everything cannot be my disciples. (Luke 14:28–33)

I send you out like sheep among wolves. You will be handed over to local councils and whipped in synagogues. You will be brought before governors, kings, and Gentiles to be my witnesses. You will be hated by everyone because of me, and you should go elsewhere when you are persecuted. Don't be afraid of dying — nobody can kill your soul. (Matt 10:16–18,22–23,28)

Unfortunately, many who claim to be Christian don't produce good fruit. People must do more than start the journey. Deciding to follow Jesus involves daily decisions to choose the right path. Being a disciple means constantly improving our understanding of what God requires of us and acting on that knowledge. It's an inward journey that accompanies our outward journey, our time on the mountain between our times in the valley, which gives us the strength to fly like eagles before we run and walk without fainting.

Part of the work in our faith journey includes challenging the status quo and the values of this world, just as Jesus did when he walked the earth. The gospel is counter-cultural in many ways and calls us to change ourselves and challenge ungodly actions and policies that occur in society (see chapter 15).

But changing ourselves and society is hard. We all resist change — we are creatures of habit and live without thinking much of the time. Change upsets our routines and presents risks of the unknown, which makes us feel uncomfortable. We want what is safe, known, and convenient. Jesus talked about this when he discussed new wine being poured into old wineskins (Luke 5:36–39, discussed in chapter 8). New ideas may be incompatible with our usual ways of thinking, and sometimes we need to give up some of our beliefs and ideas.

Change requires movement toward a different goal, and for Christians, this means becoming more like Christ. For this to happen, we need a clear understanding of who Jesus was and what he taught. We also need to evaluate ourselves to see how Christ-like we are. The difference between where we are and where we want to be is where we need to focus our attention for growth. James Baldwin wrote, "Not everything that is faced can be changed, but nothing can be changed until it is faced."

Relatively few believers make a significant difference in the world because doing so requires making changes to pursue God's priorities, not our own. Making a difference requires self-sacrifice, sometimes to the point of death (the word "martyr" comes from the Greek legal term *martus* and means "witness", which is mentioned in Acts 1:8). Following Jesus requires people to sacrifice some worldly pleasures in order to help others. Although entering the kingdom has no entrance fee, there can be a high personal cost to those who follow the countercultural teachings of Jesus.

A life of service may be exhausting and sometimes dangerous, but it need not include burnout. The branches of a tree don't struggle to make fruit — they simply stay connected to the living tree. Those who thirst for fresh water in a dry desert find a well and pump the handle until it brings up water. As long as the pump's line extends deep enough into the vast resources of fresh water, the pump effortlessly produces water. The pump is an instrument to bless those in need, and it works no matter how many times it's cranked. The secret to staying fresh for sustained service is staying connected to the dynamic and living source that sustains life.

CARE FOR THE EARTH

Genesis tells us that God created the entire physical world, including all the plants and animals that were to multiply on land and in the water and air. It was all very good and people were given the responsibility and take care of it (Gen 1:11–12,20–31; 2:8–9,15,19–20). The world (*kosmos* in Greek) is the universe that is orderly and beautiful. God loves it and Jesus came to it — John 1:10 and 3:16 use *kosmos* as the term for the world.[33] While the world is full of evil, the earth and nature are good

---

[33] *Kosmos* is used more than 180 times in the New Testament. The term can refer to life on earth and but also to evil influences in the world (e.g., John 7:7, 14:30, 18:36; Tit 2:12,

and belong to the Lord (Psa 24:1, 104:10–15). Noah saved every living creature and food from the evil in the world, and God promised never to destroy all of humanity again (Gen 6:19–21; 9:9–16). The land was even given a Sabbath to keep it from being overworked (Lev 25:2–5).

The Bible mentions the environment in positive ways. Plants and animals provided food to eat, to enjoy in feasts and festivals, and for survival. God's speech to Job (38–41) notes the majesty of creation and humbles us. Jesus mentioned plants and animals in his stories, including how God clothed the lilies in the fields and sustained birds in the sky (Matt 6:26–29, 10:29; Luke 12:6,27). Water was mentioned in very positive ways, which is essential for all living things. The air was rarely mentioned because unclean air wasn't a problem. Water and air make earth unique — life can't exist without them.

Since God's creation is beautiful and belongs to the Lord, we should be good stewards and take care of the earth. God put limits on what the Israelites could do to trees and birds (Deut 20:19, 22:6–7). A healthy environment is essential for human survival, and as noted in chapter 7, God communicates with humans through the wonder and beauty of the earth. A soiled earth prevents people from seeing its wonders.

Every part of the environment is connected, so everything we do affects others, especially the air and water, which flow across borders. The welfare of each species relates to the welfare of all other species. The idea that we can neglect the earth or use its limited resources for our own benefit without thinking of others or what we leave for our descendants is a selfish and unjust perspective. The loving and just thing to do is to ensure the earth's resources are shared and remain sustainable for future generations, which is an act of loving our neighbor. Joseph helped his family (climate migrants) when he determined a drought would last several years, and he developed a plan to help everybody survive. Science can help us identify and address problems that exist and develop ways to both improve and sustain the environment.[34]

Jam 4:4). Its meaning is determined by the context.

[34] Many in-depth essays about the Bible and the environment are found in *The Oxford Handbook of the Bible and Ecology*, H. Marlow & M. Harris, editors (2022), New York: Oxford University Press.

CHAPTER 15

UNUSUAL PERSPECTIVES

The Bible introduced new concepts about God to the ancient world through the patriarchs, Moses, and other Israelite leaders. The one Israelite God was flawless and loving — the Jews didn't have many gods that were angry and had to be pleased to ensure peace in their society. God made humans, is knowable, and wants an exclusive relationship with us. God gave humans a moral code to show people how to live together through our ethical conduct — we are to treat everybody fairly. God made unexpected people heroes and used flawed leaders to accomplish great things that showed God's power. Religion can be described as humans' efforts to find God and earn God's favor, but the Israelites believed God reached out to them. These concepts were and are still unlike all the other religions of the world.

Jesus expanded and clarified what was taught in the Old Testament by using two literary techniques to make his points: parables and hyperbole. His parables often included unusual characters and surprise endings, and he exaggerated his examples to get our attention (they weren't meant to be taken literally).

- The parables Jesus told often had a twist. The story of the vineyard workers reveals favorable unfairness when those who worked for one hour were paid a day's wage. The parable of the prodigal son illustrates that love, grace, and forgiveness are given to an immoral person, not justice. The parable of the proud Pharisee and the tax collector teaches that those who appear righteous are cursed while a remorseful sinner is honored. Jesus said he used parables so those who "had the ears to hear and eyes to see" would understand what he was saying (Matt 13:13–17).

- Jesus used hyperbole when he gave new perspectives on the laws of Moses in the Sermon on the Mount. He equated being angry with murder and looking at a person with lust with adultery. He said we should cut off our hand or cut out our eye if they offended us or caused us to stumble (Matt 5:21–22,27–32; 18:8–9). He said if we want to follow him, we must hate our family (Matt 10:37, Luke 14:26), and that if we had a tiny bit of faith, we could move a tree or mountain with a command (Luke 17:6; Matt 17:20–21, 21:21; Mark 11:23). Jesus used extremes and vivid images to emphasize a point and convey intense emotions, which prompt us to look seriously at our own thoughts and actions.

In many ways, Jesus's life story, how he behaved, and what he taught conflicted with common sense and is best described as "radical." He taught the opposite of what we intuitively think — the weak are strong, the first will be last, the least are the greatest, becoming great requires servanthood. Jesus turned logic on its head. This chapter summarizes these unusual and counter-cultural perspectives.

Jesus Was Radically Different

The life of Jesus began the opposite of what we would expect for a future king. He wasn't born and celebrated in royal fashion. Instead, he was a child of an unwed mother, born in a barn, and raised in a poor family. Mary's song when visiting Elizabeth foreshadowed a Messiah who would bring surprises: he would exalt the poor and weak and send away the rich. The Messiah, a king, would be a suffering servant who would give up his power rather than use it to take control. His army would not wield weapons but the Word. Paul summarized this strange example of how to live, which includes obedience and humility:

> Although Jesus was God, he didn't consider being equal to God as something he should use to his advantage. Instead, he came to earth as a human and became a humble servant. He obeyed his Father to the point of being humiliated and killed on a cross! (Phil 2:6–8)

Other than the unusual nature of his birth and escape to Egypt, he lived a traditional life until he started his ministry. His parents observed the rules expected of all Jews: they had him circumcised and consecrated after being born and every year they went to Jerusalem for the Passover festival. Jesus was traditional in some respects: he was baptized and taught in the synagogue and Temple, and he told those he healed to report to the priests.

But when his ministry began, Jesus immediately turned people against him. He wasn't afraid to disagree with normal traditions and beliefs. He honored foreigners and disrespected oppressive religious rituals. He intentionally broke the Sabbath to show a different perspective — love for others was more important than obeying oppressive rules. He touched lepers and talked to Samaritans.

Jesus wasn't lukewarm and didn't show moderation on important things, like those in Laodicea did (Rev 3:15–16). His approach wasn't incremental and he didn't try to negotiate. He used violence to chase merchants out of the Temple, and he alienated people when he spoke the truth. He said if somebody wanted to follow him, they had to deny their own desires. Eventually, Jesus became so much of a religious and political risk that those he threatened arranged to have him killed. Ironically, the Jewish religious leaders thought the sacrifice of one man would save their religion, but it ended up saving the world!

SOME TEACHINGS ARE RADICALLY DIFFERENT

Many teachings of the Bible are the opposite of what one would expect — God's principles and guidance often contradict prevailing earthly values and priorities. The previous chapters that relate to sacrificial love, mercy and grace, and how we are to view money show how different the gospel is compared to how the world operates. The counterintuitive nature and paradoxes of biblical teachings are at the heart of some of the most difficult actions God wants Christians to follow.

No message in the Bible is more opposite of common sense than the command to love our enemies and to be kind to them. Although it may not make sense to us, it's required of those who love God. In the context of the foreign domination when Jesus said it, the idea was treasonous. The Old Testament introduced the idea of loving our enemy and being kind and generous to them, and it was repeated by Jesus and the apostles many years after Jesus left the earth (2Ki 6:20–23; Prov 16:7, 25:21–22; Matt 5:40–48; Rom 12:14, 17–18,20; 1Pet 3:9).

Another example of a strange teaching is that we are to rejoice when bad things happen. In the Beatitudes, Jesus said, "You are blessed when others revile and persecute you and say all kinds of bad things against you because of me. Rejoice, be glad, for your reward is great in heaven, for the prophets who came before you were also persecuted"

(Matt 5:11–12). We are to embrace hardship because God causes all things to work together for good (Rom 8:28). Every situation has a silver lining, so we should stay optimistic and know pain has its advantages. Paul says, "Rejoice in our sufferings because it produces endurance, which produces character, which produces hope, and hope doesn't put us to shame" (Rom 5:3–5). As noted in chapter 12, good things can come from bad things. The story of how Joseph went from being sold as a slave by his brothers to being the highest-ranking civilian leader in Egypt shows that God sees the future and uses scandal and trauma for good purposes.

Jesus taught other twists on common sense. The norm of reciprocity is universal, practiced in all cultures, which brings an equilibrium to our relationships. When somebody helps us, we help or repay them in a similar way. But Jesus changes this social norm. He says that if we are attacked, we are to "turn the other cheek" instead of retaliating, for those who use weapons will be killed by weapons (Matt 5:38–39, 26:52; John 18:36).[35] We are to give to those who can't repay us (Luke 6:30,34; 14:12–14; Matt 5:42, 10:8). We are to help the poor and sick and strangers, even though we will get nothing in return (Matt 25:31–46). Forgiveness wipes out the need for retaliation, and generosity and grace help others promote peace.

Social Relationships

The gospel has a different perspective on our social relationships. Good Jews didn't associate with Gentiles, and it's natural for us to be friends with those who are like us, who share our views about the world, religion, politics, etc. We are often quick to judge and label others who are not like us, and we make generalizations about them. But the gospel removes the labels and makes no distinction about groups of people. "There is neither Jew nor Gentile, circumcised or uncircumcised, barbarian or refined, slave or free, male or female; you are all one in Christ" (Eph 2:10–22, Gal 3:28, Col 3:11). We are not to judge others (Matt 7:1–5; Luke 6:37,41–42; John 7:24, 8:3–11; Rom 2:1–3, 14:4–13; 1Cor 1:10–15; Jam 4:12; Tit 3:1–2). Jesus ate with

[35] Chapter 17 discusses non-violent resistance.

sinners, talked to women, touched lepers, and affirmed Gentiles and Samaritans. Jesus loved the entire world and Gentiles were invited to become part of God's kingdom. Unity, love, and inclusion within the diversity of the worldwide church was a new and compelling example of how we should live together on earth and bring peace to the world. One's looks, culture, citizenship, gender, and health are irrelevant.

Jesus emphasized compassion, not condemnation. During Old Testament times, strict rules had to be followed, and those who didn't follow the rules were judged and punished. Jesus did the opposite, often teaching and showing compassion instead of judgment. He came to the world to save it, not condemn it (John 3:17). He didn't condemn the woman caught committing adultery — the law said she should be stoned to death, but Jesus gave her another chance (John 8:3–11). His teachings about grace, mercy, generosity, and forgiveness were the opposite of punishment (justice). He associated with "worldly people" who led sinful lives, but there is no record that he judged them. He reserved his condemnation for religious people who were judgmental — they focused on minor sins or things that were not sins at all. He hold them to "remove the log from your own eye so you can see clearly and remove the speck of dust from another person's eye" (Matt 7:1–5). Their focus on little things came at the expense of seeing more important priorities, and they should have known better.

We often base our social relationships on appearances and focus on improving how we look so others will like us. We judge others based on what we can see, but what counts is what's inside us. We should therefore focus on having inward beauty (1Sam 16:7, 1Pet 3:1–7). Jesus was especially hostile toward the religious leaders who wanted to look good to others but were dead inside beautiful graves.

> The scribes and Pharisees do everything to be noticed by others; they broaden their phylacteries and lengthen the tassels of their garments. They love the place of honor at banquets and the seats of honor in the synagogues, how people greet them in the marketplaces and call them Rabbi. Woe to you, scribes and Pharisees, hypocrites! You clean the outside of the cup and dish, but inside you are full of robbery and self-indulgence. Don't be blind! First clean the inside of the cup and dish so the outside will be clean as well. You hypocrites — you're like whitewashed tombs that are beautiful but inside they are unclean and

full of dead bones. You appear righteous to others, but your insides are full of hypocrisy and lawlessness. (Matt 23:5–7,25–28)

Another principle of God's kingdom is working together within the community of believers (the Greek word *koinonia*, a term that refers to fellowship and community, appears many times in the New Testament). The emphasis is on being interdependent, not being independent. The "church" (*ekklēsia* in Greek) is an "assembly" of people who are called to work together in God's name.[36] All the parts of the body of Christ are to work together, exercising their gifts, supporting and accepting each other, correcting and serving others in love, and bearing each other's burdens (Rom 15:1–2,7,14; 1Cor 12:4–27; Gal 5:13, 6:2; Eph 4:2,11–16,29; Col 3:13–16; 1Th 5:11–14; Heb 3:13, 10:24–25).

Thus, we aren't meant to be alone. We are to depend on God and others in the church, not ourselves. "We, who are many, are one body in Christ and individually members of one another, honoring and devoted to one another" (Rom 12:5,10). The church is the Christian's extended family, and we are to support that family. Christians can't live faithfully and effectively in an evil world without the support of other church members. We need each other for emotional, psychological, economic, and spiritual support. Healthy social relationships, along with our faith, reduce fear, anxiety, and stress, which give us peace and enhance our well-being. Moreover, without being part of a loving community, a person can't show the world sacrificial love for other believers. The Jews knew how important it was to stick together, and Christians need to realize the same thing.

New believers need to be welcomed into a loving church. We are made to relate to others, and we get our identity with a group, such as a family, club, team, local bar, gang, or those who gather based on a shared interest. Thus, effective evangelism should be coupled with ways to include new believers in the church. If those who repent and start a new life with Jesus don't find a spiritual home, they will lack the Christian companionship and spiritual support needed for spiritual

---

[36] The word *ekklēsia* is first used in the Septuagint in Deuteronomy 4:10 and is first used in Matthew 16:18 in most English New Testament translations. A different Greek word, *kuriakon*, means "a holy place of worship" and has also been translated into English as "church."

growth. This lack of support makes them more susceptible to evil influences (Matt 12:43–45).

Power

The gospel also gives new perspectives about power, the ability to influence and control others and life in society. People can have power because of their money, knowledge, position, or personal charisma. Organizations also have power, and those who lead them can be very powerful if they are also wealthy, smart, and personable. Those with power have an elevated status that gives them prestige and privilege. Like money, power can be used for good or bad purposes.

Jesus had some aspects of power. Growing up poor in a disrespected region, he lacked money, status, and prestige. He didn't work in a respected profession and had no official training, but his knowledge and insights about the scriptures were unparalleled, which gave him the ability to debate respected scholars with authority. He had charisma and great powers of persuasion, and he understood common people. His ability to perform miracles instantly gave him power and popularity. His lack of stature and training raised questions about him among the religious leaders.

But unlike those who have power, Jesus didn't use his powers to coerce or control others or promote himself. Instead, he spoke the truth and let people make their own decisions about what to believe and do. As the Good Shephard, he calls his sheep who know his voice, and he doesn't drive or chase them. He promoted compassion for others and a greater cause, the kingdom of God. He was reluctant to show his power at the wedding in Cana before it was time to start his ministry (John 2), and he always used his power to help others. He spoke truth to power and didn't show the usual respect for Jewish traditions and attitudes, which alienated him from respected people. He knew what he said wouldn't make him popular. He was a humble servant, which was not a characteristic of powerful men.

Humility and Servanthood

During ancient times, receiving honor was valued and humility was associated with failure and shame. People still seek money and power so they can look good, be liked and respected, and influence others. Having these goals leads to a desire to always win and never lose and not admitting failure or showing weakness. But the Bible has the opposite view of humility. Jesus modeled it and said, "Those who exalt themselves will be humbled, and those who humble themselves will be exalted" (Matt 23:12, Luke 18:9–12). The apostles praised the virtue of being humble (Phil 2:3,9; Col 1:24; Jam 4:10; 1Pet 5:5–6). Jesus told this story about humility.

> When you are invited to a wedding feast, sit in the lowest place, so your host may say to you, 'move to a better place' and you will be honored in the presence of all who sit at table with you. For those who exalt themselves will be humbled, and those who humble themselves will be exalted. (Luke 14:10–11)

A related teaching says greatness is earned by being a servant, a slave, and a child. Unlike the Roman authorities that liked to show their power over the Jews, Jesus said, "Whoever wants to be great among you must be your servant; those who will be first among you must be your slave. Those who humble themselves like a child are the greatest in the kingdom of heaven" (Matt 20:26-27, Luke 22:25–26, Mark 10:42–44, Matt 18:4). Jesus washed the dirty feet of the disciples during their last meal together, a job normally assigned to servants and slaves. Peter protested, but Jesus said, "If I, the Lord and Teacher, wash your feet, you should wash each other's feet. I gave you this example so that you will do what I did for you" (John 13:14–15). But the disciples still didn't understand his messages of servanthood and humility, even though they had followed him daily for three years. They even argued about who would have places of honor the evening of his arrest (Matt 20:20–29).

Paradoxical Perspectives

Sometimes the teachings in the New Testament represent a paradox, a truth that appears to be a contradiction. Paul says slaves who are called to Christ are free, that those who are free are Christ's slaves (1Cor 7:22). Although many stories praise the wise, Paul says the wise were fools while fools were wise (Rom 1:22; 1Cor 1:20,27, 3:18–20). Chapter 11 describes what the Bible says about the dangers of riches and the benefits of poverty.

The Bible says being weak is a strength because it can show God's power. The Old Testament tells us about insignificant people and small armies that were victorious over larger enemies. These include the stories of David killing Goliath, the 300-man army of a reluctant Gideon from a small tribe that defeated the Midianites, the army led by Deborah and Barak that defeated the huge well-equipped army of Hazor, and how Jephthah, an illegitimate and homeless bandit, defeated the Ammonites. Paul says we are strong when we are weak (1Cor 1:26–28; 2Cor 11:17,30, 12:9–11; Rom 8:26).

Another paradox is that we must lose our life in order to save it; we must be willing to sacrifice our life to be a disciple (Matt 10:38, 16:24–25; Mark 8:34–35; Luke 9:23, 14:27). Baptism is symbolic of dying to sin and coming back as a new person with a new life, and we are to be a living sacrifice (Rom 6:4–8, 12:1; Gal 2:20, 5:24). Interestingly, we have learned that "losing" our life for a greater purpose has longevity benefits — those who live to be 100 years old have a meaningful reason to live, which "saves" their life.

These concepts are unusual, unpopular, and not easy to follow. The cost of taking Jesus seriously is high — following Jesus changes our priorities and how we spend our time and resources. It may mean we will lose friends, alienate family members, and damage our reputation. When we tell others about Jesus, they need to know that following him comes with a high price. When people know the true cost of discipleship before making a decision, they are more likely to persevere and keep the faith when their faith is challenged.

* * * * * * *

The Bible is a complex book that teaches many interesting lessons, and many of them are counter-cultural, which makes living a faithful Christian life very challenging. In many ways, the gospel is irrational, which makes having friends with a similar mindset important for our sanity and faith commitment. Yet in some ways, the guiding messages of the gospel are very simple. We are to be like children and follow basic principles. Robert Fulghum said we learn everything we need to know in kindergarten. God says, "provide justice, love mercy, and walk humbly with God" (Mic 6:8). We simply need to understand and then follow the example and teachings of Jesus.

CHAPTER 16

THE END OF HISTORY

Fear of the future is a common feeling. Many people are afraid of when and how they will die and what happens next. The concepts of hell and heaven were discussed in chapters 9 and 12, but they don't relate directly to how the world and earth may end. Fears of nuclear holocaust and environmental catastrophes don't seem farfetched these days. This chapter looks at what the Bible says about the future of this world.

THE COMING KINGDOM

During his ministry, Jesus talked about the kingdom of God (or kingdom of heaven) as if it already existed on earth but also that it was still to come. He talked about how a king would judge people like a shepherd separates sheep from goats, sending the sheep to heaven and the goats to hell. Jesus spoke privately with his disciples late in his ministry when they asked him about the events at "the end of the age." Jesus told them:

> You will hear about wars and rumors of wars, earthquakes, and famines, but these are just the beginning birth pangs. There will be tribulations and nations will hate you because you follow me. Many will fall away and betray others, and false prophets will lead many astray. The gospel must be preached to all nations, then the end will come. When you see the Antichrist standing in the Temple as Daniel predicted, you need to flee as fast as you can. The persecution will be like no other, and if the times were not cut short, nobody would survive. False prophets will tell you Jesus has returned and the end is coming, but don't believe them.
> (Matt 24:6–11,14–17,21–24)

Christians initially thought Jesus was the Messiah and would save the Jews from oppression and persecution, and later they thought he would return soon as a king to save them. Their hope was not that they would avoid terrible times but that they would soon be reunited with

Jesus. He had told parables about being ready for the time he returned — believers needed to be prepared like virgins who wait for a possible husband who could show up at any time, or like servants who are ready to unlock the door for their master when he returns in the night after a party.

But by the end of the first century AD, it was clear Jesus was not returning to earth anytime soon. The Romans had destroyed Jerusalem and the Temple, and according to the predictions related to the return of the Messiah, both needed to exist. The predictions and promises that he would return, eliminate evil, and judge all who lived in the world could still be fulfilled, but nobody knew when these events would happen.

During his ministry, Jesus told a parable about the coexistence of the good and the bad (Matt 13:24–30).

> The kingdom of heaven is like what happened to a man who sowed good seeds of wheat in his field. While everybody slept, the man's enemy came and sowed weed seeds into the wheat field and then left quietly. When the wheat sprouted, the weeds also appeared. The farmer's workers asked him, "Sir, didn't you sow good seed in your field? Where did the weeds come from?"
>
> The farmer replied, "An enemy did this." The servants asked the man, "Do you want us to pull the weeds up?"
>
> The farmer answered, "No, if you pull up the weeds, you will also uproot some of the wheat. Let both of them grow together until the harvest. Then I will tell the harvesters to collect the weeds and tie them in bundles that will be burned. Then I will tell them to gather the wheat and bring it to my barn."

It was therefore possible that Jesus would not return for a very long time while believers lived alongside those non-believers. The faithful would live on earth with their citizenship in heaven, and churches would be like small colonies in an evil world, showing the rest of the world a bit of what heaven will look like. The kingdom of God has come in part but would be complete for the faithful when Jesus returns for good and evil is destroyed.

UNCLEAR PREDICTIONS ABOUT THE FUTURE

Many predictions had already come true related to the Israelites and the Messiah, but there were still a few predictions about what would happen in the future that had not yet been fulfilled. These predictions mainly related to the "end of time" return of the Messiah and the separation of people going to either heaven or hell. Some of these prophecies were highly symbolic and filled with imagery, and the prophets who received them didn't know what they meant. But they wrote them down so others could make sense of them in the future. Because of the ongoing persecution, Christians were very interested in any details they could get about when their pain might end. They endured with hope rather than in self-pity.

Near the end of the first century, John, the fisherman who was one of the first disciples, was a pastor and lived in Ephesus. He had written about Jesus's life based on his firsthand experiences, and later he wrote letters of instruction and encouragement to various churches. He was eventually exiled to Patmos, a Greek island relatively close to Ephesus, because he was an influential Christian. John was part of the Christian resistance movement in a Roman world bent on killing those whose allegiance and worship focused on Jesus, not the emperor. This was similar to what happened when Daniel lived in Babylon and didn't worship King Nebuchadnezzar.[37]

Difficulty Understanding Apocalyptic Literature

As noted in chapter 4, John's "revelation" (*apocalypsis* in Greek, meaning "unveiling") was written in highly symbolic languages that was popular at the time. This form of literature was used by Old Testament prophets and some New Testament authors. Its symbolism lacked important details and was hard to understand, so there are different ways to interpret the texts.

---

[37] Two Roman emperors severely persecuted the Christians late in the first century AD. Nero's persecution occurred from 64 to 68, and Domitian's persecution occurred late in his reign during the 90s. Most scholars believe Revelation was written around 95 AD. Domitian had given himself the title "Lord and God" and wanted everybody to worship him.

Christians were being persecuted for not obeying Roman laws that violated the principles of their faith, and John wanted to communicate with the church from a distance. To protect those who received his letter, John used terms with double meanings and language that would only be understood by believers (this is similar to how missionaries in areas hostile to the gospel use certain terms to convey what is happening, knowing their mail will be read by others); some of what he wrote wasn't meant to be taken literally.

For example, he talked about the evils of Babylon, but he was really talking about the evils of the Roman empire. He used the number seven to symbolize completeness (e.g., seven cities, seven seals). It's not clear if the events he wrote about would happen consecutively or overlap with each other.

John described the final events of history in terms of a "tribulation" (years of intense persecution of Christians, accompanied by many natural calamities and warfare), a "beast" (an evil power using its powers against the Christians), the Antichrist (a false prophet identified by the number 666),[38] a final battle between good and evil at Armageddon (a valley in northern Israel), a "millennium" (1,000 years of peace), and the return of Christ who defeats the powers of darkness and throws all evil into hell. God's kingdom will then be established in heaven and on earth without any evil being present.

The idea of a "rapture" doesn't appear in John's revelation but is based on other Biblical passages (Matt 24:40–41, Luke 17:34–37, 1Th 4:15–17, 1Cor 15:51–52). Many Christians mistakenly view the rapture as an event that takes them to heaven, saved from the wrath of God, while non-Christians are left behind on earth. But these passages indicate that those left behind are the *faithful* ones, and non-believers will be taken to a place of death and judgment. When Christians rise into the sky, it is to accompany Jesus back to earth when a trumpet

---

[38] The meaning of 666 is unknown. Attempts have been made to identify the person using a numbering system associated with the alphabet. Many scholars think it symbolized incompleteness (the number 7 symbolized completeness, so 666 is not quite 777), and it may refer to a Roman emperor. Others think it's a mark on a person's head or represents six figures or symbols in three columns or rows. The Dutch thought it related to the year when they lost a major naval battle 1666. Many claimed Adolf Hitler met the conditions of the Antichrist.

sounds (they don't go to heaven). Believers who had died will rise first and lead the procession. This sequence of events was the normal way to greet an arriving king — a trumpet announces his arrival and dignitaries precede him.

How all these characters and events work together is subject to debate and speculation. Some believe in a pretribulation rapture, premillennial visitation scenario. In this view, the rapture comes first, then the tribulation, followed by the second coming of Christ, which ushers in the millennium. Then a final rush of evil occurs, after which Christ comes back a third time and defeats evil in one final battle. Others believe that Christians will experience the rapture *after* the tribulation; after that comes the millennium, followed by the return of Christ and the final judgment. Another view is that we are already in the millennium, and the tribulation will come before the rapture.

Other combinations are possible, but the mysteries of the symbolism and the vague details about how and when the events will occur mean that nobody knows how everything will unfold. Many scholars believe the events apply in a general sense and can be interpreted within the context of events at multiple times of history, with the key point that Christians should persevere and have hope during times of hardship. In this perspective, the revelations are not meant to predict specific events in the future. For many believers, it's enough to know there is a happy ending despite a painful process.

A sign that the end of time is approaching is the construction of the Temple for the third time in Jerusalem. (Solomon built the first one, and it was destroyed by the Babylonians. It was rebuilt during the time of Haggai and Zechariah, only to be destroyed by the Romans in AD 70.) The Antichrist is predicted to serve in the Temple, only to turn on the Jews and persecute them. Thousands of people are predicted to be protected from the tribulation. Many natural disasters (e.g., earthquakes, famine, darkened skies) are predicted to occur in the final days.[39] John confirmed some details that Isaiah and Paul said would

---

[39] The creation of the nation of Israel in 1948 after nearly 1,900 years without a national status has prompted some Christians and Jews to believe it's a sign that the end of time is coming soon. More severe natural disasters, changes in the world's climate, and discussions in Israel about rebuilding the Temple support their beliefs.

happen about the return of Jesus: those who have died will come back
to life again as Jesus did, and every creature, dead or alive, will bow and
honor Jesus as the King and Lord of the universe.

A BRIEF SUMMARY OF REVELATION

The first three chapters of Revelation were directed to seven churches
in Asia Minor — Ephesus, Smyrna, Pergamum, Thyatira, Sardis,
Philadelphia, and Laodicea. They were all connected by a major road
built by the Romans. The letter was designed to be passed from one
church to another along a circular route.

Persecution was occurring in each city and had caused believers
to compromise their beliefs and actions in order to blend in with
nonbelievers. John wrote to encourage Christians in each city to resist
the temptation to worship the Roman emperor and stay true to their
beliefs. Believers should have hope because God was in charge and
would ultimately win the war against evil.

John tailored his messages to the specific circumstances each
local church faced. For example, Laodicea was a prosperous city, and
its church was complacent and self-sufficient. Although the city was a
center for banking, John said the church was spiritually poor; although
the city produced beautiful clothes, John said the believers were naked;
although the city had a medical school, he said the church was blind.
The hot springs in the area were good for bathing, and cold water
was refreshing in the heat. But the hot water flowing to the city from
several miles away via aqueducts turned tepid by the time it reached
them. People used this lukewarm water to induce vomiting. John told
those in the church the following words from God (Rev 3:15–17,19):

> I know your deeds, that you are neither cold nor hot. I wish you were
> one or the other. Because you are lukewarm, I'm about to spit you out
> of my mouth! You say, "I am rich, I have acquired wealth and don't
> need anything." But you don't realize you are wretched, pitiful, poor,
> blind, and naked. I rebuke and discipline those I love.

But despite the church's complacency, John continued by reminding
the church of God's goodness. God says, "I stand at your door and
knock. If you hear my voice and open the door, I will come in and
eat with you" (Rev 3:20). The choice is always there for an individual

to respond, without being forced, to the invitation to know God. A central theme of the scriptures is that God's grace, not punishment, follows judgment.

The End of History

After writing to the seven churches, John switches to visions of the future by describing a set of events associated with the end of time when Jesus will return from heaven. John's revelation came from God through an angel as a message to all believers. There are "birth pangs" that reveal the final events are coming, and then the final events will occur. Here is a summary of those events.

John first received visions of scrolls and trumpets. He saw all kinds of amazing sights and creatures that sing and worship a shining king who sits on a throne. Seals on a scroll must be broken, and only Jesus is qualified to do this to reveal God's will for the future. (At that time, a person's will was recorded on a scroll that was sealed closed by witnesses. When the person died, those who sealed it had to be present to break all the seals and reveal the contents of the will.) Since God is in charge of the entire universe, "God's will" is sealed by God and can only be opened by God. The "Lion of Judah, the Root of David," is the only one qualified to break the seals and reveal God's will for the future. This causes every creature in the universe to rejoice and sing loudly, *"Worthy is the Lamb who was slain to receive power, wealth, wisdom, strength, honor, glory, and praise"* (Rev 5:12).

After the last scroll is revealed, heaven will turn silent for a while — it's a calm before all of hell breaks loose. Angels then blow seven trumpets, one after the other, and after each trumpet sounds, more awful events occur. (There are strong parallels between the plagues and Passover in Egypt before the exodus and the images associated with all these predictions.)

Before the last trumpet sounds, evil has grown so strong and widespread in its all-out desperate attempt to defeat the forces of good that God gets ready to fight the final battle. When the seventh trumpet sounds, it's time for the judgment — evil must be destroyed. Evil forces led by Satan invade heaven but are defeated by many angels, led by the archangel Michael. Angels proclaim the gospel to all those living on earth and announce, "Babylon has fallen!" A voice from heaven says, "Blessed are those who die in the Lord. They will rest from their work" (Rev 18:2, 14:8,13) This calls for patient endurance by God's people to keep God's commands and remain faithful.

Many plagues then affect the earth and a battle among many nations takes place in Armageddon (Hebrew for "mountain of Megiddo"), a valley 20 miles southeast of modern-day Haifa. The description of the battle closely resembles modern-day warfare — flashes of light, rumbling earth, and widespread destruction with the sounds of thunderous jets, bombs, and missiles falling from the sky. "Babylon" is destroyed because of its immorality, false religions, and the comforts of materialism. Those living in heaven rejoice at its destruction and sing, "Hallelujah, for the Lord, God Almighty, reigns. Let us rejoice and be glad and give God glory!" (Rev 19:6–7).

Once the powers of the world are destroyed, individuals are judged. An angel gathers nonbelievers and crushes them like grapes in a winepress. Having vanquished the powers of the world and the individuals who are not among the chosen, God then deals with the evil powers. Eventually the beast and Antichrist are captured and thrown into the fiery lake of burning sulfur.

But the dragon (Satan) is still on the loose. An angel comes from heaven and locks it in the Abyss where it stays for 1,000 years. While in the Abyss, the dragon has no influence on the earth, leading to 1,000 years of peace on earth. This shows people what life can be like without the influence of evil. (The length of time is symbolic and may not be 1,000 literal earth years.) The righteous who were martyred rise from the dead and share in ruling the earth. (This encouraged believers to remain faithful and not fear death.)

When the millennium concludes, Satan will be released from prison and gather with other evil forces that still exist. These forces will surround the people of God, but fire will come from heaven and kill all those who are evil. Satan is thrown into the lake of burning sulfur and is finally held accountable — Satan will be tormented day and night for eternity.

Then a king will sit on a throne and everybody, dead and alive, stands before the throne. The book of life will be opened, and everybody will be judged according to what is recorded in the book.

Anyone whose name is not found written in the book of life will be thrown into a lake of fire.

Once all evil in the world is destroyed, the holy city of Jerusalem is restored on earth. Jesus is on the throne and people will be in heaven where he says "there will be no more tears in their eyes and no more death or crying or pain — the old things have passed away and I have made everything new! It is done. I am the Alpha and the Omega, the Beginning and the End" (Rev 21:4–6, 22:13). The foundation and walls of the holy city are spectacular. There is no sun or moon because the glory of God provides the light; there is no darkness or night. Nothing impure ever enters the city. Those whose names are in the book of life live as the bride of God forever. Just as in the book of Job, the pain and suffering of God's people are eventually rewarded — perseverance of the faithful results in a happy ending. Spiritual battles have been epic through the ages, but the war is now over. There is total victory, and evil is gone forever.

John ended his letter by saying it was Jesus who told him to share the contents of this vision to the church. Jesus concludes by saying to everybody that he will return soon.

What the Future Holds

Nobody knows when the events associated with the end of history will take place and in what order. Instant worldwide communications make us aware of all types of atrocities and plagues, and it seems like the world is getting worse all the time. This is partly due to frequently-used information sources focusing on controversy, death, and destruction because many people follow these topics closely. Moreover, biased news sources paint a negative picture of those who don't hold their viewpoint.

But good things are happening all the time, too. Progress is constantly being made around the world in many areas. Most important worldwide indicators, including poverty rates, infant mortality, and life expectancy are now the best in history, not getting worse. People are healthier and smarter, which makes us more able to solve world problems. Can you think of a time in history when things were better worldwide than they are now? Probably not. Imagine life without electricity and the telephone, both of which were first widely used less than 150 years ago (the first plane flew in 1903). Things seem worse because we are instantly aware of crises far away via our integrated global communications systems and because the different forms of media tend to focus on bad news.

Nevertheless, our morals and cultures seem to be deteriorating, and we face threats to the existence of the human race — war using powerful weapons, freshwater shortages, climate change, and events in the Middle East are the most obvious. Worst-case scenarios could lead to some of the apocalyptic events cryptically described in the Bible. Nobody in their right mind would want these events to occur.[40]

There could be a peace before the tribulation occurs. Threats to our existence could instead lead to global cooperation that addresses our global problems. Given the progress now being made around the globe, it's possible we are about to enter a period of worldwide collaboration that could lead to a long period of peace, although major evil forces would first need to be tamed. The example of Christians who love others provides a kingdom model for the world to see that sacrificial and forgiving love brings peace and justice.

We know how the story ends. Isaiah wrote the good news that the Messiah will rule a kingdom that dominates the world, brings peace, and triumphs over the godless.

> In the last days, nations will go to the Lord together and learn how to work with each other in the right way. God will be the judge between people and will settle all the disputes nations have with each other. Nations won't fight with each other, and their people won't train for war anymore. They will beat their swords into plowshares and their spears into pruning hooks. (Isa 2:2–4)

---

[40] Some Christians want the end to come because they think they will escape the tribulation and want to see Jesus sooner rather than later. However, Christians have never escaped suffering, and being persecuted is normal in the Christian experience. Our hope is in our eternal life, not avoiding suffering.

PART THREE

SPECIAL TOPICS

CHAPTER 17

GOVERNMENT, POLITICS, AND CITIZENSHIP

The Bible is full of stories and teachings related to both spiritual and earthly powers and our role in our earthly setting. Every society and belief system that develops over time has a starting point and context that must be understood in order to understand and appreciate the nuances of the society. This chapter summarizes the Bible's stories and teachings related to government, politics, and citizenship and the related themes of laws, taxes, submitting to authority, nationalism, patriotism, and freedom.

BACKGROUND[41]

A *government* is a system that oversees, supports, and regulates people who live in an area that is not controlled by another power. These systems have different sizes and responsibilities, ranging from small local entities to large international organizations. Governments exist to protect people from harm and ensure society functions smoothly and fairly. This requires a wide range of activities that relate to nearly all aspects of life. Governments also often provide support in different ways to people living in their jurisdiction and work to increase people's happiness. Governments do this by establishing policies and priorities to meet their desired goals. Government leaders have different views about how to accomplish these goals, which leads to spirited debates about what to do, how to do it, when to do it, and how much it will cost.

---

[41] In the interest of full disclosure, readers should know I worked more than 30 years in various non-partisan public service positions at the local, state, national, and international levels and that I have a master's degree in public administration (MPA). My experiences provide me with unique insights into these topics but do not bias me to favor or oppose governments or politics.

Politics is different from the government — it relates to power that individuals and groups use to make decisions related to strategies, policies, priorities, and the use of resources. This means politics relates to far more than government. Every organization has some form of political activity. The Jewish religious leaders in the Bible were not government workers, but they had political power because they influenced certain aspects of Jewish society, and they cooperated and negotiated with Roman leaders. Politicians are leaders who work in governmental settings. One way to address the danger of people abusing their power is to divide their responsibilities. Having a balance of power makes the work less efficient, but this is preferable to having an efficient system controlled by people who abuse their power.

Citizenship is an entitled status people are given by a government when they meet certain legal criteria. Citizens have more rights than a non-citizen, and it typically includes the ability to vote and receive certain benefits when certain conditions are met. Citizens may also have some responsibilities, such as serving in the military. Citizenship gives people a sense of collective consciousness and companionship with others. Increasingly, the term is being applied to a wider geography (e.g., a "global" or "world" citizen) because countries are increasingly interdependent.

How Government Functions

Government models differ, and each model can be either good or bad. A *theocracy* is a government with God as its leader with humans having delegated authority to make decisions and rules in the name of God. A national government led by one person is an *autocracy* or *monarchy* (usually led by a king, queen, or emperor, who may inherit the role through their family ties). Autocrats and monarchs who pursue their own interests instead of the common good are often called *tyrants* or *dictators*. A government can also be led by a small group of people (*aristocracies* and *oligarchies*) or by a majority of its citizens (*democracy*).[42]

---

[42] Aristotle didn't favor democracy because it allows the majority to oppress the rights of those in the minority. He favored a monarchy because it's more efficient, but he worried that too much power in the hands of the wrong person would lead to a dictatorship, the worst kind of government.

Governmental units have leaders with similar responsibilities but have different names (e.g., governors and mayors, legislatures and city councils). Usually there are rules about how leaders are replaced, but sometimes these rules are not clear or are not followed. In all these models, many or some people (and in some cases, nobody) have a say in who the leader is.

Governments rely on many people to carry out their work. Leaders appoint others to oversee the activities and policies of the government and represent the leaders' interests. A vast public sector (*bureaucracy*) carries out the day-to-day duties of the government.

Governments create laws and rules that people must follow to ensure society runs smoothly and serves justice for all people. A judicial system (courts, judges, juries) makes judgments about whether a person has followed the rules, and if not, what their punishment will be. Without the laws, rules, and people to enforce them, anarchy would exist, which would then require some type of authority and enforcement system to bring peace to society.

But laws may not provide justice. Sometimes selfish people pursue power and create laws that benefit themselves. My father told me about an inner-city pastor who went to court to defend a man who unintentionally broke a minor law while providing help to another person. When the judge said the man was guilty, the pastor asked the judge, "Where is the justice in this system?" The judge looked sternly at the pastor and said, "This is a court of law. If you want justice, change the law."

Some laws are a double-edged sword. When we allow the freedoms of speech and the press, people can protest for justice and expose scandals, but they can also spread lies and print pornography. Freedom also allows people to pursue selfish goals, act in immoral and unethical ways, and endanger others. As a result, some freedoms need to be restricted for the good of society.

A government's role doesn't include enforcing morality or controlling people's lives, except when it comes to ensuring justice and an orderly society. Governments usually provide people with the freedom to choose where they live, what jobs they take, what or who to worship, how to spend their free time, and who they associate with, including who they marry. Authoritarian governments restrict these freedoms, and in a theocracy, the government will impose rules and restrictions based on religious beliefs. Those living in a theocracy will view other governments as permitting immoral behavior. Some people in some religions (Christians, Hindus, Muslims) are openly hostile against others within their country who don't believe as they do, as if they all live in a theocracy.

Taxes

Nobody likes to pay taxes, but they are necessary for the proper functioning of society — funds to pay for government activities must come from somewhere. Taxes are involuntary contributions to support organizations that provide what people need in order to live productive lives. Often the work that must be done is on a massive scale, so having a centralized authority makes sense to carry out all the activities. Thus, government is a major part of any society: taxes help pay for schools, national safety (military and its equipment), transportation infrastructure (roads, bridges, ports, public transport systems), and systems for justice (police, courts, prisons). Taxes also fund safety-net systems to help those who lack the ability to support themselves successfully (e.g., widows, orphans, and those with disabilities, diseases, and limited income).

The Bible doesn't provide any information about how much people spent on taxes compared to their total income, but when we consider the substantial needs of Israel's military and the amount of support the Israelites needed to ensure all their needs were met, the amount was likely substantial. This was on top of the command to tithe 10% of their resources to pay for the work of the Levites.

In biblical times, paying a required tax was done in different ways. Contributions could be anything of value, including money, precious metals, spices, and agricultural products (animals, crops). The amount owed depended on a person's circumstances. Jesus didn't object to paying taxes — he paid the temple tax and said people should give Caesar what is owed to him. He was known as a friend of tax collectors and he told the Pharisees they were worse than the tax collectors. Paul said, "Pay your taxes, for the authorities are God's servants who work full time at governing. Give everybody what you owe them: If you owe taxes, pay them; if you owe others revenue, respect, or honor, pay them" (Rom 13:6–7).

FOREIGN NATIONS INFLUENCED THE ISRAELITES

The relatively small nation of Israel grew and declined over a 650-year period in a politically-charged region. Canaan was a relatively small and narrow strip of fertile land squeezed between many other small nations, the Mediterranean Sea, and a vast desert. This made it a battleground for large empires that fought for control of its resources and strategic location.

God used other nations to both help and punish Israel as it grew into a strong nation. The Philistine King Abimelech was helpful to Abraham and Isaac, but the Philistines were usually hostile neighbors. The Egyptians were both supportive and hostile toward the Israelites. Pharoahs sold them food during droughts and accepted immigrants from Israel, but a different Pharoah made them slaves. Egypt harbored Joseph, Mary, and Jesus for two years when Herod was looking to kill Jesus.

Like the Philistines and Egyptians, Israel's other neighbors were both helpful and harmful. The Israelites had good relations with the Phoenicians to the north, and the Midianites in the southeast were initially helpful. However, the Israelites were constantly battling the Amalekites, Ammonites, Amorites, and Moabites, and they had hostile relations with the Edomites and Jebusites.

God used foreign empires to punish the Israelites for their unfaithfulness. Prophets said the Israelites would be taken away as slaves by the Assyrians, and it happened in 722 BC under King Sennacherib. Prophets said the Southern Kingdom (Judah) would fall to the Babylonians, which happened in 536 BC under King Nebuchadnezzar. The Persians eventually controlled the region, and its kings (Cyrus, Darius, Xerxes, Artaxerxes) supported the Israelites.

During the 400 years between the end of the Old Testament and when Jesus was born, other empires controlled Canaan. While the Bible doesn't talk about the Greeks and Alexander the Great who conquered the Egyptians, Assyrians, Babylonians, and Persians, the Greeks brought new ways of thinking about the world through their religious and political ideas. The Greek language became widely spoken and written throughout the empire, and educated Israelites were literate in both Greek and Hebrew.

The Romans conquered Palestine and took control of Jerusalem in 63 BC. They didn't tolerate rebellion and they ruthlessly executed many priests and Jewish leaders. In 37 BC Herod the Great was declared the king of the Jews and started constructing many buildings, including a larger Temple in Jerusalem. When he died in 4 BC, Rome put other leaders in his place.

Roman leaders played key roles in some of the main events of the New Testament. The census of Caesar Augustus required Joseph and Mary to travel to Bethlehem, the city where the Messiah was to be born. Herod the Great tried to kill the baby Jesus, Pontius Pilate was the governor of Judea who approved Jesus's crucifixion, and Felix and Festus oversaw Paul's trial in Caesarea. Many years later, Nero and Domitian were Roman emperors who persecuted Christians.

The Christian movement benefited from the widespread use of the Greek language and being in the Roman Empire. Paul communicated in Greek to the churches he established and used Roman laws and his Roman citizenship to his advantage to spread the gospel in the Mediterranean region. The church expanded rapidly throughout the Roman Empire thanks in part to the 200 years of peace in the empire at the time (Pax Romana) and an excellent road system, both of which made it possible for people to travel safely over long distances.

Government Characters in the Bible

Many Old Testament characters held governmental positions. The first one, Joseph, led the nation of Egypt — only the Pharaoh had more power. Unnamed Israelites worked with the Egyptians to supervise workers and argued with Moses when he tried to set the Israelites free. Moses went on to lead the new nation of Israel, a theocracy.

When the job became too big for Moses, his father-in-law (Jethro, a Midianite priest) told him to delegate less important duties to faithful men he could trust. Moses set up a system of hierarchical supervision to let these leaders and judges provide advice and handle minor disputes.

By sharing the burden of work, Moses was able to work longer, and life was better for everybody.

Moses faced much opposition to his leadership, and the Israelites constantly complained about the hardship of their lives. Moses also faced several major rebellions. After he came down from Mount Sinai and saw people worshipping a golden calf, he told those who chose to follow the Lord to come to his side. About 3,000 men didn't come forward and were killed by the Levites, casualties in the war against evil. (There was no jail in the wilderness where rebels could be fed and rehabilitated.) Later, Moses said anybody who defiantly sinned had to leave the community. Then after Moses told the Israelites they had to live in the wilderness another 40 years because the lack of faith of the 10 spies, many respected Jewish leaders confronted Moses and Aaron and questioned their authority. In an amazing show of power and anger by God, all those who rebelled against Moses were killed in an earthquake, and an outbreak of a disease took many more lives.

After Moses died, Joshua continued the theocracy and led the Israelites in their conquest of Canaan. When the conquest was complete, each of the 12 tribes of Israel selected their own leaders, and they all met occasionally to solve common problems, which usually dealt with how to fight foreign invaders. Various judges, including Samuel and Deborah, handled disputes in the region, and Deborah worked with Barak to defeat the superior army of Hazor. Military judges Othniel and Ehud led battles and defeated foreign powers, and other military leaders, including Jephthah, Gideon, and Samson played important roles in defending the Israelites from other nations.

Israel Gets Its King

With each family controlling its own land, the nation lacked cohesion and national prestige. The 12 tribes had no coordinating political structure to defend themselves, so the Israelites wanted a king so it would be like other nations. Samuel said they were rejecting God as Israel's leader and that having a king would mean the Israelites would have to hire more people to serve the king and protect the kingdom; there would also be taxes they would resent. But the people didn't listen and insisted on having a king. God told Samuel to give them what they wanted (1Sam 8:7), even if it wasn't a good idea, and he led the search for the nation's first king. God was clearly present in the selection process, and Saul became Israel's first king.

But like many of the previous Israelite leaders, Saul had major flaws. A young David distinguished himself in battle against Goliath and the Philistines, and Saul became jealous of David's popularity. Saul's insecurities and paranoia led him to rule badly and obsess about killing David.

When Saul died in battle, David became Israel's second and most famous king. He expanded Israel's national boundaries with many victories against foreign powers, but his personal shortcomings led to various tragedies. He eventually had a son, Solomon, who became the third king and became known for his great wisdom. But he also was known for his immorality and unfaithfulness to God.

When Solomon died, the nation had a crisis. No succession plan was in place and several men said they should be king. This led to a civil war and the nation split in two, the Northern and Southern Kingdoms. This began a disgraceful period when most of the kings in both kingdoms were very evil (appendix D rates the kings who served during this time). Eventually, God punished the two kingdoms and most of the Israelites were led away to the lands of their captors (the Assyrians and Babylonians).

Jewish Leaders Served Other Nations

Several Jews served in key government roles in these other nations. When Daniel and three other Jews (Shadrack, Meshach, Abednego) arrived in Babylon, King Nebuchadnezzar picked them to learn Aramaic, the main language of international trade and diplomacy. When Daniel correctly interpreted the king's dream, the king made him the ruler over the entire province of Babylon and put him in charge of all its wise men. Daniel later had the king appoint his three Jewish friends as administrators over the province of Babylon while he worked in the royal court.

After Babylon was conquered by the Persians, Daniel worked for the Persian king, and his integrity as a government official was flawless. People were jealous of his power but he was always able to avoid the plots against him. His enemies had the Persian king create an irrevocable order they knew Daniel would not obey: everybody had to worship the king, and those who didn't obey this order were to be thrown into a den of lions. When Daniel's enemies found him worshiping God, he was thrown to the lions. The king hated what happened, but God closed the mouth of the lions. Daniel was not harmed, and when he was pulled out of the den untouched, the king had his enemies thrown to the lions.

Two Persian kings, Cyrus and Darius, encouraged the Jews to return to Jerusalem, but many Jews chose to stay in Persia. This led to a Jewish woman becoming its queen when the Persian king (Xerxes) decided to replace his queen for disobeying his order at a public banquet. Young virgins from across the empire were brought to the king's harem so he could pick a new queen. Esther was a Jew who was brought to the harem. She had been adopted by her older cousin Mordecai and lived in the capital city of Susa. She impressed the king so much that he picked her to be his new queen. After Mordecai reported a plot to kill the king and Esther confronted the prime minister who was trying to get rid of the two million Jews who lived in the empire, Mordecai was made the prime minister.

Nehemiah was a highly loyal Jew who worked for King Artaxerxes to ensure his drinks tasted good and were not poisoned. When he looked sad while serving drinks to the royal family, the king asked him what was wrong. Nehemiah said he had learned Jerusalem and his homeland were in bad condition. The king gave him permission and supplies to return to Jerusalem to repair and secure the city. Nehemiah traveled back to Canaan and made a thorough evaluation of the city's condition. He created a plan to make repairs quickly and all the Jews worked in some way to make the necessary repairs and defend the city during the construction period. Taxes on the poor and interest on their debts were waived because they couldn't do their normal job while they worked on the repairs. After the walls and gates were strong again, Nehemiah set up security systems to protect the city, and he worked with Ezra, a well-educated Levite who had earlier earned the trust of King Artaxerxes, to strengthen the religious activities of the Jews. Later, he became a prophet who warned the people not to ignore God's commands.

In sum, God used many foreign nations and their leaders, as well as brave Jews who worked within those governments, to carry out God's holy purposes. A remnant of Jews that returned to the Promised Land resumed their faith in God.

Other Public Service Roles in the Old Testament

Thousands of men served in the military on a daily basis throughout Israel's history. Wars and battles were a normal part of the Israelites' existence due to the threats from their surrounding enemies (this is still true today). The Israelites sent scouts on reconnaissance missions to gather information about their opponents. Moses sent 12 "spies" into Canaan to gather intelligence on its inhabitants. Joshua sent two scouts into Jericho to assess its defenses (if Rahab hadn't protected them with her lies, they would have been caught). Other leaders used spies to determine the conditions of other cities before Israelite attacks.

The Levites were responsible for carrying out various religious functions. Although technically they were not filling public service roles, religion was a central aspect of Jewish society, and the Levites were supported by the people's tithes rather than through taxes.

Government Characters in the New Testament

The Romans dominated the political scene in the New Testament, but unlike the Old Testament times, few Jews held government positions. Working for the Roman oppressors was viewed by the Jews as a form of treason, and Jews who collected taxes were despised in part because their money supported the Romans. Matthew was a tax collector before becoming a disciple, and Zacchaeus was a corrupt tax collector before he decided to carry out his duties honestly. Jesus referred to tax collectors in some of his stories.

Political power among the Jews during the New Testament times was held by several groups that emerged during the 400-year period between Malachi's book and the birth of Jesus. Greek (Hellenistic) ways of thinking became attractive to many of the Jews during that time, and differences emerged about how Jews should interact with the Hellenistic world while preserving their faith. Chapter 3 discussed how different Jewish groups wielded power before Jesus was born (the Pharisees, Sadducees, and Sanhedrin). *Scribes* were experts in the law and served as teachers and interpreters of the scriptures and were usually associated with the Pharisees; some of them were members of the Sanhedrin.

A number of key characters in the New Testament interacted with or were impacted by Roman authorities. The emperor Caesar Augustus ordered the census that forced Mary and Joseph to go to Bethlehem. King Herod searched for Jesus after the wise men said another king had been born, which forced the family to flee to Egypt. The king also had the head of John the Baptist cut off to please his new wife. Jesus appeared before two Roman governors in the region, Pontius Pilate and Herod, during his trial. Roman soldiers carried out orders to torture and kill him and guard the tomb. Jesus and Peter both interacted with Roman centurions, and Paul had numerous interactions with Roman soldiers and authorities. Paul used his Roman citizenship to appeal his case to the emperor in Rome.

OLD TESTAMENT COMMANDMENTS AND LAWS

As noted above, governments create laws and rules that people must follow to ensure society runs smoothly and justice serves all people, and the theocracy of the nation of Israel was no exception. In his role as God's spokesman, Moses issued 10 general commands and then wrote many laws that applied to many areas of life. These were meant to ensure the survival of the Israelites in the wilderness and provide specific guidance on how to live together peacefully. The instructions were practical and helped maintain the people's health, and most related to ensuring right living and providing justice.

- There were detailed health-related instructions about what to eat and not eat, what could be touched and not touched. For example, people were not to eat rats or lizards or drink any form of blood. Those with a skin disease had to be quarantined and practice social distancing until they were healthy, and new washing techniques had to be followed. These instructions gave the Israelites advantages in battle and longevity.
- There were laws about personal injuries (e.g., a person who kills or kidnaps another person was to be killed; if there was a fight, the

eye).

- There were laws about property rights (e.g., if a person's fire spread to burn the grain owned by another person, the person who started the fire had to make restitution).
- There were laws about relationships (e.g., a sorcerer and those having sex with an animal were to be killed; strangers were to be treated kindly and not oppressed; widows and orphans were to be treated fairly, and those who treated them badly were to be killed).
- There were laws about money and principles for correct living. For example, money loaned to the poor couldn't require interest. Those seeing their enemy's animal in trouble must help the animal. People were commanded to "love your neighbor as yourself" (Lev 19:18).
- There were laws to promote justice and economic equity. People couldn't conspire and lie in court, and giving or taking a bribe was forbidden because it subverted justice. The rich and poor were both to be judged in the same way, and foreigners were to be accepted and loved just like everybody else. Farmers had to let their land rest every seventh year to let needy people eat from it. Israelite slaves had to be freed after six years, and in the Year of Jubilee, the possessions of the poor that had been purchased so they could survive had to be returned to the original owners. Six cities of refuge were created to shield people from immediate retribution until their case was heard in court.

The abundance of these detailed laws led to legalism and a sense that religion and obeying God is mostly about following rules. But laws and rules have a limited purpose — they ensure a safe and civil society and promote fairness. When many people live close to each other, there must be laws and rules so everybody can live together in peace.

The New Testament did not focus on any new laws for a society because people didn't live in a theocracy. The laws of Moses only applied to the Israelites, and Roman laws were respected during New Testament times. Rather, the New Testament reinforced the legal principles of the Old Testament (e.g., the 10 commandments, love your neighbor, provide justice), and it went further by showing that the law of loving God and others is a guiding principle that supersedes the law in certain situations. Jesus said he didn't come to abolish the law but to fulfill it (Matt 5:17), and loving God and our neighbor fulfills all the Old Testament laws (Matt 22:37–40). In sum, we are to follow the *spirit* of the law, not the *letter* of the law.

The New Testament also changed the punishments for breaking the law — mercy and grace (forgiveness and generosity) were to be practiced by God's people. The New Testament also did away with ceremonial laws (e.g., touching an unclean person, eating unclean food, cleaning ourselves in certain ways, working on the Sabbath) because we are saved by God's grace; we are to follow the law of love and are no longer bound by rules.

BIBLICAL PRINCIPLES RELATED TO GOVERNMENT

The Bible teaches a number of principles related to government authority and power. The first principle is that *God is the supreme authority*. The Old Testament has many verses that say God is sovereign over the kings on Earth (Prov 8:15–16; Isa 9:6–7, 45:1; Dan 2:21,37; 4:17; 5:21; Job 12:23). The Psalms say, "It's God who executes judgment, putting down one and lifting up another" (Psa 75:7) and "Kingship belongs to the Lord, who rules over the nations" (Psa 22:28). Jesus claimed to have authority over governments and told Pilate, "You would have no authority over me if it hadn't been given to you from above" (John 19:11). Just before Jesus left the earth, he told the 11 disciples, "All authority in heaven and on earth has been given to me" (Matt 28:18).

As the supreme authority, *God establishes and delegates authority to human governments to maintain peace and order as they restrain evil and avert anarchy*. "He changes times and seasons; he removes kings and sets up kings" (Dan 2:21). The Israelite leaders then delegated authority to levels closer to the people. For example, God had Moses appoint judges and officers in all the towns who were to judge the people with righteousness (Deut 16:18–20); King Solomon appointed 12 district governors over all Israel who supplied provisions for the king and the royal household (1Ki 4:7). Other verses apply to this principle (Dan 2:37–38, John 19:11, Rom 12:19).

Several other principles related to government are described in Romans 13, the Bible's most complete description of the role of government. Paul's letter was sent to believers in Rome who feared persecution. They didn't like the Roman rule, but Paul told them to submit to it.

> Everyone should submit themselves to the governing authorities, for there is no authority except what God has established. Those who rebel against their authority are rebelling against what God has instituted, and they bring judgment on themselves. For rulers don't threaten those who do right, but those who do wrong. Do you want to be free from fear of those in authority? Then do what is right and you will be thanked. For those in authority are God's servants for your good. But if you do wrong, be afraid, for rulers don't bear the sword for no reason. They are God's servants, agents of wrath to bring punishment on wrongdoers. So you should submit to the authorities, not only because you might be punished if you don't, but as a matter of conscience. This means you should pay your taxes, for the authorities are God's servants who work full-time in their governing. (Rom 13:1–6)

This passage leads to the next principle: *we are to submit to government authorities.* Since governments are authorized and ordained by God to function for the good of society, we are to obey its rules. This means paying our taxes, following laws and regulations, and being good citizens. Those who resist authority are opposing God and may be punished. A law-abiding society benefits all people. Paul used the Roman system of justice to help him share the gospel in the Mediterranean region. Jeremiah 29:7 says, "Seek the welfare of the city where I have sent you into exile, and pray to the Lord on its behalf, for in its welfare you will find your welfare." Since governments provide benefits to society, it would be hypocritical to receive the benefits without paying for them. Without taxes, a government collapses and society is left in anarchy.

The "sword" Paul refers to doesn't mean leaders had the power to kill people — only Romans in the military could do this. Rather, it represents the general right the government has to punish those who break the law, which can include the death penalty. Paul may have been warning the Christians in Rome not to be rebellious — if they were, they would probably be killed. The best way to create change is to work within the system rather than to try to overthrow it, especially when the odds are stacked against you. Submission can be an act of self-preservation.

Other New Testament passages stressed the need for Christians to obey the government. Paul told Titus to have people in his congregation obey the secular leaders (Tit 3:1), and he told Timothy to have his congregation pray for them (1Tim 2:1–2). Peter's first letter told Christians to submit to human authorities:

> Submit yourselves for the Lord's sake to every human authority: whether to the emperor, as the supreme authority, or to governors, who are sent by God to punish those who do wrong and to commend those who do right. For it's God's will that by doing good you should silence the ignorant talk of foolish people. Live as free people, but don't use your freedom to cover up evil; live as God's slaves. Show proper respect to everyone, love other believers, fear God, and honor the emperor. (1Pet 2:13–17)

Finally, while human governments have God-given authority, God doesn't approve of everything they do. Peter referred to Pontius Pilate as one of many "godless men" (Acts 2:23, 4:27) but Jesus affirmed Pilate's authority (John 19:11). In other words, God *allows* things to happen *but doesn't necessarily direct or cause* them to happen. The Bible doesn't recommend any form of government, and many governmental structures are mentioned in the scriptures. But they are all created to promote peace, safety, and justice.

Opposing the Government

Paul wrote other letters that provided additional insights into a Christian's relationship with human authority. He said *our true citizenship is in heaven* and *we are God's representatives (ambassadors)* to those who live on earth (Phil 3:20, 2Cor 5:20, Eph 6:19–20); Peter said we are "a chosen people, a royal priesthood, a holy nation, foreigners" (1Pet 2:9–11). Our ultimate loyalty is to God, not an earthly authority; we represent God and should not obey rules that conflict with God's rules.

My experience living for many years outside the United States has given me insights into these verses. I served five years as a diplomat for the United States government while I lived in Europe and traveled to many countries in Africa, Asia, and the Middle East. I had to obey the rules of the countries where I went, but I didn't give up my U.S. citizenship. During my time abroad, if I was ordered to do something that violated the oath I took to the U.S. Constitution, such as pledging my allegiance to another country or revealing a secret I was sworn to keep private, I would not follow that order. I met with ambassadors who had the same perspective — they represented their country as they lived in another country. While they lived *in* another country, they had different loyalties and represented the perspectives of their own country.

In the same way, those who follow Jesus are ambassadors who represent the kingdom of heaven to others on earth. We are to live in this world but not violate God's mandates. So as citizens of heaven, *we are not to obey governments that require us to violate God's commands and laws.* Being God's representatives on earth can be a dangerous and uncomfortable job, and standing against those in power can even be fatal. The prophets, apostles, and early Christians were jailed, persecuted, and martyred (Heb 11:35).

Those who stayed true to God's teachings used three non-violent methods to oppose ungodly rules and practices.

- *God's people speak truth to power.* When the Israelites and their leaders disobeyed God's commands, prophets said they needed to repent and change their ways. Some of them were killed, and some were harassed and persecuted. John the Baptist told King Herod that he should not have married his brother's wife, and the king honored his wife's request for John's head.

- *God's people engage in civil disobedience.* This form of resistance involves intentionally disobeying a government rule or requirement that violates God's laws. The Hebrew midwives disobeyed Pharaoh's command to kill newborn boys. When Shadrach, Meshach, and Abednego defied the Babylonian king's order to worship a statue of himself, they told the king, "If you throw us in the fire, our God can deliver us from it. But even if our God doesn't save us, we want you to know that we won't worship another god or bow to the golden image you set up" (Dan 3:17–18). The three men were then forced into the burning furnace. Daniel defied the Persian requirement to worship the king and was thrown to the lions. Obadiah, a faithful leader in the government of the evil king Ahab and queen Jezebel, disobeyed a command to kill all the prophets, and he saved 100 men by hiding them in a cave. Many of the disciples defied orders to stop preaching, and some were thrown into prison for it. Peter said, "We must obey God rather than men" (Acts 5:29).

- *God's people flee evil.* There are many examples of how faithful people left a situation in an act of self-preservation to escape the dangers of evil forces. Lot and his family fled Sodom, the Israelites fled from Egypt, David fled from Saul, and Elijah ran away twice to avoid the armies Jezebel sent to kill him. In the New Testament, Christians fled for their lives because Jewish leaders were arresting and killing them. Paul and his traveling companions were constantly being threatened, which forced them to move to other cities.

None of these three methods of opposition involved physical rebellion or violence. (The only possible exception was when Samson killed himself and several thousand Philistines in an act of suicide that brought down the roof and walls of their house of worship. But as a blind prisoner, he had no other options.) When armed men came to arrest Jesus, Peter moved quickly to defend him and cut off the ear of a man who approached Jesus with his sword. But Jesus told Peter, "Put away your sword; those who use the sword will die by the sword" (Matt 26:52). There is no Biblical basis for individuals to use violence against others or to overthrow a government. God tells us not to seek revenge or use evil means when evil is done to us. God says, "Vengeance is mine, I will repay; overcome evil with good" (Deut 32:35, Prov 20:22, Rom 12:17–21, Heb 10:30).

Those who act as agents of the government have different responsibilities. As noted in chapter 5, commands for individuals are different for governments, which God uses to administer justice and protect people. So judges need to follow the law, even if the law could be considered immoral. Soldiers must follow orders to kill their enemies because they are part of a government that is responsible for protecting others, including taking lives when lives are taken (Gen 9:6). Resisting evil is an act of love, and governments have this responsibility. Some acts of violence in the Old Testament were justified because they were carried out against evil people by those representing God.[43]

However, there are exceptions when the human authorities issue orders that are not legal or moral. We are not to lie or take bribes to protect those with evil motives. When soldiers are given orders to kill others without a good reason, soldiers must not obey the orders — blind compliance to such a command is unlawful and considered murder; "following orders" is not an acceptable excuse for murdering others. Some people "flee" and avoid required military service on the grounds they feel the actions of the military are unjustified and morally wrong.

Finally, there is no scripture or precedent to support the idea that God's people should try to change a secular government into a theocracy or have it follow God — that's not why governments exist. In fact, a government should protect a person's right to believe what they want, for God always gives us a choice. The Israelites who were captured by the Assyrians and Babylonians didn't try to convert their captors to Judaism or change the government. The armed rebellion against immoral Greek orders by the Maccabees in the 2nd century BC was never mentioned in the New Testament. Jesus, his disciples, and the apostles made no attempt to rebel or question Roman authority, even though it exerted harsh control throughout its empire; this would be inconsistent with obeying God's delegated authority. They focused instead on informing people about our spiritual condition and beliefs. The angry Crusaders used force to restore Christian values and traditions in Palestine, which damaged the reputation of the Christian faith.

NATIONALISM, PATRIOTISM, CITIZENSHIP, AND FREEDOM

The issues of obeying the law, submitting to human authorities, and citizenship bring up the issues of nationalism, patriotism, and our

---

[43] Usually the violence was conducted by Jews toward other Jews who had abandoned God within their theocracy. This "violence" was really a form of justice being administered by those in charge of the government. For example, Moses had rebels killed several times and Elijah had 850 prophets of Baal killed.

earthy citizenship and freedoms. This section discusses these concepts and the biblical principles related to them.

Nationalism and Patriotism

While people define terms differently, *nationalism* is generally defined as a political belief that a person's loyalty, devotion, and allegiance to a group of people who share a history, culture, language, and religion takes priority over the interests of individuals or other groups. It can be expressed in different ways, including the promotion of and adherence to the group's culture, religion, and economic system. In this sense, a *nation* is different than a *country*, which is a political term that applies to an area of land. For example, the United States is a country, not a nation, because it consists of many different groups of people who share the same history, culture, language, and religion; some of these "nations" are formally recognized, such as those of native American tribes. Nationalism implies a belief that one's own group is better than other groups and should be defended against other groups, which makes it "exclusive." Nationalist movements currently exist around the world to defend a group's race, language, history, and way of life. The "nation of Israel" had no land of its own for many centuries but still retained its identity.

Patriotism is similar to nationalism but focuses on love, support, and the defense of one's country (*patrios* in Greek, meaning "of one's father" as in "fatherland"). It assumes a defense of all people who live in the country, even those who have a different way of life. However, it doesn't imply an advocacy for the country's interests in the world, and it doesn't imply one's country is better than others. But like nationalism, it implies a willingness to fight to defend one's country. In some cases, the two terms apply to ethnic groups rather than a country because there may not be a political entity that represents the group. Like the term "citizenship," the two terms imply a sense of collective companionship with others. Charles de Gaulle, the leader who led France against Nazi Germany during World War II, defined patriotism and nationalism this way: "Patriotism is when love of your own people comes first; nationalism is when hate for people other than your own comes first." In a diverse society, patriotism and nationalism can be enemies.

Starting with Abraham, the Israelites and Jews developed a collective identity as God's chosen people, the nation of Israel, which gave them a nationalist perspective and a sense of superiority. God blessed the Israelites, but part of the covenant required them to honor God and provide justice to others, not just other Jews. All people were to be treated fairly. While the Israelites were proud of their nation and many fought to keep it safe, the military expansion by David and Solomon beyond Canaan represented nationalism, the extension of power and use of foreign lands and resources at the expense of others.[44]

Gentiles were later adopted into God's kingdom after Peter's exchange with Cornelius, but some Jews rejected the idea because they loved their nation above any others and wanted to keep God's blessing to themselves. Later, the Jews who followed Jesus wanted Gentile believers to follow the same Old Testament laws they followed. But at the Council of Jerusalem, the apostles decided this wasn't necessary, that one's faith didn't include following rules set up for a different time. It was always God's intention to include *all* people in the Kingdom: *God loved the world* and *Jesus saved the world* (John 3:16–17; Gal 3:26–29; 1Cor 12:12–14). The good news is that all people can access a loving God who wants a relationship with all people without regard to their tribe, gender, race, age, or birthplace and without regard to what they do or believe. The gradual increase in the revelation of God's desires for the world reveals a movement from exclusiveness to inclusion — there is no longer favoritism or special privileges for a selected people.

---

[44] Today, *Zionism* is the nationalistic belief held by some Jews that Israel is for Jews with Judaism as its religion, a mixing of political and religious beliefs. The movement began when Theodor Herzl wrote *The Jewish State* (1896) that proposed the idea that Jews needed a nation, with its own land, to provide safety from worldwide persecution. (The last Jewish nation ended in AD 70 when the Romans defeated a Jewish rebellion in Jerusalem and destroyed the city and Temple; Jesus predicted this in Matthew 24:2. After another revolt failed, the Romans expelled the Jews from the region.) Zionists believe any Jew living anywhere in the world can be an Israeli citizen. Many Israelis want to occupy the West Bank of the Jordan River which was controlled by Jordan after the nation of Israel was formed in 1948. Many permanent settlements have been created, but many Jews (as well as the non-Jews who have lived in the region for centuries) oppose the creation of these settlements.

Citizenship

As noted earlier, Christians are citizens of heaven and God's ambassadors in this world. We live in the world with temporary citizenship under an earthly authority, but our ultimate allegiance is to God's kingdom. We are told to love God, our neighbors, other Christians, and our enemies. The Bible has no verse that supports loving one group over another, and there is nothing biblical about loving one's country. This doesn't mean it's wrong to love one's country — it's natural to appreciate our own land, people, and customs, and it's appropriate to honor those who serve and celebrate freedom from tyranny and oppression — the Jews had similar celebrations. But for Christians, our allegiance to and love for our country must never take priority over the commands to love God and our neighbors.

Given that God loves all people, it's inconsistent for Christians to love God and our neighbors but then show favoritism to one group or civil authorities or those who share our earthly citizenship. In some countries, the flag is a widely-visible sacred symbol of national pride and may become closely associated with the cross. But blending the two symbols as equals, a nation's flag and a cross (love of country and love of God), is a form of idolatry (extreme love or devotion for something or someone) and syncretism (blending beliefs). It's similar to the sins of the Israelites who proudly valued their special status as much as, if not more than, worshiping God. Jesus said, "Where your treasure is, there your heart will be. Nobody can serve two masters" (Matt 6:21,24). We must not pledge to Caesar what belongs to God, which is our total allegiance.

At a minimum, we should use our right to vote to advocate for justice and a better society in the country of our citizenship. Using non-violent methods, we should oppose improper rules and practices and speak truth to power. Working within a government is another way to promote just causes and a civil society. Serving in the military and the diplomatic corps are unique roles that can help promote justice and peace within a country and in other parts of the world. Voting for leaders who value promoting world peace and justice is another way to show our love for the world. When good people do nothing, evil grows at home and abroad.

The command to show a special love for other Christians affirms a Christian's duty to have an international perspective. Most Christians live in Latin America, Africa, and Asia, and millions of them live in severe poverty. We know that major disparities in wealth and justice exist, so we have no excuse for not helping our Christian brothers and sisters who are in need and live outside our country. We can't honestly say to the king, "When did we see you hungry, thirsty, a stranger, naked, sick, or in prison, and didn't help you?" (Matt 25:44).

Thus, Christians should have an international focus rather than an allegiance to their country. God loves the world, and before Jesus left the earth, he told his disciples to "make disciples of all the nations" and be his witnesses "in Jerusalem, in all Judea and Samaria, and to the ends of the earth." These verses are collectively known as the Great Commission (Matt 28:19–20, Acts 1:8). Most Christians initially stayed near Jerusalem, but God used persecution to move them out of their comfort zone. As they moved elsewhere to be safe, they shared the gospel with others. As a result, the gospel has been heard around the world.

Being an effective world citizen requires a better understanding of world issues. My experiences living in and traveling to many countries has opened my eyes to the cultures, beliefs, and needs of others. Global migration patterns also bring to us those from other countries who have different religions and cultures — God brings the world to us so we can share the gospel with those who have never heard it. To communicate effectively with those from other countries and cultures, we need to understand their context.

As a Christian who takes the Bible very seriously, I have pledged my total allegiance to being a citizen of the kingdom of God, which carries with it an unwritten pledge to serve the world. When I worked for the government, I also temporarily pledged my limited allegiance to serving my country. I use my rights as a citizen to pick good leaders and advocate for just laws and services that help others and improve society as a whole, including what is good for the world, not just my country. Finally, I have used the privileges and freedoms that come with my citizenship to make vocational and life choices that focus on helping others, both at home and abroad.

Freedom

The term *freedom* is used in different ways in the Bible. The freedoms that governments provide are implied in the biblical narratives. People were free to live and travel where they want, to do business with others and spend their money how they want, to follow and believe different religions and philosophies, to choose their vocations and friends, to discuss and debate the merits of an argument, and to act in immoral ways that don't interfere with the freedoms and safety of others. Good governments don't try to control these aspects of society, don't intrude into a person's private life, and don't force people to do something against their will. Some governments include these basic principles in their charter or constitution.

God never forces people to obey — good relationships never depend on force and control. We are given freedom to choose, including the freedom to make bad decisions, for which there will be consequences. But hopefully we learn from our mistakes and the mistakes of others.

Adam and Eve were free to live as they chose in the Garden of Eden and they had only one restriction. Both Moses and Joshua told the Israelites that they had a choice about how they could live. In Deuteronomy 30, Moses said, "Walk in obedience, love and serve the Lord with all your heart and with all your soul. Keep God's commands and decrees I'm giving you today for your own good. This isn't too difficult for you. Today, I set before you life and prosperity, death and destruction. Choose life." When Joshua was about to die, he said people should stay faithful and concluded, "If serving the Lord seems hard for you, then you need to choose who you will serve, whether the gods of your ancestors or the gods of the Amorites where you live now. But as for me and my family, we will serve the Lord" (Josh 24:15). When the Israelites didn't follow God and made bad decisions, they were eventually punished. In the story of the prodigal son, the father set his son free to pursue his earthly desires but hoped and prayed he would come back home.

Of course, freedoms need to be restricted to ensure the safety and well-being of society. Laws are created to ensure justice, fairness, and public safety. Parents put restrictions on their children for their own good and for the good of the family, neighborhood, and society. Those who grow up without restrictions and accountability become reckless and selfish and endanger society. But laws should not oppress or exclude some people in order to benefit others. Sometimes selfish people who wield power create laws and rules that keep themselves in power and favor their own interests at the expense of others. When this happens, we should speak the truth and call for changes in the laws and rules.

The term "freedom" is explicitly used in two ways in the Bible. First, it referred to the literal freedom people had from being controlled by others. The Israelites were freed from working as slaves for the Egyptians, and Moses and many others often reminded them how God saved them from slavery. The Israelites lost their freedom and were taken prisoners of the nations that conquered them. The apostles were set free from jails. Paul and Peter wrote that one's freedoms should not be abused. "You say you have the right to do anything, but some things are not helpful. You were called to be free, but don't use your freedom to indulge the flesh; instead, serve one another humbly in love" (1Cor 6:12, Gal 5:13). "Live as free people, but don't use your freedom to cover-up evil; live as God's slaves" (1Pet 2:16).

The Old and New Testaments also talk about "freedom" in the spiritual and emotional sense, and it was often contrasted with a spiritual form of slavery and bondage. The first public speech by Jesus included a reading from Isaiah 61, which referred to the Messiah:

> The Spirit of the Lord is on me: God has anointed me to proclaim good news to the poor. God sent me to proclaim freedom for the prisoners and recovery of sight for the blind, to set the oppressed free and proclaim the year of Jubilee. (Luke 4:18–19)

Jesus was using the terms both literally and metaphorically as he claimed he was fulfilling Isaiah's prophecy (the Jews thought of the terms literally). The year of Jubilee was the 50th year when all debts were released, giving freedom to those who had long-term debts. The Psalms also refer to freedom this way (Psa 18:5, 119:45). Justice can bring both literal and emotional freedom for those who are oppressed and falsely accused.

Many New Testament passages talk about the spiritual dimension of freedom and slavery. Jesus talked about freedom and truth when he talked to Jews who believed him: "If you embrace my words, you are my disciples; you will know the truth, and the truth will set you free. If the Son sets you free, you will be truly free" (John 8:31–32,36).

Paul wrote to the churches about freedom and slavery in a spiritual sense.

> Our old self has died; we are no longer slaves, and we have been set free from sin and have become slaves to righteousness. The law of the Spirit of life has set you free in Christ Jesus from the law of sin and death. So those who follow Christ are no longer condemned. The law of the Spirit who gives life has set you free from the law of sin and death. God's Spirit doesn't make you a slave and make you afraid again.
> (Rom 6:6–7,18,22; 8:1–2,15)

Paul told the churches in Corinth and Galatia the same thing: "Where the Spirit of the Lord is, there is freedom. Christ has set us free. Stand firm and don't become burdened again by a yoke of slavery" (2Cor 3:17, Gal 5:1).

People become slaves to those they follow (Rom 6:16), so those who follow Jesus take on a different kind of slavery, a devotion to Christ. "When you were slaves, God called you and made you free. Those who are free are now Christ's slaves; you were bought with a price, so don't become slaves of others" (1Cor 7:22–23).[45] But this is not too big of a burden. Jesus said his yoke is easy and light, like the yoke on animals that guide them (Matt 11:29–30).

* * * * * * *

The Bible contains many passages and teachings related to governments and politics, including the topics of justice and living peacefully in society. Although Christianity was an illegal religion and many believers were killed throughout the Roman empire, Christians tried to be good citizens and didn't use violence to defend themselves. The faith grew quickly, and according to Tertullian's *Apology* written in about AD 200, Christians "filled the cities, islands, fortresses, towns, marketplaces,

---

[45] Many forms of slavery existed during Biblical times, and it was different from how we think of slavery today. Sometimes it was an economic arrangement that had specific conditions, like paying off a debt. However, slavery could be involuntary and cruel, and both Nehemiah and Paul condemned it (Neh 5, 1Tim 1:10).

the army itself, tribes, companies, the Imperial Palace, the Senate, the Forum" (in other words, Christians were found everywhere). The spread of Christianity was also influenced in part by the promises of life after death to believers and by the predicted downfall of the Roman Empire. Justin Martyr tried to convince the Roman authorities that Christians were good citizens, even though they would not worship the Roman gods, but he was beheaded with some of his disciples in AD 165. Other Christian leaders were persecuted and killed in spectacular and gruesome fashion. Because of the strong persecution against the Christians, most believers at the time thought they were in the midst of the tribulation. It wasn't until AD 313 that the Romans stopped persecuting Christians during Constantine's rule. But persecution has continued on a smaller scale, and Christians are still persecuted and ostracized in some parts of the world.

In the entrance to the CIA headquarters building in Virginia, there is a structure that says: "You will know the truth, and the truth will set you free" (John 8:32). The verse has merit as part of the CIA's mandate to provide accurate information to America's political leaders about what is happening in the world. However, Jesus's words were not about political or individual freedom. While the truth can lead to political freedom, we are to put our trust in God, not in our nation, military, money, or minds.

CHAPTER 18

WOMEN IN THE BIBLE

The cultures of the ancient world are traditionally described as patriarchal — most woman were not respected and were near the bottom of a caste-like system in society (the poor, sick, and immoral women were at the very bottom). To estimate the size of a crowd, only the men were counted, and nothing a woman wrote was read by men. The typical genealogies named only the men, and a child's "last name" was their father's name.

While most of the women mentioned in the Bible were nameless, the Bible names 163 women (about 6% of all the people named), and less than 50 of the named women are quoted. Some of the women have the same name — there are at least six different women named Mary mentioned, not including two women named Miriam, a Hebrew word for Mary. Most of the women are minor characters, but some had significant roles, and some were involved in scandals. Jesus had an unusually positive view of women as shown in his respectful treatment of different types of women.

Both males and females were created in God's image. Genesis 2:18 says Eve was created as Adam's "helper," but the Hebrew term used, *ezer*, doesn't mean she was his "assistant" or "servant." The word *ezer* is mentioned 21 times in the Old Testament, and a better translation of the term is "rescuer" or "protector" as in "God is our help." Eve wasn't created to serve Adam but to serve *with* him; the verse says it was "not good for a man to be alone." Hence, Eve was made to be a co-partner with Adam, not his subordinate. God gave both the man and the woman the tasks of creating families (populating the earth) and subduing the earth (to be stewards of God's creation).

This chapter provides an overview of the wide range of women that are mentioned in the Bible, and it ends with a discussion of issues raised about the role of women in the church.

EARLY DESCRIPTIONS OF WOMEN/FEMALES

Genesis has two accounts about the creation of women. Genesis 1:27 says a male and female were both made in God's image at the same time, and both have some of the same characteristics of God. In Genesis 2:7,20–23, God made man from dust and a woman from the man's side, and they were called Adam and Eve. In Genesis 3, they both sin and neither accepts any responsibility (Adam blamed Eve and she blamed the serpent). The story says the serpent's deception of Eve and her desire for something that looked good caused sin in the world. As a result, women would experience pain during childbirth and Adam was to lead the family. (Men would experience difficulty working the ground to survive.)

Many of the women mentioned in the Old Testament were wives of famous men. In some cases, the wives played minor roles, and their primary role was producing sons who become important figures in the Biblical narrative. For example, Noah's wife and the wives of his three sons were not named. Wives were portrayed in negative or positive ways, and in many cases, the women dealt with infertility, which sometimes led to unusual ways for their husbands to have children.

For example, Sarah was Abraham's first wife, and we know almost nothing about her. We are told that she was very beautiful and because of her beauty, Abraham told her to lie about her relationship with him to the Egyptians (which she did to protect Abraham). God's promise that he would have many descendants weighed on her so much that, after many years of trying to get pregnant, she let her Egyptian servant Hagar bear his first child (Ishmael). When Hagar became pregnant, Sarah was jealous and mistreated Hagar. Sarah laughed when hearing she would have a son of her own because she was well past childbearing age. But as predicted, she soon had Isaac, her first son.

Abraham's nephew, Lot, lived in Sodom and offered his daughters to men who wanted to have sex with the handsome angels he was harboring. His curious unnamed wife disobeyed God's command and stopped to look at what was happening to the city when God destroyed it. As a result, hot embers from the inferno fell on her head and she died as she was covered by the salty brimstone. Lot's two daughters escaped with him after leaving their fiancés behind. They wanted children, but since all the men in Sodom died, they got Lot drunk, had sex with him, and both got pregnant. The names of his daughters were not given, but their children were named.

Wives of Isaac and Jacob

Abraham sent an adviser to northern Mesopotamia to find Isaac a wife. He wanted the woman to be a family relative, have a gracious spirit, and be friendly to strangers. The advisor met Rebekah, who met all these conditions, and she was also very beautiful. (This is the only example of an arranged marriage in the Bible.) Isaac married Rebekah, but the couple struggled with infertility for many years. Eventually they had twins, Esau (Isaac's favorite) and Jacob (Rebekah's favorite).

As the two boys grew up, Jacob took advantage of Esau and traded food for the rights normally given to the first-born son. When Isaac was almost blind and about to die, he wanted to bless Esau, but Rebekah had Jacob dress up like Esau and get the blessing. Jacob didn't like this idea, but he did it anyway and insisted he was Esau when Isaac doubted his identity. Isaac ended up blessing Isaac and said, "May God give you fertile ground and plenty of grain and wine. May people and nations serve you. Those who bless you will be blessed, and those who curse you will be cursed" (Gen 27:28–29).

When Esau found out Jacob tricked his father and gained the blessing, he was furious. He had lost both his birthright and his father's blessing to Jacob, but Isaac didn't revoke the blessing and didn't bless Esau. Rebekah's plan to have her favorite son receive the blessing had worked.

Esau plotted to kill Jacob, so Rebekah told Jacob to run far away to be safe. Rebekah also complained to Isaac that Esau and his wives, who were from another tribe, had caused problems in the family. When Esau realized his wives were not accepted, he moved away with his wives.

Jacob moved to an area where Rebekah had lived, and he fell in love with his cousin Rachel, a beautiful shepherd girl. He wanted to marry her and told her father Laban (a brother of Rebekah) that he would work seven years as payment for the marriage. But after working off that debt, Laban said his first-born and less-attractive daughter,

Leah, had to be married first. So Jacob worked another seven years as payment to marry Leah.

As Jacob worked for Laban, he started his family with the two wives. Jacob loved Rachel more than Leah, which caused a division between the sisters. Leah had four sons — Reuben, Simeon, Levi, and Judah — but Rachel was barren, which added to this division. Rachel was jealous of Leah and wanted children of her own, so she agreed to let Jacob have her maid Bilhah as another wife; Bilhah's offspring would be considered Rachel's descendant. Bilhah had two sons, Dan and Naphtali. As Leah watched Rachel's family grow, she decided to give Jacob her maid, Zilpah, as his wife. Zilpah had two sons, Gad and Asher. Then in a series of surprise pregnancies, Leah had two more sons, Issachar and Zebulun, and a daughter Dinah. Finally, after all the years of being barren, Rachel had a surprise pregnancy of her own, and she gave birth to Joseph. Later, Rachel died while giving birth to another son, Benjamin.

To summarize, here are the names of Jacob's 12 sons and one daughter. After Jacob's name was changed to Israel, they were known as the children of Israel.

- From Leah: Reuben, Simeon, Levi, Judah, Issachar, Zebulun, and Dinah
- From Rachel: Joseph and Benjamin
- From Bilhah: Dan and Naphtali
- From Zilpah: Gad and Asher.

Joseph and Potiphar's Wife

Joseph was the little brother who told his father all the things his older brothers did that were forbidden. As a result, his older brothers hated him, and eventually they sold him to traders who took him to Egypt. Joseph was then sold to Potiphar, the leader of the bodyguards for the king (Pharaoh). Joseph was smart and wise and became such a success that Potiphar put him in charge of everything in his household.

Joseph was young and handsome, and Potiphar's wife tried to seduce him many times. But Joseph resisted each attempt. One day when only Joseph and the wife were home, she tried to embrace him passionately, but Joseph ran out of the house. To get revenge, she told

Potiphar that Joseph tried to rape her. Potiphar then threw Joseph into the king's prison.

Joseph eventually worked his way out of prison and into the second highest position in Egypt. He was then reunited with his family after an amazing series of events. During this time, he started a family with his Egyptian wife and had two sons, Manasseh and Ephraim.

Women in Egypt and the Wilderness

Women played key roles when the Israelites lived in Egypt. Joseph had arranged for his extended family to move to Egypt during a famine, and eventually the number and strength of the Israelites in the region threatened the Egyptian powers. Pharoah issued a decree that all male Israelite babies should be killed.

But the Egyptian midwives respected the Israelite's God and didn't follow these orders. Instead, they said Israelite women delivered babies so fast that their children were born before the midwives arrived. Pharaoh then said all the Israelite baby boys had to be thrown into the Nile River.

An Israelite couple (Amram and Jochebed), who had a boy (Aaron) and girl (Miriam), had a third child during this time. It was a boy and they hid him for three months, but they couldn't hide him any longer. So they put the baby in a basket and pushed it into the reeds along the Nile River shore. Miriam hid to see where the basket went.

Pharaoh's daughter was bathing in the river and saw the basket. She retrieved it and saw that it held an Israelite baby boy. He was crying and she took pity on him. Mariam came out of hiding and asked Pharaoh's daughter if she needed a wet nurse to take care of the child for her. Pharaoh's daughter agreed and Jochebed nursed him until he was weaned. Eventually the mother brought the boy to Pharaoh's daughter, who adopted him as her own. She named him Moses because "I drew him out of the water."

As Pharaoh's adopted grandson, Moses became well educated. He eventually realized he was adopted and got to know his birth parents and siblings. He grew to love the Israelites and watched as they were oppressed. He killed an Egyptian who was beating an Israelite worker and had to escape to avoid being killed by Pharaoh.

Moses went to Midian, a wilderness region several hundred miles away to the east. There, he met some women at a well who had come to get water for their family's flocks. But some shepherds arrived and drove the women away. Moses got the women the water they needed and then watered their flocks. The women told their father Jethro, a Midian priest, what happened, and Jethro invited Moses into their home. Moses became part of their family and married one of Jethro's daughters, Zipporah, and the couple had two sons, Gershom and Eliezer. She was a Cushite (an ethnic group that lived mainly in northeast Africa). The family traveled together, but his wife and sons probably went back home before Moses reached Egypt. He saw them again when he traveled through the region during the exodus, and he was criticized by Aaron and Miriam for marrying a non-Jew (Num 12).

During the exodus, God issued many laws, through Moses, to the Israelites, and some of them related to women. For example, a sorceress was to be killed and people must respect widows.

When the Israelites were about to enter Canaan, they were camped near the Moabites, east of the Jordan River. Some of the men had sex with Moabite women and made sacrifices to their gods. God was enraged and told Moses to kill all the men who interacted with the Moabite women. Later, a man brought the daughter of a Midianite leader into the camp as a secret lover. God spread a plague among the people until Phinehas killed both of them at the same time while they clung to each other. The Midianites were then considered an enemy, and the Israelite army attacked the Midianites. All the Midianite kings were killed, their towns and camps were burned, and all the women were killed (except for the virgins) because they followed other gods, were part of the deception, and would be a bad influence on the Israelites.

Before moving into Canaan, Moses said that men must not marry women of other nations because it would lead the Israelites to follow other gods. Rules were made to handle inheritances, and five daughters of a man who died without having any sons appealed to Moses to get an inheritance. Up until then, no woman received an inheritance. After praying about it, Moses said it was right for women to get a family inheritance, but only when a man had no sons. If there were no sons or daughters, a man's belongings were to be given to the man's brothers or uncles — wives got nothing.

Rahab

Before Joshua led the Israelites into Canaan, he sent two spies to learn more about Jericho, the first city they would face in battle. The spies met a prostitute named Rahab who told them that everybody in Canaan knew about the Israelites, their powerful God, and their goal to take over the region. But the spies were spotted visiting Rahab, and city guards went to her home and told her to release the spies. But she hid the spies on her roof and lied to the guards, saying the spies had come but had left. The guards believed her and continued their search elsewhere. Rahab then asked the spies to spare her and her family from the coming destruction — she had saved them, so she wanted to be saved as well. The spies promised not to harm her and told her to leave a scarlet rope at her window as a sign of where she lived (her home was part of the city wall). As long as she didn't tell anybody about their visit and didn't move from her home when the city was invaded, she and her family would survive the assault. She then let the two spies down to the ground by rope through a window in the wall, and the two men returned to their camp.

After the Israelites crossed the Jordan River, the army carried out an unusual strategy to take the city. The walls of Jericho collapsed and the army went into the unprotected city and killed every person and every animal, except for Rahab, her parents, and the siblings hiding with her. Because she hid the two spies, she and all her relatives were allowed to live with the Israelites for many years. Rahab, the lying prostitute, became the mother of Boaz and is mentioned as an ancestor of Jesus, and she is mentioned in Hebrews 11:31 as a woman of faith.

WOMEN ASSOCIATED WITH ISRAELITE LEADERS

Many other women are mentioned, either briefly or at great length, in the Old Testament. They were heroes, villains, and innocent minor characters in the stories. Some are mentioned by name, and others are either not named or are lumped into a general category of women. This section discusses women associated with important Old Testament leaders.

Samson

The story of Samson includes several women. His father was Manoah, but his mother was unnamed and barren. An angel told her she would have a special son and he should follow a special diet when she was pregnant. Her son would be a Nazarite and save the Israelites from being dominated by the Philistines. His name was Samson and he was to become famous for his great strength.

When Samson grew up, he liked an unnamed Philistine woman and married her, but at the wedding, she manipulated him into telling her the answer of a riddle he told Philistine men at the wedding party. As a result, Samson lost a bet with them, prompting him to leave the wedding party and kill many Philistines to get what he needed to pay off the debt. When he returned, his wife had been given to the best man at the wedding to be his wife. Samson was so angry that he tied torches of fire to the tails of foxes that ran through fields of grain, vineyards, and olive trees, burning them before the harvest. The Philistines retaliated by killing the woman and her father.

Samson later fell in love with a Philistine woman named Delilah. The Philistine leaders wanted to learn the secret of Samson's strength, and they told Delilah that if she could get Samson to reveal his secret, they would give her a large amount of silver. After multiple manipulative attempts to find out his secret, Samson finally told her — it was the length of his uncut hair. Delilah had somebody cut his hair as he slept so the Philistines could capture him. They did so and took him away as their prisoner.

Naomi and Ruth

During turbulent times, members of the Israelite tribes moved around the region. During a famine, a family that lived in Bethlehem moved to Moab. The husband died and left behind his wife Naomi and two sons. The sons married Moabite women, Orpah and Ruth. But the sons died, so the family was composed of Naomi and her two daughters-in-law.

Naomi heard there was food in Judah, so she left Moab with Orpah and Ruth. But Naomi told the two widows to go back to Moab so they could get married again. Orpah returned but Ruth insisted on staying with Naomi, telling Naomi, "Where you go, I will go; where you live,

I will live. Your people will be my people, your God will be my God. Where you die, I will die, and I will be buried there. May the Lord deal with me severely if I let anything other than death separate us" (Ruth 1:16–17). She gave up her Moabite lifestyle and committed to following the ways of the Israelites.

Ruth ended up working in the barley fields that were being harvested. The fields belonged to Boaz, a wealthy landowner who was a relative of Naomi's dead husband. Boaz saw Ruth and changed her job so she could work with the women who worked directly for him. Ruth was surprised that he favored her, a foreigner. But Boaz said he had heard about her and wanted to help her.

Naomi coached Ruth about how to build a relationship with Boaz, and eventually Boaz married Ruth. They had a son named Obed who later became the father of Jesse, who was David's father. Ruth's status had changed dramatically because of her integrity and her courage to change her allegiance. She went from being a childless widow from a hated nation to a respected woman who married a well-off Israelite and had a child whose descendants would include Israel's greatest leader and Jesus.

Hannah

A childless woman named Hannah came to the tabernacle one day and desperately wanted a child. Her sister had children and made rude remarks to her about being childless, which made her cry and lose her appetite. For many years, she asked God to let her have a son. She made a vow to God: "If you see my misery and give me a son, I will give him to you for all the days of his life. The hairs of his head will never be cut" (1Sam 1:11).

Eli, the high priest, saw Hannah praying with such passion that he thought she was drunk. After she told him why she was praying so passionately, he told her, "Go in peace. May the God of Israel grant you what you have asked" (1Sam 1:17). She went away encouraged and started eating. The next day, she and her husband made love, and she became pregnant. She had a son and named him Samuel (meaning "God has heard"). When Samuel was weaned, Hannah took him to the tabernacle and dedicated him to the Lord. Samuel worked in the tabernacle and took his duties seriously. His parents visited him often and supported his ministry. Eli blessed the parents and Hannah had five more children.

Women Associated with David and Solomon

Saul was Israel's first king, and his daughter Michal loved David, who had become Saul's rival. David and Michal got married, and David's happiness so angered Saul that he sent men to kill David. But Michal warned David, who escaped and traveled far away to avoid Saul's men, leaving Michal behind.

While David was in hiding, he met Abigail, a smart and beautiful woman who had been mistreated by her husband. After she gave David and his men food and supplies, her husband died and David took her as another wife. David also took Ahinoam as his third wife. These two wives were kidnapped by Amalekite invaders. David led an attack on their tribe and rescued them. Saul had given Michal to another man after David left, and after Saul died, David arranged to have her become his wife again.

When David became king, he defeated foreigners who had occupied Jerusalem, and the city became known as the City of David. He had a large palace built that became David's home. He danced in the streets of Jerusalem when the Ark of the Covenant came into the city. Michal was disgusted at the sight of him dancing in front of the people he would lead. He told her he was celebrating for good reasons and would likely behave disgracefully again in her eyes. Michal then became barren because of her contempt for him.

David practiced polygamy, and some of his wives had political connections — besides Michal, Saul's daughter, he married Maacah, the daughter of Talmai, the king of Geshur. It was common for a leader to have a large harem, and David had many wives and concubines and many children. (Polygamy was an important part of ancient society and is discussed in more depth in chapter 19.)

David had a strong sex drive that led to a major crisis. While walking on the roof of the palace, he saw a beautiful young woman bathing. He found out her name was Bathsheba and was married to Uriah, a military leader who was fighting in a battle far away. David had her come to his room and they had sex, and she became pregnant. David arranged to have her husband killed during a battle, and he thought he had gotten away with both adultery and murder. Bathsheba mourned the loss of her husband, and soon afterward, David took her as another wife.

God gave the prophet Nathan insight about what happened and confronted David about his crimes. Rather than being angry with Nathan, David repented. The Lord forgave his sin, but because of his sin, Nathan said Bathsheba's baby would die. Soon after the baby was born, it became sick and died after living seven days. David comforted Bathsheba as she mourned, and soon they had another baby boy — his name was Solomon.

After David retired, Solomon became king and was known as a very wise man who knew how to deal with complex and unusual cases. In one case, two women came to him, both claiming to be the mother of a child. Solomon said since both claimed to be the mother, he would cut the child in half and give each woman part of the child. Hearing that, one mother said she would give up the child to the other, thereby showing that she was the true mother. People from all over the world visited Solomon to learn from his wisdom. When the Arabian queen of Sheba visited him with many riddles, he answered all of them. She was so impressed that she gave him several tons of gold, many precious jewels, and many spices before she returned home.

Solomon became the richest man in the world. As he expanded Israel's empire through trade, he met women with different value systems and beliefs, which Solomon tolerated in the spirit of religious inclusion. Despite Moses's warning not to marry foreigners, he had many wives from many nations; his harem had 700 wives and princesses and another 300 concubines. Success and prosperity tainted his judgment, and he gradually compromised his values and acquired idols of worship and built altars to worship gods associated with his wives.

Women Leaders in the Old Testament

Two women distinguished themselves as leaders, Deborah and Esther. Deborah was an Israelite prophet and judge who lived in the hills of

Ephraim, about 15 miles north of Jerusalem.[46] She handled disputes among the Israelites while witnessing their oppression by the Canaanites based in Hazor. God told her to visit Barak and say the Lord wanted him to lead an alliance of forces against Hazor and its strong army with its new ironclad chariots. God promised Barak a victory, but he said he would go only if Deborah was with him. She agreed, and together they led forces against Hazor's army in the valley of the Kishon River, where they were victorious. The retreating commander of Hazor's army was killed by a foreign woman, Jael, when she nailed a tent peg through his head while he was sleeping and hiding from the pursuing Israelite army. Deborah and Barak wrote a song together to celebrate the victory, which started 40 years of peace.

Esther

After the Israelite kingdom split up and weakened, the Israelites were conquered by different empires, resulting in mass migrations to foreign lands. Millions of Israelites (then known as Jews) lived outside Palestine, and two million Jews lived in areas controlled by the Persians. When the queen of the Persian King Xerxes disobeyed an order to appear at a banquet in the capital city (Susa), Xerxes decided she should be replaced. (If he let her get away with such defiance, word would spread and women would stop obeying their husbands.) So young virgins from around the empire were brought to the king's harem so he could select a new queen. Each woman went through a year of beauty treatment before seeing Xerxes.

Esther was among those brought to the harem. She was a young and faithful Jew who also lived in Susa. She had been adopted by her older cousin Mordecai when both of her parents died. When it was her turn to meet the king, she impressed him so much that he chose her to be the next queen. But Mordecai told her not to tell anybody that she was adopted or a Jew.

The Persian prime minister, Haman, hated Mordecai because he refused to bow to him on the streets. Haman found out Mordecai was a Jew and devised a plan to get rid of all the Jews in the kingdom. He told

---

[46] Prophets spoke God's thoughts and teachings to the people and leaders, and they sometimes made predictions about the future.

King Xerxes that a group of people kept themselves separate and had different customs and didn't obey the king's laws. He had the king issue a decree that all Jews would be killed on a specific day 11 months later.

Esther found out about this plan and decided to talk to the king. But nobody was allowed to see the king in his inner court of the palace unless he invited them in; those who entered on their own were killed by his guards. Mordecai told Esther that it was her duty as a Jewish leader to do something — she might not be spared because she was a Jew. Esther told him to have all the Jews in Susa pray for her for three days, and then she would enter the king's inner court. She told Mordecai, "If I die, I die" (Est 4:16).

After three days, Esther went into the king's inner court and stood in front of his room. He invited her into his room and was relieved that she wasn't arrested and killed. She asked the king if she could host a dinner with just him and Haman. He agreed, and that night during their dinner together, the king asked Esther what she wanted. She said she would answer him the next day when the three of them could eat dinner together again.

The next night, Esther told the king she wanted him to spare the Jews, her people. The king had forgotten who thought of the idea to kill all the Jews, so he asked who was responsible for the order. She said it was Haman, the man sitting with them! The king left in a rage, but Haman stayed behind and begged Esther for his life. When the king returned, he saw Haman kneeling at Esther's feet and thought he was trying to molest her. The king ordered his attendants to kill Haman, and the king gave Haman's estate to Esther and made Mordecai his new prime minister.

But the decree to kill all the Jews was still in place. Esther begged the king to issue another decree to remove the order to have all Jews killed. The king had Mordecai write the new decree. It was quickly written, translated into every language spoken in the empire, sealed with the king's ring, and sent to every province using the king's fastest horses. When the news arrived, Jews in every province were overjoyed. Their courageous queen and new prime minister had spared them. Jews now celebrate the two days of Purim to remember how they got relief from their enemies, and the story of Esther is read in dramatic fashion.[47]

Other Women in the Old Testament

There were also Israelite women who held leadership positions but abused their power. Jezebel was King Ahab's wife and sent men to kill the prophet Elijah after he started a drought due to the evil being practiced in the Northern Kingdom. He hid in the wilderness and then in the home of a very poor widow in Zarephath. When he emerged and won a battle of spiritual powers against the prophets of Baal, Jezebel tried to kill Elijah again. Jehoram was an evil king in the Southern Kingdom, and when he and his sons died, his wife Athaliah, the daughter of Jezebel, took over and killed all the potential successors. She used her power during her 6-year reign to establish the worship of Baal in Judah.

Several females had minor but noteworthy roles in the Old Testament.

- Hosea married a prostitute to understand how God feels when dealing with an unfaithful partner. Israel was like a prostitute and had not been faithful to God, so God would leave them because they had committed adultery.
- Josiah found the original book of the Law written by Moses in the rubble of the Temple and was appalled when he realized how far the Israelites had deviated from God's ways. He consulted the female prophet Huldah for advice. She told him God's judgment was unavoidable — the Jews had not obeyed the laws and commands God gave Moses. Ignorance of the Law was not an excuse to avoid punishment.
- The daughter of Jephthah willingly sacrificed herself because her father had made a vow to God.

---

[47] The inclusion of the book of Esther in the Old Testament is controversial. The author is unknown, and the words *God* and *Lord* do not appear in it. The story is mostly about Jewish nationalism. But Esther and Mordecai were courageous and faithful Jews who served authority faithfully and used their positions of power to fight injustice and evil within the political system. They are examples of how God's people carry out God's will on earth in many ways.

- The Song of Solomon is a love story about an ideal relationship between a man and a woman.
- The last chapter of Proverbs has 22 verses that describe the qualities of a wife with noble character.
- Several women are mentioned in Job. The story begins with Job having three daughters, but they all died in a house that collapsed. Later, his wife tells him to curse God, the only verse in which she speaks. At the end of the story, Job has three more daughters and their names are given (Jemimah, Keziah, and Keren-Happuch). They are said to be the most beautiful women in the entire region. As mentioned in chapter 2, the author may have been a woman advocating for women's rights.

WOMEN IN THE GOSPELS

Many women are mentioned in the New Testament. They first appear in the first chapter of Matthew's gospel, a genealogy of Jesus that includes the names of four women: Tamar, Rahab, Ruth, and Mary. Luke's gospel begins with the stories of the birth of John and Jesus.

Elizabeth and Mary

Elizabeth was a devout Jew who was married to Zechariah, and although they had prayed many times to have a child, Elizabeth couldn't get pregnant. Both were very old when an angel told Zechariah that Elizabeth would have a child, and the boy's name would be John. Zechariah didn't believe the angel, and as a result, he wasn't able to speak until the boy was born.

Six months after this happened, the same angel appeared to Mary, a young teenager who lived in Nazareth and was Elizabeth's relative. She was engaged to Joseph, a descendant of King David. The angel told Mary, "Greetings, you are highly favored! The Lord is with you!" Mary was confused and afraid when she heard this from a total stranger who suddenly appeared. But the angel said, "Don't be afraid. You have found favor with God. You will have a son, and you are to call him Jesus. He will be great and be called the Son of the Most High. God will give him the throne of King David, and he will reign over Jacob's descendants forever" (Luke 1:28–33).

Mary wondered how this could happen since she was still a virgin. The angel told her the Holy Spirit was the father, and the angel told Mary that Elizabeth was also pregnant, even though she was very old. Mary immediately went to see Elizabeth, who lived nearly 100 miles away. When Mary entered the room and greeted Elizabeth, the baby inside Elizabeth jumped and the Holy Spirit gave her insight into what happened to Mary. She told Mary, "You are blessed among women, and blessed is the child of your womb! I am so blessed that the mother of the Lord has come to me" (Luke 1:42–43). Mary stayed with Elizabeth for three months until just before John was born, and everybody was surprised that her son was named John (boys usually were named after their father).

Luke 2 and Matthew 1–2 describe the events associated with the birth of Jesus. Mary was engaged to Joseph, who was surprised to find out Mary was pregnant. But in a dream, an angel told him God's spirit was the father — Mary had been faithful to him. In the morning, Mary and Joseph got married.

After Jesus was born, Mary and Joseph took him to the Temple to be dedicated. An old widow named Anna came up to him to give God thanks. She was a prophet and worshipped at the Temple day and night and probably saw Simeon's reaction when he saw Jesus at the Temple (God told Simeon he would see the Messiah before he died). Anna then spoke about Jesus to everybody who looked forward to the coming Messiah — she was the first to tell others the Christ had finally arrived.

Every year the family went to Jerusalem for the Festival of the Passover. When Jesus was 12 years old, Mary and Joseph accidentally left him behind after attending the Passover Festival in Jerusalem, many miles from their home. They traveled for a day with their friends and relatives before they realized Jesus was missing from their caravan (Mary was clearly not a controlling mother). They returned to Jerusalem and found him in the Temple courts, sitting with the teachers, listening to them, and asking questions. Mary scolded him for staying in Jerusalem on his own, and said, "Why have you done this to us? Your father and I have been very worried as we looked for you" (Luke 2:48). Jesus was surprised they had difficulty finding him, for he was simply in his "father's house."

We don't know much more about Mary. She is the only woman mentioned in the Quran, which has more references to her than the Bible (she is often called the Virgin Mary, but the Bible never refers to her this way). She and Elizabeth were probably close friends who spoke often because they shared the secret about who Jesus was as their boys became life-long friends. At the wedding in Cana, Mary asked Jesus to intervene when the wine was running out, and she was at the cross when he was crucified. She was also with the disciples in the upper room after Jesus went to heaven, but she isn't mentioned again. She may have moved with John to Ephesus where she would have died.

Jesus Treats Women with Unusual Kindness

Jesus broke many cultural norms during his ministry, which included treating women with respect and healing them. Perhaps the best example was when he walked with his disciples through Samaria, a region the Jews often avoided, and had a long and meaningful conversation with a sinful woman at a well. She was shunned by her community, so she had to go to the well in the heat of the day to avoid being among those who despised her. But Jesus started talking to her, stunning her because Jews didn't associate with Samaritans. His nonjudgmental interaction led to her conversion, and Jesus told her to tell others about him. She became an evangelist who spread the good news that the Messiah had come, but the people in town didn't believe her (a woman's testimony wasn't considered valid). So people went to see Jesus for themselves. He stayed in Samaria two more days, and many Samaritans came to believe he was the Messiah.

Jesus had another encounter with a sinful woman and was not judgmental. John 8:3–11 tells the story of a woman who was caught in the act of adultery. She was brought to Jesus in front of a crowd in the Temple, and the religious leaders said the law said she should be stoned to death. When Jesus was asked what should happen to her, he bent down and doodled in the dirt in silence. When he was questioned again, he stood up and said, "Let the person who is without sin throw the first stone" and then he bent down again to doodle in the dirt. Eventually everybody in the crowd left, leaving just Jesus and the woman alone. Jesus stood up and asked her where everybody went and if anybody condemned her. She said nobody condemned her. Jesus told her, "I don't condemn you, either. Go and don't sin again." She was given another chance to lead a good life. (We don't know what happened to her.)

Jesus also healed girls and women. For example, a Jewish leader named Jairus pleaded with him to heal his young daughter who was dying. As Jesus was going to his house, the crowds almost crushed him. A woman who had bled continuously for 12 years had not been able to find anybody who could heal her. She thought she would be healed if she could simply touch Jesus's cloak. She touched the edge of his cloak, and immediately her bleeding stopped. Jesus quickly stopped and asked who touched him. When nobody said anything, Simon Peter said the entire crowd was pressing against him. But Jesus said somebody touched him and he felt power leave him. The bleeding woman fell at his feet, and everybody listened as she told him why she touched him and that she had been healed.

While Jesus was speaking to her, someone told Jairus that his daughter was dead and Jesus wasn't needed anymore. Jesus heard this and told Jairus to believe and his daughter would be healed. Jesus went to the house and raised the dead child who quickly stood up and ate some food to show she was not a ghost.

At one point in his ministry, Jesus went to the coast of Phoenicia with his disciples. A Greek woman living there asked Jesus to have mercy on her daughter who was demon-possessed and suffered terribly. Jesus ignored her and told his disciples, "I was sent only to the lost sheep of Israel. It's not right to take the children's bread and give it to the dogs." The woman persisted and became a nuisance, and she knelt before Jesus and asked for help. She said, "Lord, even the dogs eat the crumbs that fall from their master's table." Jesus said to her, "Woman, you have great faith! The demon is gone." She went home and found her child lying on the bed without the demon (Matt 15:21–28).

In another act of compassion for women, Jesus was in the town of Nain when he met a large crowd carrying a dead man on a stretcher. The man was the only son of his mother, a widow. Jesus had compassion for her and told her not to cry, and he touched the stretcher and told the dead man to get up. The dead man sat up and began talking.

Mary Magdalene and Martha

Jesus had a close relationship with Mary Magdalene, another sinful woman. Their first encounter was probably when Jesus removed seven demons living in her that made her life miserable. She became a changed woman and started following Jesus, and she was probably the "sinful woman" who went to a dinner party being held for Jesus by a Pharisee and his friends. Mary poured expensive oil on his feet, kissed them, and wiped them with her hair. The guests knew her reputation and were appalled Jesus let her do this to him. Jesus then told the men in the room a story that showed the host had not been kind to him like Mary had, and he spoke highly of her kindness.

Mary Magdalene stayed devoted to Jesus to the end. She supported him financially and was at the cross when he died. She went to the tomb when he was buried because she planned to anoint his body with spices after the Sabbath. When she went to the tomb early Sunday morning, she couldn't find him and started crying. She didn't recognize Jesus through her tears when he asked her why she was crying. But she knew his voice, and when he spoke her name, she recognized him and hugged him passionately. Jesus told her to tell the disciples that he was alive and would see them in Galilee. Mary ran to tell the 11 disciples that Jesus was alive and she had seen him. But the disciples didn't believe her, so Peter and John ran to the tomb and found it empty.

Martha, the sister of Mary and Lazarus, is mentioned several times and is more action-oriented and practical than her more reflective sister.[48] She invited Jesus into their home and stayed busy making sure all the details of his visit were addressed. She was dismayed that Mary was listening to him and wasn't helping her, so she asked Jesus to tell Mary that she should help her. But Jesus said she was worried and bothered by too many things, and it was more important for Mary to listen to him (Luke 10:38–42). Later, Jesus was notified that Lazarus was nearing death but delayed coming to him. Jesus loved him and his sisters and told his disciples that Lazarus had died. Jesus arrived four days later and Martha acted immediately when she heard he had finally

---

[48] Historically, Mary Magdalene and Mary, the sister of Martha and Lazarus who lived in Bethany, were believed to be the same person. Some evidence supports this view, but other evidence suggests they were different people.

arrived. She went to him while Mary stayed home and had an important discussion with Jesus where she showed her faith and insights about him.

> Martha told Jesus, "Lord, if you had been here, my brother wouldn't have died. But I know God will give you whatever you ask." Jesus told her, "Your brother will rise again." Martha told him, "I know he will rise again in the resurrection on the last day." He then told her, "I am the resurrection and the life. Those who believe in me will live, even when they die. Everybody who lives and believes in me will never die. Do you believe this?" Martha told him, "Yes Lord, I believe you are the Christ, the Son of God who has come into the world." (John 11:21–27)

Martha then went and told Mary that Jesus had arrived and wanted to see her. Mary got up quickly and left the village to see him, and those mourning with her followed. Jesus had compassion on everybody who was crying about Lazarus, and he wept as well. He went to the tomb, a cave covered by a stone, and ordered the stone removed. Martha said the dead body would smell bad, but Jesus told her to believe. Then Lazarus came out of the cave. Martha should be remembered as a woman of action and faith in addition to being a busy and obsessed woman who worried about appearances.

Other Stories about Women in the Gospels

Other women are mentioned in the gospels. Besides the 12 disciples, we know many women followed Jesus as well. Like Mary Magdalene, Joanna (the wife of the manager of Herod's household) was another woman who was healed, supported the disciples, and initially went to the empty tomb. Susanna also supported Jesus and the disciples with her own money. We don't know how many women followed Jesus because when the number of people was given, it usually only included men.

Herodias, the wife of King Herod, was responsible for the death of John the Baptist. John was put in prison because he said King Herod should not have married his brother's wife. As a result, Herodias hated John. When the king held a birthday party for himself and invited high-ranking officials and leaders, he had his stepdaughter dance in front of everybody. She pleased them all, so Herod said she could ask for anything and he would give it to her. The girl asked her mother what to ask for, and Herodias said she should ask for the head of John the Baptist. When the girl revealed her request, the king was distressed, but to keep his word, he sent an executioner to bring him John's head. The head was brought to the king on a platter, and Herod gave it to the girl, who then gave it to her mother.

During the trial of Jesus, several women played minor parts in the story. Two servant girls confronted Peter about being with Jesus, and Pilate's wife revealed she had a dream about Jesus and told her husband not to have anything to do with him.

Finally, Jesus used women in some of his teaching stories. He asks what a woman would do if she had 10 coins but lost one of them, and he told a parable about 10 virgins who waited for their bridegroom.

OTHER WOMEN IN THE NEW TESTAMENT

Relatively few women were mentioned in the rest of the New Testament, although the teachings of Paul and the apostles sometimes touch on issues related to women in general.

In the book of Acts, we learn about a couple, Ananias and his wife Sapphira, who lied about the price of property they sold. When they were confronted about their lie, they died on the spot. Also, when deacons were selected to supplement the ministry of the apostles, women were involved in selecting the men. Later, Peter raised Tabitha (Dorcas) from the dead in Joppa before visiting Cornelius. She was a well-respected disciple who was always doing good and helping the poor. Finally, many people gathered in the house of John's mother, where they prayed for Peter after he was arrested by King Herod Antipas.

Several women are mentioned while Paul and his traveling companions were in Philippi. They met a woman named Lydia as she prayed. She owned a large business in Thyatira (in Asia Minor), and she responded to Paul's message about Jesus. She and the members of her household were baptized and she spent time with the men learning about her new faith. Paul also drove an evil spirit out of a female slave who was a fortune teller. After Paul and Silas were arrested and beaten, they were released from jail and went to Lydia's house, where other Christians were staying and praying for them.

Paul later went to Corinth and met a Jewish couple, Aquila and his wife Priscilla. Paul worked and stayed with the couple, and the three of them made and sold tents as a profession. Later, the three of them sailed to Ephesus, a major city on the western coast of Asia Minor. Paul spent time speaking to the Jews about Jesus, and he had Aquila and Priscilla continue preaching after he left. They were still teaching there when Paul returned to Ephesus. They told him about how a Jewish scholar, Apollos, had been preaching effectively but didn't know about the baptism of the Holy Spirit. Priscilla and Aquila spent time helping Apollos improve his teaching and support for Christians. They also hosted church meetings in their home in Rome, and it's possible they were co-authors of the book of Hebrews — nobody claimed to be the author, and women authors never would have revealed they wrote such a document.

Finally, Paul names Junia (a Greek name for Joanna) as an outstanding apostle (Rom 16:7). She may be the same Joanna, a Hebrew name, identified in Luke as the wife of the manager of Herod's household, and she may have moved to Rome with her husband when Paul wrote his letter. In his letter, Paul mentions other women who he heard had made significant contributions to the church in Rome. Phoebe carried his most important letter the long way from Greece to Rome — Paul describes her as a servant and deacon, and she was obviously a very trustworthy person.

THEOLOGICAL ISSUES RELATED TO WOMEN

As mentioned earlier, both males and females were created in God's image. Eve was named as the responsible party that brought sin into the world, but Adam was an equal participant in the initial sin. Eve was deceived into eating the fruit, but Adam also knew it was wrong but ate the fruit anyway. The traditional interpretation of the Genesis account established a patriarchy and has been used for centuries by men to keep women in a subservient role, which has resulted in much harm to women. Many women are mentioned in the Bible, and in nearly all the cases, women had a minor or subservient role in society.

Jesus treated women very differently and didn't see them as minor characters or subservient characters. His interactions with women are examples of how he broke cultural norms in a patriarchal society. In addition, widows are singled out in both the Old and New Testaments as a special group that need extra help because they were powerless and neglected (they are mentioned more than 80 times). Yet thousands of years later, women still lack power and privilege in the world.[49]

The instructions Paul and others gave about a woman's role in society were given in the context of a patriarchal culture. Some of Paul's instructions were clearly meant for specific audiences at specific times. For example, he said women in Corinth should cover their heads, but men should not, and he made comments about the length of their hair (1Cor 11:3–16). He told Timothy that women should not braid their hair or wear gold, pearls, and expensive clothing (1Tim 2:9), and Peter says similar things (1Pet 3:3–4), but the Old Testament has verses that say there is nothing wrong with wearing nice jewelry (Gen 24:53; Exod 3:22, 35:22; Prov 25:12). Paul also says men should lift their hands when they pray (1Tim 2:8). All these instructions were valid because they related to the local customs at the time and could be labeled "best practices" for the situation. These instructions are clearly limited in their scope, and most Christians believe the instructions are not meant to be applied in all places at all times .

Hence, instructions in the Bible must be considered in light of the cultural context. As discussed in chapter 5, it's important to know when to take statements literally and when they apply to a specific setting. If there is a conflict between different teachings in the Bible, it's likely that the context of the author's words is relevant. (A women's role in a marriage is discussed in chapter 19.)

Women's Role in Religious Activities

In the Old Testament, only men from the Levite tribe were priests and workers in the tabernacle and Temple. However, the stories of Deborah

---

[49] In 2023, women served as the head of government in only 13 of the 193 (6.7%) members of the United Nations (Taiwan, not a UN member, also had a female President). In 1960, Sri Lanka became the first country to have a female leader among the UN nations. In 2024, only 11% of Fortune 500 companies had a female CEO.

and Huldah show there were women prophets (religious teachers and advisors), and there is no indication they were unusual in some way. Miriam led the song the Israelites sang after the Red Sea drowned the pursuing Egyptian army. In the New Testament, Priscilla was a church leader with her husband.

Paul wrote several letters to the new Christians in Corinth, a tough Greek port city with many taverns and prostitutes, and most of the new believers weren't well educated. Paul said women shouldn't talk or ask questions during worship if they didn't understand something — they should ask others about it later. Women were told not to have disruptive side conversations and to be quiet unless they were praying and teaching as part of the worship activities. While Paul said a man came first and a woman was created for him, they were to be interdependent (1Cor 11:2–15).

Paul said similar things in his letter to Timothy, who at the time led the large, diverse church in Ephesus. He said women should be quiet in church and shouldn't teach men:

> Women should learn while being quiet and submitting. I don't allow a woman to teach or assume authority over a man; she must be quiet. For Adam was formed first, and then Eve, and Adam wasn't the one who was deceived; it was Eve and she became a sinner. But women will be saved through childbearing if they continue to have faith, love, and holiness. (1Tim 2:11–15)

These verses have been interpreted in different ways by Christians. Some take the verses literally and say they apply in all situations, that women should not speak in church and must not preach or teach men. Those with this view usually say women can teach other women, but not when men are present. The Catholic church allows only men to be a priest — Jesus was a man and was the head of the church, and all his closest disciples were men, while women served in supporting roles. Paul's last statement, that women will be saved through childbearing, contradicts what the Bible says about how a person is saved, which casts doubt on the belief that his instructions in this passage should be taken literally and apply everywhere as a theological position (there are different views about what the last verse means).

Others believe Paul's instructions reflected a patriarchal world view and that he wanted to keep order within the family and church. They don't believe Paul's instructions apply literally in all situations, and they point to examples in the Old and New Testaments where women were teachers. Junia was an apostle, Paul said women prophesized in church (1Cor 11:5), and the prophet Joel predicted the Holy Spirit would be poured out on the church and "sons and daughters will prophesy" (Joel 2:28, Acts 2:17–18). As noted in chapter 14, women were also evangelists. These passages indicate that both men and women were given power and commissioned to carry the gospel to the world. Some believe it made sense not to have women in leadership positions in locations where most women were neither educated nor respected by men, but times have changed — many women are educated now and often serve in leadership positions in society.

Those who believe Paul's instructions don't apply anymore also justify their position by noting that Jesus had a high regard for women and that all Christians should use their spiritual gifts for the body of Christ. They say this applies to women who have the gifts of teaching and preaching, even when men are present. Some believe that not allowing women into positions of leadership in the church is a form of oppression and unnecessary control, that there needs to be equality and inclusiveness within the church, and we should not constrain others' aspirations or scope of influence. Finally, Paul talked about the inclusiveness of the gospel: "There is neither Jew nor Greek, there is neither slave nor free, there is no male and female — you are all one in Christ Jesus" (Gal 3:28).

As a result of all these different views about women's role in the church, some churches still have only men in leadership positions, while others use both men and women to fill teaching and preaching roles. Some Protestant denominations have divided based on these different views.

Finally, Paul sent practical messages to both Titus and Timothy about how to pick church leaders (elders/bishops and deacons). The two church leaders were to pick men who were mature spiritually and emotionally and exhibited high integrity and compassion. They also had to be faithful to their wives (Tit 1:5; 1Tim 3:2). These instructions assumed the church leaders were men. Paul also gave Timothy guidance about how to pick deacons who had a "helping role" within the church (Acts 6:1–3; 1Tim 3:8–13). The guidance assumes they were only men, and their qualifications included having a dignified wife and being the husband of one wife.

* * * * * * *

The women and girls mentioned in the Old and New Testaments represent just about every kind of female that exists. They were wives, mothers, daughters, sisters, teenagers, widows, queens, judges, prophets, teachers, business owners, slaves and servants, fertile and barren, subjects of healings, victims of crime and neglect, people of faith and perseverance, innocent victims who suffered undeserved consequences, evil leaders, girlfriends, prostitutes and adulterers, people of prayer, and people who cursed others. Many were nameless players in a massive supporting cast, and sometimes they were just mentioned as "women." In most cases, they were second-class citizens operating in a patriarchal culture whose views were devalued and their presence ignored. Jesus treated them with unusual respect and kindness and singled them out for special treatment because they were habitually oppressed. This informs us how we should treat and view them today — as equals who are made in the image of God.

There are still many controversies related to women in the church today. Divisions have occurred because of different interpretations of the scriptures that relate to their role in the church, including being elders, pastors, preachers, and other types of leaders. Some modern translations of the Bible have been made gender-neutral, which has increased tensions within the church. Moreover, recent movements to be more accepting of those with different sexual orientations further divide the church and have caused splits in many churches and denominations (this is discussed in more detail in chapter 19).

No doubt there will always be differences based on the interpretation of scripture in a culture that is constantly changing. The challenge for Christians is to remember that our primary purpose is to love God, love each other, love others, and promote justice. We are not to judge others — condemnation and judgment are God's responsibility (Rom 14:3–12).

CHAPTER 19

SEX, MARRIAGE, AND FAMILIES

The Bible contains a surprising amount of content related to sex, marriage, and families. Many important stories, such as the creation and the birth of Jesus, include a sexual component. However, many things about these topics are *not* said, and some of what was written relates to a local context and doesn't apply everywhere at all times today. As a result, there are many different views about these topics.

We haven't developed a clear understanding of the Biblical texts related to sex in part because we rarely discuss the topic publicly — it's a private and personal matter. Public sex-related behaviors have always been considered unusual and abnormal, although lately, expressing one's sexuality publicly has become a symbol of sexual freedom and pride. Discussions related to sex and sexuality have become charged emotionally, and many have hardened their positions without taking time to understand the Biblical texts and others' points of view.

This chapter summarizes the main Bible stories and teachings on the wide range of topics related to sex and sexuality, marriage and divorce, and families. This information provides a framework for understanding and discussing these topics today.

BACKGROUND

The Bible's main theme relates to love, but it contains little romance. The Bible describes close emotional interactions among people, and a few stories about sexual encounters are largely scandalous. This first section provides general definitions and information about terms used today and is followed by Bible stories related to sex, marriages, and families.

Explanation of Relevant Terms

Gender, sex, and sexuality are defined in many ways and are sometimes used in the same way, but they mean different things. A person's *gender* refers to their identity and can change. Most people refer to themselves either as male (boy/man/he) or female (girl/woman/she), but one's gender can be described in other ways because the medical field has the ability to change a person's body. Some people don't identify with one gender and refer to themselves with plural pronouns (they/them).

The term *sex* has been used as a synonym for a person's gender, but since sex means other things, "gender" is also used. Sex relates to a person's biological characteristics (e.g., chromosomes, hormone functions, sexual anatomy), and it also refers to different types of physical interactions between two people, usually involving some kind of physical contact with another person's genitalia and erogenous areas (*eros* in Greek, meaning "physical love"). Less intense forms of physical contact (e.g., hugs and kisses) between people are not called sex. *Rape* is any form of sexual penetration that involves one or more people forcing themselves on another person sexually without that person's consent. Males and females of any age can be either a victim or a perpetrator of rape.

The term *sexuality* applies to all aspects of one's gender identity and sexual behaviors, and it also describes the type of a person's *romantic attraction or desire* to be intimate with others. Most people are attracted to those of a different gender (heterosexual), but some are attracted to those of their own gender (homosexual). Some have desires for both genders (bisexual), and some aren't attracted to anybody (asexual). The term *orientation* is used to describe one's attraction for another person, which is different than one's *behaviors*. There is also a range in the level of the attraction (from intense to little or none). *Lust* is a strong desire that leads to inappropriate action related to that desire. Those who lust for power or fame take action to get them. It's not lust if a married person is attracted to somebody they don't know, but lust occurs when the person takes steps to initiate a relationship with the other person .

Marriage is a legally or formally recognized union of two people as partners in a personal relationship, and it can take many forms. *Monogamy* is a marriage between only two people and the physical intimacy is exclusive in the relationship. *Polygamy* is a marriage involving more than two people at the same time (*polygyny* refers to relationships in which a man has more than one wife, while *polyandry*, which is rare, is when a woman has more than one husband). *Concubines* were legal wives with an inferior status who didn't participate in the usual ceremonies reserved for regular wives. *Adultery* occurs when a person has sexual intercourse outside a marriage, while *infidelity* involves other forms of sexual contact by a married person outside a marriage. *Divorce* occurs when a formal marriage contract between married people ends. *Celibacy* is a person's status who has decided not to get married, and it usually means the person has decided not to engage in any sexual activity. Some adults never marry but are still sexually active and may have children.

A *family* is a group of people who are united in some way and interact with each other because of a bond they share. A family unit can be simple or complex: it includes at least one adult and may include other adults and children who may or may not be related to an adult. Families come in many forms, and new family configurations are created as norms change and religion becomes less prevalent in free societies. People are becoming less bound by tradition and family expectations, and being divorced or a single parent is increasingly acceptable.[50]

The marriage rate worldwide has been declining over the past 50 years. In western societies, people are less likely to get married or to marry young and stay with each other their entire lives. In "serial monogamy," people get divorced and remarry, and some simply move from one partner to another. Many factors have caused the marriage rate to decline, including the increased acceptability of staying unmarried while a couple lives together, the rising cost of raising children while making ends meet within a family, the ability of women to support themselves, the impact that divorce has on those who contemplate getting married, and the declining poverty rate that makes it less important to have children to support older family members later in

---

[50] The main family groups include *nuclear* families (two adults with at least one child of their own); *single-parent* families (one adult, who may or may not have been married, living with at least one child); *extended* families (multiple people who are related in some way, e.g., parents, grandparents, children, cousins, aunts or uncles); *childless* families (couples who either cannot or choose not to have children); *step-families* or "blended" families (a combination of family members merged into one unit, often due to divorce or the death of a spouse); *grandparent* families (adults who raise grandchildren, often due to a parent's death, addiction, incarceration, or abandonment); and *singles* (unmarried, divorced, widowed). Other configurations may include foster or adopted children and those living with roommates, partners, or in a group.

life. The marriage rate varies considerably by geography, race, and ethnicity.

The declining marriage rate has led to declining birthrates worldwide. In 1950, women had an average of 4.7 children in their lifetime. By 2020, the rate had declined by 50%.[51] Nearly every country could have shrinking populations by the end of the century. This decline is projected to have negative consequences in the future because there won't be enough people to generate enough resources to support a growing population of older adults. It is also expected to change the structure of societies and families. It could also have some positive effects, such as less consumption of limited resources.

Changes in society have created changes in the family. In traditional families, men work outside the home and women work in the home and care for children. Now, many women work outside the home while many men handle work within the home — taking care of children is often a shared responsibility. Multi-generational families are common: they provide support and companionship to those with a range of needs, and they pool and preserve financial resources. Family members live in many types of homes in cities, the suburbs, and rural areas. Some families are homeless and may live in cars or temporary housing, with other non-relatives, or outside with little or no shelter. In short, there is no such thing as an "average" or "normal" family.

Non-Traditional Orientations and Genders

In the past, psychologists categorized sexual orientations other than heterosexuals as abnormal deviancies because they were often associated with other mental problems. Now, these "non-traditional" orientations are considered abnormal only in a statistical sense — they simply occur much less often in the general population and are no longer considered a mental illness. In the first *Diagnostic and Statistical Manual of Mental Disorders* (DSM) issued in 1952 by the American Psychological Association, homosexuality was listed as a "sexual deviation" within the category of personality disorders, along with other sexual deviations. When the DSM-II was updated in 1974, homosexuality was considered

---

[51] Estimates made by researchers at the University of Washington's Institute for Health Metrics and Evaluation, *The Lancet*, Vol. 396, Issue 10258, Oct. 17, 2020.

a mental disorder only when a person's sexual orientation caused them distress. Different forms of therapy have been tried to "cure" the orientation, but these treatments have been ineffective. The DSM-5, published in 2013, has no classification based on a person's sexual orientation, and the standard psychotherapy now used in developed countries encourages people to accept their sexual orientation. In 2020, for the first time in U.S. history, people could indicate on the census form that they were part of a same-sex couple, either married or unmarried.

The percentage of those who don't view themselves as heterosexual or who have had a non-traditional experience isn't well known because these have been considered a deviancy and were therefore rarely discussed. With more acceptance of non-traditional orientations and genders, estimates of their frequency have increased, and recent generations are much more likely to identify with a non-traditional orientation. In 2022, nearly 20% of those living in the United States ages 18–25 (generation Z) identified with some kind of non-traditional orientation, and 11% of those ages 26–42 (millennials) thought of themselves in non-traditional terms. In contrast, less than 4% of those born between 1946 and 1980 (baby boomers, generation X) viewed themselves this way. The percentage of all people in the U.S. with a non-traditional orientation doubled in a 10-year period, from 3.5% in 2012 to 7.2% in 2022, according to Statista 2023 (Life/Love & Sex).

Non-traditional sexual orientations are found worldwide and among all socio-economic groups. The percentage of people who identify themselves in this way increases as a society becomes more accepting of these orientations. European countries are the most accepting of non-traditional orientations, while African countries are the least accepting. The degree to which people accept others who aren't like themselves also varies across and within cultures and countries.

Evidence increasingly suggests that one's sexual orientation is much more complex than we initially thought. For some, their orientation is not a choice. We all have certain attributes which cannot be changed (e.g., skin and eye color), and the percentage of people who are born with a non-traditional sexual orientation is estimated to be about 8%. In addition, gender is complex and nuanced, not simple and binary. The fields of biology and neurobiology have identified plants and animals that can reproduce without sexual activity, and some animals can be male or female at different times of their lives. Analyses of the human brain reveal that most people have a brain structure that is typically male or female, but all our brains have a combination of male and female characteristics. Finally, one's attractions to others can be fluid and change over time. Some people simply prefer spending quality time with somebody of the same gender, and sexual attraction is one reason this occurs.

We don't know why some people have non-traditional orientations, but it could be due to many factors that interact with each other over time. These include biochemical, genetic, hormonal, and environmental influences and what happens to an embryo and fetus prior to birth. This lack of a clear understanding about why an unusual condition exists also applies to medical and psychological conditions that some people have or develop during their lives. Human life is complex and simple answers to questions that involve such complexity are rarely the correct ones.

Sex, Marriage, and Families in the Bible

The Bible has many stories about sexual encounters, marriages, and families. Nearly all are in the Old Testament and most involve scandals of some kind. The marriages and families in the Bible were very different from each other, and many involved polygamy. Moreover, many of the Israelite leaders married foreigners (non-Jews). Since some of the stories have been discussed earlier in this book, this chapter only mentions the main details.

Polygamy

During ancient times, polygamy was a common form of marriage. It was first mentioned in Genesis 4:19 when Lamech had two wives. The law required it if a married man died without leaving a male heir; his brother was required to marry the widow even if he already had a wife. This provided her with support when she was old (if she didn't have a son) and passed on the family name (Deut 25:5–6). Polygamy was allowed in other circumstances, with the only restriction being that a man shouldn't marry two sisters (Lev 18:18).

Polygamy sometimes included concubines when a wife was barren. Some concubines were captives or purchased slaves, and they could be discarded with a divorce decree. Multiple wives were justified because many people were killed during battles, so many children were needed to keep the population strong. Moreover, the wives of men who died or were killed in battle needed a man to support them. The extent to which polygamy was practiced is unknown, but some scholars don't think it was common because it required significant wealth, and when it occurred, husbands probably didn't have many wives.

Other cultures in the region didn't practice polygamy, and many Jews who lived outside Palestine got used to the principle of men having only one wife. The Romans allowed it among the Jews, but outside Palestine, it was forbidden. It gradually declined before Jesus was born, and there is no direct reference to polygamy in the New Testament. However, Paul said church leaders should only have one wife, which implies it still occurred in the early church (1Tim 3:2,12; Tit 1:6). Having only one wife allowed a church leader to focus his duties on church matters. Jews continued practicing polygyny for many centuries.[52]

The First Families

The first couple in the Bible was Adam and Eve. They disobeyed God, became aware of their nakedness, and were expelled from paradise. Later, they had two sons, and Cain was sent away after he killed Abel, and then the couple had more children.

The story of Lot and his family is one of the most graphic sex-related stories in the Bible (Gen 18–19). Lot was a successful rancher who lived in Sodom, one of several prosperous cities on the south end of the Dead Sea. The cities had become lawless and full of injustice and sexual deviancy — everybody in Sodom, except for Lot and his family, was living a lawless and immoral life. Two handsome men (angels) went to his home and told him to leave with his family because the cities were going to be destroyed due to their wickedness. Many old

---

[52] The Ashkenazi Jews in Europe banned polygamy around 1000 AD. Sephardic Jews and their descendants (those from Spain, Portugal, North Africa and the Middle East) have continued the practice in countries where it is common.

and young men from the city surrounded Lot's house and demanded that he release the angels to them so they could rape them, but Lot offered them his two engaged virgin daughters instead. But the men didn't want them and the angels blinded the men so they couldn't get into the house.

In the morning, the angels escorted Lot, his wife, and his two daughters out of the city to safety. Soon after they left, an explosive fire burned Sodom and the other cities to the ground. Lot's wife defied the angels' instructions and watched the cities burn from a distance. She was killed when embers burned her alive and totally covered her. Since everybody in the region had died, the daughters worried they would never have children. So they both got Lot drunk and slept with him, and both became pregnant. The daughters were unnamed, but they had sons named Moab and Ben-ammi, whose descendants became the Moabites and Ammonites.

Abraham, Isaac, and Jacob

Abraham's family story is complicated. He and his wife Sarah moved a long way with his extended family to Canaan, but because she was barren, she gave him her Egyptian servant (Hagar) as a concubine so he could have a child (Ishmael). Sarah then wanted a child of her own and treated Hagar and Ishmael harshly, causing them to leave home. Sarah had Isaac, and after she died, Abraham married Keturah, who had six sons. But only Isaac inherited his estate and received God's blessing (the six sons received special gifts before moving out of the area).

Isaac married Rebekah, his only wife, and the couple had two sons, Esau (favored by Isaac) and Jacob (favored by Rebekah). Jacob took advantage of Esau and got his birthright as the oldest son as well as Isaac's blessing. When Esau realized Jacob tricked Isaac to get the blessing, Esau wanted to kill Jacob, who escaped and went to Haran, more than 500 miles north. There he fell in love with his cousin Rachel, but her father (Laban) tricked him into working for seven years to get her as his wife. After working off the debt, Laban told Jacob he first had to marry Leah, the oldest daughter (this was the tradition). So Jacob worked seven more years and was married to both women. Rachel was barren and let Jacob take her maid, Bilhah, as a concubine. Leah then said he could have her maid, Zilpah, as a concubine. The four wives produced 12 sons and one daughter (Dinah).

When Jacob and his extended family traveled back to Canaan, they stopped in Shechem where the son of the city's leader raped Dinah. Her brothers found out what happened and played a trick on the men in the city. A few days after Dinah and her rapist got married, the brothers entered the city at night and killed the groom, his father, and all the men in the city. They also looted the city and took all its riches, the wives and children, and all the animals. Jacob found out what they did and was very upset, but the sons said they had to do it to save the honor of Dinah and the family. Jacob then moved his extended family much further south toward the area where Isaac owned land.

Genesis 38 tells the story of Judah, one of Jacob's sons, who married a Canaanite woman. The couple had three sons, and his oldest son, Er, grew up and married Tamar. But Er was wicked and died before the couple had any children, so Jacob told his other second son, Onan, to sleep with her so she could get pregnant. But on multiple occasions, Onan didn't complete the sex act, which God considered to be wicked, and he died. Jacob told her to live as a widow with her father until his third son grew up. But Jacob didn't let his third son sleep with her, and after Jacob's wife died, Tamar posed as a prostitute and slept with Jacob. Three months later, Jacob was told Tamar was pregnant, and he wanted her killed. But she proved to him that she was the "prostitute" he approached earlier, and he said of her, "She's more righteous than I am, for I didn't give her to my son" (38:26). He had not provided her with another husband as required by the law (Deut 25:5–10). He didn't sleep with her again and she became the mother of twin boys. (Tamar is listed in Matthew's genealogy of Jesus.)

Joseph and Moses

After being barren for many years, Rachel had a son, Joseph, who became Jacob's favorite son. His 10 older brothers resented this favoritism and staged his death after selling him to traders headed to Egypt. The traders sold Joseph to Potiphar, the leader of the bodyguards for the king (Pharaoh). Potiphar's wife tried to seduce Joseph many times, and after one advance failed, she accused him of trying to rape her, and he was sent to prison. Joseph was later released and put in charge of the entire Egyptian kingdom. He married an Egyptian wife and fathered two sons.

Moses was another Israelite who gained fame in Egypt who had a non-Jewish wife. After being adopted by the daughter of a different Pharaoh, he grew up and realized he was an Israelite. After killing an Egyptian, he escaped to Midian, a wilderness area several hundred miles away. There, he married a Cushite woman, with whom had had at least one son.

Before the Israelites entered Canaan, some of the men got involved sexually with Moabite women and made sacrifices to their gods. God had Moses kill all the men who interacted with the Moabite women. When an Israelite man brought the daughter of a Midianite leader to his tent as a secret lover, God brought a plague among the people, which stopped when the man and his lover were killed. The Israelite army then killed all the Midianite kings, destroyed all their towns, and all the boys and Midianite women, except for 32,000 virgins.

Naomi and Ruth

The story of Naomi and Ruth started out tragically but turned out well. Both were widows who lived during a famine but returned to Bethlehem where Ruth started working for Boaz, a wealthy relative of Naomi's dead husband. He had Ruth work for him, which surprised her because she was a foreigner. But Boaz knew about her character, how she had the courage to move and live with people she didn't know. Naomi told Ruth that Boaz was a good man and advised her to visit Boaz where he slept during the harvest and lay at his feet. When Boaz woke during the night, he was surprised to find her at his feet. Boaz covered her with some of his blanket while she stayed at his feet, and in the morning, he gave her a large amount of barley to take back to Naomi. She then left without being seen.

The next day, Boaz met with a man who had an obligation to help Naomi's family. The men negotiated a deal and Boaz bought land and Ruth, and then Boaz married her. They had a son named Obed, who later became the father of Jesse and the grandfather of David, Israel's greatest leader.

Events During Times of Conflict and Prosperity

The Bible documents some sordid and heart-breaking stories after the Israelites occupied Canaan and judges oversaw the tribes. Samson was a leader who was famous for his strength because he never cut his hair. However, he lacked good moral character — he slept with prostitutes, married foreigners, and was tricked by his girlfriend Delilah into telling her the secret of his strength. This resulted in his capture by the Philistines.

Unity among the tribes didn't exist, there was no king, and each tribe acted in its own self-interest. As a result, the tribes sometimes fought each other because an offense occurred between members of different tribes. People stole from each other, including taking women from other tribes as wives.

Judges 19–20 gives an example of this tribal warfare. It tells the story of a Levite and his unfaithful concubine as they traveled home to Ephraim from Bethlehem. They stopped to sleep in Gibeah, an area where members of the tribe of Benjamin lived. An old man saw them in the town square and invited them to spend the night with him. But a gang of men saw the couple and went to the man's house, demanding to have sex with the Levite. The man offered the concubine instead, and she was raped all night and died at his doorstep. In the morning, the Levite took her home, cut her into pieces, and sent parts of her body to the tribes of Israel and told them what happened. Most of the tribes then formed an army and attacked the Benjamites as punishment for this heinous crime. They slaughtered the Benjamites and burned down all their towns.

One of Israel's unusual heroes was Jephthah. His mother was a prostitute and his two half-brothers mistreated him because he was illegitimate. So he ran away and lived with a gang of homeless bandits at the edge of the desert and became a fearless warrior. The elders in the region asked him to lead a battle against an enemy that had taken some of Israel's land. They said that if he won the battle, they would make him the leader of everybody in the region. He agreed, and after diplomacy failed to resolve the dispute, Jephthah made a bargain with God, that if God let him defeat the enemy, he would sacrifice whatever came out of the door of his house when he returned home. Then he destroyed the 20 cities of Ammon.

When Jephthah went home, his young daughter and only child ran out to greet him. He saw her and cried out, "Oh no! I made a vow to God I cannot break." After telling her what he had vowed, she told him, "Dad, you must keep your word to the Lord. Do to me what you promised because God gave you the victory. But I have one request. Give me two months to roam the hills and cry with my friends, because I will never marry" (Judg 11:35–37). Jephthah let her go and mourn the fact that she would die without getting married or having children. When she returned two months later, Jephthah killed her.

An important child was born many years later. Hannah was a faithful woman who went to the tabernacle and prayed desperately for a child. Her sister was harassing her because she was childless, and for many years she asked God to let her have a son with her husband. She vowed that if God gave her a son, she would give him to the Lord for his entire life. The high priest blessed her and she soon got pregnant and had a son named Samuel. He grew up to be a great leader and helped identify Israel's first king, Saul, who was eventually replaced by David.

The marriages and families of Saul, David, and Solomon are discussed in chapter 18. Their lives show us that those holding high positions and who have great wealth and power are not immune from marital and child-rearing problems and sex-related scandals that lead to their downfall.

The Divided Kingdoms and Prophets

A power struggle developed to determine Solomon's successor, resulting in a civil war and the nation broke into the North and South Kingdoms. Nearly all their kings were evil and rampant immorality occurred. The Israelites followed the usual cult religious and fertility practices of its neighbors. "Shrine prostitution" occurred in "high places" around the country (1Ki 14:22–24), and by the time of King Asa, it was taking place in the Jerusalem temple. The king, and later his son Jehoshaphat, fired the male prostitutes (1Ki 15:11–13; 22:45–46). Micah and Isaiah both mentioned these types of sins (Mic 1:7, Isa 57:1–13). Temple prostitution was common and God warned Israel about it (Exod 34:15–16, Deut 23:17–18). Eventually God punished the Israelites by having them conquered by their enemies.

The prophet Ezekiel lived in Babylon and God called him to speak to the Jews living in exile who wanted to return to Palestine. Ezekiel 16 is a scathing chapter that says Jerusalem is like a prostitute, and he said God would punish its people because of their sexual immorality and injustice. They were worse than those who lived in Sodom, and Jerusalem would be destroyed.

Hosea was one of the last prophets to warn the Northern Kingdom of its coming doom. God was horrified by the prostitution that was taking place in Israel (Hos 4:10–14) and told him to marry a prostitute and have children so he would know how God feels when dealing with an unfaithful partner. The symbolic names of the children were associated with evil and indicated Israel was like a prostitute — they had not been faithful and had fallen in love with other gods. So God would leave them because they had committed adultery.

Life During Exile

The Bible has two noteworthy stories about marriages and families after the Israelites were taken captive by foreign powers. Esther lived in Persia and was adopted by her cousin Mordecai because her parents died. She became the queen of Persia when she married King Xerxes after winning a beauty contest. There is no record of her having any children, but she probably did.

Ezra moved to Jerusalem after living in Babylon and saw that Israelites had intermarried with people from other cultures and religions and had adopted non-Jewish practices. He was furious and told all the Jews about the danger of marrying non-Jews. He discovered that every priest who had returned from exile had married a non-Jew, and he had all of them divorce their wives.

Song of Solomon

The unknown author of the Song of Solomon uses a dialogue to describe an ideal love story between a young woman and her lover. The romance has sensuous and erotic dimensions, and the author uses significant imagery of plants and animals to describe the couple's attraction to each other. There is no reference to the sacrificial form of love, which affirms the sacredness of physical love within the context of marriage.

A man with significant social and economic standing falls in love with a young woman when he first sees her and dreams of his wedding day. They long to be with each other and fantasize about the features of the other's body and movements. The woman has external and internal beauty and has erotic dreams about him; she is sad when she wakes up and he is not there. When they meet and leave on their honeymoon, they become one. She tells him:

> Place me as a necklace hanging next to your heart, like a bracelet on your arm, exposed for all to see, for love is as strong as death; its jealousy as unyielding as the grave. Love burns like a blazing fire, like a divine flame. Many waters cannot quench love, no river can wash it away. (Song 8:6–7)

The story concludes with the wife recalling the sad days of her youth when she was immature and unappreciated. Once she matured and is adored for the person she is, those days are over.

New Testament Stories and Characters

The gospels and the rest of the New Testament have only a few stories related to sex and marriage. We know Jesus interacted in positive and forgiving ways with several women who lived immoral lives: Mary Magdalene, the Samarian woman at the well, and the woman caught in adultery. His first miracle changed water into wine at a wedding, and John the Baptist went to prison because he said King Herod should not have married his brother's wife.

We know little about the families and marital status of the main New Testament characters. John the Baptist and Jesus both came from unusual families (Elizabeth was old and barren, Mary was an unmarried virgin, probably in her mid-teens when Jesus was born), and there is no evidence that either were married. We don't know much about Joseph, the "father" of Jesus. While nothing he said is recorded in scripture, he was an honorable man who listened to God through his dreams. He saw that Mary was pregnant when she returned from being with Elizabeth, but rather than divorce her openly for being unfaithful or have her killed, he planned to divorce her quietly. But his dream that God was the father convinced him to take her as his wife, and the couple kept the identity of the true father a secret.

After Jesus was born, Joseph had another dream and the couple traveled as refugees to Egypt to escape persecution. The couple later had other children. The family was relatively poor (a simple sacrifice was made when Jesus was consecrated). The only story about Jesus's childhood was about the family's trip to Jerusalem for the Passover when he was 12 and he was left behind (Jesus knew he was God by that age). He grew up in Nazareth, had siblings, and became a routine carpenter. So it appears that Jesus was raised in a normal, faithful Jewish family, and nobody other than John and his two parents, Mary, and Joseph knew he was the son of God until he revealed it during his ministry. They kept his status a secret for decades as he grew strong and wise.

Mary isn't mentioned in Matthew's genealogy of Jesus (Joseph is, but he's not really the father, and Mary is mentioned as his wife), but she was also a descendent of David through Nathan, who is listed in Luke's genealogy (2Sam 5:14, Luke 3:23–31).

Jesus loved children and said that to be great in God's kingdom, we need to be like humble children (Matt 18:1–5). He supported the fifth commandment for children to honor their parents, and he probably supported his mother somehow during his ministry — when he was killed, she was a widow and he told John to take care of her (Mark 7:9–13, John 19:26–27). Jesus's request of John infers that the fifth commandment means more than just being an obedient child — it also means honoring one's parents later in life.

Almost nothing was written about the wives or families of any of the disciples or apostles. Paul said he wasn't married (perhaps his "thorn in the side" was sexual in nature), and Peter had a mother-in-law, so he was married (Matt 9:14). The intense nature of the persecution of the apostles, the demands on their time, and the lack of any mention of their marital status in the Bible makes it unlikely that the other apostles were married. However, women weren't valued at that time, so it's possible some of them were married and nothing about their families was mentioned.

BIBLICAL VIEWS OF SEX AND MARRIAGE IN THE OLD TESTAMENT

In addition to the stories that have sexual content, the Bible has several passages that discuss sex and marriage in general. However, some teachings aren't consistent with each other because the authors' understandings changed as God's work on earth evolved and the teachings were clarified by Jesus and the Spirit. In addition, some topics are *not* discussed at all, and authors and Bible translators used different terms to talk about a subject. For example, sexual intercourse was referred to by the word "know" and phrases like "become one flesh" and "uncovering the nakedness" and "slept with" when converting the original text to English (Gen 4:1, 2:24, 19:32–35; Lev 18; Mark 10:6–9; 1Cor 6:16). All these factors, plus the variation in the Bible stories, can lead to misunderstandings and different opinions about the topics.

The overall theme of the Bible is that sex is a gift from God that shouldn't be considered evil or sinful when practiced in the proper context. We are made in God's image — we aren't animals that simply follow a reproductive instinct. But what God made to be good can be corrupted by evil forces. Just as the *love* of money is evil, the *abuse* of sex is evil.

Any discussion about these topics must start with the two creation accounts (Gen 1:27–28,31; 2:7–25). God created two human forms, male and female, man and woman, which were "very good." They were told to have sex, "be fruitful and multiply." In the second account, they became "one flesh." The goal was sexual pleasure, not procreation like in the first account. This means sex is a good thing, and the consequences of the sin by Adam and Eve didn't make it a bad thing. The two stories emphasize the equality of men and women, recognize our need for companionship and helpers in life, and affirm our sexuality for both procreative and recreative purposes.

The Song of Solomon provides another example about the goodness of the pleasure of physical love. These passages are used to assert that monogamy is the ideal relationship, but polygamy was widely practiced (sometimes it was required) and was never forbidden. So while monogamy may be ideal, other forms of marriage can be acceptable if they are not illegal or described in scripture as immoral.

The Bible says our bodies are good and can be attractive. Some of the main characters are described as being beautiful or handsome (e.g., Rebekah, Rachel, Joseph, Moses, Saul, David, Bathsheba, Solomon, Absalom, Daniel, Esther). Several stories talk of attractions between men and women and the beauty of their bodies: Jacob and Rachel fell in love at first sight, as did the man in the Song of Solomon. Divine beings were said to have desired the beautiful women (Gen 6:2). While the Bible has many verses that imply there's nothing wrong about wearing things to be attractive, it focuses on inward beauty (1Sam 16:7) and has no verses about an ugly person (Leah, who was probably cross-eyed, wasn't described in a positive way, and Jacob didn't love her). Isaiah said the Messiah wouldn't be attractive (Isa 53:2); it was his character, behavior, power, and words that attracted people. (Jesus probably looked like a typical Palestinian Jew with a brown complexion, brown eyes, dark hair, and a beard.)

God gave Moses many laws for the Israelites to follow after they left Egypt, some of which related to sexual relationships. One commandment was that people must not commit adultery and another said people were not to desire anything that belongs to their neighbor, including their wife. Many sex-related acts were forbidden: people were not to have sex with close relatives (incest), animals, and those of the same gender (Lev 18:6–23). Men were not to have sex with women during menstruation (Lev 20:18) and a man who rapes a virgin had to pay her father a fine and marry her (Deut 22:28–29). In some cases, the death penalty applied to inappropriate sex acts.

However, the law was silent on all other sexual activities, including premarital sex — they were neither forbidden nor were they said to be valid. In fact, the word "fornication," which is usually translated as sexual immorality, is only mentioned when prophets describe Israel's compromised value system that abandoned God — it committed adultery by being unfaithful. Given the many detailed laws Moses gave about sexual sins and the fact that humans have a natural sex drive, one can infer that the law's silence on other sexual activities means they were common and not forbidden practices.

Moses also gave many laws related to marriage and divorce, and some of them were quite complex to ensure they related to every possible situation (Num 30, Deut 22). For example, if a man slept with a woman who was engaged or married to another man, both the man and women were to be killed (Deut 22:22–24). A man could marry a woman who was taken from an enemy after a battle, and she couldn't be sold as a slave. There were also rules about the property rights of a first son who was born to a wife a man didn't love (Deut 21:10–17). Priests could marry a virgin but not a widow or divorcee (Lev 21:14).

A man could divorce his wife fairly easily — if he found some fault with her, he simply had to give her a certificate of divorce (Deut 24:1–4). If a man wanted a divorce because his wife wasn't a virgin but there was no proof of it, he was fined and had to keep her as a wife. But if she wasn't a virgin, the wife was to be killed (Deut 22:13–21). A wife couldn't divorce her husband, but some wives probably behaved badly to initiate a divorce. We don't know how often divorce occurred, but we know many marriages were in turmoil and stayed intact. Remarriage probably occurred often due to the death of a spouse and because polygamy was permitted.

Late in his 40-year reign, Solomon wrote most of Proverbs that includes many passages about sexual morality and avoiding sex-related sins, especially having sex with a prostitute. In the last chapter, King Lemuel describes the characteristics of an excellent wife (Prov 31:10–31). Solomon probably also wrote Ecclesiastes, which views wisdom more realistically. Instead of following fixed rules in every situation, the right thing to do depends on the context — there's a right time for everything: "a time to embrace and a time to stay apart" (Eccl 3:5). He lived a long, prosperous life and tried everything to be happy, which included being sexually active. But eventually he concluded that "everything is meaningless" and trying to improve one's life is like "chasing after the wind — nothing is gained under the sun" (Eccl 1:2,9,14). He also wrote about the benefits of having a close bond with another person:

Two are better than one. They can do more when they work together. For if one of them falls, the one can lift up the other. But woe to the those who fall when nobody is there to help them. When two lie down together, they both stay warm — one can't keep warm alone. Also, though one is overpowered by a foe, two can defend themselves. A cord of three strands is not quickly torn apart. (Eccl 4:9–12)

The Old Testament has at least one story that relates to unmarried sex that isn't condemned. Tamar's seduction of Jacob when she posed as a prostitute involved extramarital sex that was celebrated, not condemned. Some scholars believe Naomi told Ruth to lay down near Boaz and "uncover his feet" (Ruth 3:4–8), which could imply that some sexual activity took place (at a minimum, it signaled she was interested in a marital relationship with him).

BIBLICAL VIEWS OF SEX AND MARRIAGE IN THE NEW TESTAMENT

Most of the discussions about love in the New Testament relate to *agape* (sacrificial love for others without expecting anything in return), and *philia* (a close friendship or reciprocal love) is mentioned a few times. However, sex and marriage were also discussed by Jesus, Paul, and others.

New Testament teachings about sex mostly use general terms such as lust, impurity, debauchery, lasciviousness, lewdness, and fornication to condemn unspecified sexual immorality. These terms refer to behaviors that reflect excessive indulgences in sensual pleasures with little or no regard for another person's desires or honor. The Greek word *porneía*, from which we get the word "pornography," is usually translated as "sexual immorality" in the Bible and was condemned by Jesus, Paul, and others (Matt 15:19; Mark 7:21–23; Acts 15:20; Rom 13:13; 1Cor 5:11, 6:18, 10:8; 2Cor 12:21; Gal 5:19–21; Eph 4:19, 5:3; Col 3:5; 1Th 4:3–5; 1Pet 4:3; 2Pet 2:6–14; Heb 13:4; Jude 4,7,18–19).

The New Testament specifically forbids some sex-related actions but is surprisingly silent about other sex-related issues. Adultery and coveting are clearly condemned (Matt 5:27–32, Rom 7:3, Heb 13:4), which is consistent with the laws of Moses, and like the Old Testament, some verses condemn homosexual practices and being with a prostitute (Rom 1:26–27, 1Cor 6:9,15–16, 1Tim 1:10). But like the Old Testament, the New Testament is silent about the morals of polygamy and specific sexual interactions outside a marriage. Paul was asked whether it was good for men to have sex with women (1Cor 7:1–2), and English translations of the verses are different. Based on the other verses in this section of scripture, the issue probably related to the effects that abstinence had on a couple during a marriage, but it could have also related to celibacy. Paul clarified that his views weren't commands from God.

We are told to have self-control and avoid situations that can tempt us to commit sexual sins (1Th 4:3–5, 2Tim 2:22, 1Pet 4:3). We are not to desire what belongs to others, which is a form of jealousy, envy, and loving ourselves, which leads to worse sins. We are to guard our bodies, which are good and "temples" where God lives (1Cor 6:18–20). Jesus understands our temptations because he experienced them himself, but he didn't sin (Heb 4:15). It's how we respond to temptation that counts.

The Bible is also totally silent on self-stimulation to orgasm (masturbation), which is a common practice. In the early 1600s, several verses were interpreted as implying it was sinful (Gen 38:9–10; Mic 2:1, 1Cor 6:9), but these verses are better understood now. Those who say self-sex is sinful base their view on general verses about sexual immorality. By the middle of the 20th century, doctors and psychologists believed it caused no physical or mental illness, and people began encouraging it because it felt good, was legal and always available, wasn't harmful to one's health, and released tension to help avoid sex outside of marriage. One Christian author called masturbation a "gift from God" (Charlie Shedd, *The Stork Is Dead,* 1968). Others support its private use on a limited basis, while others say it's always sinful. This is an example of how people interpret the scriptures differently when nothing specific is mentioned about an issue. When this happens, the context and the general concepts found elsewhere in the Bible should be used to arrive at a position.

Jesus had some extreme views about sex-related sins. He didn't support the law of Moses to kill a woman who was caught in adultery (John 8:3–11). He probably saw the hypocrisy of the religious leaders who brought the woman to him but not the man — the law said the man who was involved in the affair was to be killed as well. After all the men who condemned her left without throwing a stone (they may have also committed adultery), Jesus didn't condemn her — he was guided by the laws of love and forgiveness, not judgment.

On the other hand, Jesus was *more* strict than the law. Not only did he affirm the commandments about adultery and coveting (lusting) and link them to each other, but he used hyperbole to make his point.

> The law of Moses says, 'Do not commit adultery.' But I say, anyone who even looks at a woman with lust in his eyes has already committed adultery with her in his heart. So if your eye causes you to lust, gouge it out and throw it away; if your hand, even if it's your good hand, causes you to sin, cut it off and throw it away. For it's better for you to lose one part of your body than for your entire body to go to hell. (Matt 5:27–30)[53]

He also said a man who marries a divorced woman or divorces his wife and marries again has committed adultery (Matt 5:31–32, Mark 10:11–12, Luke 16:18). The disciples were alarmed by this position.

Marriage, Divorce, and Celibacy

In the New Testament, a marriage was both a sacred commitment and a legal union. Jesus quoted Genesis about the divine origin of marriage and added to it, "… the two become one flesh. So nobody should separate what God has joined together" (Matt 19:4–6, Mark 10:9). A marriage was meant to last until one person died, and the marriage bed was to be kept pure (Rom 7:2–3, Heb 13:4).[54] As noted earlier, monogamy was the ideal but not the only acceptable type of marriage.

Paul wrote several long passages about the relationship between a husband and wife (1Cor 7:1–14, Eph 5:21–33). To those in the Corinth church, he said that both a husband and wife are to submit to each other and give their bodies to each other, and not withhold intimacy from each other. Neither party has authority over the body of the other. He said a wife must not leave her husband, but if she does, she must either

---

[53] He used similar hyperbole when condemning those who cause others to stumble (Matt 18:6–9).

[54] The Pharisees asked Jesus a long question about who a man's wife would be in heaven after a man had many wives on earth. Jesus told them that nobody will be married in heaven (Mark 12:25). Their question shows how religious leaders focused on tiny details rather than larger principles when discussing topics related to God.

stay unmarried or return to him. If she leaves, the husband is not to divorce her (he approved a "separation" phase of a marriage).

Paul wrote briefly to the Colossians about marriage (Col 3:18–21) and gave a longer explanation to those in Ephesus.

> Submit to one another out of respect for Christ. Wives, submit yourselves to your husband as you do to the Lord. The husband is the head of the wife as Christ is the head of the church. As the church submits to Christ, wives should submit to their husbands in everything. Husbands, love your wives like Christ loved the church and gave himself for her to make her holy and without a blemish. So husbands should love their wives as their own bodies. He who loves his wife loves his own body. Love your wife as you love yourself, and a wife must respect her husband. (Eph 5:21–28,33)

This passage starts with a message of mutual submission, then transitions to a view of a traditional relationship. In this passage, Paul is more emphatic about the superiority of the husband in the marriage. However, husbands receive a much longer explanation of what they must do. Submitting is relatively easy compared to loving in a sacrificial way. Women were used to submitting, but husbands rarely loved their wives in a sacrificial way.

Peter said similar things about how a couple should behave in a marriage, giving more details to wives and reasons for submitting.

> Wives, submit to your husbands so that if they don't believe what you say, your behavior and the purity of your lives will win them over without words. Your beauty shouldn't come from your outward appearance, with your fancy hairstyles, gold jewelry, or fine clothes. Rather, it should be your inner self, the unfading beauty of your gentle and quiet spirit, which pleases God. This is the way holy women of the past adorned themselves. They submitted to their own husbands (Sarah obeyed Abraham and called him her lord). Husbands, be considerate as you live with your wives, and treat them with respect as the weaker partner. (1Pet 3:1–7)

Marriage was meant to last a lifetime, but Jesus said divorce was made easy because of a man's "hard heart" and was only justified due to sexual immorality or infidelity (Matt 19:8–9, Mark 10:2–9). Paul said divorce is a reasonable response when an unbelieving spouse wants to leave a believer, but he encouraged believers to stay married to an unbeliever because it could benefit the family (1Cor 7:12–17).

In the Old Testament, celibacy was not desirable, but the New Testament has a different view. Jesus said being unmarried is honorable (Matt 19:3–12,18; Mark 10:2–9,19) and Paul said voluntary celibacy is a good gift because it enables people to serve God and others more freely. He also said being unmarried or a widow was a good idea, but for those who burn with passion for another person, it was better to be married (1Cor 7:7–9). He also saw benefits in being unmarried and negative aspects of being married (1Cor 7:24–40).

The New Testament has little to say about how children should behave or be raised. In most cases, verses about children related to the spiritual immaturity of new Christians. Paul spoke briefly about the duty of children within the family, saying they should obey their parents and that "honor your father and mother" was the first commandment with a promise (it would give them a good life). Parents were not to frustrate their children and were to raise them with a knowledge of the Lord (Eph 6:1–4). Paul likened immature Christians to children, telling those in Corinth, "As infants in Christ, I gave you milk you could handle. But you're still not ready for solid food" (1Cor 3:1–2). He also wrote that when he was young, he thought and talked in simple ways like a child, but when he matured, he "put away childish things" (1Cor 13:11).

Historical Views

Christian leaders have held different positions about sex, marriage, and celibacy through the centuries. The early church leaders believed sex was sinful if it didn't relate to procreation. Being celibate and a virgin were virtues, and both male and female leaders vowed to abstain from all sexual activity. The leaders of the Reformation viewed sex more positively, and in the 1600s, the Puritans viewed sex within marriage as part of romantic love as well as a duty and a gift from God. But sex was only acceptable in marital relationships — the Puritans opposed adultery, homosexuality, masturbation, and any form of premarital sex, even kissing in public.

Eventually, romance and the need to support each other for survival became important parts of marital decisions. During the Victorian times in the 1800s, Christian views toward sex became more conservative and prudish. Thoughts and feelings about sex were repressed, and women were thought to lack sexual desire. (Sigmund Freud's psychological theories evolved in part from his discovery of people's repressed sexual thoughts.) Patriarchal views continued to prevail, which eventually led women to seek more equality and control over their lives.

In a free society, sex can become a dangerous force. Historical traditions, a lack of understanding about what the Bible teaches about sex, and fears about the dangers of sex have led to strict views about sex in some circles. In light of the Bible's silence about many sex-related activities, children and teenagers in many families and churches are told the Bible teaches abstinence until marriage. Like matches in the hands of a child, it's easier to have clear and fixed rules that forbid their use rather than give general guidelines and allow judgment that risks starting an accidental fire. Sex, like fire, is a wonderful thing when it's controlled, but both are dangerous and destructive when unconstrained. Small fires and passions can lead to bigger and more dangerous ones.

Non-Traditional Relationships

The traditional view of what the Bible teaches about same-sex relationships is that they are immoral. This view is based on seven clear passages of scripture that says homosexual behavior is a sin (Gen 19:1–38; Lev 18:22, 20:13; Rom 1:25–27; 1Cor 6:9; 1Tim 1:9–10; Jude 6–7).[55]

Some believe other passages support a broader and less literal view of these relationships. They base their position on the following principles.

- The Bible doesn't address issues related to sexual orientation. We now know that a small minority of people are naturally attracted to others of the same gender. Since sex is good, is not just for procreation, and people can't change their natural attractions, same-sex relationships are unusual but not sinful.

---

[55] Deuteronomy 22:5 has a related passage: "A woman must not wear men's clothing, and a man must not wear women's clothing — God detests anybody who does this."

- The context of homosexuality during ancient times is different from our current context. Men at that time had a low view of women and often used teenage boys to satisfy their sexual urges (*pederasty*). The Bible condemns rape and vices of excess, including promiscuous sex, drunkenness, and gluttony, which reflect selfishness, indulgence, and a lack of self-control. This context doesn't relate to consensual, loving, and exclusive same-sex relationships. Since these relationships didn't exist at the time, nothing was written for or against them. Those holding this position say that when the Bible is silent on a topic, one's theological position about an issue should be based on its general principles.
- Christians have reinterpreted scripture in the past based on general Biblical principles, our knowledge of the local context, and new information. This includes not requiring Gentiles to follow all the laws of Moses, changing our views about slavery and polygamy, and providing more rights to women. Many commands aren't followed because we know they applied to a specific context, not for all times in all places (we don't kill people who commit adultery or work on the Sabbath). Some Old Testament laws express God's will to manage sins at a particular time, but not for all of time (Jesus said some of the laws of Moses were outdated and meant for a certain time). Science has provided new evidence about the universe that is different from what the Bible says.
- The Bible's overriding theme is love for others. One's sexual orientation isn't discussed in the Bible, which describes great diversity in marriages. Relationships should be judged by their intentions and fruits, not by literal interpretations of a few verses made within a different culture at a different time (Leviticus has verses that prohibit having sex with a menstruating woman). The love between Jonathan and David and between Ruth and Naomi show the value of same-sex relationships.
- Finally, those who have a less literal view of the scriptures say same-sex relationships should be allowed because sex is a private matter and same-sex marriage is a legitimate bond between two people who commit to love each other. Therefore, governments should allow people to be free and make their own decisions about who to love and how love is expressed. From a justice and family

point of view, those holding this position say same-sex marriages should be legal so it carries with it the rights of married people. As noted in chapter 17, governments create laws and rules to provide fairness, equal treatment, and safety to those under their care — they provide people with many individual freedoms, including who they want to live with.

Christians on both sides of the debate agree that excessive, unwanted, and selfish sexual activities are always sinful and that being attracted to another person is part of human nature. Both sides also agree that some commands aren't meant to be taken literally all the time. We are told that if somebody burns with desire for another person, they should get married because sexual pleasure is good, even without a procreative purpose (1Cor 7:9).

The question then becomes, what should Christians do if they are attracted to somebody of the same gender? The traditional answer is that they must remain celibate and not engage in any sexual activities. Those holding a less literal interpretation of the scriptures say that celibacy is a gift, not a command to be single and sexually inactive, and that the Bible affirms the need for companionship (Gen 2:18, Eccl 4:9–12).

The extent to which churches accept people who engage in a non-traditional relationship varies. Some churches won't associate with them at all (Matt 18:15–17, 1Cor 5:11) or won't allow them to be members. Other churches allow them to attend or be members, and some allow them to serve in leadership positions. These variations are a result of how the scriptures are interpreted, and church organizations have split based on these different interpretations.

Changes in Identity

The Bible includes references to people whose sexuality was changed. Eunuchs are mentioned several dozen times (*saris* in Hebrew, *eunouchos* in Greek), and English translations use different terms when referring to them (e.g., palace officials, guards). Eunuchs were men who had some or all parts of their sex organs removed (e.g., castration), which led to sterility and a loss of their sex drive (some were born with defective genitals). The changes affected other aspects of their physical appearance (their voice, beard, and breasts). These men usually worked for a leader or women or protected women (many eunuchs are mentioned in the book of Esther). Sometimes the sons of a captured king were castrated to stop the lineage of a royal family.

Eunuchs eventually became an accepted part of society. Castration was a common practice in the region and was used to shame people — others despised them because they couldn't fulfil the duties of marriage or be a natural father. They were initially forbidden to be part of God's "assembly" but were later accepted (Deut 23:1, Isa 56:3–5). Jeremiah was likely rescued by an Ethiopian eunuch (Jer 38:7–13), and Jehu had the eunuchs who guarded Jezebel kill her by throwing her out her window (2Ki 9:30–33). Some believe Daniel, Shadrach, Meshach, and Abednego may have been eunuchs who served Nebuchadnezzar (Isa 39:5–7; Dan 1:3–7).

Two passages in the New Testament discuss eunuchs in a neutral manner. Jesus mentions them when discussing who wasn't fit for marriage: those who are castrated, are born as eunuchs, and are voluntarily celibate (Matt 19:12). He accepted all people, including those who had an unusual body and sexuality. Philip explained the gospel to a high-ranking Ethiopian official who was a eunuch and who became a Christian and took the gospel to Africa (Acts 8:27–39).

Another way people changed their identity was through the tradition of using a new or different name. This was a common practice in biblical days — a name gives a person a new identity, and many people in the Bible had more than one name. In some cases, God changed a name: Abram and Sarai became Abraham and Sarah, Jacob was called Israel, and Simon became Peter. Some people were given new names by others or referred to themselves with a different name, sometimes in another language. Naomi called herself Mara ("bitter") because God made her suffer, and Tabitha was also known as Dorcas. When Daniel and his three friends were taken to Babylon, they were given new names to encourage their assimilation. Several of the original 12 disciples, besides Peter, had other names: Matthew was known as Levi (his Hebrew name), Bartholomew was called Nathaniel, Thomas was known as Didymus, and Mark was also known as John Mark. Saul was known as Paul, his Greek name, because he traveled in Greek-speaking areas.

Names were very important because the words had meaning and gave people an identity. God told some parents to name their child in a non-traditional way because the name had a special meaning. Jesus and God were given many different names. The different names for the same person can make understanding the Bible a challenge.

* * * * * * *

Sex is good and one of the most powerful forces among humans, and it's closely associated with love, another powerful force. It can be personal and meaningful but also impersonal, selfish, and perverted. When used appropriately, sexual intercourse can provide pleasure, strengthen a marital relationship, and produce children. But sex can be misused — we are all sexual beings and Satan corrupts what is good. The value of human sexuality comes when a relationship involves two people who commit themselves to one another in a binding covenant.

God's people have had different views of sex and marriage throughout history. The silence of the Bible on certain topics and the different context of its teachings require us to examine all the scriptures carefully and apply its main principles to determine what we should believe about acceptable actions. Our culture influences our beliefs, and the growth and accessibility of sex-related content and experiences in the world makes discerning the right position difficult. Sexual control, modesty, and chastity are viewed by some as being outdated.

On controversial issues, Christians need to agree to disagree with humility and not insist that one position is correct and demonize those holding other positions. We should examine all scriptures and not form a position based on a few verses that may have a specific context. All people are born in God's image, but there is tremendous diversity among us — we are not all the same. But all people deserve love and respect. Christians are to be known by our love for all people and how we reflect the characteristics of Christ; Christians who disrespect others soil Christ's reputation.

Finally, we should always remember that freedom from rules and laws shouldn't be used as an excuse to act in sinful ways or to cause others to stumble (Rom 14:20–21, 1Cor 10:23, Gal 5:13, 1Pet 2:16).

EPILOGUE

The Bible is a long and complicated book that is hard to understand because of how many documents are included and the way they were written and compiled. Its many authors didn't know that what they wrote would be read for centuries by millions of people. Many of them didn't take time to write concisely, and they usually didn't revise their work. (Mark Twain once apologized for writing a long letter and said he didn't have time to write a shorter one.)

When we look closely at the Bible, some of what it contains is surprising, and some of what it *doesn't* say is surprising. Besides its scandalous stories and captivating journeys and encounters, it contains new ideas and controversial topics. If the entire Bible were made into a movie, it would be R-rated. Conventional thinking about what the Bible says has been passed on to us through generations, but sometimes what we believe is true is not consistent with what the Bible actually teaches. Moreover, what the Bible *says* may not be what it *means*, and interpreting scripture is a challenge — different interpretations lead to different conclusions. In some cases, the Bible is silent on a topic, leaving us to come to our own conclusions about what we should believe and do. When the Bible is silent, we make educated guesses about what to believe, but our positions shouldn't be rigid and uncompromising because others can come to different conclusions based on scripture. Christians are known by their love, not their "correct" theology, and we are not to judge others.

This book has summarized the major events and teachings of the Bible, but entire books have been written on the various topics. A deeper study of its main stories and themes reveals new insights that show us how close we are to being people who please God. We often don't do what the Bible says we should do. We are all works in process, and those calling themselves disciples of Jesus should be learning constantly, growing in our understanding of all the scriptures, and maturing in our faith. Christians are warned not to be seduced by the culture, but rather be transformed continually by having a different mindset. This should translate into changed attitudes and behaviors that reflect our citizenship in heaven.

NEXT STEPS

Paul spent a significant amount of time and energy starting and building the church in Corinth. Before he visited them a third time, he wrote them again and said they should reflect on how their attitudes and actions had changed because of their new faith. Had they heard him and followed his instructions?

> Examine yourself to see if you are in the faith; test yourself. Don't you realize that Christ Jesus is in you, or have you failed the test? I trust you will discover that we haven't failed the test. We pray that you won't do anything wrong — not so others will see we passed the test, but so you will do what is right, even though we may seem to have failed. (2Cor 13:5–7)

We all need to evaluate how well we have done on God's test, to become more like Jesus. Do we reflect the fruits of the Spirit: love, joy, peace, patience, kindness, goodness, faithfulness, self-control? Do we exhibit the qualities of God's character: generosity, forgiveness, servanthood, humility, showing mercy and grace to others, speaking up for fairness, loving our neighbors and enemies? Will Jesus say to us when we meet him, "Well done, good and faithful servant," because we addressed the needs of those we met? After doing this personal inventory, reflect on how much growth has occurred over time in your life and what contributed to that growth. Finally, identify what areas of your life need attention and what needs to be done next to become more like Jesus.

Christians are called to fight the forces of evil with love, generosity, compassion, forgiveness, and promoting fairness to others without regard to their beliefs. Believers are to be motivated by the prophet's words, "This is what God requires of us: act justly, love mercy, and walk humbly with God" (Mic 6:8). Jesus chastised the Pharisees for making their religion a show but neglecting these three things. In fact, the only time Jesus got very angry was when he spoke to hypocritical and judgmental religious people and saw religion turned into a business.

The prophets mainly condemned God's people for not acting how they should.

Micah's message is simple but hard to live. While some people have a dramatic conversion experience, the process of becoming more like Jesus requires a slow and steady transformation led by God's spirit. It took Paul several years to figure out how Jesus fit into his life. The task of transformation is easier when our cause is just and we are supported and encouraged by mature believers.

The kingdom of God on earth expanded rapidly because the early Christians loved others in unusual ways. They were the sheep who fed the hungry, gave drinks to the thirsty, invited the stranger in, clothed the naked, cared for the sick, and visited those in prison. We were delivered from sin for a reason, and while we need to worship God and be thankful for our salvation, the validity of our faith and beliefs is revealed by our actions in the world. Faith without action is no faith at all.

The first priority is staying connected to Jesus, the true vine. God is the gardener that cuts off branches that bear no fruit. God also prunes branches to produce more fruit. Jesus said:

> Remain in me as I remain in you. No branch can bear fruit by itself; it must remain attached to the vine. You can't bear fruit unless you remain in me. If you don't remain in me, you will be like a branch that withers and is thrown away; these branches are picked up and burned in a fire. This is to my Father's glory, that you bear much fruit, showing yourselves to be my disciples. (John 15:4,6,8)

I'm convinced that love for others is what the world needs now more than ever. Jesus used his power to serve others, not promote himself. Those who study and follow his radical example of love in emotionally charged settings will make the world a better place. In a world that lacks peace and reconciliation, Christians need to be peacemakers who are called "children of God" (Matt 5:9). By staying connected to the vine, we become more like Christ, and our heart changes. This eventually leads to peace in the world. Confucius wrote about this 2,500 years ago. He said that goodness in one's heart leads to beauty in their character, which leads to harmony in the home and then order in the nations. When order is in the nations, we will have peace in the world.

Being a peacemaker and loving others the way Jesus did can be risky. Søren Kierkegaard, a Christian philosopher from Denmark, said we become anxious when making changes and taking risks, but one doesn't truly live to the fullest without taking risks. Speaking the truth, especially to those in power, is risky but necessary for the world to become a better place. Throughout history, those who have risked speaking the truth have lost their jobs, been arrested and put in prison, and have even been killed. But true believers who stay connected to the vine serve and speak the truth in love with confidence as they stand up for what is right. Taking risks may lead to failure in the eyes of others, but God uses flawed people to bring about desired changes. That way, God gets the glory, and those who obey God never really fail.

Jesus said, "To be great, you need to serve others; to be first, you need to be a slave to others, just as the Son of Man didn't come to be served but to serve" (Matt 20:26–28). Those who love God don't have a choice, for Jesus said, "If you love me, obey my commandments" (John 14:15). This includes sharing the good news about God's love for everybody to everybody. In order for Christians to be heard, our lives must reflect his character.

Current conditions in the world and conflict within the church have created doubts about the merits of Christianity and have discouraged some from keeping the faith. Some people have totally rejected the faith because of how parts of the church have acted. One must be careful not to let the influences of evil prevail over the truth of the good news that Jesus has saved us from sin. We must not throw out the baby with the bathwater. We must constantly be aware of the filth of the bathwater and take steps to deal with it.

In the second sentence of the Lord's Prayer, Jesus says to God, "May your kingdom come and your will be done here on earth, just as it is in heaven." We should all want kingdom values and principles to be carried out now, here on earth, before they become a reality forever everywhere. Christians are to be people of hope and optimism because of our faith and confidence in a great God. Bringing peace to the world is part of the Christian's call in this world — blessed are the peacemakers, for they shall be called children of God. Let us all be like

Jesus, the Prince of Peace, who loved the world, so others will know the true God. Amen.

* * * * * * *

Time and space prevent this book from discussing other themes discussed in the Bible. For example, this book is silent on what the Bible says about how we should respond to personal struggles (e.g., grief, death, fear, anxiety, anger, trauma), how to raise children, and how to study the Bible. Readers should continue their faith journey by seeking guidance about these and other issues from sources while keeping Christ as the solid cornerstone who sets the direction of our lives.

Compiling and summarizing the main ideas of the Bible in a clear way is a challenge. Some readers will disagree with the perspectives found in this book or may think key points have been omitted. It's possible that some key points have been missed or even misrepresented. To keep the text concise, some verses related to a particular point have not been cited. In addition, there may be errors or omissions that weren't caught in the editing process. Readers are encouraged to provide feedback on these issues so the next version of the book can reflect the necessary revisions. Send comments and suggestions for changes to the email or website listed on the credits page in the front of this book.

APPENDICES

CHRONOLOGY OF MAIN BIBLICAL CHARACTERS AND EVENTS

(dates are approximate)

Old Testament	
Prehistory	
• Adam and Eve	Creation of the world
• Noah	Great flood
• Patriarchs (1850–1240 BC)	
• Abraham and Sarah	Promises to become God's people
• Isaac and Rebekah	Isaac blesses Jacob
• Esau, Jacob, Rachel, and Leah	Jacob leaves then returns to Canaan
• Jacob and his 12 sons	Jacob and his family move to Egypt
• Moses and Aaron	Exodus from Egypt, God gives laws
• Joshua	Israelites enter and occupy Canaan
Judges and Oppressors (1240–1050 BC)	
• Deborah and Barak	Victory over Canaanites in Hazor
• Gideon	Victory over raiders from the east
• Jephthah	Victory over Ammonites
• Samson	Victory over Philistines
• Eli and Samuel	Battles with Philistines
• Boaz and Ruth	Foreigner's child precedes future king
Kings (1050–930 BC)	
• Saul	First king of Israel with many flaws
• David	Most significant Israelite hero/king
• Solomon	Wise king expands Israel's territory
Divided Kingdom (930–586 BC)	
• Amos, Elijah, Elisha, Isaiah	Israelites in Northern Kingdom enslaved by the Assyrians (722 BC)
• Isaiah, Micah, Jeremiah	People of Southern Kingdom (Judah) eventually exiled to Babylon
Exile and Return (586–400 BC)	
• Ezekiel and other prophets	Jews settle in Babylonia, many return
• Daniel and Esther	Jews thrive in Babylonia and Persia
• Ezra and Nehemiah	Jerusalem and Temple are rebuilt

New Testament

Jesus's Birth and Preparation (5 BC–AD 7)

- Mary, Joseph, and Jesus   God becomes a human
- John the Baptist   Predictions of the Messiah come true

Jesus's Ministry (AD 25–28)

- Twelve disciples   Miracles attract large crowds
- Jewish religious leaders   New ideas challenge existing rules
- Roman political leaders   Jesus is killed but comes back to life

Leaders Spread Good News (28–95)

- Twelve disciples   News about Jesus spreads in Israel
- Saul (Paul)   Good news is extended to Gentiles
- Believers in Asia and Europe   Apostles encourage struggling churches

APPENDIX B
SUMMARY OF EACH BIBLE BOOK

This appendix provides a very brief summary of what is covered in each of the 66 books of the Bible in the order they appear (they are not in chronological order).

Book	Main Content
Genesis	Stories of creation and early events, Noah, Abraham, Isaac, Jacob and his children (especially Joseph)
Exodus	Israelites living in slavery in Egypt are led by Moses and God in the wilderness, major laws are given
Leviticus	God gives more rules about worship and religious festivals
Numbers	Another account of the Israelites wandering in the wilderness
Deuteronomy	Stories about life in the wilderness and Israelite rebellions against Moses battles as the nation approaches Canaan
Joshua	Joshua leads Israelites in their conquest of Canaan and distributes land to the tribes after all their victories
Judges	Israelites go through a cycle of turning away from God, then returning to God, while judges lead the people
Ruth	Naomi and Ruth lose their husbands and return to Canaan, Ruth meets and marries Boaz, and the couple have a son
1 Samuel	Samuel becomes Israel's spiritual leader, Saul becomes the first king and becomes jealous of David's popularity
2 Samuel	David becomes Israel's next king, expands the kingdom, and commits several crimes and experiences several family crises
1 Kings	Solomon builds the Temple and expands kingdom, but the nation divides into the Northern and Southern Kingdoms
2 Kings	Both kingdoms fail to honor God, prophets warn the people of the consequences of their sin, and the kingdoms are conquered by the Assyrians and Babylonians
1 Chronicles	Summary of history from Adam to David, with many details about David's family
2 Chronicles	More details about David as king, Solomon builds the Temple, and the Babylonians conquer Judah and destroy the Temple
Ezra	Israelites live in foreign lands and a few return to Jerusalem and rebuild the Temple, Ezra leads the people back to God
Nehemiah	Leader who returns to lead the rebuilding of Jerusalem's walls to ensure the people's security, later calls Jews to live like they should
Esther	Woman who becomes the queen of Persia and saves the Jews from extinction by taking bold actions with the king
Job	Story of how Satan caused very bad things to happen to a righteous man who remains loyal to God through his troubles

Psalms	A collection of 150 emotional poems that praise God and appeal for God's protection
Proverbs	A collection of moral sayings and stories that teach about wisdom and how to live in the world
Ecclesiastes	A philosophical reflection about the meaning of life
Song of Solomon	A romantic story about a man and woman who fall in love with each other
Isaiah	Prophet issues warnings about the consequences of Israel's sins and predicts a coming servant king (Messiah) will be killed, then save the people and rule the world
Jeremiah	Prophet warns Israel about their capture of the Babylonians
Lamentations	Sadness described about the fall of Jerusalem to the Babylonians, which was justified
Ezekiel	Priest and prophet condemns Judah and other nations and promises God will restore the land to the Israelites
Daniel	Brave political leader honors God, survives a king's punishment with his three friends, and predicts strange future events
Hosea	Prophet calls Northern Kingdom to avoid God's judgment
Joel	God sends plagues to judge Israel and calls them to repent, predicts other nations will be judged as well
Amos	Prophet preaches against injustice in other nations, then says the same thing about the Northern Kingdom
Obadiah	Prophet warns the Edomites that they will be judged for helping to destroy Jerusalem and for their injustice
Jonah	Prophet runs away from God but later goes to Nineveh to preach repentance, then is sad when they repent
Micah	Prophet says both kingdoms will be captured by foreign powers because they didn't honor God and others, predicts a future leader will come from Bethlehem
Nahum	Prophet predicts God's judgment of the Assyrians in Nineveh because of their violence and immorality
Habakkuk	Prophet tells Judah that God will use the Babylonians to punish them, but would then be conquered themselves, and Israel would rise again
Zephaniah	Prophet tells Judah that God's punishment would come because of their godless behavior and Jerusalem would fall, but a few Jews would return and show their humility
Haggai	Prophet encourages people to rebuild the Temple and predicts the new Temple would be better than the first one
Zechariah	Prophet predicts Jerusalem would rise again, a humble king would remove the sins of all people in one day but Jews would reject him, and God will return to rule the world
Malachi	Prophet warns people that they will be judged if they don't honor God and live properly, predicts a Messiah will come
Matthew	Long account of the life of Jesus, written to the Jews by an eyewitness
Mark	Short account of the life of Jesus written by a friend of Peter
Luke	Chronological account of the life of Jesus written by a Gentile doctor and friend of Paul

John	Different account of the life of Jesus written by his closest friend
Acts	Persecution starts after the disciples, Paul, and others receive the Spirit and preach the gospel throughout the region
Romans	Paul summarizes the good news about Jesus in a long and well-designed letter to believers in Rome
1 Corinthians	Paul answers questions from the church in Corinth (a port city in Greece) and provides advice about how to act
2 Corinthians	Another letter with instructions from Paul to the church in Corinth
Galatians	Paul's letter to churches in cities in the region of Galatia (central Turkey) that he previously visited
Ephesians	Paul's letter to the church in Ephesus (a major city on the west coast of Turkey) about the implications of the faith
Philippians	Paul's letter of encouragement, thanks, and instructions to believers in Philippi (a major Macedonian city)
Colossians	Paul's letter of instructions to the believers in Colossae (a city east of Ephesus) about their new faith
1 Thessalonians	Paul's letter of thanks and instructions to believers in Thessalonica (a large city in Macedonia)
2 Thessalonians	Paul's second letter to believers in Thessalonica with instructions to keep working hard
1 Timothy	Paul's letter to his traveling companion about correct beliefs and how to lead the church
2 Timothy	Paul's last letter, written from prison, encouraging Timothy to continue preaching while suffering
Titus	Paul's letter to his friend, a Greek Gentile, about how to lead the church on the island of Crete
Philemon	Paul's letter to a friend about how to treat a runaway slave who was returning to him
Hebrews	General essay written to Jews to convince them that Jesus was superior to the major Old Testament characters and that the New Covenant was better than the Old Covenant — Jesus was the last sacrifice and faith is needed to persevere during difficult times
James	Letter to Jews who had become Christians that stresses the practical implications of following Jesus and the importance of acting in addition to believing
1 Peter	Letter to encourage Gentile believers to stand firm in the faith and live correctly while being persecuted
2 Peter	Short letter about resisting false teachings and evildoers
1 John	Letter to encourage and strengthen believers who faced false teachings by Gnostics within the church, stresses obeying Jesus's commands and loving one another
2 John	Very short letter warns the church about false teachings
3 John	Very short letter about an authoritarian church leader
Jude	Short letter warns false prophets and teachers about being punished by God
Revelation	Letter of encouragement to seven churches in Asia Minor, followed by highly symbolic predictions about future events related to the end of history, hell, and heaven which gave Christians hope during their persecution

APPENDIX C
THE BIBLE IN A NUTSHELL

The Bible is a collection of 66 documents written by many authors over about 1,600 years. The documents ("books") were not organized in chronological order, so this appendix is a condensed summary of all 66 books in 24 sections that are put in chronological order. These sections cover the contents of the 24 chapters that appear in *The Simplified Short Bible: A Short Chronological Summary of the Old and New Testaments*. Each section indicates the parts of the Bible that are summarized.

THE OLD TESTAMENT

1 – THE BEGINNING *(Genesis 1–31)*

A loving God created a wonderful world and humans in God's image. But evil forces infect the world with sin, causing people to disobey God. God tells Abram to move to Canaan where he eventually has a son, Isaac. Abraham proves he trusts God and is told he will lead a special group of people who live in Canaan — his descendants will be countless as long as they obey God; they will be blessed, and every nation will be blessed by them. Isaac marries Rebekah and has twins, Esau and Jacob, and Jacob tricks Esau into giving away the normal blessings that belongs to his older brother. Esau wants to kill Jacob, who escapes to live with his relatives hundreds of miles away. Jacob work with his relatives for many years, and he eventually had 12 sons and a daughter with Rachel and his three other wives. God tells him he will be blessed and have many descendants, the same promise God made to Abraham. When Isaac decides to return to Canaan, his awkward departure strains his relationship with his relatives. Eventually, they work out their differences and leave each other as friends.

2 – JACOB RETURNS TO CANAAN *(Genesis 32–48)*

Jacob returns to Canaan and God changes his name to Israel. He mends his relationship with Esau, and his wife Rachel dies when she has a son, Benjamin. Joseph is Rachel's first son and is Jacob's favorite. His older brothers hate him and stage his death and sell him to traders who take him to Egypt. Joseph is so wise that the Egyptian leader (Pharoah) puts him in charge of the entire country, including supervising food sold to foreigners during a long famine. When his brothers come to Egypt to get food, they don't recognize him — they all think he is dead. At first, Joseph doesn't let them know who he is, but later he tells them the truth — he is alive and will take care of them. God had used the evil done they had done to him to bless them. Joseph arranges for all his relatives to move to Egypt where they are given the best farmland in the Nile delta.

3 – Life in Egypt *(Genesis 48–50, Exodus 1–12)*

Members of Jacob's tribe are called Israelites and speak Hebrew. Their population grows powerful and threaten a new Pharoah who makes the Israelites his slaves. An Israelite baby named Moses is saved from death and adopted by Pharoah's daughter. When he is fully grown, he is upset with how the Israelites are treated, and he kills an Egyptian soldier and escapes to avoid arrest. While living in the wilderness for many years, God appears to him in a burning bush. God tells Moses to go back to Egypt and tell Pharoah to let the Israelites leave Egypt, and his brother Aaron will help him. God gives Moses special powers to show Pharoah God is on his side, but the king makes life more miserable for the Israelites. Moses tells the people God is on their side and will deliver them from Egypt, but they don't believe him. Moses confronts Pharoah many times and creates many problems for the Egyptians by using God's power, but the king doesn't let the people go. After God kills all the first-born children and animals one night (but not those of the Israelites who put blood around their doors so death would "passover" their homes), the king orders all the Israelites to leave, who start heading back to Canaan with Moses as their leader.

4 – The Israelites Leave Egypt *(Exodus 13–40, Leviticus)*

Pharaoh soon tries to recapture the Israelites, but Moses uses God's power to open a path through vast waters, and the pursuing Egyptian army drowns when the water return to its normal depth. The Israelites understand God saved them, and God faithfully provides water and food as they travel in the wilderness. Moses is God's spokesman, and an agreement is made — God will love and protect the Israelites if they obey God. While camping near Mount Sinai, Moses receives many commands and rules from God that the people must obey in order to create a just, healthy, loving, and holy society. There are rewards and blessings if people obey God's laws, but punishment will occur if people don't follow God's commands. When they disobey, the people are to seek forgiveness and make high-quality sacrifices and offerings to God. Shedding blood is a key sacrifice to mending a broken relationship, and God forgives those who are sorry for their disobedience. God warns the Israelites that if they continue to break their agreement with God, they will lose their land and be enslaved by their enemies. God lives in a special tent (tabernacle), and male descendants of Levi, one of Jacob's sons, become priests to lead the people's worship of God. When people rebel against God and Moses, the Levites kill them.

5 – Life in the Wilderness *(Numbers, Deuteronomy)*
When the Israelites get close to Canaan, 12 "spies" go into the region to learn about its conditions. When they return, 10 of them say it will be impossible to conquer the region. However, Joshua and Caleb disagree and say that if God is on their side, they will occupy the land. The Israelite leaders are angry that Moses led them out of Egypt to a land they can't occupy. As punishment for their lack of faith, God has the Israelites wander in the wilderness for 40 years. During this time, the people constantly complain about their living conditions. After 40 years, they travel toward Canaan and defeat the armies they meet on the way. They camp on the banks of the Jordan River and Moses provides instructions about what they should do when they cross into Canaan. Moses reminds the people several times to love and obey God because the Lord first loved them. If the Israelites don't obey God's commands, they will lose their land. They are stubborn, but the wickedness of the people living in Canaan is much worse. They are to drive them all out, destroy their images of their idols and gods, and not intermarry with others because they will cause God's people to stumble.

6 – The Occupation of Canaan *(Joshua)*
Joshua leads the people across the Jordan River. The Israelites camp near the walled city of Jericho and the army marches around it many times. When trumpets blow on the seventh day, the walls fall and the Israelite army kills everybody except the prostitute Rahab and her family (she lied to shelter two Israelites investigating conditions in

Jericho). The army then conquers all the other nations in the region. During the next seven years, the Israelites conquer all the local nations, and the land is divided so the 12 tribes of Israel (descendants of Jacob) have their own land. But some areas are not occupied, so Canaanites continue living in the region. Joshua reminds everybody to be faithful to God and not mix with the Canaanites, and that God will destroy them if they behave in evil ways. They all agree to do this.

7 – ISRAEL STRUGGLES IN CANAAN *(Judges, Ruth)*

The nation of Israel is a disjointed set of tribes that don't work together effectively. They don't follow the warnings of Moses and Joshua, and the people adopt the ways of the local Canaanites. As a result, God takes away the blessings promised to them. When the tribes are attacked by other nations, leaders sometimes rise and use God's power to lead the Israelites into periods of peace. But these good times are always followed by periods when the people return to their evil ways. A young Moabite widow travels to Bethlehem with her mother-in-law during a famine and marries a wealthy landowner, and the couple have a son (his descendants will lead the Israelites).

8 – CROWNING A UNIFYING KING *(1 Samuel)*

The Israelite tribes fight each other and neighboring powers and don't follow the God who blessed them. God calls Samuel, a prophet and judge, to lead the people back to the Lord. The leaders of the tribes ask him to appoint a king so the Israelites can be unified and be like other nations. Saul is crowned the first king, but he lacks the personal qualities needed to be a good leader. A young shepherd, David, is picked to eventually become the next king, and he proves his courage and faith in God by killing Goliath in a dramatic confrontation with their enemy, the Philistines. Saul is jealous of David's fame and tries to kill him, but David always escapes.

9 – KING DAVID AND KING SOLOMON
(2 Samuel, 1 Kings, 1–2 Chronicles)

Saul dies in battle and David becomes the king and defeats many foreign powers, extending the land of the nation in every direction. Jerusalem becomes the political and religious center of the nation. King David has an affair with Bathsheba and has her husband killed. After being confronted, he repents but their child dies. Their next child, Solomon, becomes the king after David died. Solomon builds an elaborate Temple where God will live, and he is known around the world for his great wisdom. But his wealth and fame lead him to adopt other customs and ideas that are not consistent with God's values.

10 – THE DIVIDED KINGDOM *(2 Kings, Amos, Hosea, Isaiah, Micah)*
There is no plan to pick the next king, and when Solomon dies, a leadership struggle develops into a civil war. The nation divides into two kingdoms, Judah in the South and Israel in the North. As a divided nation, the kingdoms are weak and often attacked by foreigners. Both kingdoms have many kings, and most of them don't honor God, although some kings lead religious and social reforms that lead to periods of peace and prosperity. Various prophets warn the people and leaders of both nations about the negative consequences of being corrupt, not providing justice, and not following God. They say other nations will conquer them and God's blessings will be taken from them if they continue doing these things. Micah say people are to "act fairly, love kindness, and walk humbly with God." Isaiah harshly condemns the moral decline of the Israelites, saying people will be judged based on justice and correct living. He also predicts a servant king will come, a Messiah, who will be a descendent of David and lead a worldwide kingdom that lasts forever. The blood of the Messiah's death will save all people, including those of other nations, from their sins.

11 – BOTH KINGDOMS FALL *(Jeremiah, Joel, Zephaniah, Obadiah, Nahum, Habakkuk, Lamentations)*
The Assyrians are the first foreign power to conquer the Israelites, who are now collectively known as Jews (from the term Judah). The Assyrians occupy the Northern Kingdom and take thousands of Jews captive. The Assyrians who move into the region intermarry with the Jews that still lived there (people living in the region are called Samaritans because Samaria is the main city). In the Southern Kingdom, several kings are faithful to God, and the Kingdom lasts 136 years longer than the Northern Kingdom. But prophets warn the people that God will judge them as well for their disobedience. They are to repent because God is merciful and forgiving; those who don't repent and obey will be captured, but there is hope for those who love God and survive. Eventually the Babylonians conquer the Southern

Kingdom; the Temple is looted and Jerusalem is burned to the ground. The Jewish leaders hadn't listened to the prophets' warnings, and the people suffer as God said they would.

12 – LIFE IN EXILE, THEN RESTORATION *(Ezekiel, Daniel, Haggai, Zechariah, Esther, Ezra, Nehemiah, Malachi)*

While the Jews live in the land of their conquerors, they become active in the local economies and maintain their distinctive way of life. A few hold leadership positions in the government (Daniel, Nehemiah, Esther) and stay faithful to God, even though they faced possible death. Many wonder when Jews can return to Canaan (Palestine), and Persian kings support their return. Several prophets encourage people to return, and those who do find Jerusalem in ruins. The city and Temple are rebuilt, and Zechariah predicts a glorious future for God's people led by a servant leader who will enter Jerusalem riding on a donkey. The Jews start waiting for the Messiah who will come and establish a new kingdom, and for a messenger who will come first to prepare the way for the Messiah.

13 – BIBLICAL POETRY AND UNIQUE BOOKS

(Psalms, Proverbs, Ecclesiastes, Job, Jonah, Song of Solomon)

The Old Testament contains six books that represent other forms of literature and are not part of the chronological history of the Israelites. Poetry in the Bible reflects strong emotions and imagery about God and the human condition. Several books provide lessons about life — wisdom for correct living and how to deal with difficult situations when life turns in unexpected directions. Stories about individuals teach different lessons.

THE NEW TESTAMENT

14 – THE MESSIAH ARRIVES *(Luke 1–5, John 1, Matthew 1–4)*

For 400 years, the Israelites wait for a Messiah to deliver them from foreign domination. The Greeks conquer the region and Jewish religious leaders develop elaborate rules so the Jews will please God and get the Messiah to come. Rebellions against the Greeks lead to temporary victories., but the Romans conquer the region. Jesus is born in Bethlehem, and when he is 30 years old, John the Baptist announces the Kingdom of God is coming. Jesus is baptized and spends 40 days in the wilderness preparing to start his ministry. He resists Satan's temptations and starts preaching and performing miracles. When he speaks in his hometown of Nazareth, he implies he is the Messiah, and the people turn against him. He leaves town and tells several men to follow him and be his disciples. Word spreads about his healing powers.

15 – THE ACTS OF JESUS

(Luke 5–10, 18–21; John 2–5, Matthew 8–9, 11–12, 14–15, 17)

Jesus spends several years performing different types of miracles and relating to people who are not respected in society — women, social outcasts, foreigners, and those with physical limitations. His powers and popularity threaten the religious leaders because he violates their traditions and reveals their misplaced values. He values people more than rules and rebukes those with religious pride. He sends trusted followers to perform more miracles and spread news about him. In a message to John, Jesus confirms he is the Messiah, the son of God.

16 – THE TEACHINGS OF JESUS

(Luke 11–21, John 6–9, Matthew 5–7, 10–25, Mark)

Most of Jesus's teachings are new to his audiences, and some of his messages are hard to understand. He changes the meaning of long-established religious laws and customs, and he says people should serve and support others without conditions, especially those with great need. He strongly condemns the views held by religious leaders and says being a loving, generous, and forgiving person is more important than following rules people are told they must follow. He says he is the human form of God, gives advice about how to communicate with God, and redefines what people need to do to gain God's favor. But his core teachings about loving, serving, and forgiving others and being merciful, generous, and compassionate to all people are counter-cultural and not easy to follow.

17 – ARREST, TRIAL, AND EXECUTION

(Luke 22–23, John 10–19, Matthew 26–27)

After Jesus travels and teaching in the region for three years, his time on earth is ending. His teachings threaten the religious traditions of Judaism, and its leaders want to kill him. Jesus clarifies some of his main teachings with his closest disciples during their last meal, and one of them betrays him. Jesus is arrested in the middle of the night and the religious leaders say he must die because he said he is God. They arrange to have the Roman leader sentence him to death. He is brutally beaten but rarely speaks, never complains, and doesn't try to avoid his death sentence. He dies a few hours after being nailed to a cross, and he is buried in a stone tomb, which is covered by a large stone and guarded by Roman soldiers.

18 – LIFE AFTER DEATH *(Luke 24, John 20–21, Matthew 28, Acts 1)*
After Jesus dies Friday afternoon, he come back to life early Sunday morning. The frightened Roman guards at the gravesite leave their post and are bribed to say the disciples stole his body. Jesus appears to many people in different areas of Israel over the next 40 days, and he explains how he fulfilled the Biblical predictions that as the Messiah, he had to die as a loving sacrifice to save the entire world. The sacrifice of the blood of a perfect man permanently allows all people to have their sins forgiven — sacrifices are no longer needed for people to be acceptable to God. Jesus tells his disciples to tell everybody what he taught them and how people should live. He say he will return in the future and that God's spirit will guide people who live on earth. Then he rises into the sky and disappears.

19 – THE DISCIPLES RESPOND AND SCATTER *(Acts 1–11)*
God's spirit soon fills the disciples, and they start healing people and preaching about who Jesus is. Thousands believe he is the Messiah, and the religious leaders start arresting the disciples. The number of people who follow "the Way" of Jesus grows, and more leaders are appointed to help new believers. Those who follow the teachings of Jesus start being persecuted, and Saul, a Pharisee, leads this effort. But Saul becomes a believer after having a dramatic experience on a trip to Damascus. He becomes known as Paul and many Jews try to kill him. Peter, the lead disciple, continues preaching and healing people, and God reveals to him that forbidden practices, such as eating unclean food, are no longer forbidden. Peter meets Cornelius, a Gentile Roman military leader, and realizes Jesus came to save all people, not just the Jews. This news spreads throughout the region and the movement keeps growing. People who follow Jesus are called Christians, and collectively they are called the church.

20 – PAUL'S TRAVELS, PART 1: TRIPS TO ASIA MINOR AND GREECE *(Acts 12–20)*

Paul takes three long journeys to spread the gospel in Asia Minor (Turkey) and Greece. He travels with different men, and many Jews and local people oppose him because they are threatened by his message about Jesus. Paul and his followers are jailed and nearly killed several times. Word about Gentiles becoming believers results in decisions about what rules should be followed — they don't need to follow Jewish rules and traditions. Paul's trips start many churches throughout the region. When he returns to Palestine after his third trip, he expects to encounter more hardships.

21 – PAUL'S TRAVELS, PART 2: FROM JERUSALEM TO ROME *(Acts 21–28)*

Paul goes to Jerusalem and is accused of false teachings by Jews who know him from his travels in Asia. After being arrested by Roman soldiers, he uses his privilege as a Roman citizen to tell the authorities why people oppose him. He avoids plots to kill him, and his false accusers can't provide any evidence against him. He wins his appeal to have his case heard in Rome. On the trip to Rome as a prisoner, his ship faces a very strong storm and the ship is destroyed on the shores of Malta. Paul provides leadership on the boat and everybody survives the shipwreck. After arriving in Rome and while he waits for his trial, he speaks to many people about Jesus being the Messiah, and he writes many letters to the Christians he met on his previous trips.

22 – PAUL'S LETTERS TO BELIEVERS

(Galatians, 1–2 Thessalonians, 1–2 Corinthians, Romans, Colossians, Ephesians, Philippians, Titus, Philemon, 1–2 Timothy)

Paul writes letters to Christians who lived in Galatia, Corinth, Thessalonica, Rome, Colossae, Ephesus, and Philippi and to three Christian leaders — Timothy, Titus, and Philemon. He describes and explains Jesus's teachings and actions and discusses what they mean for believers. He also provides practical advice and encourages those receiving his letters. Paul's longer letters include many concepts about God as he clarifies and defends the faith. Here are the main ideas in his letters.

- Jesus is the human form of God and came to earth to give himself as the final sacrifice to forgive and save all people from their sins. People can't earn God's approval by following rules and laws. God's free gift of eternal life is available to everybody — non-Jews were adopted into God's family. Being free from sin through God's forgiveness and unconditional acceptance gives people spiritual and emotional freedom, which helps them be better models of holy living and a beneficial presence in the world.

- Jesus provides us with a concrete example of how we should live and act, and those who put their faith and trust in him are called to be like him. His followers should show elements of God's character, including love for others, compassion, forgiveness, helpfulness, hope, humility, kindness, patience, peace, and perseverance.

- God's spirit lives in people and helps them become more like Jesus and do what God wants them to do. Christians must stay focused on Jesus's teachings and example and be united within their diverse community. They are to resist the distractions and alternative belief systems that exist in society.

23 – OTHER LETTERS TO BELIEVERS
(1–2 Peter, James, Jude, 1–3 John, Hebrews)

Other Christian leaders write letters to various believers. Peter's two letters offer encouragement and instruction about how to live a godly life, and he warns believers about following false teachings. The short letter by James is practical in nature, and the very short letters by Jude and John deal with false teachings that circulate in the region. A general letter, Hebrews, makes the case to Jewish Christians about how Jesus relate to the Old Testament and the importance of having faith during difficult times. These letters stress some of the same themes found in Paul's letters: Christians should love one another, live a good life, serve others through their actions, endure hardship, and resist evil and false teachings.

24 – PREDICTIONS ABOUT THE FUTURE
(Matthew 13 and 24, Revelation)

Jesus and others predicted certain things will happen in the future, including the judgment of those who are evil and rewards for those who remain faithful. These predictions are hard to understand because they use symbolism that is unclear, and nobody knows when the final judgment will occur. Christians are being persecuted because their allegiance is to God, not to the Roman leaders, and John encourages believers not to compromise their faith in order to blend in with others in society. At some point in the future, certain things will happen that indicate the final judgment is near. These include intense warfare and natural disasters and the persecution of Christians. A final battle between the forces of good and evil will eventually take place, and Jesus will return and destroy the forces of evil forever. Jesus and all his faithful followers, both dead and alive, will then live forever in heaven. The prediction of a final victory helps Christians endure during difficult times.

APPENDIX D
JUDGES, KINGS, AND PROPHETS OF THE OLD TESTAMENT

Keeping track of the many judges, kings, and prophets mentioned in the Old Testament is challenging because multiple books provide information about them. This appendix lists the judges and kings mentioned in the Bible in the order they served Israel and the Northern and Southern Kingdoms (Israel and Judah). Each king is rated based on the overall level of righteousness that occurred in society during their reign, using a scale of 1 to 5 stars, with one star (*) being very bad, and five stars (*****) being very good. The vast majority of the 43 kings were very bad, and a few started well but later became evil.

Prophets are people who speak for God. Some who spoke for God aren't called prophets because their writings are historical (Moses, Joshua, Ezra, Nehemiah). The prophets who addressed the Israelites during each king's reign are listed in *italics*. These include some prophets who didn't produce written works. The dates are rounded and are based on those used in the 1981 edition of the *Master Study Bible* of the New American Standard version (different dates are given by others).

Judges (330 years, 1380–1050 BC)
Othniel
Ehud, Shamgar
Deborah
Gideon
Abimelech
Tola, Jair
Jephthah, Ibzan, Elon, Abdon
Samson
Eli
Samuel

Kings, United Kingdom, 120 years (1050–931 BC)
Saul (40 years) ** *Samuel*
David (40 years) **** *Samuel/Nathan*
Solomon (40 years) *** *Nathan*

Kings, Northern Kingdom – Israel 210 years (931–722 BC)	Kings, Southern Kingdom – Judah 345 years (931–586 BC)
Jeroboam (22 years) * *Ahijah*	Rehoboam (17 years) * *Shemaiah*
Nadab (2 years) *	Abijah (3 years) * *Shemaiah*
Baasha (24 years) * *Jehu*	Asa (41 years) **** *Shemaiah/Hanani*
Elah (2 years) *	Jehoshaphat (25 years) ***
Zimri (7 days) * *Elijah/Micaiah*	Jehoram/Joram (8 years) *
Tibni (4 years) * *?*	Ahaziah (1 years) *
Omri (8 years) * *Elijah/Micaiah*	Queen Athaliah (6 years) *
Ahab (22 years) * *Elijah/Micaiah*	Jehoash (40 years) ** *Joel*
Ahaziah (2 years) * *Elisha*	Amaziah (29 years) **
Jehoram/Joram (12 years) * *Elisha*	Uzziah/Azariah (17 years) ** *Isaiah*
Jehu (28 years) ***	Jotham 16 years) **** *Isaiah/ Micah*
Jehoahaz (17 years) *	Ahaz (16 years) * *Isaiah/Micah*
Jehoash (16 years) *	Hezekiah (29 years) **** *Isaiah/Micah/Hosea*
Jeroboam II (41 years) * *Hosea/Amos*	Manasseh (55 years) **
Zechariah (6 months) * *Hosea*	Amon (2 years) *
Shallum (1 month) * *Hosea*	Josiah (31 years) ***** *Zephaniah/Jeremiah/Habakkuk*
Menahem (10 years) * *Hosea*	Jehoahaz (3 months) * *Jeremiah*
Pekahiah (2 years) * *Hosea*	Jehoiakim (11 years) * *Jeremiah*
Pekah (20 years) * *Hosea*	Jehoiachin (3 months) * *Jeremiah*
Hoshea (9 years) * *Hosea*	Zedekiah (11 years) * *Jeremiah*

In addition to the prophets mentioned above, other prophets or authors are mentioned in the Old Testament. They either spoke to other nations (Jonah, Obadiah, Nahum), or to the Israelites while they were in exile (Daniel, Ezekiel, Ezra), or after they returned to Jerusalem (Ezra, Nehemiah, Haggai, Zechariah, Malachi). Other prophets didn't leave written works, and two of these, Elijah and Elisha, are included in the table because they were significant prophets to Israelite kings. Although Esther was not a prophet, she spoke for God indirectly as the queen of Persia when her brave actions saved the Israelites from genocide.

APPENDIX E
THEOLOGICAL TERMS EXPLAINED

The Bible and Christians use many terms that are uncommon or specialized in the field of theology. This appendix explains most of these terms, some of which are commonly used in their conversations and could be considered "religious jargon" and are not fully understood by others.

Term	Definition
Abide	To remain, stay in a place, hold fast, or remain steadfast to the goal.
Advent	The coming of Christ, either his incarnation (*first advent*), or his future second coming (*second advent*). Also used to refer to the period of the church calendar leading up to and anticipating the celebration of the birth of Christ.
Agape	One of three Greek words for love that means sacrificing one's own desires for another, the most profound type of love (pronounced *ŭ–GAP–á*).
Agnostic	Person who claims not to know anything with certainty about God. From the Greek word *agnoeō* meaning "not knowing."
Apocalyptic/ Apocalypse	A form of literature about future events and the end of time that used highly symbolic language and numerology and often lacked important details. From the Greek word *apocalypsis* meaning "unveiling." Apocalypse is a term for a final battle, often associated with Armageddon (a valley in northern Israel).
Apocrypha	The books in Catholic Bibles that are not in Protestant Bibles. From the word *apokryphos* meaning "hidden."
Apologetics	The theological discipline related to explaining and defending the truthfulness of the Christian faith.
Apostacy	The renunciation of a profession of Christian faith.
Apostles	Messengers of God, derived from the Greek word *apostolos* meaning "one sent." The 12 disciples were named apostles in the New Testament, and five other men and one woman are also called apostles: Paul, Barnabas, Mathias, James (brother of Jesus), Andronicus, and Junia. Jesus is referred to as an apostle (Heb 3:1). Other apostles were not named.
Apostolic	Belonging or related to the early followers of Jesus (the apostles) and their teaching.
Atheist	A person who denies God's existence. In Greek, the letter ἀ at the beginning of a word means "not" and *theos* means "God."

Atone/ Atonement	To pay for a penalty, to make amends, to repair a wrong done. This is what Jesus did on our behalf — our guilt was removed and we are restored in our relationship with God through the sacrifice of Jesus and the forgiveness of our sins. Old Testament atonements offered by the high priest were temporary and foreshadowed the final atonement made by Jesus.
Backsliding	A condition resulting from spiritual apathy or disregard for the things of God. It includes departing from a confession of faith and from ethical standards prescribed for God's people.
Baptism	A sacrament that uses water as an external symbol of an internal change in a person's allegiance, from self to God. Baptism is carried out in different ways by different church groups.
Beatitude	A literary form that expresses a "blessing" on a person because of some virtue or act.
Bishop	A Christian leader of a church or set of churches, often to oversee priests or pastors.
Blasphemy	Showing contempt for God and religious matters through one's thoughts, words, or actions. From the Greek word *blasphemia* meaning profane speech, defamation, evil-speaking, or slander.
Born again	A spiritual beginning for a person who decides to be a Christian, also called rebirth or spiritual birth.
Canon	Collection of documents contained in the Bible.
Catechism	Any instruction meant to deepen a person's Christian faith. From the Greek word *katēkhein* meaning to "teach orally."
Catholic	Term used to designate the Christian church throughout the world. The word is written with a lower case "c" to differentiate it from Roman Catholic (uses a capital "C"). From the Greek word *katholikos* meaning general or universal.
Charisma/ Charismatic	A term from the Greek word *charisma* meaning "gift" that refers to different spiritual gifts given by the Holy Spirit. The theology of Charismatics is similar to Pentecostalism and usually includes a second experience or baptism in the Holy Spirit.
Charity	A term sometimes translated in the Bible meaning "love" and is one of three key theological virtues, along with faith and hope. From the Latin word *caritas* meaning love; the Greek word is *agape*.
Christ	The Greek term for Messiah (see Messiah).
Christology	The branch of theology related to the study of the person and work of Jesus Christ. From the Greek words *christos* meaning "the anointed one" and *logos* meaning "word" or account.
Church	The world community that believes and follows Jesus and who are called to work together in God's name. From the Greek word *ekklēsia* meaning "assembly."
Cleric	A clergy person. From the Latin word *clericus* meaning "priest."
Communion	Protestant term used for the Lord's Supper that includes taking the "body" and "blood" of Jesus, one of the sacraments of the church. Also called Eucharist.

Concubine	A wife with an inferior status (slave or servant) and limited rights that a man used for sexual pleasure and to produce children, sometimes because his wife was barren.
Conversion	A process of changing one's heart, mind, and will.
Covenant	An agreement that establishes a relationship between two parties and includes details about the obligations and responsibilities of both parties.
Creed	A formal statement of belief. From the Latin word *credo* meaning "I believe."
Cross	An ancient execution device used for capital offenses in which people were killed painfully and slowly through gradual suffocation. It became a universal symbol of Christianity because Jesus was crucified on a cross.
Crucifix	A cross with an image of Jesus upon it.
Cult	Any religious group that follows an unorthodox theological system, especially when it attempts to change the views of historical Christianity.
Denomination	The religious organization that operates in a self-governing and doctrinally autonomous manner.
Deuteron- canonical	Books in the Greek translation of the Old Testament that are not in the canon. Term used by Catholics to describe Old Testament books that aren't in the Bible used by Protestants. Protestants call these books the Apocrypha.
Diaspora	Initially used to describe Jews living outside of Palestine after the Babylonian exile, and now a general term to mean the religion and culture of any group living outside its native land.
Disciple	One who learns from another as a pupil. Old Testament prophets and teachers had disciples; John the Baptist and Jesus had disciples.
Dispensationalism	A relatively new religious perspective that teaches that there are seven distinct time periods within biblical history. The seventh period is the 1,000-year reign of Christ (the millennium). Dispensationalists believe that God's covenant with Israel continues into the present "church age."
Doctrine/Dogma	Doctrines are theological conclusions based on Biblical teachings. Term means "teaching" or "interpretation" and many doctrines have been developed relatively recently. Dogma is a doctrine taught by the Church to be believed by all believers, and its denial is condemned by the Church as heresy.
Doxology	A saying or writing that gives glory to God. St. Basil the Great (330–379) introduced this doxology: "Glory be to the Father and the Son and the Holy Spirit."
Ecclesiology	The study of the church as a biblical and theological subject. From the Latin word *ecclesia* meaning "congregation."

Ecumenical	A term given when the entire community of God interacts with each other. It can also apply to how Christians work with other world faiths. From the Greek word *oikoumene* meaning "the inhabited world."
Election	A doctrine that says a person's ultimate destiny (salvation or damnation) is determined by God alone prior to, and apart from, any worth or merit on the person's part. Also known as "predestination."
Epistemology	A branch of philosophy that studies human knowledge, its nature, sources, and limits. From the Greek word *episteme* meaning "knowledge" or "understanding."
Epistle	A type of literature that is written in the form of a letter
Eschatology	The study of the last things or end of the world. From the Greek words *eschatos* meaning "last."
Eucharist	Term used in Catholic and Anglican traditions to remember the last supper Jesus had with his disciples before his death. Called "communion" by Protestants. From the Greek word *eucharisto* meaning "I give thanks."
Evangelical	A general term applied to a diverse group of Christians in many denominations who usually have a common set of religious beliefs, including viewing the Bible as the highest moral authority and following the example of Jesus as the correct way to live. The label is increasingly associated with those embracing certain political and cultural positions, regardless of their religious beliefs.
Evangelism	Term for sharing the message of the gospel with non-Christians.
Evil	An act (or inaction), event, or thought that is contrary to the good and holy purposes of God.
Exegesis	The act of interpreting the scriptures by determining the original and intended meaning. From the Greek word *exegesis* meaning interpretation or explanation.
Faith	In Christianity, the intellectual belief and relational trust or commitment to Jesus. One of the three theological virtues, along with hope and love. Sometimes Christianity is called "the faith."
Fall	A Christian term for the act of Adam and Eve in which they disobeyed God (sinned) and thus lost the relationship they had with God.
Fundamentalism	In Christianity, a recent Protestant movement that seeks to preserve conservative Protestant views and values and holds specific views about the authority and interpretation of the Bible, especially when they conflict with scientific theories and practices.
Glossolalia	Literally, "tongue-speaking," an experience in which the Holy Spirit gives people a gift to speak another language. Some people speak in a "tongue" for their private use, and scripture provides guidance about when to use them.

Gnosticism	A heresy that believed all matter is evil and the spirit is good, so the death of Jesus was not important.
God	The supreme being who created and sustains the universe. Christians believe God has three "persons" that form the Trinity. Also called Lord, Jehovah, and YHWH (the Hebrew God named in the Old Testament — there are no vowels in Hebrew).
Gospel	The "good news" of what Jesus has done for us: all the sins of the world are permanently forgiven, which makes a close relationship with God possible.
Grace	An undeserved favor or reward.
Heaven	The place beyond the earth that is where God exists. In Christianity, it's the future eternal home of those who trust and follow Jesus.
Hell	The place where the dead go after death in which the wicked endure eternal punishment and experience a total separation from God.
Hermeneutics	The field of study related to interpreting the Bible.
Holy	Sacred, totally good, perfectly pure, righteous, worthy of devotion, blameless. From the Greek word *hagios* meaning "to be set apart." Used to describe God, personal character, and actions.
Holy Spirit	An invisible form of God that exists everywhere and influences and interacts with people in different ways.
Homiletics	The art of public preaching.
Hope	The positive expectation of something in the future. In Christianity, the expectation of future blessings as part of God's promise to resurrect our bodies. One of the three theological virtues with faith and love.
Humanism	A philosophy that emphasizes having human-generated moral and ethical beliefs based on reason and science that do not include God or any supernatural reality.
Idolatry	The worship of false or nonexistent gods (idols).
Imago Dei	Term used to describe the uniqueness of humans who were created with certain characteristics of God as first described in Genesis 1, Latin for the "image of God."
Immanent	The concept that God is knowable and continuously involved in creation. From the Latin *in manere* meaning "remaining in."
Immortal	Without death, never dies, imperishable, incorruptible.
Immutable	The doctrine describing God's unchanging nature, e.g., perfect, always loving, constantly present.
Incarnate	A deity that takes on a human form.
Inerrancy	The concept that the Bible is written without error.
Infallible	The characteristic of something said or written that it will not deceive or lead to error.
Inspired/ Inspiration	Terms used to describe the trustworthiness of all the scriptures because they come from God. From the Latin word *inspirare* meaning "to breathe in."

Justice	Another term for "fair" and "getting what we deserve," a concept associated with people getting a fair hearing and share of society's resources and right relationships in society.
Justification	The process of becoming righteous by God's grace through faith in Jesus which makes people acceptable to God; being pardoned from the penalty of sin.
Laity/Lay person	Term referring to people who are not officially trained for church leadership. From the Greek word *laos* meaning "people."
Limbo	An informal Catholic position about a place between heaven and hell where souls stay that have not been condemned or punished but do not experience the joys of heaven (e.g., infants who die before being baptized).
Liturgy	The organized format of worship used by people within the church. From the Greek word *leitourgia* meaning "work of the people."
Lord's Supper	Sacrament of communion/Eucharist that remembers the last meal Jesus had with his disciples in which he symbolically gave them his "body" and "blood" before his arrest.
Love	A strong feeling of personal affection, care, and desire. The Greeks had three words for love: 1) *agape* means unselfish and sacrificial love for others, 2) *philia* which is friendship, a reciprocal relationship between equals, and 3) *eros* is love that satisfies one's passions, such as physical love.
Mercy	Kind and compassionate care for all living things, especially human beings.
Messiah/Christ	The promised deliverer of Israel who would reestablish God's kingdom in society. The Hebrew word for "anointed one" (*christos* in Greek). Terms used in the Bible to describe the Messiah include King, Savior, Priest, Prophet, and Suffering Servant.
Millennium	A period of 1,000 years of peace described in Revelation that occurs before the final judgment.
Ministry/Minister	Service to God by the church and individuals; a person who serves others in the name of God (noun); the act of serving others (verb).
Orthodox	Acts and beliefs that are considered correct and proper. From the Greek words *orthos* meaning "straight" or "right" and *doxa* meaning "praise."
Pastor	A guide for people in a church, usually in a Protestant setting. From the Greek word *poimen* meaning "shepherd" which relates to a "pasture."
Peace	A time of full societal and personal well-being (not just the lack of war), *shalom* in Hebrew.
Pentecostal	A religious movement that began in the early 1900s that created Pentecostal denominations that emphasize a second experience of the "baptism in the Holy Spirit" and the gifts of the Spirit, especially speaking in a different language ("tongues").

Pentecost	A major Jewish celebration held 50 days after Passover, the Holy Spirit filled the disciples on this day after Jesus ascended into heaven.
Pneumatology	The study of the Holy Spirit. From the Greek word *pneuma* meaning "spirit."
Priest	A leader in a Catholic or Orthodox church or organization.
Prophecy	Speech and teaching on behalf of God or God's people to communicate God's will and may include predictions about what will happen in the future.
Prophet	A person who speaks on behalf of God to communicate God's will to God's people.
Propitiation	A sacrifice or payment that satisfies the wrath of God and thus averts God's wrath toward sinners.
Proselytize	To advocate or promote a certain way of thinking in order to persuade a person to change their religious or political position.
Protestant	A movement started by Martin Luther in the 1500s that protested some of the practices of the Roman Catholic Church; now a general term for groups of Christians that are neither Catholic nor Orthodox.
Purgatory	A Catholic doctrine about a process of final purification of a person's soul after death and before entrance into heaven for those who died but who were not yet perfectly purified for heaven.
Rapture	The act when Christians and non-Christians suddenly separate from each other while living on the earth.
Redemption	The concept that sinful humans are "bought back" from the bondage of sin into a renewed relationship with God through a human act or grace by a down payment, such as Jesus's death. It's a commercial metaphor applied to salvation.
Reformation	A general term for the time when reforms were taking place in the church and new organizations were formed after Martin Luther protested against the Roman Catholic Church in 1517.
Religion	The practice of piety and reverence toward God.
Repent	The act of turning around to go a different direction with humility for what happened previously. In Christianity, it's accompanied by faith in Jesus and the forgiveness of one's sins, which makes a person acceptable to God.
Resurrection	The return to life of the dead body of Jesus and others.
Revelation	The ways God reveals truth about the world and communicates with people.
Righteous	Being morally right or just. From the Greek word *dikaios*.
Sacrament	A practice or ritual that symbolizes a spiritual reality. Catholics recognize seven (baptism, communion, confession, confirmation, marriage, ordination, last rite), and Protestants recognize two (baptism and communion).
Sacred	Holy or divine, as opposed to "ordinary" or "human." From the Latin word *sacrare* meaning "set apart."

Sacrifice	Something of value offered as an act of worship or devotion to God.
Saint	A "holy one," someone set apart for God's special purposes (everybody who follows Jesus is a saint). In some church traditions, a person who displayed an extraordinary level of holiness when they were alive.
Salvation	God's activities of delivering people from sin and bringing them into a right relationship with God and with one another through the death of Jesus.
Sanctification	A gradual and ongoing transformation in which the Holy Spirit makes believers more like Jesus in every way, including their desires, thoughts, and actions; to become more pure and holy.
Sanctuary	The area in a church where worship takes place.
Scripture	Writings regarded as sacred. In Christianity, this consists of the Old and New Testaments.
Sect	A sociological term for a group with voluntary and exclusive membership and a unique identity.
Secular	A belief system that excludes God and religion.
Sin	Missing the mark or coming short of a standard, which requires forgiveness. Original sin defines human nature, while actual sins are thoughts, words, and deeds that are contrary to God's commands.
Syncretism	The blending together of views from different philosophies or religions.
Synod	A formal meeting of church leaders to deal with church matters.
Synoptic	Term used when referring to the gospels of Matthew, Mark, and Luke which often parallel each other and provide similar accounts of the life and teaching of Jesus. Greek for "seeing together."
Theocracy	A view of government in which God is acknowledged to be the supreme ruler.
Theology	The systematic study of God, based on the Greek word *theos* meaning "God."
Tithe	Term for giving God one-tenth (10%) of one's annual income (money earned, food production, etc.).
Transcendent	A characteristic of God. From the Latin word for "surpassing" meaning people cannot fully understand God (but God is also knowable, or "immanent").
Transfiguration	An event when Jesus went up a mountain with three disciples, and he began to shine and his clothes turned white. Elijah and Moses appeared and talked to Jesus and a voice said, "This is my Son, I'm very pleased with him; listen to him!"
Transubstantiation	A Catholic belief that the bread and wine used for Communion become the actual body and blood of Jesus.
Trinity	The biblical doctrine defining the one true God in three persons: Father, Son (Jesus), and Holy Spirit, similar to how an element or compound has different forms (e.g., solid, liquid, gas).

Tribulation	Term for a period of intense persecution of Christians before the final judgment occurs.
Usury	The practice of making unethical or immoral loans with a very high interest rate that unfairly enrich the lender.
Word	A broad theological term referring to the Scriptures and the words of God and personified by Jesus. God created all things with a spoken word (*logos* in Greek).
Worship	Human action that glorifies and honors God because of what has been done for us, especially by Christ Jesus. Historic Christian worship is a structured response to God in a context where his grace is received in the Word and the Sacraments.

APPENDIX F
TOPICAL INDEX

Many important topics related to the Bible are discussed in different parts of this book. This index provides the chapters where the most important concepts and ideas are discussed in greater detail.

[Note: The words *God* and *Jesus* appear in nearly all the chapters, so they are not included in this index.]

APPENDIX G
BIBLE BOOKS AND ABBREVIATIONS

The books and their abbreviations used in the citations in this book are listed below in the order the books appear in the Bible.

Old Testament

Genesis	Gen	Habakkuk	Hab
Exodus	Exod	Zephaniah	Zeph
Leviticus	Lev	Haggai	Hag
Numbers	Num	Zechariah	Zech
Deuteronomy	Deut	Malachi	Mal
Joshua	Josh		
Judges	Judg	**New Testament**	
Ruth	Ruth	Matthew	Matt
1 Samuel	1Sam	Mark	Mark
2 Samuel	2Sam	Luke	Luke
1 Kings	1Ki	John	John
2 Kings	2Ki	Acts	Acts
1 Chronicles	1Chr	Romans	Rom
2 Chronicles	2Chr	1 Corinthians	1Cor
Ezra	Ezra	2 Corinthians	2Cor
Nehemiah	Neh	Galatians	Gal
Esther	Est	Ephesians	Eph
Job	Job	Philippians	Phil
Psalms	Psa	Colossians	Col
Proverbs	Prov	1 Thessalonians	1Th
Ecclesiastes	Eccl	2 Thessalonians	2Th
Song of Solomon	Song	1 Timothy	1Tim
Isaiah	Isa	2 Timothy	2Tim
Jeremiah	Jer	Titus	Tit
Lamentations	Lam	Philemon	Phm
Ezekiel	Eze	Hebrews	Heb
Daniel	Dan	James	Jam
Hosea	Hos	1 Peter	1Pet
Joel	Joel	2 Peter	2Pet
Amos	Amos	1 John	1Joh
Obadiah	Oba	2 John	2Joh
Jonah	Jona	3 John	3Joh
Micah	Mic	Jude	Jude
Nahum	Nah	Revelation	Rev

INDEX OF SCRIPTURE CITATIONS

The scriptures mentioned in the chapters of this book are listed below in the order they appear in the Bible.

OLD TESTAMENT

Lev	18	18	19
Lev	18	22	19
Lev	19	2	1
Lev	19	15	10
Lev	19	18	9,10,17
Lev	19	28	5
Lev	19	9-10	11
Lev	20	13	19
Lev	20	26	1
Lev	21	14	19
Lev	25	2-5	14
Lev	25	8-13	11
Lev	25	35-37	11
Lev	27	30	11
Num	4	9	13
Num	5	11-31	9
Num	6	23-26	10
Num	11	12	6
Num	12		18
Num	14	19-20	9
Num	18	25-28	11
Num	22		8
Num	22	22-35	7
Num	23	19	6
Deut	4	2	5
Deut	4	25-26	13
Deut	8	7-10,18	11
Deut	8	11-18	11
Deut	9	5-6	12
Deut	10	14	11
Deut	11	17	12
Deut	12	32	5
Deut	14	22-24	11
Deut	15	1-11	11
Deut	15	7-8	11
Deut	15	10	11
Deut	16	18-20	17
Deut	17	3	12
Deut	18	12	12
Deut	20	19	14
Deut	21	10-17	19
Deut	22		19
Deut	22	6-7	14
Deut	22	13-21	19
Deut	22	22-24	19
Deut	22	28-29	19
Deut	23	1	19
Deut	23	17-18	19
Deut	23	19-20	11
Deut	24	1-4	19
Deut	24	6,10-13	11

Deut	25	5-6	19
Deut	25	5-10	19
Deut	26	15	12
Deut	28	12	11
Deut	30		17,19
Deut	30	15-19	13
Deut	32	18	6
Josh	1	9	6
Josh	2		9
Josh	6		9
Josh	24	15	17
Judg	4		8
Judg	8	27	11
Judg	11	35-37	19
Judg	19		19
Judg	20		19
Ruth	1	16-17	18,19
Ruth	3	4-8	19
1Sam	1	8-11	7
1Sam	1	11	18
1Sam	1	17	18
1Sam	2		4
1Sam	8	7	17
1Sam	16	7	15,19
2Sam	5	14	19
2Sam	12	7,13-14	19
2Sam	22		4
2Sam	24	16	6
1Ki	4	7	17
1Ki	8	27	12
1Ki	8	30	12
1Ki	13		8
1Ki	14	22-24	19
1Ki	15	11-13	19
1Ki	17		8
1Ki	18		8
1Ki	22	45-46	19
2Ki	2	23-24	8
2Ki	5		8
2Ki	6		8
2Ki	6	20-23	15
2Ki	7		8
2Ki	9	30-33	19
2Ki	13	21	8
2Ki	19		4
2Ki	20	1-6	8

NEW TESTAMENT

Matt	24	6-11,14-17	16
Matt	24	21-24	16
Matt	24	40-41	16
Matt	25		10
Matt	25	14-29	12
Matt	25	14-30	11,12
Matt	25	31-46	11,13,15
Matt	25	41	9
Matt	25	44	17
Matt	26		9
Matt	26	28	9
Matt	26	52	15,17
Matt	26	64	12
Matt	27	52-53	12
Matt	28	3	7
Matt	28	5-10	14
Matt	28	18	17
Matt	28	19	14
Matt	28	19-20	14,17
Mark	1	2-3	5
Mark	2	27	6
Mark	3	28-30	9
Mark	3	35	13
Mark	4		1,8,13,14
Mark	4	30-34	12
Mark	5	1-20	8
Mark	5	25-34	8
Mark	6		8
Mark	6	11	14
Mark	7	8-9,14-15	13
Mark	7	9-13	19
Mark	7	21-23	19
Mark	8	34-35	15
Mark	9	17-29	6
Mark	9	23	8
Mark	10	2-9	19
Mark	10	2-9,19	19
Mark	10	6-9	19
Mark	10	9	19
Mark	10	11-12	19
Mark	10	25	11
Mark	10	42-44	15
Mark	11	23	15
Mark	11	24	7
Mark	11	25	9
Mark	12	25	19
Mark	12	28-33	10
Mark	12	30-31	9
Mark	14		9
Mark	14	7	11
Mark	14	36	6
Mark	16	1-10	10

Mark	16	15	14
Luke	1	19	7
Luke	1	28-33	18
Luke	1	37	6
Luke	1	42-43	18
Luke	2	28	18
Luke	2	29	7
Luke	2	49-50	6
Luke	3	4	5
Luke	3	7-9	13
Luke	3	8-9	13
Luke	3	23-31	19
Luke	4		8
Luke	4	17-19	11
Luke	4	18	10
Luke	4	18-19	17
Luke	5	20-21	9
Luke	5	36-39	8,14
Luke	6	20-21	11
Luke	6	23,35	12
Luke	6	27-28	9
Luke	6	27-36	9
Luke	6	30,34	15
Luke	6	30,34-35	11
Luke	6	31	10
Luke	6	36	10
Luke	6	37	9
Luke	6	37,41-42	15
Luke	6	37-38	11
Luke	6	46-49	13
Luke	7		9
Luke	7	41-42	11
Luke	8		1,8,13,14
Luke	8	1	12
Luke	8	6-7,13	13
Luke	8	26-39	8
Luke	9	5	14
Luke	9	23	15
Luke	10	18	14
Luke	10	25-37	9,11
Luke	10	27	10
Luke	10	37	13
Luke	10	38-42	18
Luke	11	2-4	7
Luke	11	4	9,11
Luke	11	5-13	7
Luke	11	9-13	7
Luke	11	39,41	13
Luke	11	41	9
Luke	12	6,27	14
Luke	12	10	9
Luke	12	13-21	11

Book	Ch	Verse	Page
Acts	3	19	9
Acts	4		8
Acts	4	27	17
Acts	5		8
Acts	5	1-11	13
Acts	5	12	8
Acts	5	29	9,17
Acts	6		8
Acts	6	1-3	18
Acts	7	55-56	12
Acts	7	59-60	7
Acts	8		8
Acts	8	27-39	19
Acts	9		8
Acts	10		5,8
Acts	10	15	8
Acts	12		8
Acts	13	36	12
Acts	13	43	13
Acts	13	48	13
Acts	13	51	14
Acts	14	22	13
Acts	15	20	19
Acts	16	30-31	13
Rom	1	9	7
Rom	1	22	15
Rom	1	25-27	19
Rom	1	26-27	19
Rom	2	1-3	15
Rom	5	3-5	15
Rom	5	8	9
Rom	6	4-8	15
Rom	6	6-7,18,22	17
Rom	6	23	11
Rom	7	2-3	19
Rom	7	3	19
Rom	7	4	13
Rom	7	4,6	11
Rom	8	1-2,15	17
Rom	8	5-6	6
Rom	8	15	6
Rom	8	26	15
Rom	8	26-27	6
Rom	8	27	7
Rom	8	28	12,15
Rom	8	28,31	9
Rom	8	29	13
Rom	10	9-10	13
Rom	10	14-15	7
Rom	11	22	13
Rom	12		6
Rom	12	1	9,15
Rom	12	2	1,8,14
Rom	12	5,10	15
Rom	12	14,17-19	9,15
Rom	12	17-21	17
Rom	12	19	5,17
Rom	12	20	5,9
Rom	13	1-6	17
Rom	13	6-7	17
Rom	13	7-8	11
Rom	13	8-10	9
Rom	13	9	10
Rom	13	13	19
Rom	14	3-12	18
Rom	14	4-13	15
Rom	14	20-21	19
Rom	15	1-2,7,14	15
Rom	16	7	18
Rom	16	16	5
1Cor	1	10-15	15
1Cor	1	18-20	11
1Cor	1	20,27	15
1Cor	1	26-28	15
1Cor	2	12-13	5
1Cor	3	1-2	19
1Cor	3	5-7	14
1Cor	3	8,11-14	12
1Cor	3	18-20	15
1Cor	5	9-10	14
1Cor	5	11	19
1Cor	6	9	19
1Cor	6	9,15-16	19
1Cor	6	12	17
1Cor	6	16	19
1Cor	6	18	19
1Cor	6	18-20	19
1Cor	7	1-2	19
1Cor	7	1-14	19
1Cor	7	7-9	19
1Cor	7	9	19
1Cor	7	12-17	19
1Cor	7	22	15
1Cor	7	22-23	17
1Cor	7	24-40	19
1Cor	9	18	12
1Cor	10	8	19
1Cor	10	23	19
1Cor	11		5
1Cor	11	2-15	18
1Cor	11	3-16	18
1Cor	11	5	18
1Cor	11	30	9,12
1Cor	12		6

1Th	5	26	5
2Th	1	8-9	9
2Th	1	11-12	7
2Th	2	9	14
1Tim	1	9-10	19
1Tim	1	10	19
1Tim	1	15	9
1Tim	1	18-20	13
1Tim	2	1	7
1Tim	2	1-2	17
1Tim	2	1-3	7
1Tim	2	8	18
1Tim	2	9	18
1Tim	2	11-15	18
1Tim	3	2	18
1Tim	3	2,12	19
1Tim	3	8-13	18
1Tim	5	23	8
1Tim	6	10	11
1Tim	6	17-18	11
1Tim	6	17-19	11
2Tim	2	22	19
2Tim	3	5	14
2Tim	3	16	5
2Tim	4	8	12
Tit	1	5	18
Tit	1	6	19
Tit	2	12	14
Tit	3	1	17
Tit	3	1-2	15
Tit	3	4-6	10
Heb	3	6,14	13
Heb	3	13	15
Heb	4	14	13
Heb	4	15	19
Heb	6	4-6	13
Heb	6	18	5
Heb	8		6
Heb	8	12	10
Heb	10	17	9
Heb	10	24-25	15
Heb	10	26-29	13
Heb	10	30	17
Heb	11		4,9
Heb	11	31	18
Heb	11	35	17
Heb	12	1-2	4
Heb	13	2	7

Heb	13	4	19
Heb	13	5	11
Heb	13	8	6
Jam	1	2-4	12
Jam	1	6	7
Jam	1	12	12
Jam	1	17	6
Jam	1	27	10,14
Jam	2		9
Jam	2	5	11
Jam	2	6-7	11,12
Jam	2	8	9,10
Jam	2	13	10
Jam	2	14-26	13
Jam	2	17,26	13
Jam	3	1	9
Jam	4	3	7
Jam	4	4	14
Jam	4	10	15
Jam	4	12	15
Jam	4	13-15	11
Jam	5	13-16	7
Jam	5	16	6,7
1Pet	1	15-16	1
1Pet	2	9-11	17
1Pet	2	13-17	17
1Pet	2	16	17,19
1Pet	3	1-7	15,19
1Pet	3	3-4	18
1Pet	3	8-9	10
1Pet	3	9	9,15
1Pet	3	15	14
1Pet	4	3	19
1Pet	5	2-4	12
1Pet	5	4	12
1Pet	5	8	14
1Pet	5	14	5
1Pet	5	5-6	15
2Pet	1	20-21	5
2Pet	2	6-14	19
2Pet	3	10-13	12
2Pet	3	14-18	1
1Joh	1	9	9
1Joh	1	19	10
1Joh	2	1	6
1Joh	2	15	14
1Joh	2	19	13
1Joh	3	10-11,15-18, 23	9
1Joh	3	30	6

SCRIPTURE CITATIONS BY CHAPTER

The scriptures mentioned in each chapter of this book are listed below in the order they appear in the Bible (by book, chapter, and verse). If no verse is listed, the citation is for the entire chapter. (Note: Some verses are cited more than once within a chapter.)

Chapter 1

Lev	11	44
Lev	19	2
Lev	20	26
Mic	6	8
Matt	5	48
Matt	13	
Mark	4	
Luke	8	
Rom	12	2
Phil	2	12-13
Phil	4	8
1Pet	1	15-16
2Pet	3	14-18
Lev	11	44
Lev	19	2

Chapter 2
No verses cited

Chapter 3

Luke	15	11-32
John	21	25

Chapter 4

Gen	1	
Gen	2	
Gen	3	
Gen	4	
Gen	11	
1Sam	2	
2Sam	22	
2Ki	19	
Psa	1	
Psa	1	3-4
Psa	15	
Prov	3	5
Prov	31	
Isa	52	
Isa	53	
Matt	10	16
John	1	1-18
1Cor	13	
Heb	11	
Heb	12	1-2

Chapter 5

Gen	9	6
Exod	20	13
Lev	19	28
Deut	4	2
Deut	12	32
Prov	9	10
Prov	25	21-22
Prov	30	6
Isa	40	3-4
Mal	3	1
Matt	3	3
Matt	15	11
Mark	1	2-3
Luke	3	4
John	2	19
Acts	10	
Rom	12	19
Rom	12	20
Rom	16	16
1Cor	2	12-13
1Cor	11	
1Cor	13	
1Cor	16	20
2Cor	13	12
1Th	5	26
2Tim	3	16
Heb	6	18
1Pet	5	14
2Pet	1	20-21
Rev	22	18-19

Matt	6	5-8
Matt	6	9-13
Matt	7	7
Matt	7	7-11
Matt	9	36-38
Matt	14	30
Matt	15	21-28
Matt	18	19
Matt	28	3
Mark	11	24
Luke	1	19
Luke	2	29
Luke	11	5-13
Luke	11	9-13
Luke	11	2-4
Luke	18	9-14
Luke	18	1-7
Luke	18	1-8
Luke	21	35-36
Luke	23	42
John	17	15
Acts	7	59-60
Rom	1	9
Rom	8	27
Rom	10	14-15
2Cor	11	14
Eph	1	18
Eph	6	19-20
Eph	6	18
Phil	4	6
Phil	4	6
Col	4	3
1Th	5	16-18
1Th	5	17
2Th	1	11-12
1Tim	2	1
1Tim	2	1-3
Heb	13	2
Jam	1	6
Jam	4	3
Jam	5	16
Jam	5	13-16
1Joh	5	14
3Joh	1	2
Jude	1	9
Rev	12	7

Chapter 8

Exod	3	
Exod	4	
Exod	7	
Num	22	
Judg	4	

1Ki	13	
1Ki	17	
1Ki	18	
2Ki	2	23-24
2Ki	5	
2Ki	13	21
2Ki	20	1-6
2Ki	6	
2Ki	7	
Psa	1	1-2
Isa	61	3
Matt	4	23-24
Matt	8	
Matt	8	28-34
Matt	13	19
Matt	14	
Matt	15	
Matt	17	20
Matt	19	26
Mark	4	
Mark	5	25-34
Mark	5	1-20
Mark	6	
Mark	9	23
Luke	4	
Luke	5	36-39
Luke	8	
Luke	8	26-39
John	2	
John	6	
John	8	31-32
John	8	44
John	9	25
John	14	12-14
Acts	2	43
Acts	3	
Acts	4	
Acts	5	
Acts	5	12
Acts	6	
Acts	8	
Acts	9	
Acts	10	
Acts	10	15
Acts	12	
Rom	12	2
1Cor	13	11
2Cor	12	7-10
Phil	4	8
1Tim	5	23

Chapter 9

Gen	45	4-8

Prov	20	17		1Cor	15	51-52
Prov	22	16		1Cor	15	52
Eccl	1	2,9,14		2Cor	5	1-4
Eccl	8	12-14		2Cor	12	2-3
Eccl	8	13		2Cor	12	2-4
Eccl	9	2,12,18		Gal	6	7-9
Isa	65	17		Phil	3	20
Isa	66	22		1Th	4	13-14
Jer	12	1		1Th	4	15-16
Lam	1	5		1Th	5	10
Dan	11	36		2Tim	4	8
Dan	12	2		2Tim	4	8
Hos	13	14		Jam	1	2-4
Mal	3	15		Jam	1	12
Matt	4	45		Jam	2	6-7
Matt	5	10-12		1Pet	5	4
Matt	5	11-12		1Pet	5	2-4
Matt	5	16		2Pet	3	10-13
Matt	6	10		Rev	2	10
Matt	6	27		Rev	20	4
Matt	13	24-30		Rev	20	11
Matt	13	24-52		Rev	21	1
Matt	16	27		Rev	21	1-6
Matt	25	14-29		Rev	22	12
Matt	25	14-30				
Matt	26	64		**Chapter 13**		
Matt	27	52-53		Gen	22	16-18
Mark	4	30-34		Num	4	9
Luke	6	23,35		Deut	4	25-26
Luke	8	1		Deut	30	15-19
Luke	12	48		2Chr	7	14
Luke	18	29-30		Psa	51	7
Luke	19	15-19		Psa	69	13-14
Luke	21	33		Isa	1	18
Luke	23	43		Isa	29	13
John	3	13		Eze	18	24
John	6	31		Matt	5	19
John	6	39-40		Matt	7	15-20
John	9			Matt	7	15-23
John	11	11,13		Matt	7	19-21
John	14	3		Matt	13	
Acts	2	29,34		Matt	15	20
Acts	7	55-56		Matt	15	7-9
Acts	13	36		Matt	21	28-32
Rom	8	28		Matt	22	14
1Cor	3	8,11-14		Matt	22	1-10
1Cor	9	18		Matt	23	25
1Cor	11	30		Matt	25	31-46
1Cor	15	18,20,51		Mark	3	35
1Cor	15	20		Mark	4	
1Cor	15	42-44		Mark	7	8-9,14-15
1Cor	15	42,44, 54–55		Luke	3	7-9
				Luke	3	8-9

Luke	6	46-49
Luke	8	6-7,13
Luke	8	
Luke	10	37
Luke	11	39,41
Luke	13	23
Luke	14	16-24
Luke	19	2-9
John	3	3
John	3	14-18
John	6	44
John	10	28
John	15	16,19
John	15	
Acts	5	1-11
Acts	13	43
Acts	13	48
Acts	14	22
Acts	16	30-31
Rom	7	4
Rom	8	29
Rom	10	9-10
Rom	11	22
Rom	11	22
1Cor	15	1-2
2Cor	5	17
Gal	5	22-23
Eph	1	4-5,11
Eph	2	3-5,8
Col	1	2
1Tim	1	18-20
Heb	3	6,14
Heb	4	14
Heb	6	4-6
Heb	10	26-29
Jam	2	14-26
Jam	2	17,26
1Joh	2	19
Rev	3	5

Chapter 14

Gen	1	11-12
Gen	1	20-31
Gen	2	8-9, 15,19-20
Gen	2	17
Gen	3	1-5, 11-13
Gen	3	17-23
Gen	6	19-21
Gen	9	9-16
Exod	7	11
Lev	25	2-5

Deut	20	19
Deut	22	6-7
Job	38-41	
Psa	24	1
Psa	104	10-14
Matt	4	1-10
Matt	5	43-47
Matt	6	26-29
Matt	7	1-5
Matt	7	13-14
Matt	10	4
Matt	10	16-18, 22-23,28
Matt	10	29
Matt	13	
Matt	13	19
Matt	23	24
Matt	28	5-10
Matt	28	19
Matt	28	19-20
Mark	4	
Mark	6	11
Mark	16	15
Luke	5	36-39
Luke	8	
Luke	9	5
Luke	10	18
Luke	12	6,27
Luke	14	26-27
Luke	14	28-33
Luke	24	10
John	1	10
John	3	16
John	4	4-42
John	7	7
John	8	44
John	9	25
John	12	31
John	14	30
John	15	15-16
John	15	18-19
John	18	36
John	20	17
Acts	1	8
Acts	13	51
Rom	12	2
1Cor	3	5-7
1Cor	5	9-10
1Cor	15	33
2Cor	4	4
2Cor	6	14-17
2Cor	11	14

Gal	5	22-23
Eph	2	2
Eph	6	12
Eph	6	11-17
Col	1	13
2Th	2	9
2Tim	3	5
Tit	2	12
Jam	1	27
Jam	4	4
1Pet	3	15
1Pet	5	8
1Joh	2	15
Rev	3	20

Chapter 15

1Sam	16	7
2Ki	6	20-23
Prov	16	7
Prov	25	21-22
Mic	6	8
Matt	5	11-12
Matt	5	21-22, 27-32
Matt	5	38-39
Matt	5	40-48
Matt	5	42
Matt	7	1-5
Matt	10	8
Matt	10	37
Matt	10	38
Matt	12	43-45
Matt	13	13-17
Matt	16	24-25
Matt	17	20-21
Matt	18	4
Matt	18	8-9
Matt	20	26-27
Matt	21	21
Matt	23	12
Matt	23	5-7,25-28
Matt	25	31-46
Matt	26	52
Mark	8	34-35
Mark	10	42-44
Mark	11	23
Luke	6	30,34
Luke	6	37,41-42
Luke	9	23
Luke	14	10-11
Luke	14	12-14
Luke	14	26
Luke	14	27

Luke	17	6
Luke	18	9-12
Luke	22	25-26
John	2	
John	3	17
John	7	24
John	8	3-11
John	13	14-15
John	18	36
Rom	1	22
Rom	2	1-3
Rom	5	3-5
Rom	6	4-8
Rom	8	26
Rom	8	28
Rom	12	1
Rom	12	5,10
Rom	12	14,17-19
Rom	14	4-13
Rom	15	1-2,7,14
1Cor	1	10-15
1Cor	1	20,27
1Cor	1	26-28
1Cor	3	18-20
1Cor	7	22
1Cor	12	4-27
2Cor	11	17,30
2Cor	12	9-11
Gal	2	20
Gal	3	28
Gal	5	13
Gal	5	24
Gal	6	2
Eph	2	10-22
Phil	2	3,9
Eph	4	2,11-16, 19
Phil	2	6-8
Col	1	24
Col	3	11
Col	3	13-16
1Th	5	11-14
Heb	3	13
Heb	10	24-25
Jam	4	10
Jam	4	12
1Pet	3	9
1Pet	3	1-7
1Pet	5	5-6
Tit	3	1-2
Rev	3	15-16

Chapter 16

Isa	2	2-4

Matt	13	24-30
Matt	24	6-11,14-17,21-24
Matt	24	40-41
Luke	17	34-37
1Cor	15	51-52
1Th	4	15-17
Rev	3	15-17,19
Rev	3	20
Rev	5	12
Rev	14	8,13
Rev	18	2
Rev	19	6-7
Rev	21	4-6
Rev	22	13

Chapter 17

Gen	9	6
Lev	19	18
Deut	16	18-20
Deut	30	
Deut	32	35
Josh	24	15
1Sam	8	7
1Ki	4	7
Job	12	23
Psa	18	5
Psa	22	28
Psa	75	7
Psa	119	45
Prov	8	15-16
Prov	20	22
Isa	9	6-7
Isa	45	1
Isa	61	
Jer	29	7
Dan	2	21
Dan	2	21,37
Dan	2	37-38
Dan	3	17-18
Dan	4	17
Dan	5	21
Matt	5	17
Matt	6	21,24
Matt	11	29-30
Matt	22	37-40
Matt	24	2
Matt	25	44
Matt	26	52
Matt	28	18
Matt	28	19-20
Luke	4	18-19
John	3	16-17

John	8	31-32,36
John	8	32
John	19	11
John	19	11
John	19	11
Acts	1	8
Acts	2	23
Acts	4	27
Acts	5	29
Rom	6	6-7,18,22
Rom	8	1-2,15
Rom	12	19
Rom	12	17-21
Rom	13	1-6
Rom	13	6-7
1Cor	6	12
1Cor	7	22-23
1Cor	12	12-14
2Cor	3	17
2Cor	5	20
Gal	3	26-29
Gal	5	1
Gal	5	13
Phil	3	20
1Tim	2	1-2
Tit	3	1
Heb	10	30
Heb	11	35
1Pet	2	16
1Pet	2	9-11
1Pet	2	13-17

Chapter 18

Gen	1	27
Gen	2	7,20-23
Gen	2	18
Gen	3	
Gen	24	53
Gen	27	28-29
Exod	3	22
Exod	35	22
Num	12	
Ruth	1	16-17
1Sam	1	11
1Sam	1	17
Prov	25	12
Prov	31	10-31
Est	4	16
Joel	2	28
Matt	15	21-28
Luke	1	28-33
Luke	1	42-43
Luke	2	28

Luke	10	38-42	Judg	19	
John	8	3-11	Judg	20	
Acts	2	17-18	Ruth	1	16-17
Acts	6	1-3	Ruth	3	4-8
Rom	14	3-12	1Sam	16	7
Rom	16	7	2Sam	5	14
1Cor	11	2-15	2Sam	12	7,13-14
1Cor	11	3-16	1Ki	14	22-24
1Cor	11	5	1Ki	15	11-13
Gal	3	28	1Ki	22	45-46
1Tim	2	8	2Ki	9	30-33
1Tim	2	9	Prov	31	10-31
1Tim	2	11-15	Eccl	1	2,9,14
1Tim	3	2	Eccl	3	5
1Tim	3	8-13	Eccl	4	9-12
Tit	1	5	Song	8	6-7
Heb	11	31	Isa	39	5-7
1Pet	3	3-4	Isa	53	2
			Isa	56	3-5

Chapter 19

Gen	1	27-28,31	Jer	38	7-13
Gen	2	7-25	Eze	16	
Gen	2	18	Dan	1	3-7
Gen	2	24	Hos	4	10-14
Gen	4	1	Mic	2	1
Gen	4	19	Matt	5	27-30
Gen	6	2	Matt	5	27-32
Gen	18		Matt	5	31-32
Gen	19		Matt	9	14
Gen	19	1-38	Matt	15	19
Gen	19	32-35	Matt	18	1-5
Gen	38		Matt	18	6-9
Gen	38	9-10	Matt	18	15-17
Gen	38	26	Matt	19	3-12,18
Exod	34	15-16	Matt	19	4-6
Lev	18		Matt	19	8-9
Lev	18	6-23	Matt	19	12
Lev	18	18	Mark	7	9-13
Lev	18	22	Mark	7	21-23
Lev	20	13	Mark	10	2-9
Deut	21	10-17	Mark	10	2-9,19
Lev	21	14	Mark	10	6-9
Deut	22		Mark	10	9
Deut	22	13-21	Mark	10	11-12
Deut	22	22-24	Mark	12	25
Deut	22	28-29	Luke	3	23-31
Deut	23	1	Luke	16	18
Deut	23	17-18	John	8	3-11
Deut	24	1-4	John	19	26-27
Deut	25	5-6	Acts	8	27-39
Deut	25	5-10	Acts	15	20
Deut	30		Rom	1	25-27
Judg	11	35-37	Rom	1	26-27
			Rom	7	2-3

Rom	7	3
Rom	13	13
Rom	14	20-21
1Cor	3	1-2
1Cor	5	11
1Cor	6	9
1Cor	6	9,15-16
1Cor	6	16
1Cor	6	18
1Cor	6	18-20
1Cor	7	1-2
1Cor	7	1-14
1Cor	7	7-9
1Cor	7	9
1Cor	7	12-17
1Cor	7	24-40
1Cor	10	8
1Cor	10	23
1Cor	13	11
2Cor	12	21
Gal	5	13
Gal	5	19-21
Eph	4	19
Eph	5	21-28,33
Eph	5	21-33
Eph	6	1-4
Col	3	18-21
Col	5	3
1Th	4	3-5
1Th	4	3-5
1Tim	1	9-10
1Tim	1	10
1Tim	3	2,12
2Tim	2	22
Heb	4	15
Heb	13	4
Tit	1	6
1Pet	2	16
1Pet	3	1-7
1Pet	4	3
1Pet	4	3
2Pet	2	6-14
Jude	1	4,7,18-19
Jude	1	6-7

Epilogue

Mic	6	8
Matt	5	9
Matt	20	26-28
John	14	15
John	15	4,6,8
2Cor	13	5-7

Appendix J
MAPS

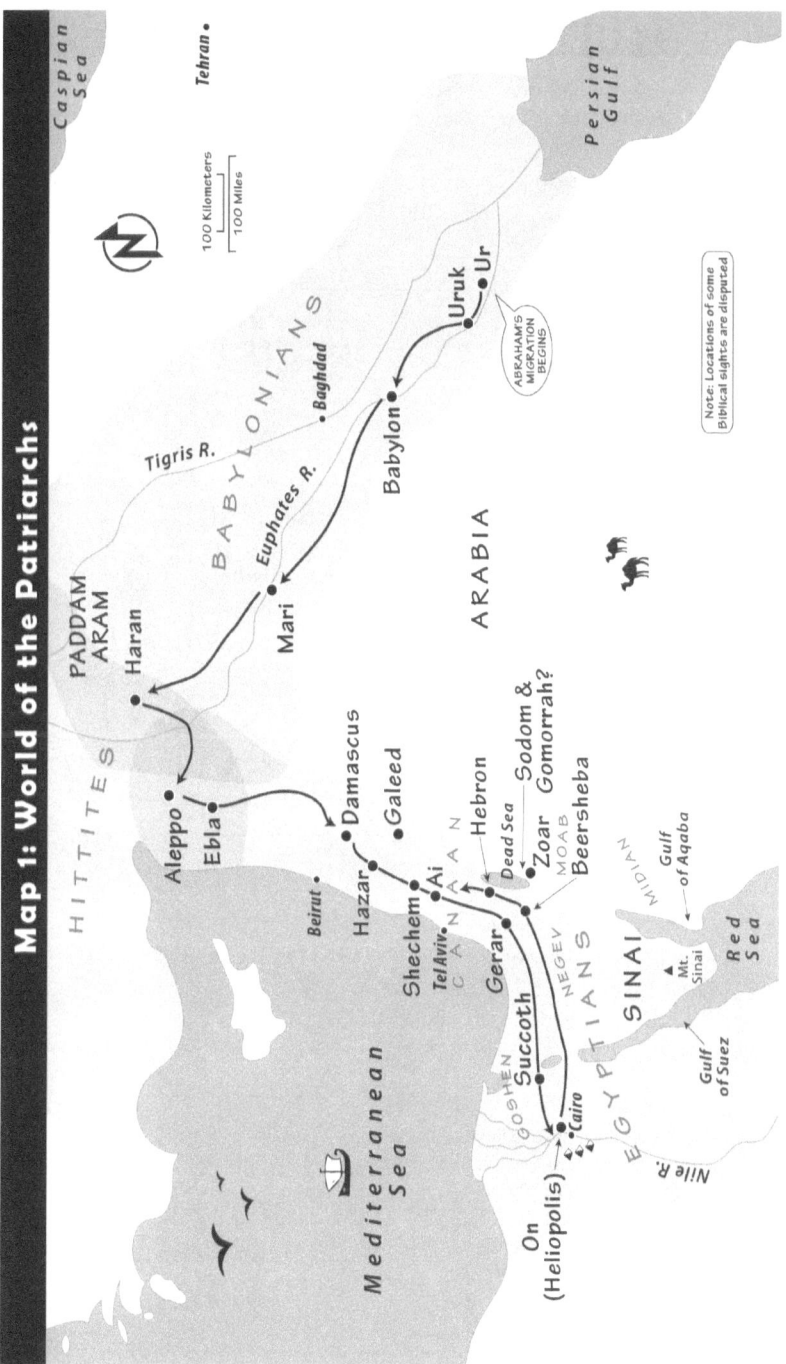

Map 1: World of the Patriarchs

Caspian Sea

Tehran •

Persian Gulf

100 Kilometers
100 Miles

HITTITES

PADDAM ARAM

Haran

Aleppo

Ebla

BABYLONIANS

Tigris R.

• Baghdad

Euphrates R.

Babylon

Mari

Uruk

Ur

ABRAHAM'S MIGRATION BEGINS

Note: Locations of some Biblical sights are disputed

ARABIA

Damascus

Galeed

Hebron

Sodom & Gomorrah?

Beirut •

Hazar

Shechem

Ai

Tel Aviv

CANAAN

Gerar

Dead Sea

Zoar

MOAB

Beersheba

NEGEV

SINAI

MIDIAN

Gulf of Aqaba

Mt. Sinai

Red Sea

Succoth

GOSHEN

Cairo

EGYPTIANS

Gulf of Suez

Nile R.

On (Heliopolis)

Mediterranean Sea

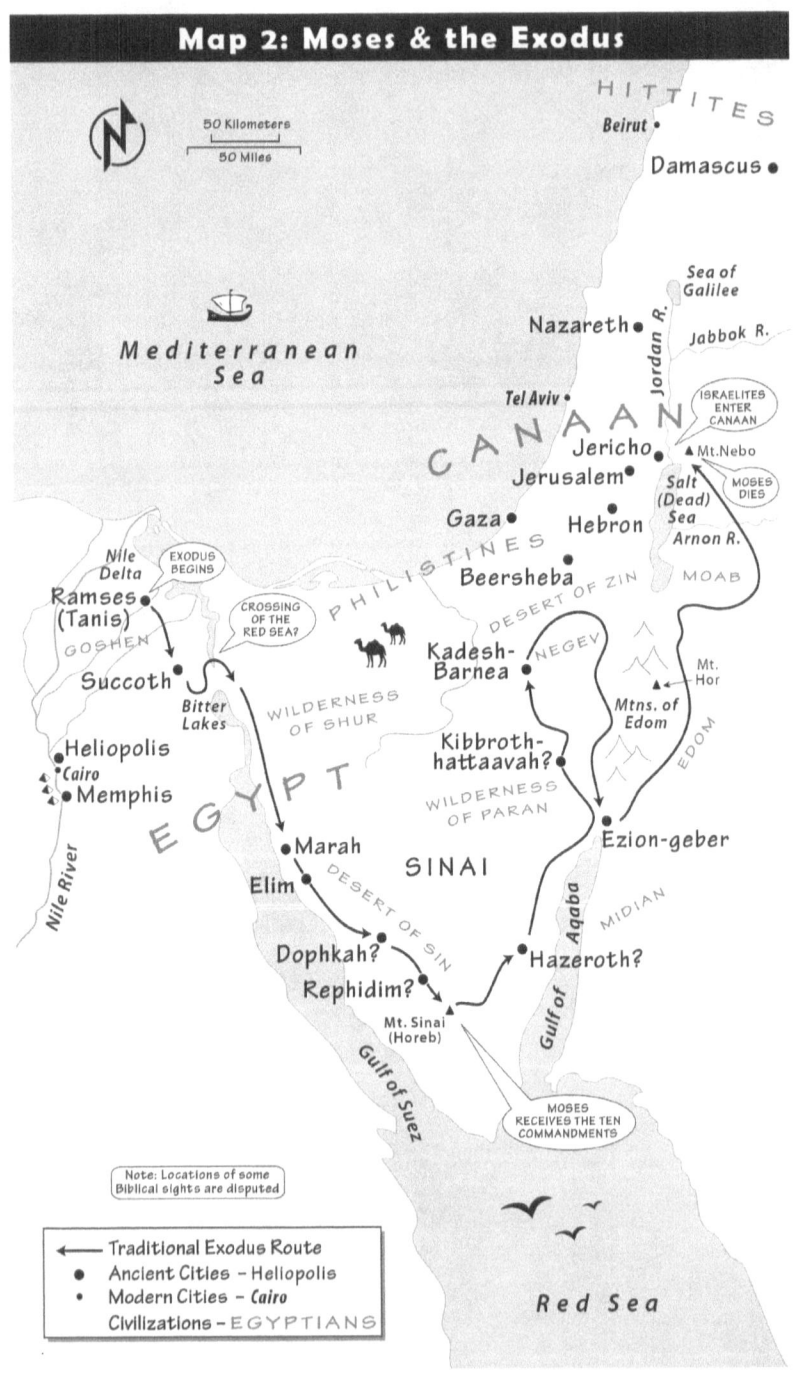

Map 2: Moses & the Exodus

50 Kilometers
50 Miles

HITTITES

Beirut •

Damascus •

Mediterranean
Sea

Sea of
Galilee

Nazareth •

Jordan R.

Jabbok R.

ISRAELITES
ENTER
CANAAN

Tel Aviv •

CANAAN

Jericho •

▲ Mt. Nebo

Jerusalem •

Salt
(Dead)
Sea

MOSES
DIES

Gaza •

Hebron •

Arnon R.

PHILISTINES

Beersheba •

DESERT OF ZIN

MOAB

Nile
Delta

EXODUS
BEGINS

Ramses •
(Tanis)

CROSSING
OF THE
RED SEA?

Kadesh-
Barnea •

NEGEV

Mt.
Hor ▲

GOSHEN

Mtns. of
Edom

Succoth •

Bitter
Lakes

WILDERNESS
OF SHUR

EGYPT

EDOM

Heliopolis •

Kibbroth-
hattaavah? •

• Cairo

▲▲ • Memphis

WILDERNESS
OF PARAN

Ezion-geber •

Nile River

• Marah

SINAI

Elim •

DESERT OF SIN

Gulf of Aqaba

MIDIAN

Dophkah? •

• Hazeroth?

Rephidim? •

Mt. Sinai
(Horeb)

Gulf of Suez

MOSES
RECEIVES THE TEN
COMMANDMENTS

Note: Locations of some
Biblical sights are disputed

Red Sea

← Traditional Exodus Route
• Ancient Cities – Heliopolis
• Modern Cities – Cairo
Civilizations – EGYPTIANS

Map 3: The 12 Tribes & Conquest of Canaan

Damascus •

Mt. Hermon

Pharpar R.

PHOENICIA

ASHER

NAPHALTI

Tyre •

Mediterranean Sea

Dan •

Hazor •

EAST MANESSEH

Merom ✳

Golan •

Sea of Galilee

ZEBULUN

Varmuk R.

Megiddo •

ISSACHAR

Taanach

10 Kilometers

10 Miles

MANESSEH

Jordan River

Jabbok R.

Shechem •

Mt. Ebal

Mt. Gerizim

Tel Aviv
Joppa •

Valley of Achor

EPHRAIM

GAD

AMMON

DAN

Bethel •

Jericho

BENJAMIN ✳

Gilgal •

Mt. Nebo

Emmaus •

Gibeon ✳

Jerusalem •

Ashkelon •

Bethlehem •

PHILISTIA

JUDAH

REUBEN

Gaza •

Hebron •

Salt (Dead) Sea

Arnon R.

En Gedi •

MOAB

AMALEC

Beersheba •

SIMEON

Zoar •

Zered R.

WILDERNESS OF ZIN

EDOM

NEGEV

✳	Major Battles
•	Ancient Cities – *Shechem*
•	Modern Cities – *Tel Aviv*
	Nations – PHILISTIA

Kadesh-Barnea •

353

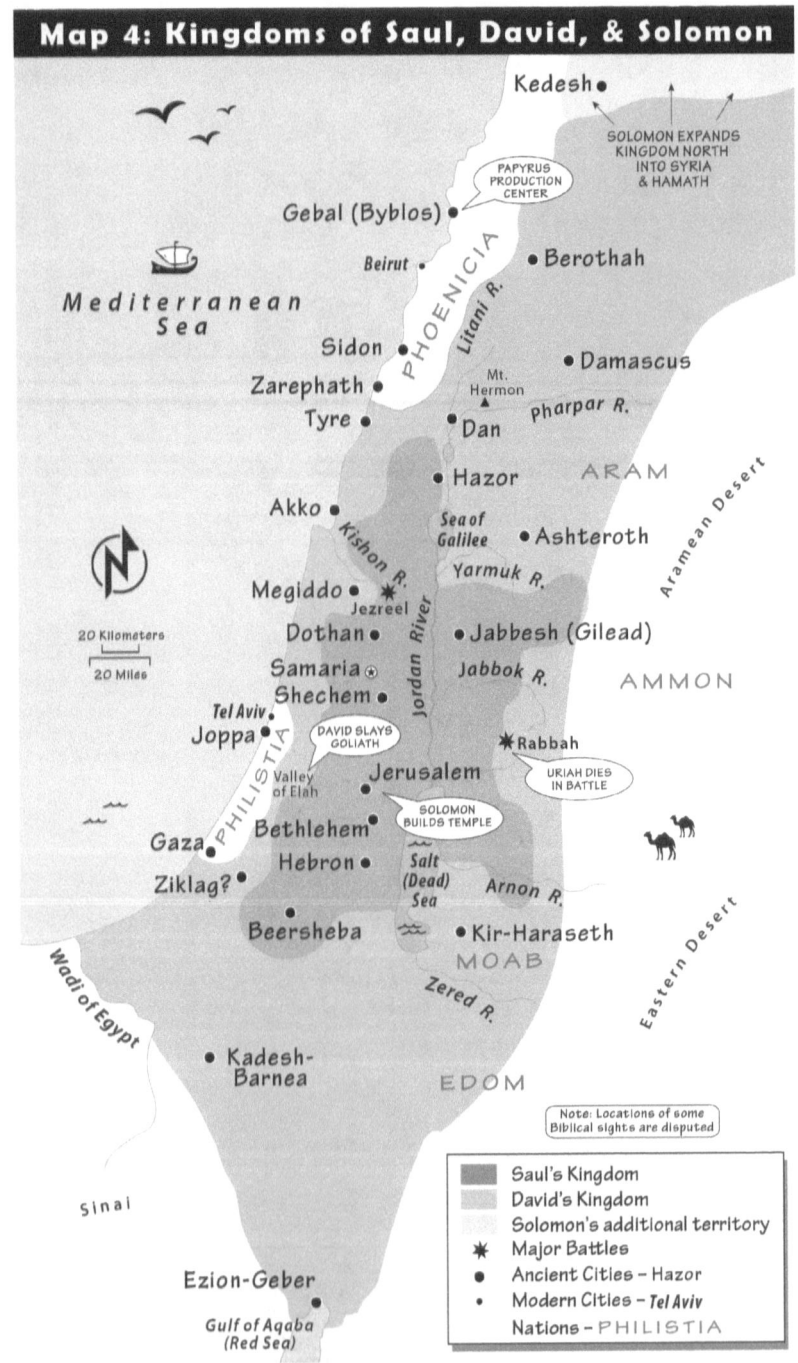

Map 4: Kingdoms of Saul, David, & Solomon

Kedesh

SOLOMON EXPANDS KINGDOM NORTH INTO SYRIA & HAMATH

PAPYRUS PRODUCTION CENTER

Gebal (Byblos)

Beirut

Berothah

Mediterranean Sea

PHOENICIA

Litani R.

Sidon

Damascus

Zarephath

Mt. Hermon

Tyre

Dan

Pharpar R.

Hazor

ARAM

Akko

Sea of Galilee

Ashteroth

Kishon R.

Aramean Desert

Megiddo

Jezreel

Yarmuk R.

20 Kilometers

Dothan

Jordan River

Jabbesh (Gilead)

AMMON

20 Miles

Samaria

Jabbok R.

Shechem

Tel Aviv

Joppa

DAVID SLAYS GOLIATH

Rabbah

PHILISTIA

Valley of Elah

Jerusalem

URIAH DIES IN BATTLE

Gaza

Bethlehem

SOLOMON BUILDS TEMPLE

Ziklag?

Hebron

Salt (Dead) Sea

Arnon R.

Eastern Desert

Beersheba

Kir-Haraseth

MOAB

Zered R.

Note: Locations of some Biblical sights are disputed

EDOM

Kadesh-Barnea

▨	Saul's Kingdom
▨	David's Kingdom
	Solomon's additional territory
✳	Major Battles
●	Ancient Cities – Hazor
•	Modern Cities – *Tel Aviv*
	Nations – PHILISTIA

Sinai

Ezion-Geber

Gulf of Aqaba (Red Sea)

Map 5: Northern & Southern Kingdoms

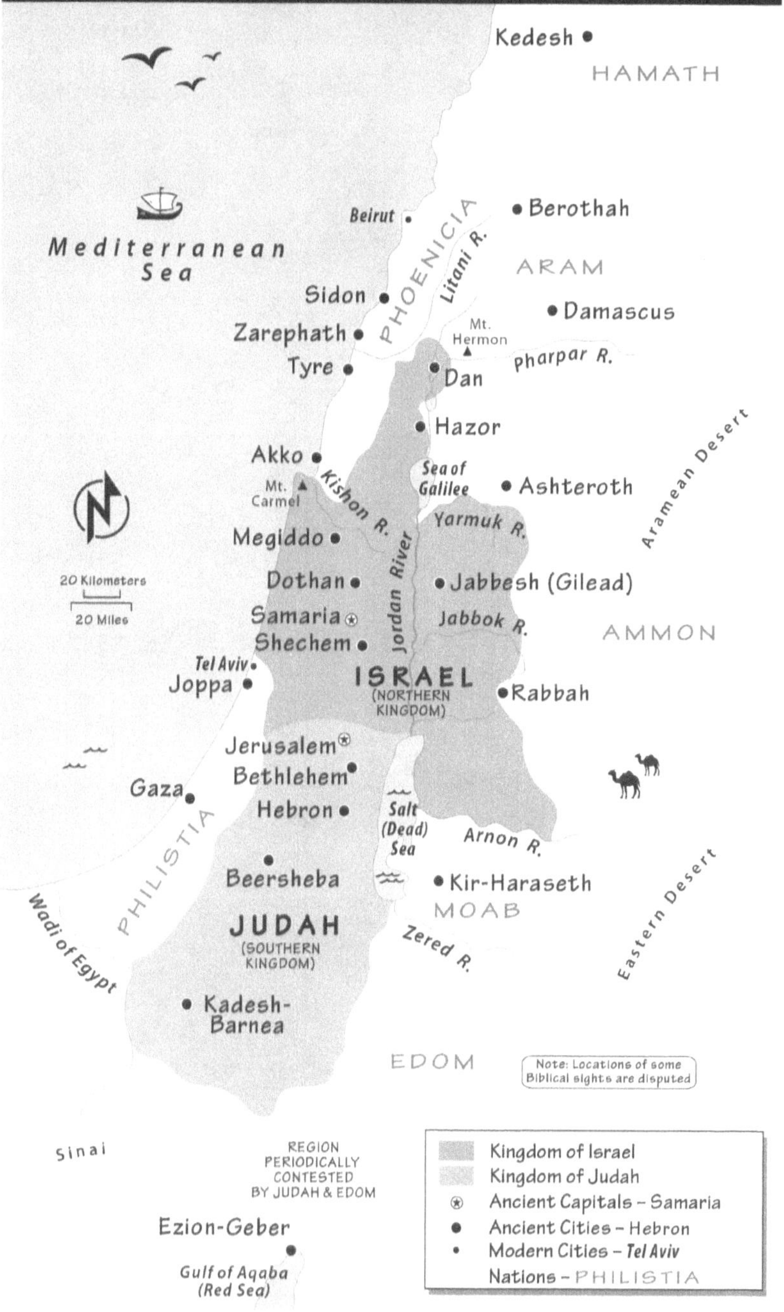

Kedesh •

HAMATH

Mediterranean Sea

Beirut •

PHOENICIA

Litani R.

• Berothah

ARAM

Sidon •

Mt. Hermon ▲

• Damascus

Zarephath •

Pharpar R.

Tyre •

• Dan

• Hazor

Akko •

Mt. Carmel ▲

Kishon R.

Sea of Galilee

• Ashteroth

Megiddo •

Yarmuk R.

Aramean Desert

20 Kilometers

20 Miles

Dothan •

Jordan River

• Jabbesh (Gilead)

Samaria ⊛

Jabbok R.

AMMON

Shechem •

Tel Aviv •

ISRAEL
(NORTHERN KINGDOM)

Joppa •

• Rabbah

Jerusalem ⊛

Bethlehem •

Gaza •

Hebron •

Salt (Dead) Sea

Arnon R.

PHILISTIA

Beersheba •

• Kir-Haraseth

MOAB

JUDAH
(SOUTHERN KINGDOM)

Zered R.

Eastern Desert

Wadi of Egypt

• Kadesh-Barnea

EDOM

Note: Locations of some Biblical sights are disputed

Sinai

REGION PERIODICALLY CONTESTED BY JUDAH & EDOM

Kingdom of Israel
Kingdom of Judah
⊛ Ancient Capitals – Samaria
• Ancient Cities – Hebron
• Modern Cities – *Tel Aviv*
Nations – PHILISTIA

Ezion-Geber
•
Gulf of Aqaba (Red Sea)

355

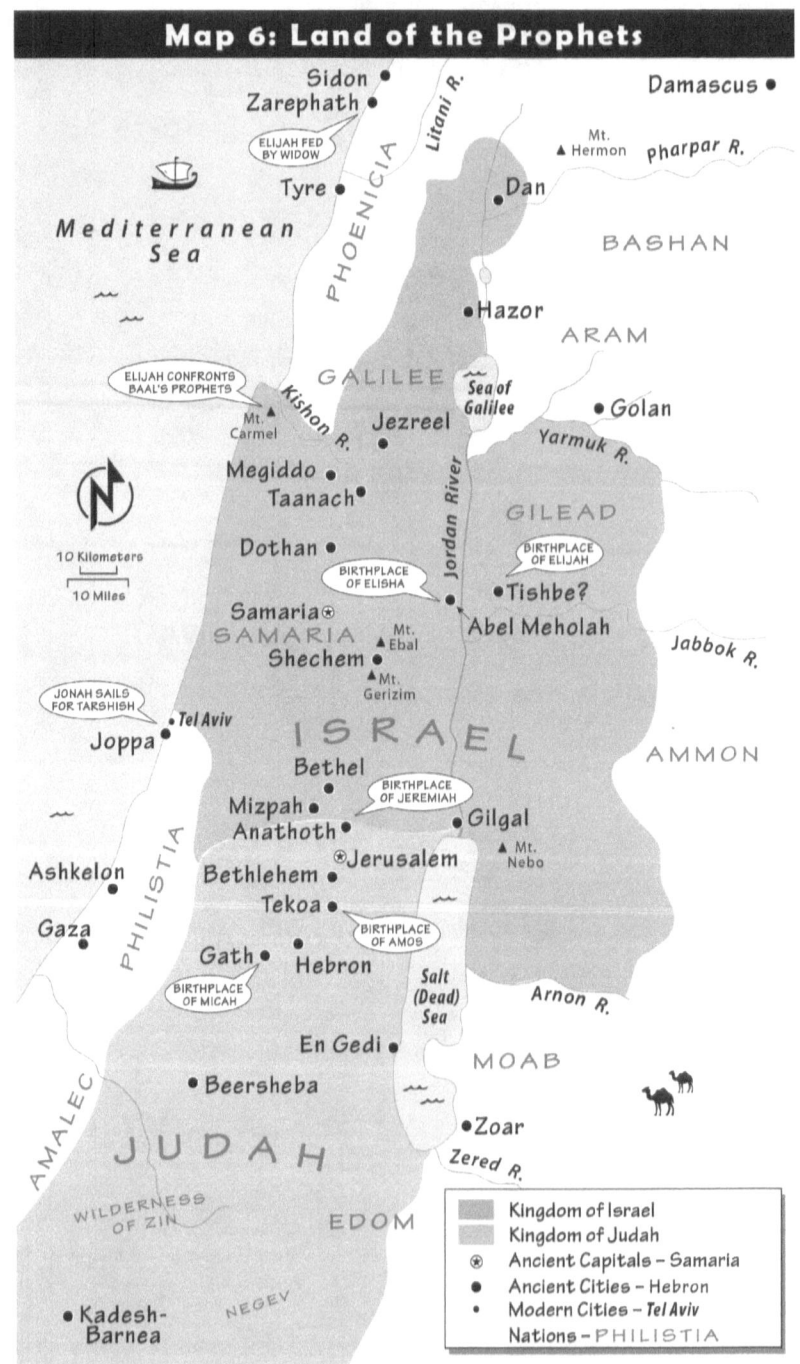

Map 6: Land of the Prophets

Sidon
Zarephath
ELIJAH FED BY WIDOW
Tyre
Mediterranean Sea

Litani R.
PHOENICIA

Damascus

Mt. Hermon
Pharpar R.

Dan

BASHAN

Hazor

ARAM

ELIJAH CONFRONTS BAAL'S PROPHETS
GALILEE
Sea of Galilee
Golan
Mt. Carmel
Kishon R.
Jezreel
Yarmuk R.

Megiddo
Taanach

GILEAD
BIRTHPLACE OF ELIJAH
Jordan River
Dothan
BIRTHPLACE OF ELISHA
Tishbe?
Abel Meholah
Jabbok R.

Samaria
SAMARIA
Mt. Ebal
Shechem
Mt. Gerizim

JONAH SAILS FOR TARSHISH
Tel Aviv
Joppa
ISRAEL
AMMON

Bethel
BIRTHPLACE OF JEREMIAH
Mizpah
Anathoth
Gilgal
Ashkelon
PHILISTIA
Bethlehem
Jerusalem
Mt. Nebo

Gaza
Tekoa
BIRTHPLACE OF AMOS
Gath
Hebron
BIRTHPLACE OF MICAH
Salt (Dead) Sea
Arnon R.

En Gedi
MOAB
Beersheba
Zoar
Zered R.

AMALEC
JUDAH
WILDERNESS OF ZIN
EDOM
NEGEV

Kadesh-Barnea

10 Kilometers
10 Miles

Kingdom of Israel
Kingdom of Judah
Ancient Capitals – Samaria
Ancient Cities – Hebron
Modern Cities – *Tel Aviv*
Nations – PHILISTIA

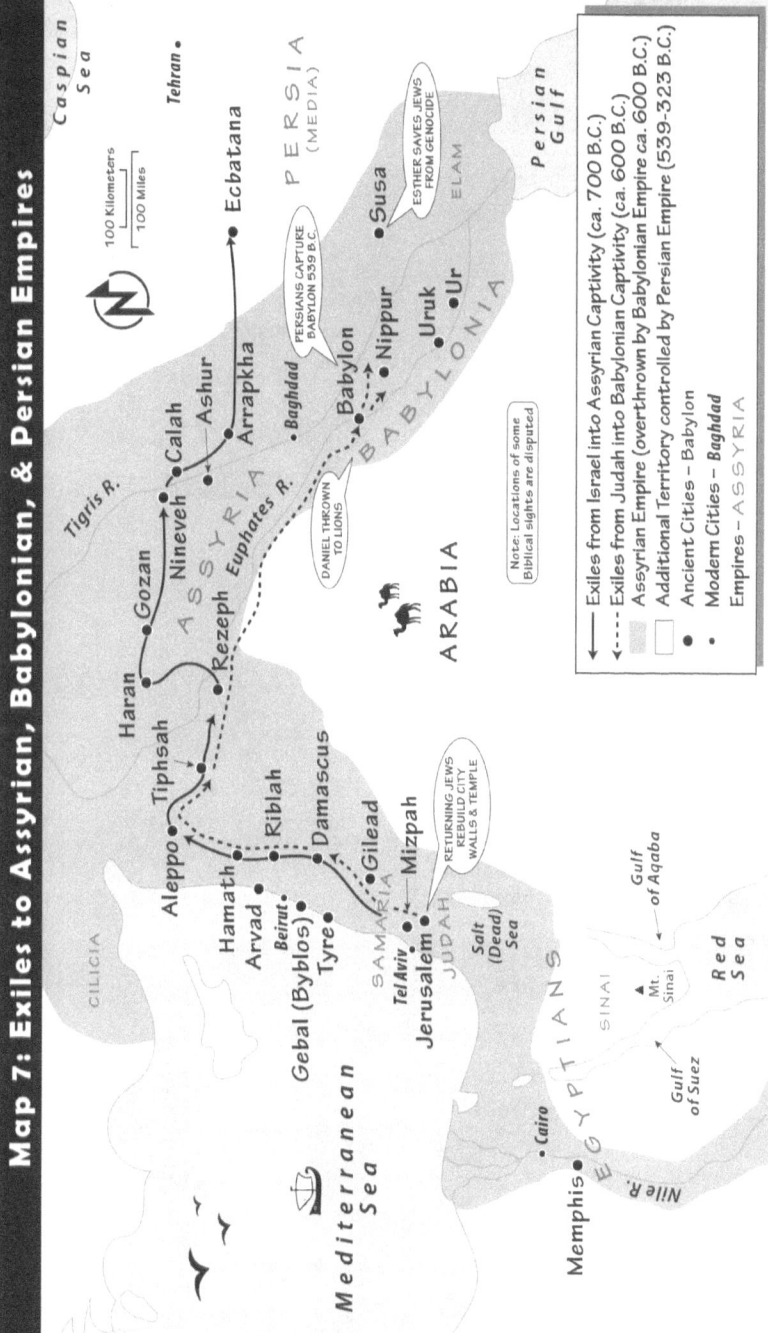

Map 7: Exiles to Assyrian, Babylonian, & Persian Empires

Caspian Sea

Tehran •

PERSIA

(MEDIA)

• Ecbatana

100 Kilometers
100 Miles

N

ESTHER SAVES JEWS
FROM GENOCIDE

• Susa

ELAM

Persian Gulf

Tigris R.

Gozan

Nineveh • Calah
• Ashur

ASSYRIA

Arrapkha

• Baghdad

PERSIANS CAPTURE
BABYLON 539 B.C.

Babylon •

• Nippur

BABYLONIA

Uruk
• Ur

Euphrates R.

Rezeph

DANIEL THROWN
TO LIONS

Note: Locations of some
Biblical sights are disputed

Haran •

Tiphsah •

ARABIA

Aleppo •

Riblah •

Damascus •

Gilead

Mizpah

RETURNING JEWS
REBUILD CITY
WALLS & TEMPLE

Hamath •

Arvad •

Beirut •

Gebal (Byblos) •

Tyre •

SAMARIA

Tel Aviv •

Jerusalem •

JUDAH

Salt
(Dead)
Sea

Gulf
of Aqaba

CILICIA

Mediterranean Sea

SINAI

Mt.
Sinai

Red Sea

Gulf
of Suez

• Cairo

E G Y P T I A N S

Memphis •

Nile R.

Exiles from Israel into Assyrian Captivity (ca. 700 B.C.)
Exiles from Judah into Babylonian Captivity (ca. 600 B.C.)
Assyrian Empire (overthrown by Babylonian Empire ca. 600 B.C.)
Additional Territory controlled by Persian Empire (539-323 B.C.)
Ancient Cities – Babylon
Modern Cities – *Baghdad*
Empires – A S S Y R I A

Map 8: Jesus' Ministry in Palestine

10 Kilometers
10 Miles

Damascus •

PHOENICIA

Mt. Hermon ▲   Pharpar R.

Caesarea Philippi •

Tyre •

HEALS CANAANITE WOMAN'S DAUGHTER

Mediterranean Sea

MEETS FIRST DISCIPLES, HEALS PARALYZED MEN

SERMON ON THE MOUNT?

HEALS BLIND MAN

Chorazin •
Capernaum • •Bethsaida
TURNS WATER INTO WINE   •Cana   •Gerasa

GALILEE   Sea of Galilee

CASTS OUT DEMONS

Nazareth •   ▲ Mt. Tabor   WALKS ON WATER

BOYHOOD

Nain

RAISES MAN FROM DEAD

Caesarea •

PEREA

SAMARIA

DECAPOLIS

Sychar •   Mt. ▲ Ebal
▲ Mt. Gerizim

Jabbok R.

SPEAKS WITH SAMARITAN WOMAN AT WELL

Tel Aviv •
Joppa •

Jordan River

TEMPTATION BY SATAN IN WILDERNESS?

APPEARS AFTER RESURRECTION

Bethel •

BAPTIZED BY JOHN? (TRADITIONAL)

Emmaus •

Mount of Olives

Jerusalem •
Bethlehem •   Bethany

▲ Mt. Nebo

Ashkelon •

BIRTHPLACE

RAISES LAZARUS FROM DEAD

Gaza •

JUDEA
Hebron •

LAST SUPPER, CRUCIFIXION

Salt (Dead) Sea

Arnon R.

To Egypt

Masada •

• Beersheba

Zered R.

Note: Locations of some Biblical sights are disputed

• Ancient Cities – Sychar
· Modern Cities – Tel Aviv
Nations – PHOENICIA

Kadesh-
• Barnea

Map 9: Apostles' Early Travels

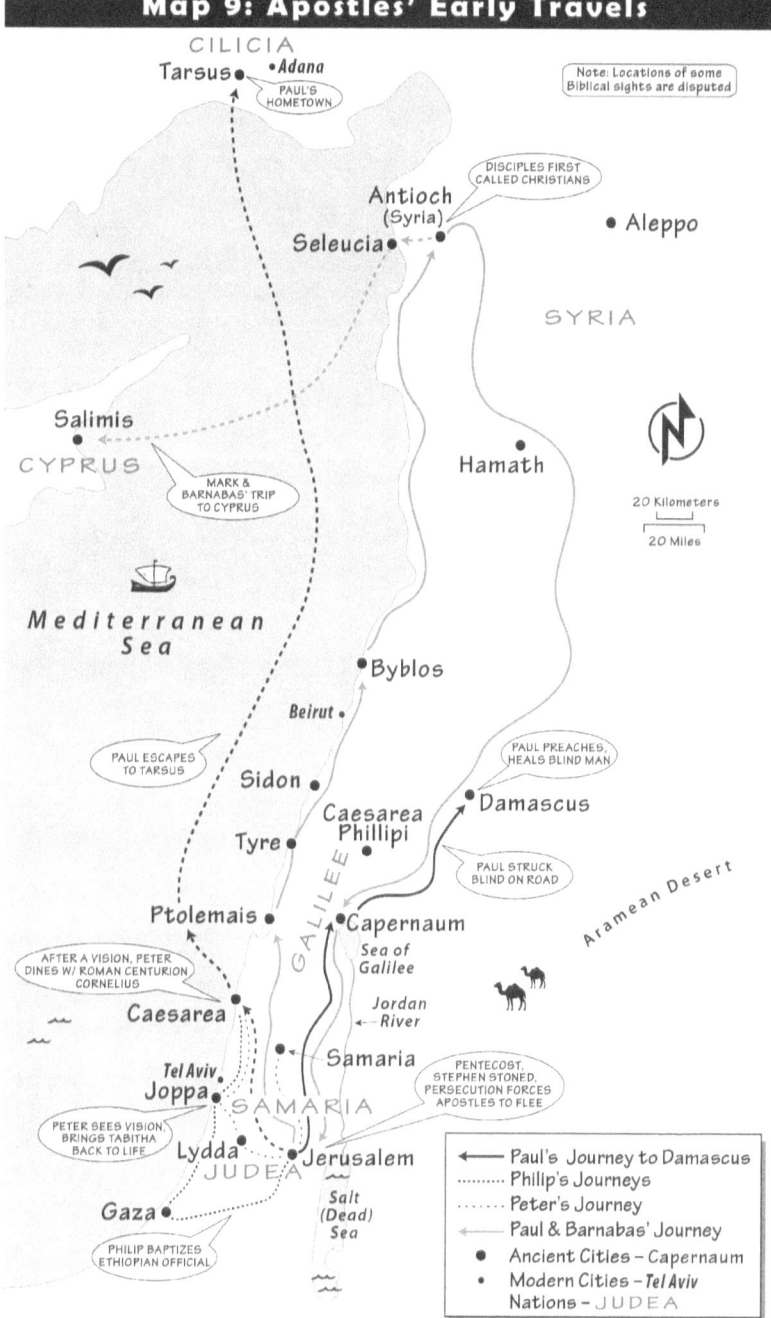

CILICIA

Tarsus • Adana
PAUL'S HOMETOWN

Note: Locations of some Biblical sights are disputed

Antioch (Syria)
DISCIPLES FIRST CALLED CHRISTIANS

Seleucia •
• Aleppo

SYRIA

Salimis
CYPRUS
MARK & BARNABAS' TRIP TO CYPRUS

Hamath

20 Kilometers
20 Miles

Mediterranean Sea

• Byblos

Beirut •

PAUL ESCAPES TO TARSUS

Sidon •

Caesarea Phillipi

Tyre •

PAUL PREACHES, HEALS BLIND MAN

• Damascus

PAUL STRUCK BLIND ON ROAD

Aramean Desert

Ptolemais •
GALILEE
• Capernaum

AFTER A VISION, PETER DINES W/ ROMAN CENTURION CORNELIUS

Sea of Galilee

Jordan River

Caesarea •

Tel Aviv
Joppa •
SAMARIA

Samaria

PENTECOST, STEPHEN STONED, PERSECUTION FORCES APOSTLES TO FLEE

PETER SEES VISION, BRINGS TABITHA BACK TO LIFE

Lydda •
JUDEA
Jerusalem •

Gaza •

Salt (Dead) Sea

PHILIP BAPTIZES ETHIOPIAN OFFICIAL

Paul's Journey to Damascus
Philip's Journeys
Peter's Journey
Paul & Barnabas' Journey
• Ancient Cities – Capernaum
• Modern Cities – *Tel Aviv*
Nations – JUDEA

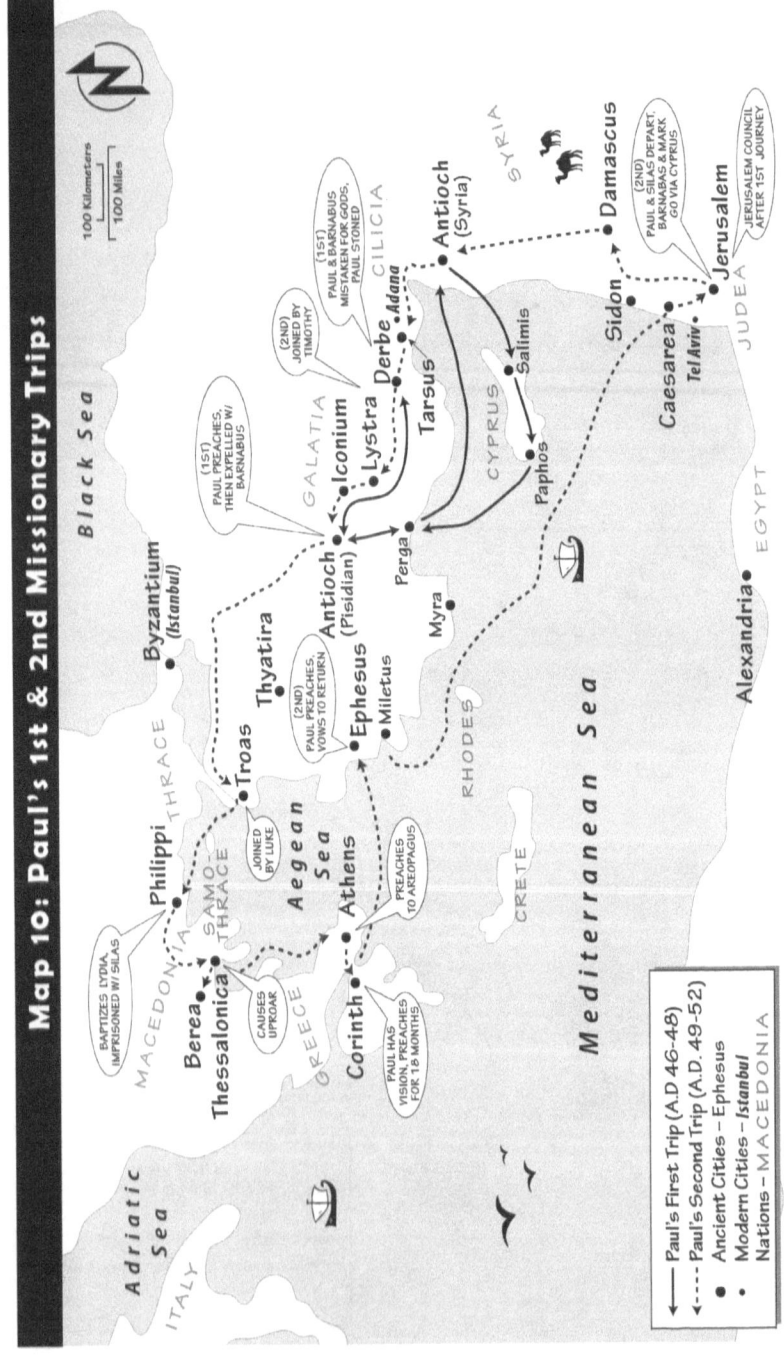

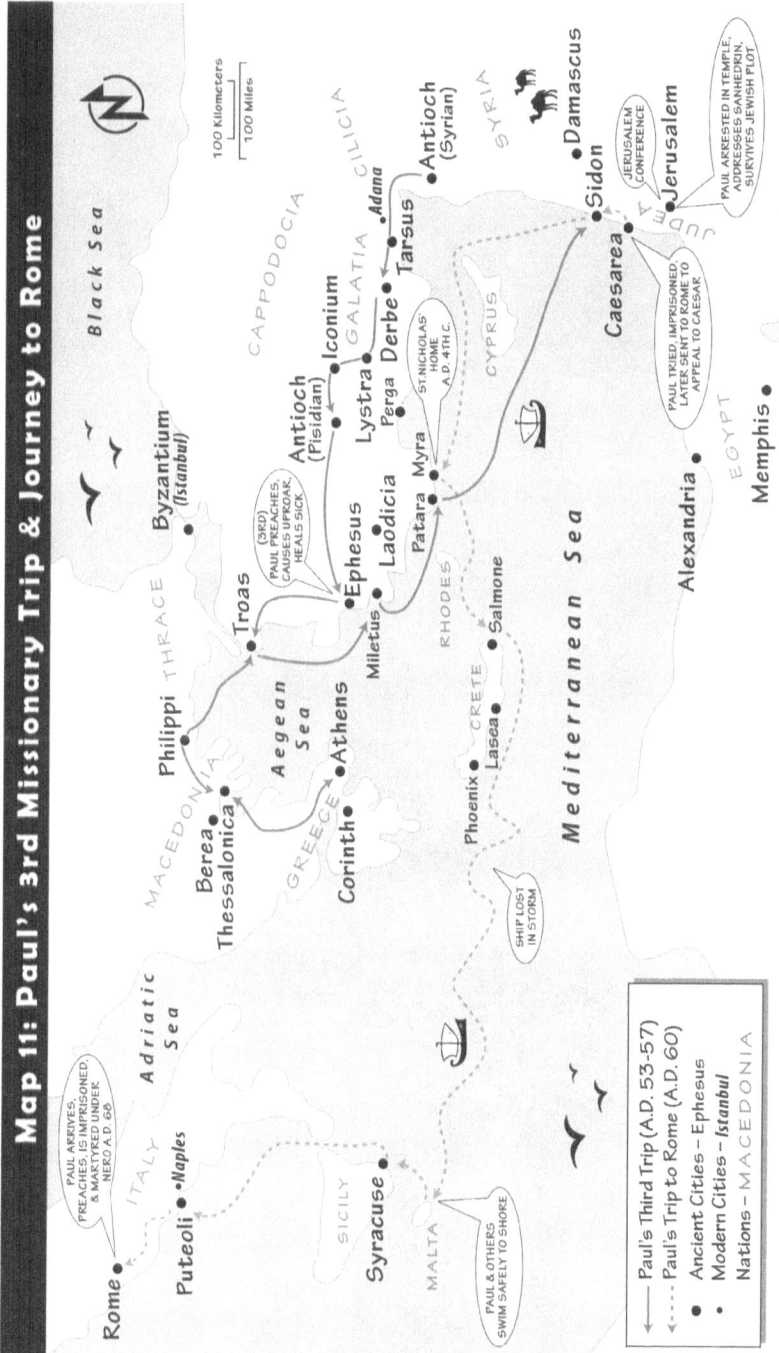

Map 11: Paul's 3rd Missionary Trip & Journey to Rome

N

100 Kilometers
100 Miles

Black Sea

Byzantium
(Istanbul)

THRACE

Philippi

MACEDONIA

Berea
Thessalonica

Aegean
Sea

GREECE

Athens

Corinth

Troas

CAPPODOCIA

Antioch
(Pisidian)

GALATIA

Iconium

Lystra

Derge

Adana

CILICIA

Tarsus

Antioch
(Syrian)

SYRIA

Damascus

Sidon

PAUL PREACHES,
CAUSES UPROAR,
HEALS SICK

(3RD)

Ephesus

Laodicia

Miletus

Patara Myra

Perga

ST. NICHOLAS
HOME,
A.D. 4TH C.

RHODES

Salmone

CYPRUS

JUDEA

Caesarea

Jerusalem

JERUSALEM
CONFERENCE

PAUL ARRESTED IN TEMPLE,
ADDRESSES SANHEDRIN,
SURVIVES JEWISH PLOT

PAUL TRIED, IMPRISONED,
LATER SENT TO ROME TO
APPEAL TO CAESAR.

EGYPT

Memphis

Alexandria

Mediterranean Sea

Phoenix

CRETE

Lasea

SHIP LOST
IN STORM

Adriatic
Sea

ITALY

Naples

Rome

Puteoli

PAUL ARRIVES,
PREACHES, IS IMPRISONED,
& MARTYRED UNDER
NERO A.D. 66

SICILY

Syracuse

MALTA

PAUL & OTHERS
SWIM SAFELY TO SHORE

Paul's Third Trip (A.D. 53-57)
Paul's Trip to Rome (A.D. 60)
Ancient Cities – Ephesus
Modern Cities – Istanbul
Nations – MACEDONIA

Peter J. Bylsma has studied the Bible for more than 50 years and has researched many complex topics in an objective manner and summarized the issues for busy leaders. He is the author of The Short Bible series (including Simplified and Very Short versions) that summarize and explain the Bible while organizing all 66 books in chronological order. Books in the series have been translated into several other languages (see www.shortbible.com). Dr. Bylsma earned his BA in psychology from Wheaton College (IL), MPA in public administration, and doctorate in education leadership and policy from the University of Washington (Seattle).

www.ingramcontent.com/pod-product-compliance
Lightning Source LLC
Chambersburg PA
CBHW021607120626
46545CB00001B/114